The Scottish witch-hunt
in context

MANCHESTER
UNIVERSITY PRESS

To the memory of Christina Larner
(1934–83)

The Scottish witch-hunt
in context

edited by Julian Goodare

Manchester University Press

Manchester and New York

distributed exclusively in the USA by Palgrave

Published by Manchester University Press
Oxford Road, Manchester M13 9NR, UK
and Room 400, 175 Fifth Avenue, New York, NY 10010, USA
www.manchesteruniversitypress.co.uk

Distributed exclusively in the USA by
Palgrave, 175 Fifth Avenue, New York,
NY 10010, USA

Distributed exclusively in Canada by
UBC Press, University of British Columbia, 2029 West Mall,
Vancouver, BC, Canada V6T 1Z2

British Library Cataloguing-in-Publication Data
A catalogue record for this book is available from the British Library

Library of Congress Cataloging-in-Publication Data applied for

ISBN 0 7190 6023 0 *hardback*
0 7190 6024 9 *paperback*

First published 2002

10 09 08 07 06 05 04 03 02   10 9 8 7 6 5 4 3 2 1

Typeset in Minion
by Northern Phototypesetting Co. Ltd, Bolton
Printed in Great Britain
by Bell & Bain Ltd, Glasgow

Contents

Figures

Preface

The idea for this book arose among a number of scholars connected with the University of Edinburgh, and it soon attracted international interest. It says much for the state of research into the subject that the book contains contributions from scholars in England, the United States and Canada, as well as Scotland.

A lively and well-attended conference was held in Edinburgh in February 2000 at which earlier versions of seven of the present chapters were presented and discussed. Joyce Miller, one of the speakers, kindly acted as conference administrator. Those who attended have reason to be grateful to the cheerful efficiency of the four conference assistants, all members of my honours course on the Scottish witch-hunt: Claire Bartlett, Susan Macrae, Natasha Reid and Katie Trout.

Manchester University Press showed early interest in the project and has been a supportive publisher.

Julian Goodare
August 2001

Abbreviations

APS   *The Acts of the Parliaments of Scotland*, 12 vols, eds T. Thomson and C. Innes (Edinburgh, 1814–75).

Balfour, *Historical Works*   Sir James Balfour of Denmilne, *Historical Works*, 4 vols, ed. J. Haig (Edinburgh, 1824–5).

BL   British Library, London.

Black, *Calendar*   G. F. Black, *A Calendar of Cases of Witchcraft in Scotland, 1510–1727* (New York, 1937).

Calderwood, *History*   David Calderwood, *History of the Kirk of Scotland*, 8 vols, eds T. Thomson and D. Laing (Wodrow Society, 1842–9).

CSP Scot.   *Calendar of State Papers relating to Scotland and Mary, Queen of Scots, 1547–1603*, 13 vols, eds J. Bain *et al.* (Edinburgh, 1898–1969).

DNB   *Dictionary of National Biography* (1885–1996).

HMC   Historical Manuscripts Commission.

James VI, *Daemonologie*, in *MPW*   James VI, *Daemonologie*, in James VI & I, *Minor Prose Works*, ed. J. Craigie (Scottish Text Society, 1982).

Larner, *Enemies of God*   C. Larner, *Enemies of God: the Witch-Hunt in Scotland* (London, 1981).

Larner, *Witchcraft*   C. Larner, *Witchcraft and Religion: the Politics of Popular Belief* (Oxford, 1984).

Larner *et al.*, *Source-Book*   C. Larner *et al.*, *A Source-Book of Scottish Witchcraft* (Glasgow, 1977).

NAS   National Archives of Scotland, Edinburgh.

NLS   National Library of Scotland, Edinburgh.

Pitcairn (ed.), *Trials*   *Criminal Trials in Scotland, 1488–1624*, 3 vols, ed. R. Pitcairn (Edinburgh, 1833).

RMS   *Register of the Great Seal of Scotland (Registrum Magni Sigilli Regum Scotorum)*, 11 vols, eds J. M. Thomson *et al.* (Edinburgh, 1882–).

RPC   *Register of the Privy Council of Scotland*, 38 vols, eds J. H. Burton *et al.* (Edinburgh, 1877–).

SCA   Stirling Council Archives.

SHR   *Scottish Historical Review*.

SHS   Scottish History Society.

SJC   *Selected Justiciary Cases, 1624–1650*, 3 vols, eds S. I. Gillon and J. I. Smith (Stair Society, 1954–74).

Spalding Misc.   *Miscellany of the Spalding Club*, 5 vols (1844–52).

SWHDB   S. Macdonald, 'Scottish Witch-Hunt Data Base' (CD-Rom, forthcoming).

Notes on contributors

Edward J. Cowan is professor of Scottish history, University of Glasgow. His most recent books are *The Ballad in Scottish History* (East Linton, 2000) and (with Lizanne Henderson) *Scottish Fairy Belief: a History* (East Linton, 2001). Other publications include (ed. with Douglas Gifford) *The Polar Twins* (Edinburgh, 1999), (ed. with R. Andrew McDonald) *Alba: Celtic Scotland in the Medieval Era* (East Linton, 2000), and (with Richard Finlay) *Scottish History: the Power of the Past* (Edinburgh, 2002).

Julian Goodare is a lecturer in Scottish history, University of Edinburgh. He is author of *State and Society in Early Modern Scotland* (Oxford, 1999), and co-editor (with Michael Lynch) of *The Reign of James VI* (East Linton, 2000). He is a publication secretary of the Scottish History Society, an associate editor of the *New Dictionary of National Biography*, and director of the Survey of Scottish Witchcraft in the University of Edinburgh.

Lizanne Henderson is editorial assistant of the journal *Folklore*, and a postgraduate in history, University of Strathclyde. She is co-author (with Edward J. Cowan) of *Scottish Fairy Belief: a History* (East Linton, 2001), and editor of *Fantasticall Ymaginations: the Supernatural in Scottish Culture* (East Linton, forthcoming).

Ronald Hutton is professor of history, University of Bristol. His most recent books are *The Pagan Religions of the Ancient British Isles* (Oxford, 1991), *The Rise and Fall of Merry England: the Ritual Year, 1400-1700* (Oxford, 1994), *The Stations of the Sun: a History of the Ritual Year in Britain* (Oxford, 1996), *The Triumph of the Moon: a History of Modern Pagan Witchcraft* (Oxford, 1999), and *The British Republic, 1649–1660* (2nd edn, London, 2000).

Brian P. Levack is John Green Regents Professor of History, University of Texas at Austin. He is author of *The Civil Lawyers in England, 1603–1641: a Political Study* (Oxford, 1973), *The Formation of the British State: England, Scotland, and the Union, 1603–1707* (Oxford, 1987), and *The Witch-Hunt in Early Modern Europe* (2nd edn, London, 1995). He edited a 12-volume series of 'Articles on witchcraft, magic and demonology' for Garland Publishing in 1992, and is currently writing a book on possession and exorcism in Reformation Europe.

Stuart Macdonald is Director of Basic Degree Studies and Theological Field Education, Knox College, University of Toronto. He is the author of *The Witches of Fife: Witch-Hunting in a Scottish Shire, 1560–1710* (East Linton, 2002). He is currently revising for electronic publication his 'Scottish Witch-Hunt Database', a corrected and expanded version of Larner *et al.*'s *Source-Book of Scottish Witchcraft*.

Lauren Martin is a research associate with the Survey of Scottish Witchcraft, University of Edinburgh. As a postgraduate student in anthropology, New School of Social Research, New York, she is currently completing a doctoral dissertation on 'The Devil and the Domestic: Witchcraft, Women's Work and Marriage in Seventeenth Century Scotland'.

Joyce Miller is a research fellow with the Survey of Scottish Witchcraft, University of Edinburgh. She has written several popular works on Scottish history, including *Magic and Myth: Scotland's Ancient Beliefs and Sacred Places* (Musselburgh, 2000). She is currently revising for publication her University of Stirling Ph.D. thesis on charming in seventeenth-century Scotland.

James Sharpe is professor of history, University of York. His most recent books are *Judicial Punishment in England* (London, 1990), *Instruments of Darkness: Witchcraft in England, 1550–1700* (London, 1996), *Early Modern England: a Social History, 1160–1760* (2nd edn, London, 1997), and *The Bewitching of Anne Gunter* (London, 1999). He is director of a research project on violence in early modern England.

Michael Wasser is a faculty lecturer in history, Bishop's University, Lennoxville, Quebec. He is the author of several articles on crime and witchcraft in Scotland, and is currently working on a book incorporating his doctoral and post-doctoral researches on violent crime in late sixteenth- and early seventeenth-century Scotland.

Louise Yeoman is a curator of manuscripts, National Library of Scotland. She is author of *Reportage Scotland: History in the Making* (National Library of Scotland, 2000) and co-director of the Survey of Scottish Witchcraft in the University of Edinburgh. She broadcasts regularly on Scottish history, and is working on a study of religious belief and experience in early modern Scotland.

1

Introduction

Julian Goodare

Early modern Scottish society was indelibly marked by witch-hunting. For centuries before about 1550, people had believed in witches; malevolent old women casting evil spells were standard folkloric characters. However, medieval people do not seem to have been *haunted* by these beliefs, and they had not acted on them; there had been no witch-hunt. Now, with the Reformation and the growth of the modern state, there was. The witch-hunt is important partly because it was bound up with these colossal forces shaping the modern world. And it is also important in its own right. Between a thousand and two thousand people, most but not all old, most but not all women, were tortured, strangled and burned at the stake for something that most readers of this book will regard as an impossible crime. Over twice that number were accused. Both witches and witch-hunters were people much like us. No wonder we want to understand them.

This is the first book for a long time to discuss the Scottish witch-hunt as a whole. For two decades, scholars interested in the subject have unanimously turned to Christina Larner's book *Enemies of God: the Witch-Hunt in Scotland* (1981). This brilliant work so dominated the field that until recently it was difficult for anyone to think of new things to say about it. Larner's book, although quite short, was a comprehensive and cogently-argued general survey of the Scottish witch-hunt. It combined a thorough knowledge of recent European historical scholarship with a sophisticated sociological framework. It drew on a statistical survey, directed by Larner herself, of all witchcraft accusations then known in Scotland. But witchcraft is about individual people, and above all Larner's book was built on a close and persuasive reading of many individual cases of witchcraft. It was, and remains, a winning combination.

However, interest in the witch-hunt has grown, and fresh research on the subject elsewhere in Europe has begun to make parts of Larner's interpretative framework look dated. The works to which we most often turn on the European witch-hunt were published well after 1981.[1] Larner herself would have been unlikely to rest on

---

[1] To mention just a few: B. Ankarloo and G. Henningsen (eds), *Early Modern European Witchcraft: Centres and Peripheries* (Oxford, 1991); B. P. Levack, *The Witch-Hunt in Early Modern Europe* (2nd edn,

her laurels – her 1982 Gifford lectures indicate one direction of her intellectual quest – but, sadly, she died in 1983.[2] Several scholars have recently begun, not only to build on her work, but also to open wholly new perspectives on the Scottish witch-hunt. Detailed studies of particular episodes, regions or themes have found ways to take the subject further.[3]

Hence the idea for a collection of essays that would draw together the best of these new approaches. As we shall see, the time is not yet ripe for a new synthesis, but this book's contributors cover a range of issues that have something new to say about the whole subject. They range from beginning to end of the period of witch-hunting in Scotland – from the late sixteenth century to the early eighteenth (and indeed after). They deal with witch-hunting as a top-down, state-directed process, and also with popular belief, community interaction and ritual practice. They offer close readings of some fascinating cases, and also general interpretations of major themes in the light of the latest European research. The book's title is carefully chosen: it aims to set the Scottish witch-hunt *in context*. Indeed it addresses two contexts: the Scottish context of related social trends, and the comparative context of Scotland's position in the wider world.

I

In seeking to place the Scottish witch-hunt in context, we are in some ways following in Larner's footsteps. The first two chapters of *Enemies of God* were a review of recent European research – hardly about Scotland at all; the third was about the Scottish social context. Scottish witch-hunting became her main subject only in Chapter 4. But the broad contextualising of the subject goes back further. Sir John Graham Dalyell, in his remarkable and erudite gathering of Scottish beliefs and ritual practices first published in 1834, ranged the entire world for comparative material – and not just the world of his own day, but European civilisation back to classical times. Turkey, Mexico, Malabar and Ceylon rubbed shoulders in his pages with Virgil and the ancient Franks.[4]

There will never again be as cosmopolitan a work as Dalyell's, but Ronald Hutton's chapter runs it close – and provides a far more focused way to make global comparisons. Drawing on a hundred anthropological studies of tribal societies, he shows that witch-beliefs and witch-hunting were remarkably widespread, though far from universal. The distinctiveness of the shamanistic cultural region centred

London, 1995); J. Barry *et al.* (eds), *Witchcraft in Early Modern Europe: Studies in Culture and Belief* (Cambridge, 1996); R. Briggs, *Witches and Neighbours: the Social and Cultural Context of European Witchcraft* (London, 1996); S. Clark, *Thinking with Demons: the Idea of Witchcraft in Early Modern Europe* (Oxford, 1997).

   [2] These lectures are the centrepiece of her posthumously-published collection of essays, *Witchcraft and Religion: the Politics of Popular Belief* (Oxford, 1984).

   [3] For these see the 'Further reading' section below.

   [4] J. G. Dalyell, *The Darker Superstitions of Scotland* (2nd edn, Edinburgh, 1839), pp. 125, 128, 263, 306, 419.

on Siberia is particularly striking; it extended into parts of Scandinavia that were in socio-economic terms similar to Scotland. The Scottish Highlands and Gaelic Ireland, in which misfortunes tended to be blamed on fairies rather than witches, form another distinctive cultural region. Hutton also compares the witchcraft panics that were so common in Scotland with similar events elsewhere. And he looks back to the witches of the ancient European world to argue that the sixteenth-century growth of witch-hunting was in fact a *revival* after a long medieval 'hiatus'. After Hutton's work, no general explanation of witchcraft will satisfy unless it addresses the global nature of the phenomenon.

One reason for the medieval 'hiatus', in Hutton's model, was the autonomous power of Christianity and the separation of church and state – quite unusual in a global context.[5] The medieval church, secure in its vast wealth and status, did not try to control secular rulers or to construct a unified theocracy. It sometimes wanted to promote crusading or to repress heresy, but was generally satisfied with a *status quo* in which both secular rulers and the common people respected its rights and its rites. Such a mood of complacency was not one that would foster witch-hunting; people at all social levels believed in witches, but did not feel threatened by them. Witchcraft accusations occasionally became a political weapon; the first known executions of witches in Scotland occurred in 1479 when John, earl of Mar, was accused of having employed them to bewitch his brother, James III. This was an isolated episode confined within the tiny world of elite politics. It did not represent a sustained effort to modify the behaviour of the common folk, or to address their own concerns about witchcraft.[6]

This lack of concern was partly because the late-medieval ruling class was quite a small group.[7] King, nobles, lairds, bishops and abbots formed its core – a group numbered in dozens. Below them there were bailies, chamberlains and other estate officials, personal servants and followers, and (for the clergy) cathedral canons. There were also swarms of humble parish priests and chaplains, but they were mostly recruited from the common folk and were members of their local communities rather than 'rulers'. The number of people *from the elite* who were in regular contact with the common folk was small, so there were few people who might be faced with the challenge of 'ruling' them in the sense of getting them to modify their behaviour. One group who did try to modify people's behaviour, the preaching friars, operated mainly in towns and entirely by persuasion.[8]

In the sixteenth century, the century of the Reformation, this began to change. Lairds became more numerous with the 'feuing' (alienation in return for a fixed feu-duty) of church and crown land. Professional groups arose, notably lawyers and Protestant ministers, who were *not* part of the community. With a growth in statute law and bureaucracy, this expanding elite's own activities were more closely

[5] Cf. S. E. Finer, *The History of Government*, 3 vols (Oxford, 1997), i, pp. 4–5; ii, pp. 855–95.

[6] N. Macdougall, *James III* (Edinburgh, 1982), pp. 130–3; cf. R. Kieckhefer, *European Witch Trials: their Foundations in Popular and Learned Culture, 1300–1500* (Berkeley, Calif., 1976), pp. 10–13.

[7] The term 'ruling class' is used in the cautious way that Larner used it: *Enemies of God*, p. 1.

[8] I. B. Cowan, *The Scottish Reformation* (London, 1982), pp. 44–8.

enmeshed in governmental regulation than before.[9] Newly-established lesser lairds and parish ministers were in daily contact with the common folk, but were not subject to community values. They remained above the peasants, and knew that it was their duty to rule. Familiar with the community as they were, they were confronted daily with aspects of its lack of conformity to newly-received norms of decent and godly behaviour. It was from the ranks of lesser lairds and parish ministers that the great majority of local witch-hunters were drawn. Louise Yeoman's chapter offers a portrait of some of these men, and shows how they used local institutions and elite connections to pursue their own quarrels and obsessions in the guise of serving the state. The quarrelsomeness of witches is often noted, but the quarrelsomeness of witch-hunters is a remarkable finding that deserves careful attention.

Perhaps, though, the witch-hunters' abrasive and confrontational nature should not surprise us. This is not so much because of the tortures that they inflicted, since the usual Scottish torture, sleep deprivation, was actually less intense and horrifying to carry out than physical tortures (though the experience of the witches is another matter). What was confrontational was the overall structure of godly discipline within which the witch-hunters operated. With the kirk session (the parish disciplinary committee) in the front line, all the institutions of church and state were now committed to a campaign of moral reform that aimed to effect a thorough transformation of the behaviour of the common folk. Previously, the church had accepted and incorporated a great deal of popular folk belief; now it was consistently hostile to popular 'superstition', including both surviving Catholic practices (pilgrimages to holy wells, observance of Christmas) and rituals involving such things as fairies.

These rituals often involved healing or divination, which went under the general name of 'charming'. Witchcraft accusations by peasants could be linked to dissension about charming; it was believed that those who could heal could also harm, and healing spells that went wrong could be blamed on the charmer. Joyce Miller sets witch-hunting in this context, showing how the common and minor offence of charming sometimes became transmuted, in the minds of neighbours or kirk sessions or both, into the rarer but very serious offence of witchcraft. Some practices of charming were very ancient and drew on widespread cultural motifs. Miller's chapter comes closest to Ronald Hutton's in its breadth of geographical and chronological vision. The relevant point here is that her charmers, in their own eyes, were not witches. Indeed they might claim to cure illnesses induced by witchcraft, which sometimes led on to them identifying the witch responsible. In practice, charmers were self-defined, whereas witches were defined by other people.

The witchcraft statute itself tended to blur the distinction between charmer and witch. It ordained that nobody should 'tak upone hand in ony tymes heirefter to

    [9] I. D. Whyte, *Scotland before the Industrial Revolution: an Economic and Social History, c.1050–c.1750* (London, 1995), pp. 155–6; J. Goodare, *State and Society in Early Modern Scotland* (Oxford, 1999), chs. 2–3.

use ony maner of witchcraftis, sorsarie or necromancie, nor gif thame selfis furth to have ony sic craft or knawledge thairof, thairthrow abusand the pepill'.[10] This was not very helpful in providing a definition of witchcraft, and in practice it was left to the courts to define the crime through custom and practice; but the statute clearly regarded witches as self-defined public practitioners. The mention of 'witchcraftis' (plural) indicates that the authors of the statute intended to punish *acts* of witchcraft – specific spells, curses or malefices – rather than the thought-crime of *being* a witch. Yet it was this thought-crime for which many eventually suffered once it became customary to define a witch in the courts as someone who had made a pact with the Devil.

Witch-hunting in Scotland was a Protestant business. The witchcraft statute was passed in 1563, just three years after the Reformation. There was of course little or nothing distinctive about Protestantism when it came to witch-hunting, and many Catholic countries pursued witches with equal zeal. Larner memorably charac-terised the process as 'Christianization': early modern reform movements, whether Protestant or Catholic, were seeking to impose a new model of Christianity in which ordinary people would be personally responsible for their salvation, and deviants from the godly norm could face punishment.[11] Studies of how religious doctrine was inculcated in post-Reformation Europe have tended to focus on the most direct means, particularly (for Protestants) preaching and catechising.[12] Surely, though, Larner was right to see the coercive attack on ungodliness as an important part of the process whereby people were marshalled into godliness. If they listened to the sermons, they were expected to have in mind what could hap-pen to them if they did not. In Scotland, kirk sessions spent much effort punishing fornication, adultery, sabbath-breaking and other such common offences; witch-craft was relatively rare. But when it occurred, its punishment was so dramatic that it must have done a great deal to colour people's attitude towards the religion that the authorities were imposing on them.

The witchcraft act was not in itself a panic measure, but it soon led to panics. Larner's view of 1590 as the effective starting date for Scottish witch-hunting has been modified by Michael Wasser's research into a serious panic of 1568.[13] There was also a major local panic in Easter Ross in 1577, resulting in the trial and likely exe-cution of about thirty witches unknown to Larner; one of them, Coinneach Odhar, was later remembered as the 'Brahan Seer' to whom remarkable prophecies were attributed.[14] As for Larner's claim that the eighteenth century 'saw only a few isolated prosecutions', a pair of witches were executed in Perth in 1715, and multiple cases

[10] *APS*, ii, p. 539, c. 9.

[11] Larner, *Enemies of God*, ch. 12.

[12] G. Parker, 'Success and failure during the first century of the Reformation', *Past and Present*, 136 (Aug. 1992), 43–82.

[13] M. Wasser, 'Ambition and failure: Scotland's unknown witch-hunt, 1568–1569', unpublished paper.

[14] W. Matheson, 'The historical Coinneach Odhar and some prophecies attributed to him', *Transactions of the Gaelic Society of Inverness*, 46 (1969–70), 66–88, at pp. 68–74.

continued to occur until at least 1723.[15] Ted Cowan and Lizanne Henderson's chapter argues that it was still possible in the early eighteenth century to envisage a recurrence of really large-scale witch-hunting. The 1563 statute was repealed only in 1736; Scotland was haunted by witchcraft for a long time.

The statute set in motion a complex legal machine. It had three main components: the local church courts (kirk sessions and presbyteries); the criminal courts in which accused witches were actually tried; and the organs of central government, notably the privy council. My chapter on the state shows how they fitted together. Church courts often co-ordinated the pre-trial stage, in which a suspected witch was identified and evidence assembled against her or him – often including interrogation under torture. The trial itself tended to be a foregone conclusion, at least when it was held (as it most often was) in the locality rather than in the Edinburgh court of justiciary. But a local criminal court required central authorisation – and this was the crucial stage. The privy council examined all the prosecution's evidence, and sent the case for trial only if this was convincing. The real decision on the guilt or innocence of Scottish witches was made at the highest level of central government.

Stuart Macdonald's chapter complements this by drawing on evidence from the lowest levels of government – the kirk sessions that often co-ordinated the gathering of pre-trial evidence in the locality. He argues that many local cases were purely about malefice, and those mentioning the Devil often did not mention the demonic pact explicitly. This seems to have been because the demonic pact was not necessary to the kirk session's view of the witch as ungodly: of course she was ungodly, just as fornicators, adulterers, sabbath-breakers and the other victims of godly discipline were. Here we see witch-hunting as inseparable from its Reformation context.

II

Most of the evidence for Scottish witch-hunting was created in the trial process – particularly neighbours' depositions and witches' own confessions, either surviving in their own right as pre-trial documents, or rewritten and incorporated into the dittays (indictments) used in court. It should be mentioned that while historians of witch-hunting all over Europe use such court records as their basic source material, there has been increasing interest in literary sources, notably pamphlets on individual witchcraft cases. Such pamphlets are less common for Scotland than for a few countries, notably England;[16] but they do begin to appear in numbers towards the end of the witch-hunting period, and are discussed in Michael Wasser's chapter on the regional panic of 1697–1700. Wasser is fortunate in not having to rely solely

---

[15] Larner, *Enemies of God*, p. 60; Larner *et al.*, *Source-Book*, pp. 228–9.

[16] Where they are discussed by M. Gibson, *Reading Witchcraft: Stories of Early English Witches* (London, 1999). A literary turn to English witchcraft scholarship is natural because the survival of English court records has been so patchy. In Scotland, we have more comprehensive records of witchcraft cases and so can pursue social-scientific questions involving numbers and distribution.

on such evidence, since he can complement it with actual court records. The same is true for the best-known Scottish episode generating literary material: the North Berwick witchcraft panic of 1590–1. Lawrence Normand and Gareth Roberts, who recently produced a detailed new edition of this material, the pamphlet *Newes from Scotland* and James's treatise *Daemonologie*, wisely included a large body of court records also.[17]

What general approach should be taken to such court records? The simplest way of posing the problem is to ask: do they represent spontaneous popular testimony, or do they originate with elite interrogators, who shaped the testimony with leading questions? But we should also consider how far the elite themselves accepted much of popular culture. Beliefs about what witches did could have been shared by both groups – at least to the extent that these beliefs were congruent with the sophisticated demonology of the elite. Or the common folk could have adopted the demonic ideas of the elite as they were disseminated in sermons.

There are no definitive answers to this in the book, but several contributors grapple with the nature of witchcraft belief, notably Stuart Macdonald – who finds a low demonic content in local trials – and Lauren Martin – who finds a high demonic content in central trials. Macdonald also argues that much of what appears in the trials as demonic originated as folklore about fairies. Joyce Miller focuses on popular magic which was definitely not learned from the elite, but which could well have been shared by the elite, at least in part. We should also recall Larner's characterisation of early modern Scotland as a 'middle ground' society. It was neither pre-literate – with a homogeneous belief-system – nor fully modern – with a wide range of beliefs but heavily influenced by science and technology.[18] This states the problem and provides a context for it, but does not solve it. There is much work to be done on the nature and sources of witchcraft beliefs.

Witch-hunting and gender were inextricably linked. The stereotype witch was always a woman, and 85 per cent of actual Scottish witches were women. A recent study has sought to explain this as a combination of male fears about female sexuality with the impact of the Reformation's programme of moral discipline. The main moral offence in Scotland was fornication: women witches were effectively fornicating with the Devil.[19] Several chapters discuss aspects of this subject. Lauren Martin's chapter uses the frequent references to the demonic pact in central trial records to elucidate the way it was conceptualised. Witch and Devil did not primarily have a 'feudal' relationship, as Larner argued, but rather one analogous to marriage – particularly irregular marriage, which though legally binding was clandestine and wrongful. This adds another link between witchcraft and female sexuality. However, Martin is not convinced that her Scottish evidence would support conclusions recently drawn in England and elsewhere about the central

[17] L. Normand and G. Roberts (eds), *Witchcraft in Early Modern Scotland: King James's* Demonology *and the North Berwick Witches* (Exeter, 2000).

[18] Larner, *Enemies of God*, pp. 11–13; *Witchcraft*, pp. 159–60.

[19] J. Goodare, 'Women and the witch-hunt in Scotland', *Social History*, 23 (1998), 288–308.

role of motherhood to the image of the female witch. She points out that women also had work to do – not just childcare, but also farming, producing goods for sale, and providing services like healing or wet-nursing. As they promoted and defended their households in the community economy, the quarrels that arose could lead to recognisable patterns of witchcraft accusation.

Martin's witches belong to the peasant class. Those of Louise Yeoman belong to the elite, bringing out another aspect of attitudes to women: the problematic nature of female inheritance. Yeoman agrees readily with Carol Karlsen's conclusion (based on research into New England witch-hunting) that heiresses were anomalous in a male-dominated society. However, she shows that we need not assume that heiresses accused of witchcraft were quarrelsome; before doing so, we should look at the witch-hunters. Those who orchestrated accusations of rich witches were difficult, quarrelsome men, often in financial trouble, and over-eager to conclude that the problems this brought on them were caused by external, demonic agency. Witch-hunting was very much about women – so much so that it was about men too.

When Larner wrote, witchcraft scholars tended to draw a distinction between 'Continental' and 'English' patterns of witch-hunting. Continental witch-hunts were seen as driven by elite fears about diabolical conspiracy; torture, mass panic and multiple executions were common. In England, witch-hunts remained rooted in village quarrels; there was hardly any torture, no panics, and prosecutions were of one witch at a time. Larner noted some 'English' features of Scottish witch-hunting – notably the importance of neighbourhood concerns, and the use of juries rather than judges to determine guilt; but in general she set Scotland in the 'Continental' model of severe witch-hunting driven by the state.

However, witchcraft scholars no longer believe that the 'English' and 'Continental' models were two separate things. James Sharpe, who contributes a chapter comparing England and Scotland, has done much to undermine the idea of English uniqueness; England generated in 1645 a witchcraft panic as intense in its way as most of the Scottish ones. Earlier scholars dismissed this panic as 'untypical', but this will not do; it happened, and is ineluctably part of what the English were capable of doing.[20] By contrast, as he points out, we now know that Continental witch-hunting often arose from neighbourhood quarrels, and appreciate more fully the diversity of European experience. My chapter on the state, for instance, offers a briefer comparison between Scotland and Bavaria, and calls for further studies of medium-sized states. England, we now see, was one among many European countries with mild witch-hunting.

An English–Scottish comparison nevertheless retains its interest, both from a socio-economic and a political point of view. Alan Macfarlane's famous model of English witchcraft involved socio-economic change, as prosperous, modernising householders turned wandering beggars from the door, and the beggars' curses, followed by misfortune, led to witchcraft accusations against them. Lauren Martin

---

[20] J. Sharpe, *Instruments of Darkness: Witchcraft in England, 1550–1750* (London, 1996), ch. 5.

also sees curses followed by misfortune in Scottish cases – but the curses were prompted by quarrels between social equals in a way that does not fit the Macfarlane model. Sharpe notes that witch-hunting was more intense in regions of Scotland that *were* apparently modernising, and suggests that further research might establish a link between these trends. As for politics: Sharpe, noting Larner's focus on the state, observes that seventeenth-century Englishmen made fewer attempts to construct a godly state than did their northern counterparts. He wonders how thorough even Scotland was in this respect, but has no doubt that the godly state and witch-hunting were linked.

What form did this link take? Larner wrote of 'the conspicuous and unequivocal way in which the ruling elite controlled and manipulated the demand for and the supply of witchcraft suspects'.[21] This is not wholly wrong, but far from being 'conspicuous and unequivocal', the process was tacit and indirect. Larner was probably thinking here of the governmental initiative of 1591 which she frequently described as establishing a 'general commission' (or 'standing commissions') for witchcraft trials which was (or were) revoked in 1597. She saw this 'general commission' (or 'standing commissions') as playing an important role in making witch-hunting routine in the Scottish localities after the dramatic North Berwick witchcraft panic of 1590–1. However, it has recently been argued that no 'general commission' (or 'standing commissions') ever existed. The order of 1591 was a temporary and indeed evanescent measure, part of the North Berwick panic rather than a successor to it; the order of 1597 was part of the panic of that year, with no connection to any earlier measure. Throughout the 1590s (as before and afterwards) the framework for witch-hunting remained constant, with local witchcraft trials being authorised by the crown.[22]

This does not of course rule out central initiative – far from it. Peasants always knew of a few likely witches in their community; who would determine whether they would be prosecuted? Clearly it would be the elite – prompted either by a quarrelsome and vindictive individual, as in Louise Yeoman's cases, or by a local church court concerned for godly discipline, as in Stuart Macdonald's. It could be argued that they were simply responding to peasant concerns, but no evidence for this view has ever emerged, with one exception: the much-quoted complaint of the earl of Haddington in 1661 that his tenants were threatening to leave his lands because of witchcraft. But Brian Levack, who first drew attention to this complaint, assigned it at best a secondary role. Haddington was mainly concerned about the demonic pact, and a witch-pricker was already active in the area to identify witches who would have had no prior reputation among the tenants. Similarly the Aberdeenshire witch-hunting commissioners of 1597 overrode the reluctance of parish authorities in their determination to seek out witches.[23] More research is needed on the question of

[21] Larner, *Enemies of God*, p. 14.

[22] J. Goodare, 'The framework for Scottish witch-hunting in the 1590s', *SHR*, 81 (2002, forthcoming).

[23] B. P. Levack, 'The great Scottish witch-hunt of 1661–1662', *Journal of British Studies*, 20 (1980), 90–108, at pp. 97–8; J. Goodare, 'The Aberdeenshire witchcraft panic of 1597', *Northern Scotland*, 21 (2001), 17–37, at pp. 24–5.

where the initiative for prosecution lay, but my chapter on the state provides a good deal of evidence for witch-hunting as a centralised operation.

The most obvious way in which Larner was right about elite initiative relates to the five great national panics that dominate the story of Scottish witch-hunting. Neighbourhood disputes led to the denunciation of handfuls of individual witches in most years. It is just not credible to suggest that such disputes could accelerate to produce hundreds of denunciations in a matter of months. Robin Briggs, who argues persuasively that 'many reasons' are needed to explain witch-hunting, seems to think that state initiative was *not* one of these reasons.[24] Whatever the usefulness of this claim for some other countries, it is not helpful in understanding Scotland. This book contains a chapter on one of the five great panics, that of 1597, showing the active role of organs of the state and notably the king himself. Much has been written on the role of James VI in witch-hunting, particularly in view of his book *Daemonologie* published in 1597. My chapter on the panic of that year brings out the king's active role in it, and argues that *Daemonologie* was published as a response to the critics of the panic's excesses.

III

We think we have a good idea why witches were hunted. This is worth saying, since witchcraft scholars used to struggle to construct a coherent answer to this basic question. No doubt we still have much to learn, but we have at least largely disposed of the fundamentally misleading interpretations that dogged earlier generations.[25] But in explaining the witch-hunt so successfully, we have set ourselves a problem. Once started, how could witch-hunting ever stop? This book has been planned to provide an answer to this question – or rather to provide *answers*, since several chapters address the question in different ways.

Here we should pay tribute to Larner's argument, expressed throughout her works, that witchcraft needed to be studied as a crime – an act that was not primarily evil *per se*, but was defined by the authorities as deserving of specific punishment in the courts. Her colleagues in sociology were realising that 'crime' was not something innate in acts defined as criminal, but was a label applied to those acts by specific societies at specific times. The ways in which certain people were labelled as witches were not intrinsically different from the ways in which other people were labelled as thieves or fraudsters, and might change over time. This insight has become generally accepted, but has not been used to take the subject of Scottish witchcraft further – probably because not only witchcraft, but also the criminal law, have been neglected subjects for research. But it is vital for the issue of decline. If witchcraft could become a crime, it could also cease to be one.

[24] R. Briggs, '"Many reasons why": witchcraft and the problem of multiple explanation', in Barry *et al.* (eds), *Witchcraft in Early Modern Europe*, pp. 52–3.
[25] Though the discredited idea that witches were members of an organised cult lingers on in P. G. Maxwell-Stuart, 'Witchcraft and the kirk in Aberdeenshire, 1596–97', *Northern Scotland*, 18 (1998), 1–14. For a critique of this, see Goodare, 'Aberdeenshire witchcraft panic', pp. 26–32.

This is where Brian Levack's chapter comes in. He discusses lawyers' views of witchcraft in detail, arguing that they demanded higher standards of evidence in the courts. Here, scrutiny of criminal procedure actually tends to detach witchcraft from other crimes. Higher standards were not being applied to all criminal trials, and the lawyers' main target was practices specific to witch-hunting – particularly sleep deprivation to extort confessions, and pricking for the witch's mark. He argues that judges continued to believe in witches, but lost confidence in the ability of conventional methods of prosecution to separate the innocent from the guilty. One strength of this approach over Larner's is its unified focus. Larner wrote that 'Between 1680 and 1735 the witch-belief disappeared almost without comment from the cognitive map of the ruling class, and retired to the secret, uncharted areas of peasant exchange', but also that 'The proportion of acquittals to convictions increased and the number of prosecutions declined while the witch theory was largely intact and its general possibility still largely accepted'.[26] Levack takes issue with the first of these statements, but provides convincing detail – and a broad European perspective – to validate the second.

Elsewhere in the book we find further reasons for being less surprised that witch-hunting stopped. The seeds of decline were always present. It would be a mistake to assume that witch-hunting was normal, even at the height of the prosecutions. People always had to *persuade* themselves that it was important to prosecute witches, and things often happened to discourage them. My chapter on 1597 argues that the panic of that year backfired. Injustice was done, and was seen to be done. There was public disagreement within the government about how to respond, with the king wanting to continue the prosecutions but some of his councillors wanting to stop. James had composed his book *Daemonologie* as a response to the previous witchcraft panic of 1590–1, but revised and published it in 1597 as a contribution to the debates generated by the events of that year.[27] The business left a nasty aftertaste, and it was a long time before the next panic. Louise Yeoman shows us another of the early processes of decline. Long before judges began arguing in any systematic way for restrictions on evidence and procedural caution, an important category of witchcraft suspects had been eliminated: the elite themselves. In medieval times, and up to the North Berwick panic of 1590–1, it was credible to think that a gentlewoman could be a witch; already by 1629 it was not.

Nevertheless Levack is surely right to emphasise the importance of the panic of 1661–2, the last and greatest of Scotland's five national panics; the central government had initially encouraged it, but in April 1662 reined it in sharply in the belief that it had got out of hand. My own chapter on the state complements this by arguing that elite belief in witches was translated into large-scale prosecutions only when religion was used directly to buttress state power – something that became less

---

[26] Larner, *Enemies of God*, pp. 78–9, 176.

[27] Normand and Roberts provide a good deal of detail on the composition of *Daemonologie*, arguing persuasively for an early date close to 1591: Norand and Roberts (eds), *Witchcraft in Early Modern Scotland*, pp. 327–34. However, they say little or nothing about the events of 1597.

necessary once the Glorious Revolution of 1689 overthrew divine-right monarchy and began the reluctant move towards religious pluralism. When the state began to stop persecuting people for having the wrong version of Christian religion, it lost the imperative need to persecute witches. This argument could be seen as a case-study in support of Stuart Clark's general European contention that witchcraft was a particularly heinous political crime under divine-right monarchy.[28]

But the early stages of religious pluralism were painful. Many leaders of the newly-presbyterian Church of Scotland could not see why they should not be allowed to persecute their opponents. Witchcraft accusations offered a weapon for those seeking to restore official religious uniformity, and to attack 'Sadduceeism' (denial of spirits) and 'atheism'. These were often parish ministers, who had always been crucial in the early stages of witchcraft accusations. They and their parish elders were the men who arrested and interrogated suspected witches, took depositions from neighbours, and prepared the prosecution case before trial. However, the men who controlled the actual trial process – those in central government – no longer shared their concerns.

What this would lead us to expect in the 1690s would be a major local witchcraft panic, fuelled by ministers' concerns about official tolerance of ungodliness. When the local accusations entered the trial process, however, central government would no longer authorise the witch-hunting ministers' colleagues to hold local trials; instead they would send the cases for trial centrally, and ensure that the trials ended in acquittal. And this is what we find in Michael Wasser's chapter, an important case-study of the decline and survival of witch-hunting attitudes. Wasser puts the famous 1697 case of Christian Shaw in its proper context for the first time, showing not only how a dramatic case of apparent demonic possession could still light the flames of witch-burning, but also how quickly the flames would be quenched by governmental doubts about evidence. Since 1662, as Levack points out, the extraction of confessions under torture had been curtailed. Now the testimony of demoniacs like Shaw was also receiving critical scrutiny in the light of the scientific revolution. Some people, as Wasser shows, seized on evidence of demonic possession: they hoped that it would validate scientifically, not only witch-belief, but Christianity itself. This opens up a fascinating subject, and there is surely more to be said on the relationship between witchcraft and intellectual ideas in this formative period between the Reformation and the Enlightenment. However, Wasser concludes that the evidence generated in the Glasgow region failed to convince the people who mattered: the politicians. It is no accident that Levack, Wasser and I all quote a politician, Secretary Johnstone, expressing the most thoroughly sceptical view about witchcraft that Scotland had heard since the witch-hunt began.

The Glasgow ministers could generate witchcraft accusations only in a climate of popular witch-belief. Survival of witchcraft is addressed in more detail by Ted Cowan and Lizanne Henderson, carefully disentangling the popular beliefs of the eighteenth and early nineteenth centuries from subsequent accretions. They also

---

[28] Clark, *Thinking with Demons*, ch. 40.

provide a much-needed clarification of the last known execution, in Dornoch in 1727. Accidents of survival may lie behind the fact that most of their cases come from parts of Scotland where relatively little witch-hunting had occurred – Galloway, the Highlands, Caithness and Sutherland; but this shows how widespread witch-belief was, while the tenacity of popular witch-belief is certainly striking. It was, after all, part of an animistic or magical world-view that made good sense to those who had not been schooled out of it, as it had done throughout the witch-hunt and for many centuries before it. In a sense, as Cowan and Henderson conclude, such beliefs are 'beyond history'.

IV

So what goes around, comes around. Once the specific machinery for witch-hunting – the laws, the commissions of justiciary, the traditions of how to extract a confession – had been removed, Scotland was back where it had begun in the late middle ages. Witches existed in the popular mind, but they had to be coped with in the same ways that they had been coped with before witch-hunting began. Some of Cowan and Henderson's post-1736 'witches' were, in their own eyes, charmers like Joyce Miller's, whose repertoire included spells for counter-magic against witchcraft. As Ronald Hutton points out, witch-beliefs are common in the modern world, and even witch-hunting persists today in some places.

Yet Enlightenment Scotland had two relevant differences from the late middle ages. Firstly, the elite had a different relationship with the witch-believing common folk. The late-medieval elite had been few and distant: the elite was now numerous and in touch with the common folk, but sceptical about witchcraft. Sir Walter Scott in 1830 commented on James VI's book of 1597: it was 'a deep work on Demonology, embracing, in their fullest extent, the most absurd and gross of the popular errors on this subject'.[29] James, like all demonologists, did draw on popular beliefs as these presented themselves in witches' confessions – but he also displayed consistent scepticism about any popular testimony that did not fit his intellectual system. Scott did not even recognise that James had *had* an intellectual system. The collapse of intellectual demonology during the Enlightenment had been so complete that the intellectuals of Scott's day could no longer see anything rational beyond the luxuriant, romantic and fascinating undergrowth of popular superstition.[30] When witch-belief was regarded as popular superstition, it would be tolerated but not allowed to influence public policy.

The second difference was that among the common folk themselves, the legacy of witch-hunting could not be erased. The lynching of Janet Cornfoot in 1705, described by Cowan and Henderson, occurred because the public had learned to expect the state to execute witches and found their expectation suddenly

[29] W. Scott, *Letters on Demonology and Witchcraft* (New York, 1830), p. 210.
[30] Cf. C. O. Parsons, *Witchcraft and Demonology in Scott's Fiction* (Edinburgh, 1964), pp. 134–51, 177–204.

frustrated. Although this lynching may well have been unique, this does not mean that the legacy of witch-hunting was short-lived. There were repeated attempts to use local judicial machinery to act against witches, even after the repeal of the witchcraft statute in 1736. Belief in witches was strong among highlanders in the nineteenth century: should we attribute this to popular traditions about rowan trees and the like, or to the fact that these were God-fearing folk who had read Exodus 22:18 and believed what it said?[31] Witchcraft and Christian biblicism could never be entirely separated.

V

Collections of essays that aim at presenting innovative research cannot also aim at comprehensive coverage of their subject. Several issues calling for further research have already been mentioned, and a few more may be touched on here. Scottish theology presents an unsolved problem. Most theological writings said little of witchcraft, and its place in systematic theology is unclear. Harm and suffering could be inflicted by God, as a punishment for sin or to harden the believer's faith. Witchcraft and even the Devil seem to have been marginal.[32] The Protestant tendency to hesitate before attributing misfortune to witchcraft, outlined by Stuart Clark, was open to these theologians.[33] Yet they did not espouse it openly, and it was often churchmen who promoted witch-hunting, while its critics tended to be lawyers. Larner grappled with this problem, but a solution has still to be found.[34] Then there is much to be done on the regional pattern of witch-hunting. Why so much in east-central Scotland and so little in the Highlands? Why so much in small towns and so little in Edinburgh? Then there is the issue of witchcraft testimonies as texts or narratives. Diane Purkiss has shown something of what might be done here;[35] we need more studies of how confessing witches and aggrieved neighbours shaped the stories they told, perhaps focusing on the interaction between popular and elite beliefs. This would tell us much about early modern culture as a whole.

One way in which the call for further research may be met is through the Survey of Scottish Witchcraft, a project currently being undertaken in the Department of

[31] Cf. M. Bennett, *Oatmeal and the Catechism: Scottish Gaelic Settlers in Quebec* (Edinburgh, 1998), pp. 50, 55, 58, 129–30.

[32] For an important recent study of Scottish theological concerns see D. G. Mullan, *Scottish Puritanism, 1590–1638* (Oxford, 2000).

[33] Clark, *Thinking with Demons*, pp. 530–2; S. Clark, 'Protestant demonology: sin, uperstition, and society, c.1520–c.1630', in Ankarloo and Henningsen (eds), *Early Modern European Witchcraft*.

[34] Larner, *Enemies of God*, pp. 157–9. Cf. C. Larner, 'Two late Scottish witchcraft tracts', in S. Anglo (ed.), *The Damned Art: Essays in the Literature of Witchcraft* (London, 1977), and C. J. Larner (née Ross), 'Scottish Demonology in the Sixteenth and Seventeenth Centuries' (Ph.D. thesis, University of Edinburgh, 1962).

[35] D. Purkiss, 'Sounds of silence: fairies and incest in Scottish witchcraft stories', in S. Clark (ed.), *Languages of Witchcraft: Narrative, Ideology and Meaning in Early Modern Culture* (London, 2001).

Scottish History, University of Edinburgh.[36] This is a survey of central and local records of Scottish witch-hunting, extracting a wide range of information on each case and placing them on an online database. Many new cases are being uncovered. The trial process is being recorded, as are over a hundred qualitative themes – from fairies, rowan trees and south-running water to witch-pricking, the precise appearance of the Devil and the citation of demonological authorities. The Survey will allow researchers to ask a wide variety of new questions about the recorded scale and distribution of such themes, from which a new synthesis of knowledge on the subject may eventually emerge.

In the meantime, the chapters that follow provide detailed answers to a range of questions that *can* be asked about the Scottish witch-hunt and its context. In the process, they illuminate many aspects of early modern Scottish society – a society that can be fully understood only when its witch-haunted nature is grasped.

[36] For more details see the Survey's website: www.arts.ed.ac.uk/witches. The four members of the project team (Lauren Martin, Joyce Miller, Louise Yeoman and myself) are all contributors to the present book. When complete, the Survey will replace both Larner's 1977 *Source-Book* and Stuart Macdonald's more recent electronic revision of it, the 'Scottish Witch-Hunt Database'.

2

The global context
of the Scottish witch-hunt

Ronald Hutton

I

To suggest that the trials for witchcraft in early modern Scotland should be set within a world context is not to advocate a new approach, but to revert to an old one. During the 1960s a global perspective was dominant in the study of witchcraft. Far more attention was paid to the subject by anthropologists working among tribal peoples than by experts in European history, and when those anthropologists pooled their ideas in edited collections, the latter would routinely include one or two papers on early modern Europe, as if the phenomenon under investigation was essentially the same across space and time.[1] Conversely, historians at work on early modern British witchcraft beliefs during the same decade acknowledged the importance of research into those in the developing world;[2] indeed, that research was one of the forces which powered the upsurge of scholarly interest in witchcraft studies among early modernists during the last three decades of the twentieth century. The overwhelming majority of them were carried out in Africa, and driven by the feeling that Europeans needed urgently to understand Africans at a time when independent modern states were rapidly appearing all over the continent.

The situation has now reversed, with more research being carried out by European scholars into witchcraft beliefs and accusations in Europe itself. Much of it consists of a close study of a single community, case or text, and while cross-comparison is still the norm, it very rarely takes in data from outside European cultures. The alteration has partly been due to the sheer volume of research, and of inter-disciplinary insights, with which specialists in early modern studies now have to reckon; with so much reading to be done in one's own corner, it is very hard to find time to move out of it. It has also been propelled by a shift of attitude among

---

[1] E.g. J. Middleton (ed.), *Magic, Witchcraft and Curing* (Austin, Texas, 1967); M. Marwick (ed.), *Witchcraft and Sorcery* (Harmondsworth, 1970); M. Douglas (ed.), *Witchcraft Confessions and Accusations* (London, 1970).

[2] E.g. A. Macfarlane, *Witchcraft in Tudor and Stuart England* (London, 1970); K. Thomas, *Religion and the Decline of Magic: Studies in Popular Beliefs in Sixteenth and Seventeenth-Century England* (London, 1971).

anthropologists themselves, who have been inclined since the 1970s to insist on the unique nature of each society, of the difficulties of translating concepts between cultures and languages, and of the special danger of projecting European mental constructions onto other peoples. The change has also, however, been the result of a general sense of loss of contact between the European world and its former colonies as decolonisation has proceeded.

It can result at times in some very stark limitations of vision. The study of accusations of witchcraft in the English colonies in North America, and especially of the sensational episode at Salem, is invariably related to those in the parent society in Europe. This is natural enough, but both in terms of duration and of numbers of victims, colonial witch persecutions were trivial affairs compared with those among native American peoples as different and as widely dispersed as the Iroquois, the Navaho, and the Tlingit.[3] For this reason alone, it would seem a logical exercise to attempt comparisons across ethnic and cultural boundaries. Furthermore, anthropological theory is itself altering, once again, in ways which make such comparisons seem more desirable. There is a call for analyses which demonstrate how cultural systems communicate between themselves as well as internally.[4] One of the key texts of the change of attitude in the 1970s was John Saliba's attack on Mircea Eliade, which defined anthropology in terms of holistic field-work in a small-scale society using participant observation, void of all comparative and diachronic interests and sceptical of generalisations across cultures.[5] For almost two decades this was repeated virtually as a credo, but by 1992 another anthropologist could describe it as 'a good example of misunderstanding and academic narrowness', which had cut the discipline off from the history of religion.[6] The present chapter will represent one attempt to reunite anthropology and history in the field of research into witchcraft beliefs.

II

It draws upon studies of a hundred tribal groups made between 1890 and 1990: sixty in sub-Saharan Africa, five in the Indian subcontinent, twenty-one in Oceania (New Guinea, New Zealand and the Pacific Islands), nine in North America (including Greenland) and five in South America.[7] A comparison of these studies

---

[3] A. F. C. Wallace, *The Death and Rebirth of the Seneca* (New York, 1972); C. Kluckhorn, *Navaho Witchcraft* (Boston, Mass., 1944); F. de Laguna, 'Tlingit: people of the wolf and raven', in W. W. Fitzhugh and A. Crowell (eds), *Crossroads of Continents: Cultures of Siberia and Alaska* (Washington, DC, 1988), pp. 58–63.

[4] E.g. G. E. Marcus and M. J. Fischer, *Anthropology as Cultural Critique* (Chicago, Ill., 1986).

[5] J. A. Saliba, *'Homo Religiosus' in Mircea Eliade* (Leiden, 1976).

[6] A.-L. Siikala, 'Introduction', in A.-L. Siikala and M. Hoppal, *Studies on Shamanism* (Helsinki and Budapest, 1992), pp. 15–16.

[7] W. Crooke, *An Introduction to the Popular Religion and Folklore of Northern India* (Allahabad, 1894), pp. 347–67; A. Lyall, *Asiatic Studies: Religious and Social: 1st Series* (London, 1899), pp. 99–130; H. A. Junod, *The Life of a South African Tribe* (Neuchatel, 1912); B. Malinowski, *Argonauts of the Pacific* (London, 1922); A. M. Hocart, 'Medicine and witchcraft in Eddystone of the Solomons', *Journal of the*

throws up a number of obvious points. One is that the research involved is far more thorough and comprehensive than any carried out into witchcraft in early modern Europe, because the societies concerned are relatively small and self-contained. In most cases it seeks to relate witchcraft beliefs and accusations not just to social and economic structures but to the whole tribal system of beliefs concerning religion,

Royal Anthropological Institute, 55 (1925), 229–70; H. A. Stayt, *The BaVenda* (Oxford, 1931); R. F. Fortune, *Sorcerers of Dobu* (London, 1932), pp. 133–75; P. H. Buck, *Regional Diversity in the Elaboration of Sorcery in Polynesia* (New Haven, NJ, 1936); M. J. Field, *Religion and Medicine of the Ga People* (Oxford, 1937); E. E. Evans-Pritchard, *Witchcraft, Oracles and Magic among the Azande* (Oxford, 1937); E. J. Krige and J. D. Krige, *The Realm of a Rain-Queen* (Oxford, 1943), pp. 250–70; Kluckhorn, *Navaho Witchcraft*; H. Kuper, *An African Aristocracy* (Oxford, 1947); C. M. N. White, 'Witchcraft, divination and magic among the Balovale tribes', *Africa*, 18 (1948), 81–104; J. T. Munday, E. M. Voules and G. W. Broomfield, *Witchcraft* (London, 1951); G. Lienhardt, 'Some notions of witchcraft among the Dinka', *Africa*, 21 (1951), 303–18; J. Middleton, *The Kikuyu and Kamba of Kenya* (London, 1953), pp. 94–5; C. Mitchell, *The Yao Village* (Manchester, 1956); M. M. Edel, *The Chiga of Western Uganda* (Oxford, 1957), pp. 164–8; D. Forde, 'Spirits, witches and sorcerers in the supernatural economy of the Yako', *Journal of the Royal Anthropological Institute*, 88 (1958), 165–78; P. Bohannan, 'Extra-processual events in Tiv political institutions', *American Anthropologist*, 60 (1958), 1–12; J. Middleton, *Lugbara Religion* (Oxford, 1960); M. Hunter, *Reaction to Conquest* (Oxford, 1961), chs. 6–7; J. Middleton and E. H. Winter (eds), *Witchcraft and Sorcery in East Africa* (London, 1963); B. Reynolds, *Magic, Divination and Witchcraft among the Barotse of Northern Rhodesia* (London, 1963); V. Turner, 'Witchcraft and sorcery: taxonomy versus dynamics', *Africa*, 34 (1964), 314–24; M. G. Marwick, *Sorcery in its Social Setting: a Study of the Northern Rhodesian Cewa* (Manchester, 1965); P. Lawrence and M. J. Meggitt (eds), *Gods, Ghosts and Men in Melanesia* (Oxford, 1965); J. R. Crawford, *Witchcraft and Sorcery in Rhodesia* (Oxford, 1967); M. Fortes, *The Web of Kinship among the Tallensi* (Oxford, 1967), pp. 32–5; Middleton (ed.), *Magic, Witchcraft and Curing*; R. W. Lieban, *Cebuano Sorcery: Malign Magic in the Philippines* (Berkeley, Calif., 1967); D. J. Parkin, 'Medicines and men of influence', *Man*, new ser., 3 (1968), 424–39; Douglas (ed.), *Witchcraft Confessions and Accusations*; M. Gluckman, *Custom and Conflict in Africa* (Oxford, 1970), pp. 81–108; Marwick (ed.), *Witchcraft and Sorcery*; A. Harwood, *Witchcraft, Sorcery, and Social Categories among the Safwa* (Oxford, 1970); G. Wagner, *The Bantu of Western Kenya* (Oxford, 1970), pp. 95–113; Wallace, *Death and Rebirth of the Seneca*; R. W. Wyllie, 'Introspective witchcraft among the Effutu of southern Ghana', *Man*, new ser., 8 (1973), 74–9; W. D. Hammond-Tooke, 'The Cape Nguni witch familiar as a mediatory construct', *Man*, new ser., 9 (1974), 128–35; M. D. Jackson, 'Structure and event: witchcraft confessions among the Kuranko', *Man*, new ser., 10 (1975), 287–403; W. Bleek, 'Witchcraft, gossip, and death: a social drama', *Man*, new ser., 11 (1976), 526–41; H. Ngubane, 'Aspects of Zulu treatment', in J. B. Loudon (ed.), *Social Anthropology and Medicine* (London, 1976), pp. 328–37; D. Offiong, 'The social context of Ibibio witch beliefs', *Africa*, 53 (1982), 73–82; A. Strathern, 'Witchcraft, greed, cannibalism and death: some related themes from the New Guinea Highlands', in M. Bloch and J. Parry (eds), *Death and the Regeneration of Life* (Cambridge, 1982), pp. 111–21; N. Barley, *The Innocent Anthropologist* (London, 1983), pp. 103–39; S. Heald, 'Witches and thieves: deviant motivations in Gisu society', *Man*, new ser., 21 (1986), 65–78; de Laguna, 'Tlingit'; M. Rowlands and J.-P. Warnier, 'Sorcery, power and the modern state in Cameroon', *Man*, new ser., 23 (1988), 118–32; T. Gregor, 'Uneasy peace: intertribal relations in Brazil's Upper Xingu', in J. Haas (ed.), *The Anthropology of War* (Cambridge, 1991); S. Drucker-Brown, 'Mamprusi witchcraft, subversion, and changing gender relations', *Africa*, 63 (1993), 531–49; D. N. Gellner, 'Priests, healers, mediums and witches: the context of possession in the Kathmandu Valley, Nepal', *Man*, new ser., 29 (1994), 33–7; C.-H. Pradelles de Latour, 'Witchcraft and the avoidance of physical violence in Cameroon', *Journal of the Royal Anthropological Institute*, new ser., 1 (1995), 599–609; A. Skaria, 'Women, witchcraft and gratuitous violence in colonial Western India', *Past and Present*, 155 (May 1997), 109–41; M. D. Jakobsen, *Shamanism: Traditional and Contemporary Approaches to the Mastery of Spirits and Healing* (New York, 1999), pp. 94–100.

magic and cosmology. No specialist in early modern European studies has attempted that to date, although Stuart Clark has come closest.[8]

A second conclusion is that the studies reveal the existence of a very widespread belief in the figure to which the name of witch is traditionally given in English, despite all differences of cultures, languages and mentalities. It is found in every inhabited continent of the world, and is identified by a combination of five major characteristics. First, it defines a person who uses apparently supernatural means to cause uncanny misfortune or injury to others. Second, this person works to harm neighbours or kin rather than strangers; she or he is a threat to other members of a community. Third, this person works not for straightforward material gain but from envy or malice. She or he is either inherently evil or is in the grip of an inherently evil force. Fourth, the appearance of such a figure is not an isolated or unique event. The witch works in a tradition, either by inheritance, training or initiation. Fifth, this person can be opposed by fellow humans, either by using counter-magic, or by forcing her or him to rescind their own magic, or by eliminating her or him directly.

A large number of variables also combine with these constant characteristics of the witch-figure, such as gender, social status, whether she or he works alone or as part of a secret society, and whether his or her actions are deliberate or involuntary. These variables mean that in practice belief in the same sort of figure operates in different contexts and with different consequences. There is no tribal society which reproduces exactly the social, economic and cultural characteristics of the witch-craft accusations found in early modern Scotland. On the other hand, most of those individual characteristics do have exact parallels elsewhere in the world, and the distinctions between the nature and operation of witchcraft beliefs in different tribal societies in the same region of Africa, or in New Guinea, are often as great as those between any of those societies and that of early modern Scots. The five definitive characteristics outlined above are, by contrast, consistent worldwide.

Almost as widespread is the presence in tribal societies of witch doctors, in the original sense of the expression: individuals who specialise in detecting and removing the magical harm inflicted by witches, often serving a community and often working for payment. In most cases in which they have existed, these specialists would be the first resort of people who suspected that they, or their dependants, relatives or neighbours, had been injured by witchcraft. Direct action against the suspected witch would usually only follow a consultation with such an expert, often acting on information provided by the latter. These figures are the precise equivalents of those found throughout early modern Europe and known by the English names of cunning folk or wise-folk. Precise statistical reckoning of their frequency is rendered impossible by the variable depth and preoccupations of the ethnographic studies used above, but they occurred in the majority of the societies in the sample.

[8] S. Clark, *Thinking with Demons: the Idea of Witchcraft in Early Modern Europe* (Oxford, 1997).

A fourth major conclusion which may be drawn from that sample is that the stereotype of the witch is worldwide but not universal. At the conclusion of his justly-admired survey of the context of witch trials in early modern Europe, Robin Briggs suggested that a fear of the witch might be inherent in humanity: 'a psychic potential we cannot help carrying round within ourselves as part of our long-term inheritance'.[9] The evidence of anthropology is that this is not so, for there are plenty of tribal peoples across the world who do not believe that humans can work destructive magic. This is because they have alternative explanations for misfortune, usually that it is inflicted by angry or evil spirits, either of the natural world or of ancestors, who must be propitiated or defeated. The Andaman Islanders of the Indian Ocean, the Korongo of the Sudan, the Tallensi of Ghana, the Gurage of Ethiopia, the Banyang of Cameroon, the Fijians, the tribes of Uttar Pradesh, and the Ngaing of New Guinea are all examples of peoples who either do not believe in witchcraft at all or do not believe that it matters in practice.[10] Remarkably, these peoples were all surrounded by others who were very similar in society, economy and cosmology, but were obsessed with the danger of witchcraft.

Tribal opinions on the matter are very resilient. There are three islands off the north-east coast of New Guinea, within sight of each other and in regular communication: Dobu, Trobriand, and Fergusson. Their inhabitants are so similar, physically and socially, that they are essentially the same people. All fear witchcraft, but to Dobuans witches can be of either sex, even though women are regarded as more dangerous, to Trobrianders they are mostly male, and to Fergussonians they are essentially female, and inspire even more terror than in the other two islands. An obvious question to be asked is whether the people in one of these societies find anything odd about the discrepancy between their beliefs and those of the other two. The answer is completely negative; when a Dobuan man visits Trobriand, he is not afraid of the local women and starts to fear the men more, while the women on Fergusson frighten him even more than those at home.[11] This is why native peoples had no problems with the fact that the modern Europeans who entered their lands professed not to believe in witchcraft; the natives simply accepted that for some reason the foreigners were immune to it.

By contrast, they usually bitterly resented and resisted the attempts by the same foreigners to convince them that their own traditions regarding witches were erroneous, and the abolition by colonial regimes of the legal penalties against witchcraft and their concomitant persecution of witch doctors. Here is a direct parallel with

[9] R. Briggs, *Witches and Neighbours: the Social and Cultural Context of European Witchcraft* (London, 1996), p. 394; and see p. 410, where he suggests that perhaps 'human beings have a "witch detector" somewhere in their consciousness'.

[10] P. Mayer, 'Witches', and S. F. Nadel, 'Witchcraft in four African societies', in Marwick (ed.), *Witchcraft and Sorcery*; P. Lawrence, 'The Ngaing of the Rai Coast', in Lawrence and Meggitt (eds), *Gods, Ghosts and Men*, pp. 198–223; Fortes, *Web of Kinship among the Tallensi*, pp. 32–5; I. M. Lewis, 'A structural approach to witchcraft and spirit possession', and M. Ruel, 'Were-animals and the introverted witch', in Douglas (ed.), *Witchcraft Confessions and Accusations*, pp. 293–309, 335–50.

[11] R. F. Fortune, 'Sorcerers of Dobu', in Marwick (ed.), *Witchcraft and Sorcery*.

the relationships between elite and popular beliefs, and between the legal system and traditional magic, in the period during and following the abolition of the death penalty for witchcraft in European states. Indeed, it was a direct extension of the same process, with some of the same European elites confronting another group of aggrieved commoners. Scots posted as colonial administrators to Uganda or Rhodesia found themselves re-enacting measures of education and coercion which their ancestors had undertaken in Fife and the Lothians two hundred years before. Whereas modern rationalism posed a dramatic and destructive challenge to traditional tribal beliefs, however, Christianity was at best an ambivalent force in the interaction. In the hands of European missionaries, it could be combined with rationalist attitudes to provide arguments against suspicions of witchcraft. At the same time, the existence in the Bible of texts which appeared to sanction and encourage the persecution of witches made it as potent a document among some modern African witch-hunters as among their early modern European equivalents. Charismatic Christian churches, formed among natives, were sometimes in the forefront of agitation for the detection and punishment of witchcraft.[12]

Reference to that agitation touches upon another revealing aspect of the ethnographic studies: that the distinction between endemic and epidemic accusations of witchcraft, familiar to scholars of early modern Europe and certainly relevant to Scotland, is a global phenomenon. All over the world at particular periods, native societies habituated to a chronic low-level fear of witchcraft, and a trickle of denunciations, would be swept by panics leading to large-scale trials. Often these would either be produced by the appearance of novel movements of expert witch-finders, or produce them in turn; such movements are recorded among the Seneca of upstate New York in the late eighteenth century, and in India and much of sub-Saharan Africa in the twentieth.[13] Large-scale witch-hunts seem to have been a

[12] J. R. Crawford, 'The consequences of allegation', and R. G. Willis, 'The Kamcape movement', in Marwick (ed.), *Witchcraft and Sorcery*; Offiong, 'Social context of Ibibio witch beliefs', 73–5; T. . Beidelman, 'Witchcraft in Ukaguru', and J. la Fontaine, 'Witchcraft in Bugisu', in Middleton and Winter (eds), *Witchcraft and Sorcery*; A. Redmayne, 'Chikanga: an African diviner with an international reputation', in Douglas (ed.), *Witchcraft Confessions and Accusations*; R. N. H. Bulmer, 'The Kyaka of the Western Highlands', and K. O. L. Burridge, 'Tangu, Northern Madang District', in Lawrence and Meggitt (eds), *Gods, Ghosts and Men*, pp. 158–9; 226–30; Wyllie, 'Introspective witchcraft among the Effutu', 74–9.

[13] A. Richards, 'A modern movement of witch-finders', and M. Marwick, 'The Bwanali-Mpulumutsi anti-witchcraft movement', in Marwick (ed.), *Witchcraft and Sorcery*; Willis, 'Kamcape Movement'; M. Douglas, 'Techniques of sorcery control in central Africa', in Middleton and Winter (eds), *Witchcraft and Sorcery*; Strathern, 'Witchcraft, greed, cannibalism and death', pp. 111–33; B. Ward, 'Some observations on religious cults in Ashanti', *Africa*, 26 (1956), 47–60; M. Douglas, 'Introduction', R. G. Willis, 'Instant Millennium', and E. Ardener, 'Witchcraft, economics, and the continuity of belief', in Douglas (ed.), *Witchcraft Confessions and Accusations*, pp. xiii-xxxviii, 129–39, 141–60; Marwick, *Sorcery in its Social Setting*, ch. 3; Bohannan, 'Extra-processual events in Tiv political institutions', 1–12; Parkin, 'Medicines and men of influence', 424–39; Offiong, 'Social context of Ibibio witch beliefs', 73–82; I. A. Niehaus, 'Witch-hunting and political legitimacy: continuity and change in Green Valley, Lebowa', *Africa*, 63 (1993), 498–530; Heald, 'Witches and thieves', 65–78; Wallace, *Death and Rebirth of the Seneca, passim*; Skaria, 'Women, witchcraft, and gratuitous violence', 130–41; P. Morton-Williams, 'The Atinga cult among the south-western Yoruba', *Bulletin de l'Institute Français d'Afrique Noire*, 18 (1956), 315–34.

response to periods of unusually severe social and economic tension, and in all the well-recorded cases this was the result of the impact of Western colonialism itself. The lack of any historical depth to knowledge of the peoples concerned precludes any firm judgement on the important question of whether epidemics of witchcraft accusation occurred within them before their world was disrupted by that impact. In a few cases, however, tribal traditions suggested strongly that they had indeed taken place before regular contact with Europeans had occurred.[14] Likewise – and here is another parallel with Europe itself – there are many recorded cases of tribal communities which believed in witchcraft and yet never seem to have experienced a panic over it. A feature of the well-recorded witch-finding movements was that they were led by individuals who, although superior in their education and cultural sophistication to most of their society, were not drawn from the top ranks of the traditional ruling elite. This has obvious parallels in Britain, where the sensational example of Matthew Hopkins is accompanied by those of the lairds and ministers who were most prominent in the investigation of Scottish accusations of witch-craft. Conversely, major tribal rulers such as Handsome Lake of the Seneca in the late eighteenth century, and Manuelito of the Navaho and Lobengula of the Nde-bele in the late nineteenth, were just as capable of using traditional witchcraft beliefs to reinforce their own inherited powers as King James VI and I.[15]

A further insight furnished by the ethnographic studies is that cosmologies do not have to be coherent mental constructions. All tribal peoples who believed in witchcraft also took other forms of supernatural agency, such as deities, ancestral spirits, animal spirits and spirits of the land, into consideration. Only particular kinds of misfortune were attributed to witches. What was important in making that attribution was the practical result, in explaining or providing means of action in what were often literally matters of life and death. The fact that the theoretical origins and operation of witchcraft seemed in some places to be at odds with general presumptions about the workings of deities and spirits, did not trouble the people concerned.[16] This needs to be borne in mind when trying to resolve the apparent complexities and contradictions in beliefs concerning Christianity, fairies and witches, among early modern European commoners.

The global context makes plain that the intensity of suspicions and accusations of witchcraft registered in early modern Europe, even allowing for regional varia-tion, is about average in the overall human experience. As said above, there are societies on record which do not believe in witchcraft, and others which admit to its existence in principle but do not take regard of it in practice. There have also, however, been others which have feared and hunted witches with an intensity known only in the worst of the major European panics. In the Chiapas Highlands

---

[14] Douglas, 'Techniques of sorcery control', pp. 123–30; Willis, 'Instant Millennium', pp. 129–39.

[15] Wallace, *Death and Rebirth of the Seneca*; Kluckhorn, *Navaho Witchcraft*, chs. 2–3; Crawford, *Witchcraft and Sorcery*, ch. 17.

[16] Evans-Pritchard, *Witchcraft, Oracles and Magic among the Azande*, chs. 1.1, 1.4, 1.8; Middleton, *Lugbara Religion*, pp. 238–50; Lawrence and Meggitt, 'Introduction', in Lawrence and Meggitt (eds), *Gods, Ghosts and Men*, pp. 16–18; la Fontaine, 'Witchcraft in Bugisu', pp. 187–220.

of Mexico, a man was being murdered because of suspicion of witchcraft on average once every two months during the 1950s. Accusation was virtually continuous.
Writing of the BaVenda of the Transvaal in 1931, Hugh Stayt commented that 'fear
of the *muloi* [witch] and her creatures hangs as a sinister shadow over all their
doings'. A study of the Kwahu of Ghana revealed that 92 per cent of the population
was involved at some point in life as an accuser, a victim or a suspect, of alleged
witchcraft. In Cameroon every village of the Bakweri tribe had its witch-hanging
tree. King Lobengula of the Ndebele presided over an average nine or ten executions per month. Among the Pondo of South Africa, the rate ran at one per day
on the eve of the British conquest and the number of accused who fled or were
punished with fines was also large. A British official serving in India during the
early nineteenth century estimated that about a thousand women had been burned
alive for alleged witchcraft on the northern plains during the previous thirty years
– a rate of attrition far more serious than that caused by the more notorious native
custom of *sati*, or widow-burning.[17]

The ethnographic material demonstrates vividly that an active belief in witchcraft
can have functional social applications which are relevant to a historian of Scotland.
All over the world, where individuals were accused of it, they tended most often to
be people who deviated from social norms; in that respect accusations reinforced
those norms and discouraged eccentricity or cultural radicalism. At other times,
they acted as midwives to social change, in that the leaders of witch-finding movements were usually (as said) drawn from outside traditional elites and legitimised
or reinforced the power of new groups. Accusations could also provide a means by
which disempowered individuals, such as children or (in male-dominated cultures)
women, could attract attention and respect. They could articulate otherwise
unspeakable fantasies, reveal and represent concealed destructive impulses within
humans, and identify and express tensions within families and communities. Conversely, by charging anti-social behaviour with apparent magical power, they could
support social virtues and discourage the expression of animosity. They could
be used to collect bad debts and enforce economic obligations. Measures against
presumed witchcraft enabled humans to act purposefully in the face of adversity.
It was for these reasons that the anthropologist Mary Douglas could sum up an
influential school of thought in her discipline as holding that witchcraft accusations
functioned as instruments of social health rather than symptoms of sickness.[18]

Mary Douglas herself, however, held a different opinion, as did others among
her colleagues.[19] All these positive functions of belief in witchcraft only acted to

---

[17] M. Nash, 'Witchcraft as social process in a Tzeltal community', *American Indigena*, 20 (1961),
121–6; J. Pitt-Rivers, 'Spiritual power in Central America', in Douglas (ed.), *Witchcraft Confessions and
Accusations*, pp. 183–206; Stayt, *The BaVenda*, p. 275; Bleek, 'Witchcraft, gossip, and death', 526–41;
Ardener, 'Witchcraft, economics, and the continuity of belief', p. 150; Crawford, *Witchcraft and Sorcery*,
ch. 17; Skaria, 'Women, witchcraft and gratuitous violence', 109–12.

[18] Douglas, 'Introduction', in Douglas (ed.), *Witchcraft Confessions and Accusations*, pp. xiii-xxi.

[19] See particularly Douglas, 'Techniques of sorcery control'; Winter, 'The enemy within: Amba
witchcraft and sociological theory', in Middleton and Winter (eds), *Witchcraft and Sorcery*.

strengthen societies, or to enable them to adjust more efficiently to changing circumstances, where the rate of accusation was low and sporadic, and subjected to firm controls. In many cases this situation did not obtain, and suspicions and accusations did not resolve fears and hostilities but aggravated them and represented obstacles to peaceful co-operation. At worst, they could rend communities apart and leave lasting resentments, or greatly compound the suffering consequent upon adaptation to new social and economic developments. Most societies which have believed firmly in witchcraft have regarded it as a scourge and a curse of which they have longed to be rid; but the only way in which they have been able to conceive of bringing this happy end about has been by destroying the witches. That Scotland eventually escaped from this vicious circle owes much to the unusual ability of early modern European elites to refashion mental constructs.

III

These general reflections are of use in showing what the Scottish experience had in common with the global patterns. They may not, however, do much to assist an understanding of the Scottish trials themselves. To place those more revealingly in context it is necessary to take advantage of that depth of historical perspective which is possible to European studies and lacking in many other parts of the world. To specialists in early modern studies, the trials often appear to represent a disturbing interlude produced by circumstances peculiar to the period. It is patently true that such events were apparently absent from most of the Middle Ages, just as they have been missing from the modern period; in that sense those of the early modern epoch are self-contained. A longer backwards projection, however, reveals that modernity is actually unique in its attitudes to magic, while the early and high Middle Ages represented a remarkable hiatus in the prosecution of witchcraft.[20] In this sense the early modern trials were a return to business as usual.

When the sources for ancient belief are brought together from all over continental Europe, including the Greek, Roman and Germanic linguistic spheres, they reveal a preoccupation with the classic global stereotype of the witch, in all the five points suggested above. It is pretty well the same image which features in the early modern period. As in most tribal societies, likewise, the ancient European penalty for committing murder by witchcraft was execution or exile. The hiatus in the Middle Ages is explicable in terms of a single solvent force, Christianity, which ended witch trials in every society in which it was adopted as the official religion. It did so with a simple and novel theological argument: that if the cosmos was controlled by a single all-powerful and benevolent deity, then magic could not operate unless that deity willed it. Witchcraft had therefore to be an illusion or a fantasy. Like the modern termination of witch trials, the early medieval one was imposed from above, by the alteration of law codes, and the change is visible in one state after

---

[20] This subject is much under-researched, but it was one of the themes of N. Cohn, *Europe's Inner Demons* (Falmer, 1975).

another, often prescribed (as in the case of Charlemagne's celebrated capitulary to the Saxons in the 780s) with savage penalties for continued witch-persecution.

The renewal of trials in Europe at the end of the Middle Ages must therefore represent one or both of two different developments. One is that Christian theology buckled under the pressure of enduring ancient beliefs, and adapted to take account of popular cosmologies. The other is that Christian theology developed as a result of its own inner dynamics, which set it on a convergence course with the old beliefs. It is notable in this context how reluctant and hesitant churchmen commonly remained about the resumption of witch trials. The latter were driven by the fears of the populace, and encouraged and justified more often by secular magistrates than by clergy. There is no sign that early modern European commoners had to be re-educated to denounce each other as witches; in most cases they were clearly acting on existing beliefs. The ancient images, therefore, really matter.

A major test case may illustrate the utility of a context which possesses both space and depth; the gendering of Scottish witchcraft accusations. It is well known that 85 per cent of the accused were female, a figure which matches well with the data from most of the rest of Western Europe, including England. Recent British specialists in the subject have provided a variety of different explanations for this feature, all rooted in the particular circumstances of early modern society. Christina Larner has drawn attention to the tendency of women to use words in situations of personal confrontation, while men were more prone to physical violence; in a culture which attributed magical efficacy to curses, this made suspicion of witchcraft easier for them. James Sharpe has pointed out that most of the alleged crimes of witches took place in the woman's sphere of work, comprising the more vulnerable areas of daily activity such as the house, domestic processes, in-field farming and the rearing of children. They therefore largely reflected tensions between women. Stuart Clark, concentrating on intellectual constructions of witchcraft, has emphasised the manner in which they opposed it to social norms, so that women dominated in it even as men controlled the public life and religion of actual society. Julian Goodare has stressed the utility of accusations in reinforcing communal pressure towards conformity and inhibiting nonconformist behaviour on the part of women in particular.[21] All these summaries of arguments do less than justice to the subtleties of the originals, and all of the latter make valid and important points about early modern society. It may still be proposed that a deepening of time and a widening of space sets them in a valuable perspective.

The former exercise underpins the early modern material very neatly, by revealing a widespread conviction across ancient Europe that witches were essentially female. Both Germanic law-codes and Roman literature testify to a belief in a being known in Latin as the *strix* or *striga*, a woman with the power to fly abroad at night inflicting death or illness. Greek and Roman texts portray female magicians on an

---

[21] Larner, *Witchcraft and Religion*, ch. 3; J. Sharpe, *Instruments of Darkness: Witchcraft in England, 1550–1750* (London, 1996), pp. 169–89; Clark, *Thinking with Demons*, pp. 108–33; J. Goodare, 'Women and the witch-hunt in Scotland', *Social History*, 23 (1998), 288–308.

ascending scale from the Pamphile of Apuleius, and Theocritus's nameless *pharmaceutria*, aristocratic women who have learned operative magic, to Horace's Canidia, a professional sorceress, to Lucan's Erichtho, a more or less superhuman being who can suspend all laws of nature and is feared by the gods themselves.[22] Early Welsh literature, like modern Welsh folklore, embodies a fear of the *wrach* (hag), most famously personified as the Black Hag killed by Arthur in *Culhwch ac Olwen* and the Nine Hags of Gloucester slain by the hero of *Peredur*.

This would all make a good fit with the pattern of religious behaviour discernible across pre-Christian Europe, whether in the traditional provinces of Graeco-Roman, Germanic or Celtic culture. Religion seems essentially to have been regarded as an aspect of political or communal duty, conducted by chieftains, kings, generals, magistrates or heads of families. More specialised male spiritual functionaries had supporting roles by reading omens, explaining occurrences and advising leaders, as soothsayers, augurs, haruspices or Druids. Men could also learn how to work magic, including destructive spells, from books or teachers. Within this system, women retained an important function as repositories or channels for natural and primeval spiritual power; whereas men had to acquire the knowledge of magic, women were believed to have it in them. Sometimes they acted as permanent representatives of natural forces, such as the Vestal Virgins. More often, they were brought on when normality broke down and the usual spiritual advisers felt out of their depth, as sibyls, oracles, prophetesses, seeresses, wise women or Druidesses. The Pythoness of Delphi, the Sibyl of Cumae, the great German prophetess Veleda, and literary figures such as the Norse Thorbjorg in *Eirik's Saga* and the Irish Fedelm from *Tain bo Cuailgne*, are all representatives of this tradition. Conversely, women were regarded as having the potential to use that 'natural' magic for bad purposes, and thus matched the global figure of the witch. It is this ancient system which underpins the early modern trials.

A broader perspective of space, however, makes such a suggestion, although still valid, somewhat less neat; and it does not have to be broadened very far. The Scottish witch trials have most commonly been compared with those of England, as in this volume,[23] or with those of Continental Europe. Such a process produces important insights, but others are thrown up by a comparison with Scotland's forgotten neighbour: Iceland. The Icelanders held their own witch trials in the same period as the Scots, on a lesser scale as would befit their much smaller and more dispersed population. Between 1604 and 1720 they brought 120 individuals to court, and executed 22 of them in four major outbreaks of accusation. So far the record is a microcosm of the usual European pattern, but with one major anomaly: of the 120 people tried, only ten were women, of whom one was executed. As

[22] Cohn, *Europe's Inner Demons*, pp. 206–9. The texts cited can be found in Apuleius, *Metamorphoses*, chs. 1–5; Theocritus, *Idyll 2*; Horace, *Epodes*, 3, 5, 17, and *Satires*, I.8, II.1, II.8; Lucan, *Pharsalia*, VI.415–830.

[23] J. Sharpe, 'Witch-hunting and witch historiography: some Anglo-Scottish comparisons', Chapter 11 below.

the historian of the Icelandic trials, Kirsten Hastrup, rather blandly remarks, Icelanders tended not to credit women with magic.[24]

To a historian of Britain, this comes, or should come, as a bombshell. Early modern Iceland was economically, socially and politically extremely similar to Scotland, or at least to parts of it, and its gender relations were virtually identical. All the functional arguments produced by British social historians for the predominance of women in witchcraft accusations therefore ought to have applied to it; but they did not, and this in itself must suggest that those functional factors were conditioning, and not fundamental, reasons for the gendering of British trials. A further broadening of the geographical perspective at first only worsens the problem. Iceland during the period was under the rule of Denmark, and yet Danish witch trials were mostly of women. It had originally been settled from Norway, but 80 per cent of the people formally accused of witchcraft by early modern Norwegians were female. Almost as high a percentage is recorded in the trials in Sweden. Not until a historian turns to Finland does a parallel to the Icelandic case appear: in the 710 recorded trials, a clear majority of the accused were male until the great panic of the 1670s, when a Western European stereotype of witchcraft was introduced and women began to be denounced in significant numbers.[25] The space on the map between Iceland and Finland is a broad one, and it seems hard to find a means of spanning it which makes sense of the unusual gender balance of accusations in both. A further broadening of perspective, however, does supply one: in the phenomenon of shamanism.

IV

Historically, the largest witch-free area of the whole inhabited planet has been Siberia. As defined by the political boundaries of the modern Russian and Soviet empires, it covers a third of the northern hemisphere and contains what ethnographers have identified as thirty-five indigenous native groups. Linguistically, socially, ethnically, and economically, these are as diverse as the vast extent of the territory concerned would lead one to expect. None has ever displayed any belief in the stereotype of the witch, as defined above; where English translators find 'witches' in native Siberian folk-tales, these are always superhuman females, worsted by heroes in creation legends.[26] Uncanny misfortune is always explained in the classic alternative fashion found among other traditional peoples without witchcraft beliefs: as inflicted by ancestral or nature-spirits, which must be

[24] K. Hastrup, 'Iceland: sorcerers and paganism', in B. Ankarloo and G. Henningsen (eds), *Early Modern European Witchcraft* (Oxford, 1990), pp. 383–402.

[25] J. C. V. Johansen, 'Denmark: the sociology of accusations', H. E. Naess, 'Norway: the criminoogical context', B. Ankarloo, 'Sweden: the mass burnings', and A. Heikkinen and T. Kervenin, 'Finland: the male domination', in Ankarloo and Henningsen (eds), *Early Modern European Witchcraft*, pp. 339–66, 367–82, 285–318, 319–38; P. Sorlin, *'Wicked Arts': Witchcraft and Magic Trials in Southern Sweden, 1635–1754* (Leiden, 1999).

[26] Cf. V. Dioszegi, *Tracing Shamans in Siberia* (Oosterhout, 1968), pp. 23–4, 204–5.

defeated or propitiated. All over Siberia, this was undertaken by specialists to whom European ethnographers, followed by international scholarship in general, have given the blanket term of 'shamans', used originally by one linguistic group. These commonly carried out their work by a dramatic performance of dancing, chanting and drumming, in the course of which they entered trances and called familiar spirits to aid them, or in which their own spirits fly forth to accomplish the necessary magical work. They also have the power to curse, and among some Siberian tribes misfortune was commonly ascribed to spirits sent by shamans serving a hostile clan or faction. A majority of Siberian shamans have generally been male, although women have been acceptable if their talent for it has been clearly pre-eminent or if no qualified man has been available.[27] Shamanism is perfectly compatible with a belief in witches; in the Arctic zone of North America native peoples had very similar practitioners to the shamans of Siberia, and one of their most important functions was to detect and expose the human workers of bad magic within their community. This pattern has been found from the Tlingit of Alaska round to the Eskimo of eastern Greenland;[28] but it did not obtain in Siberia.

The Ural Mountains form a fairly solid western limit to the shamanic cultural province, as to Siberia itself. Of the native peoples of European Russia, the Votyaks had magicians who sometimes entered ecstatic trances to accomplish their work, but the Cheremises, Chuvashes and Mordvins were served by specialists who used charms, scryed in reflecting surfaces, and cured with herbs in the manner of 'cunning folk' westward as far as the British Isles. Theirs is a world familiar enough to scholars of European folk magic, whereas Siberia is not.[29] To the north, however, the Urals peter out before reaching the ocean, allowing fairly easy passage along the coasts, and the Arctic part of Europe contains a people who, historically, had shamans of exactly the Siberian sort. They are the Saami, traditionally known to Russians as Lopar and other Europeans as Lapps. Their shamanism was suppressed by Lutheran missionaries in the seventeenth and eighteenth centuries, but not before it was well recorded.[30] Their main traditional home was in Finland, but their range extended far into northern Norway, stretching into contact with those districts which supplied many of the early settlers of Iceland.

This geographical pattern in itself suggests an explanation for the unusual gendering of early modern witchcraft accusations in both Iceland and Finland, but a use

---

[27] I am at present writing a survey of Siberian shamanism and studies based upon it. For recent general works upon it in the West, see H. H. Michael (ed.), *Studies in Siberian Shamanism* (Toronto, 1963); V. Dioszegi (ed.), *Popular Beliefs and Folklore Tradition in Siberia* (Bloomington, Ind., 1968); V. Dioszegi and M. Hoppal (eds), *Shamanism in Siberia* (Budapest, 1978); M. Hoppal (ed.), *Shamanism in Eurasia* (Gottingen, 1984); A.-L. Siikala, *The Rite Technique of the Siberian Shaman* (Helsinki, 1987); R. Hamayon, *La Chasse a L'Ame* (Nanterre, 1990); P. Vitebsky, *The Shaman* (London, 1995).

[28] De Laguna, 'Tlingit', p. 63; Jakobsen, *Shamanism*, pp. 27, 94–100.

[29] V. M. Mikhailowskii, 'Shamanism in Siberia and European Russia', *Journal of the Anthropological Institute of Great Britain and Ireland*, 24 (1895), 151–7; U. Holmberg, *Finno-Ugric and Siberian Mythology* (New York, 1964), p. 295.

[30] T. Ahlback (ed.), *Saami Religion* (Abo, 1987); T. Ahlback and J. Bergman (eds), *The Saami Shaman Drum* (Abo, 1991); L. Blackman and A. Hultkranz, *Studies in Lapp Shamanism* (Stockholm, 1978).

of historical depth adds further plausibility to the hypothesis. Iceland possesses a celebrated and very rich body of source material for its medieval culture, the famous
sagas, and as long ago as 1935 the Swedish scholar Dag Stromback proved the influence of Lapp shamanism upon the magical beliefs revealed in these.[31] Lapp or
'Finnish' shamans themselves make appearances in Vatnsdaela Saga, Ynglinga Saga,
St Olaf's Saga and Fostbroeda Saga, working in the classic Siberian manner.
Icelanders themselves employ similar methods of spirit-projection. The island, however, stands at a cultural crossroads rather than straightforwardly representing the
western limit of a Eurasian shamanic province. The spirits sent forth by magicians
commonly take animal form, blending the Siberian tradition with the European one
of shape-shifting, as believed to be practised by witches: examples are found in Gull-
Thoris Saga, Hardar Saga, Kormaks Saga, Vatnsdaela Saga, Fridtjof Saga, Hjalmpers
Saga ok Olves, Sturlaugs Saga Starfsama and other works. Furthermore, the
shamanic ability to chant invocations is associated with the general north European
ascription of magical powers to poetry and to letters, so that spoken poems and
carved runes can carry powerful curses: celebrated instances occur in the Flateyjar-
bok, Vatnsdaela Saga, Laxdaela Saga, Gisla Saga, Njala Saga, Kormaks Saga and
Grettir Saga. None the less, the shamanic element in the Icelandic matrix is clear,
and does provide an explanation for the distinction between the gender pattern of
witchcraft accusations there, and that in Scotland. The stretch of Atlantic between
them divides two different ancient conceptions of magic.

V

Scholars of the early modern European trials have already had their ears tuned to
the relevance of shamanism, but in a rather different context: that of the work of
Carlo Ginzburg. He is not only one of the most remarkable living historians but
the most prominent of those who have taken a broad view of the trials, placing
them in a perspective of pre-Christian belief and in a geographical context which,
if not global, covers most of Europe and northern Asia.[32] In two respects the
research for the present chapter would thoroughly endorse his arguments: first,
that stereotypes of the early modern witches' sabbath draw partly upon ancient
beliefs, and second, that they echo particular early European traditions, concerning spectral processions by night which often include living humans and involve
the apparent power of flight. Neither is original to Professor Ginzburg, both being
found in the earlier work of Norman Cohn and the first by a sequence of scholars
stretching backwards as far as Jakob Grimm, but he has articulated them within a
broader and richer framework of material than anyone before. Only with a third of
his arguments does the present writer find difficulty: that the tradition of the

---

[31] Cited in H. R. Ellis Davidson, 'Hostile magic in the Icelandic sagas', in V. Newall (ed.), *The Witch
Figure* (London, 1973), pp. 20–42, which is the best survey in English of its subject.

[32] C. Ginzburg, *Ecstasies: Deciphering the Witches' Sabbath*, trans. R. Rosenthal (Harmondsworth,
1992); cf. his *Storia Notturna* (Turin, 1989).

sabbath draws upon a pan-Eurasian one of the spirit-flight of shamans, which inspires folk-beliefs as disparate as the Scottish reports of a Queen of Elfane and her fairy followers, the Germanic Wild Hunt, and the Italian hosts of Diana.

This is obviously at variance with the contrast presented here, of a shamanic cultural province in the far north of Europe, linked to that of Siberia, shading through an intermediate zone into a different one, covering the rest of the continent and including the classic worldwide stereotype of the witch. To resolve the difficulty it is necessary to shift perspective again, to Professor Ginzburg's own vantage-point as a specialist in north-eastern Italian records. He made his name by revealing the *benandanti* of Friuli, a tradition of particular individuals whose spirits left their sleeping bodies at night to do battle with those of witches for the fertility of local farmland. These were assimilated to witches themselves by the Inquisition in the course of the early modern period. From the beginning Professor Ginzburg commented on the apparent connection between this tradition and that of shamanic spirit-flight.[33] The Hungarian historian Gabor Klaniczay soon located it at the western extreme of a spectrum of beliefs found across the Balkans as far as Bulgaria and Hungary, concerning humans possessed of the gift to duel at night in spirit-form with witches, or with rivals from different communities, to protect their own districts from misfortunes. Professor Ginzburg subsequently linked this material to records of magicians formerly operating in Romania, Serbia and Macedonia, who communed with spirits while in trance, as further evidence of 'typically shamanic rituals in a European setting'.[34]

Some Hungarian scholars have taken a different view. Starting from the fact that the Hungarian people, the Magyars, were a set of tribes closely related to those of western Siberia who had migrated westwards into Europe in the early Middle Ages, they have suggested that these brought shamanism with them. Hungarian folklore and history certainly contains a type of magician reputed to engage in spirit-flight, the *taltos*, and the implication of this theory is that the Balkan traditions of trance mediumship and nocturnal battles are the result of a diffusion of Magyar tradition.[35] This makes such a neat parallel to a diffusion of Saami tradition in the north that it poses an obvious temptation to the present writer; but it will not work. If Hungarian shamanism were the root of all these Balkan folk beliefs, then the latter should radiate out from an epicentre in the main area of Magyar settlement. Instead, the nocturnal spirit-battles are most strongly recorded across the Balkan region from Slovenia to Bulgaria, and look like a distinctive South Slav tradition,

[33] C. Ginzburg, *The Night Battles: Witchcraft and Agrarian Cults in the Sixteenth and Seventeenth Centuries*, trans. J. and A. Tedeschi (London, 1983); cf. his *I Benandanti* (Turin, 1966).

[34] G. Klaniczay, 'Shamanistic elements in Central European witchcraft', in Hoppal (ed.), *Shamanism in Eurasia*, 404–22; Ginzburg, *Ecstasies*, pp. 160–89: quotation on p. 194.

[35] J. Balazs, 'The Hungarian shaman's technique of trance induction', in Dioszegi (ed.), *Popular Beliefs*, pp. 53–75; Dioszegi, *Tracing Shamans*, pp. 61–4; J. Fazekas, 'ungarian shamanism: material and history of research', in C.-M. Edsman (ed.), *Studies in Shamanism* (Stockholm, 1967), 97–119; M. Hoppal, 'Traces of shamanism in Hungarian folk beliefs', and M. Hoppal, 'The role of shamanism in Hungarian ethnic identity', in Siikala and Hoppal, *Studies on Shamanism*, pp. 156–68, 169–75; Ginzburg, *Ecstasies*, p. 194 and n. 64.

with some parallels across the Black Sea in the Caucasus. Hungarian equivalents are more rarely mentioned, and found more commonly the closer to the South Slav heartland that the historian goes.[36] There is a self-evident difference between the public performances of Siberian shamans and the dream-conflicts of the Balkans. A single seventeenth-century record of Moldavian magicans, who fell into trance in spectacular public displays, does sound very like Siberian shamanism and may represent a survival of it brought by the Magyars;[37] but there is no proven connection between it and the more static and later cases of trance mediumship in the Balkans cited by Professor Ginzburg. As for the Scottish fairy queen, the Wild Hunt, the hosts of Diana, and the other nocturnal phenomena included in his dossier, they may reflect a common *prehistoric* heritage of shamanism; but this suggestion is, by its very nature, immune to proof.

None the less, those Scottish fairies may still have a thing or two to teach us. One of the more obvious, and less discussed, features of the witch trials in Scotland is their concentration in the Lowlands and Northern Isles, and their apparent absence from most of the Highlands and Western Isles – the Gaelic-speaking zone of the realm. There may be a problem of evidence here, in that the zone concerned was mostly divided into heritable jurisdictions run by local chiefs who have left no records. On the other hand, the suspicion of a cultural rather than an archival difference is much strengthened by making another cross-national comparison, with Ireland. The apparent almost complete absence of witch trials there, and the concentration of the few known cases in English areas of settlement, is one of the distinctive features of the island's history. Records for the popular culture of early modern Gaelic Ireland are few, but some retrospective insight into it is provided by the exceptionally rich collections of the Irish Folklore Commission. A recent microhistory which draws upon those collections is Angela Bourke's study of the sensational burning to death of Bridget Cleary by her husband in County Tipperary in 1895.[38] It is significant that newspaper reporters habituated to English modes of thought described it as a 'witch-burning', but it was nothing of the kind. Michael Cleary had become convinced that his wife had been abducted by fairies, and that the woman with whom he was co-habiting was a non-human being left in her place, who had to be eliminated so that his true spouse could be regained. Dr Bourke's analysis of his belief reveals a rich traditional world of rural Irish cosmology, in which the fairy folk were constantly held responsible for untoward events and uncanny misfortunes. It makes a sharp contrast with the nineteenth-century English rural culture recently investigated by Owen Davies, where witchcraft is blamed for the same phenomena in a manner familiar to any scholar of the early modern trials.[39]

---

[36] Klaniczay, 'Shamanistic elements', pp. 404–22; É. Pócs, *Between the Living and the Dead: a Perspective on Witches and Seers in the Early Modern Age* (Budapest, 1999), pp. 73–105, 121–64.

[37] Ginzburg, *Ecstasies*, pp. 188, 194; Hoppál, 'The role of shamanism', pp. 169–71.

[38] A. Bourke, *The Burning of Bridget Cleary* (London, 1999). I am very grateful to Patrick Cooke for drawing my attention to this work.

[39] O. Davies, *Witchcraft, Magic and Culture, 1736–1951* (Manchester, 1999); O. Davies, *A People Bewitched: Witchcraft and Magic in Nineteenth-Century Somerset* (Bruton, 1999).

To an anthropologist, the term 'fairy' is just the English expression for 'land-spirits' ('elf' being a British equivalent), and so Gaelic Ireland affords a classic case of a society which did not fear the witch-figure because it ascribed misfortune to other sources. If Gaelic Scotland had the same system of belief, together with all its other cultural similarities, then the absence of witch trials there is explained. So, for that matter, would be the prominence of fairies in the celebrated Scottish trials of Andro Mann and Isobel Gowdie, located precisely in that borderland of Aberdeen-shire and Nairn where Highland and Lowland cultures intermingled. If this is correct, then Iceland, Gaelic Scotland and Lowland Scotland represent between them three different ancient cosmologies, with distinct views of malevolent magic: a larger version of Trobriand, Dobu and Fergusson.

VI

It may therefore be suggested both that there is a significant global context for the Scottish witch trials, and that those trials can be better understood as a result of a global perspective. There is also, however, a further reason to be conscious of parallels in other parts of the planet; that the mobbing or trial of presumed witches is no longer part of the world which we have lost. To say this is not to refer to a residual belief in traditional magic in rural parts of Europe, nor to the revival of an interest in occultism and paganism in the modern West, nor to the parallels with witch-hunts discerned by several observers in the panic over alleged satanic ritual abuse of children which spread from the United States to Britain in the late 1980s; although all these have some relevance to the statement. It is to draw attention to a full-scale revival in the traditional treatment of alleged witches in parts of Africa after the retreat of colonialism. In the Green Valley of north-eastern Transvaal, more than 150 people were denounced as witches in two months of 1986, and subjected to informal trial by youth organisations which killed at least thirty-six. Further purges have swept the valley in the 1990s. More chilling still is the restoration of formal processes against the accused. During the early 1990s the king of the Mamprusi, in northern Ghana, began to endorse the work of a public witch-finder. Those convicted were often penned up for life in a ghetto in the old capital; 140 women were confined there by 1991. From 1980 onward the state courts in eastern Cameroon began to convict and sentence alleged witches once again, responding to popular pressure.[40] If we do indeed now live in a global village, then scholars of the early modern Scottish trials need to be aware that only a few streets away they can sit in on events which are essentially the same as those which they are treating as a feature of a now vanished society.

---

[40] Niehaus, 'Witch-hunting and political legitimacy', 498–530; S. Drucker-Brown, 'Mamprusi witch-craft', 531–49; P. Geschiere with C. Fisiy, 'Domesticating personal violence: witchcraft, courts and confessions in Cameroon', *Africa*, 64 (1994), 323–41.

3

In search of the Devil
in Fife witchcraft cases,
1560–1705[1]

Stuart Macdonald

Andrew Patrick had a certain amount of explaining to do. The presbytery of Cupar wanted to know what he was doing out so late at night and who precisely he had seen on that fateful night two years previously. His answer was that he had gone to a tailor, sent out for a quart of ale, and then walked home somewhere between eleven and twelve o'clock at night. On his way home he saw seven or eight women dancing 'with a meckle man in the midst of them'. This group took Andrew and put him into the small loch by the side of which they had been dancing. He was in the water up to his shoulder blades when a voice he recognised as that of Elspeth Seath said to the rest: 'He is but a silly drunken larde; let him goe.' Andrew Patrick was let go and he ran home afraid and wet.

To the members of presbytery who listened to this story, Elspeth Seath's name came as no surprise as she had been named as a witch four months previously by Helen Young, also of the parish of Balmerino on the north coast of Fife. Helen had confessed to being a witch in December 1648 and then stated, without giving any details, that Elspeth Seath and Helen Small in Monimail were also witches. Helen Young died eighteen days after making the accusation, but the concerns over Helen Small (who had been recognised as a notorious witch as recently as 1644) and Elspeth Seath continued. Andrew Patrick's testimony of the events of that night two years previously played a substantial role in the presbytery's questioning.

The greatest interest was shown in who he claimed to have seen at this meeting he stumbled across. Had he claimed to have seen Isobel Troylus and Helen Swan? He denied this, even though witnesses claimed to have heard him name Helen as a witch. After a considerable investigation, the presbytery brought Thomas Kenner, who had claimed he had heard Andrew Patrick call Helen Swan a witch, and censured him for 'wenting imprudently what he could not prove, caling Helen Swan a

[1] I would like to thank the faculty of history at the University of Guelph and colleagues at Knox College, Toronto, for their support in the research which this paper represents as well as the participants at the Sixteenth Century Studies Conference in Toronto, Oct. 1998, where this paper was originally presented. Thanks to the Aberdeen and North East Scotland Family History Society for permission to use their map of Fife parishes and adapt it for my research. Modern spellings of many proper names have been included in the text for ease of reading. The seventeenth-century spellings are used in the notes.

witch'.[2] Lost in all of this concern about who was present seems to be any concern for what these seven or eight were doing, or for the identity of the man who stood amidst them.

I

To modern readers what was going on by the side of the loch is obvious – here we have a description of a witches' sabbat, complete with the Devil himself in attendance. The presence of sabbats, the demonic pact and the Devil himself are characterised as what differentiated Scottish witchcraft from English witchcraft. Christina Larner in *Enemies of God* wrote of the important role played by the Devil and the demonic pact in Scotland. In confessions the 'principal emphasis was on the Demonic Pact' and nocturnal gatherings with other witches were 'a frequent but optional extra':

> The Pact, however, came to be regarded by the Scottish judiciary, despite the number who continued to be convicted on other evidence or while maintaining their inno-cence, as the single most essential element in an indictment.[3]

In one of the lectures published posthumously as part of *Witchcraft and Religion* Larner wrote that most witches were accused by other witches 'and indicted for consummating the demonic pact'. The demonic pact, the Devil and other related concepts from diabolic theory are understood to be central features of Scottish witch belief, features which distinguish it from English witch belief and make it more akin to Continental theory.[4]

Clearly the Devil was present in Scottish witchcraft cases. For example, at the most famous cases involving the North Berwick witches, Satan himself was said to have appeared in the kirk and spoke from the pulpit:

> His face was terrible, his nose was like the beak of an eagle, great burning een, his hands and legs were hairy, with claws upon his hands and feet like the griffon and he spoke with a rough, deep voice.[5]

---

[2] G. R. Kinloch (ed.), *Selections from the Minutes of the Presbyteries of St Andrews and Cupar, 1641–1698* (Edinburgh, 1837), pp. 136–41, 143, 144, 146, 150.

[3] Larner, *Enemies of God*, p. 145.

[4] Larner, *Enemies of God*, pp. 10–11, 149. In comparing Scottish and English witch belief, Larner wrote that the witchcraft Acts in the latter country 'knew nothing of the notion common to Roman Law countries such as Scotland that the crime was that of being a witch, that the primary act of witchcraft was the Demonic Pact, and that all witches were part of a Satanic conspiracy': ibid., p. 200. Cf. Larner, *Witchcraft*, p. 152. In the introduction to his volume on Scottish witchcraft articles, Brian Levack stresses th role played by torture, worship of the Devil, and the demonic pact in Scotland: B. P. Levack (ed.), *Articles on Witchcraft, Magic and Demonology*, vol. vii: *Witchcraft in Scotland* (New York, 1992), pp. ix, x. Other examples include: B. P. Levack, *The Witch-Hunt in Early Modern Europe* (2nd edn, London, 1995); G. R. Quaife, *Godly Zeal and Furious Rage: the Witch in Early Modern Europe* (New York, 1987); and R. Briggs, *Witches and Neighbours: the Social and Cultural Context of European Witchcraft* (London, 1996).

[5] Quotation from E. J. Cowan, 'The royal witch-hunt', in *The Sunday Mail Story of Scotland*, vol. ii, pt. 15 (1988), p. 407.

The confessions, extracted using torture as part of the criminal process, included information not only on the meeting but also on the attempt to murder King James VI and his bride while they returned from Denmark.[6] Similarly the demonic pact and the search for the Devil's mark (made on the witch to seal the bargain) by John Kincaid, a famous pricker of witches, was central to the massive witch-hunt that swept through Scotland in the years 1661 and 1662.[7]

Other famous cases complicate the issue. Andrew Man was accused of witchcraft in Aberdeen in 1597. While his accusers understood him to have given allegiance to Satan, Man referred to his master as a mysterious figure known as Christsonday. Andrew claimed to have visited the fairy-queen over a period of sixty years prior to his arrest and interrogation. He had attended many revels and feasts in the company of her and others many of whom, like James V and Thomas the Rhymer, were 'deid men'. Andrew Man received secret knowledge and power to heal as a result of his association with the queen of fairyland, yet his real master was this mysterious figure named Christsonday: 'The queen has a grip of all the craft, but Christsonday is the gudeman and has all power under God'. Christsonday appeared as a stag alongside the elf-queen at revels, and had such power that he was able to show Andrew the fires of hell. Andrew Man was eventually executed for witchcraft.[8] Several years previously, Bessie Dunlop from Ayrshire was executed for receiving power to heal from the ghost of Thomas Reid, a neighbour who had died at the battle of Pinkie.[9] These confessions show not only elements of demonic theory but also a strong dose of popular belief.[10] To better understand this complex interweaving of belief and also the role played by the Devil in Scottish witchcraft cases, an intense study of one region, Fife, is helpful.

[6] Cowan, 'Royal Witch-hunt'. The original version of the events can be found in *Newes from Scotland*. Other discussions include M. Murray, 'The "Devil" of North Berwick', *SHR*, 15 (1918), 310–21; E. J. Cowan, 'The darker vision of the Scottish Renaissance: the Devil and Francis Stewart', in I. B. Cowan and D. Shaw (eds), *The Renaissance and Reformation in Scotland* (Edinburgh, 1983); and M. C. Kintscher, 'The culpability of James VI of Scotland, later James I of England, in the North Berwick witchcraft trials of 1590–91' (M.A. thesis, San Jose State University, 1991).

[7] B. P. Levack, 'The great Scottish witch-hunt of 1661–1662', *Journal of British Studies*, 20 (1980), 90–108, at pp. 98–9.

[8] J. A. MacCulloch, 'The mingling of fairy and witch beliefs in sixteenth and seventeenth century Scotland', *Folklore*, 32 (1921), 229–44, at pp. 235–6. Andro Man appears as case no. 2302 in Larner *et al.*, *Source-Book*. See also *Spalding Misc.*, i, pp. 117–25.

[9] The case is discussed in J. C. Baroja, *The World of the Witches* (Chicago, 1964), pp. 125–6.

[10] It is essential in discussing belief about witches to differentiate between the ideas of the educated (the elite) and those beliefs held by the general populace. While debate continues as to who should belong in each of these groups and how we should define their culture(s), contemporary historians have found this distinction vital to their work. See R. Kieckhefer, *European Witch Trials: their Foundations in Popular and Learned Culture, 1300–1500* (Berkeley, Calif., 1976), pp. 3, 105; C. Ginzburg, *The Night Battles: Witchcraft and Agrarian Cults in the Sixteenth and Seventeenth Centuries* (Baltimore, Md., 1983).

II

Fife played a prominent role in the Scottish witch-hunt. Recent research has shown that it was the third most active shire in terms of witchcraft cases, after Haddington (East Lothian) and Edinburgh.[11] Within the Fife witch-hunt there are 83 cases where the Devil's name appears. Given that there are 420 known cases of accused witches in Fife, this means that the Devil appears in approximately 20 per cent of cases – or, to put it the other way, is absent in 80 per cent. One case in which there is no mention of the Devil or the demonic pact involved an unnamed witch who was executed in St Andrews in 1572. What makes this case interesting is that John Knox played a role, preaching a sermon against her. It is unfortunate that the sermon has not survived but in the information which has survived, including an entry by Knox's secretary, there is no reference to the Devil.[12] In 1638 Janet Durie in Wemyss was accused of witchcraft by James Keddie. Margaret Douglas in Kirkcaldy was accused in 1639 of curing and causing illness in people and livestock, while the next year Margaret Lindsay was charged with charming for spitting in a child's face in order to administer a cure. In none of these three representative cases is there a reference to the Devil or the demonic pact.[13]

It is important to look in detail at the cases where the Devil does appear, noting the kinds of sources, and the way in which he is presented. When we have seen these data several things will become clear. First, that the Devil appears most frequently in documents which arise from the central government, namely the court of justiciary and the privy council. Even in the latter, as we shall see, reference to the Devil's involvement is not always a given. Second, we shall see that even when he does appear, the 'Devil' has some strange characteristics. The relative lack of the demonic requires us to take a second look at both the motives behind the Scottish witch-hunt and our understanding of it as being distinct from the witch-hunt in England.

There are many references to the Devil which are essentially references in passing, where little attention seems to be given to sabbats, demonic pacts or other elements of elite belief in the diabolic. The Devil or Satan is seen as the ultimate source of evil but there seems to be little concern to explore his role further. For example,

---

[11] S. Macdonald, 'Threats to a Godly Society: The Witch-Hunt in Fife, Scotland, 1560–1710' (Ph.D. thesis, University of Guelph, 1997), pp. 58–60.

[12] Richard Bannatyne, *Journal of the Transactions in Scotland during the contest between the adherents of Queen Mary and those of her Son* (Edinburgh, 1806), p. 339; James Melville, *Autobiography and Diary*, ed. R. Pitcairn (Wodrow Society, 1842), p. 46. While the woman was searched for a witch's mark, it seems that this was done visually and what was being sought was a deformity, not an insensate part of her body. When a white cloth like a 'collore craig' was discovered between her legs, all attention shifted to this. She was accused of not forgiving her neighbour and of stating that she did not care if she went to heaven or hell, but not – at least according to existing records – of any pact with the Devil.

[13] NAS, Kirkcaldy presbytery, CH2/224/1, fos. 127–8; *The Presbyterie Booke of Kirkcaldie: Being the record of the proceedings of that Presbytery from the 15th day of April 1630 to the 14th day of September 1653*, ed. W. Stevenson (Kirkcaldy, 1900), pp. 136, 137, 138, 141, 148, 162, 173, 174, 178, 179, 184, 187. Margaret Lindsay's actions were described at a second meeting of the presbytery as 'practices of witchcraft': p. 189.

the presbyterian writer James Kirkton in *c.* 1693, accused the episcopalian curate of Anstruther of being a witch: 'some suspect he medled with the devil, and he was known to have a brother that was a diabolick man'.[14] Another literary reference comes from the pen of the famous Scottish legal authority Sir George Mackenzie who referred to some witches who had been burned in Culross in 1665 based upon their confessions that they had been transported to public conventions of witches by the Devil.[15]

References in passing to the Devil also appeared in church court records. On 3 January 1643, Margaret Cuthbertson was brought before the session of Dunfermline and accused as a witch. This was the first case of this year, one which saw extensive witch-hunting throughout Scotland. Six other women were also brought before the session for believing that Margaret was a witch and seeking to obtain her services. These women were called upon to make public repentance, and the matter was to be counted as a point of witchcraft against each of them. The public repentance was required so that the Devil might not 'take advantage to beguile sillie ignorant bodies therby in making them to believe such idle toys'.[16] During the English occupation of the 1650s only one case, that of Maggie from St Monans, is known. Maggie was accused of being in compact with the Devil and with doing many evil deeds. She was prodded with a horn and goad in order to keep her constantly awake in a successful attempt to get her to confess.[17]

In other situations the references were more explicit but the role played by the Devil continued to be minor. This is true both of records produced in church courts and those produced by the central government, such as privy council commissions. There was obviously a certain formula for writing commissions related to witchcraft. The first commission issued in a witch-hunt in Kirkcaldy presbytery in 1626 accused Isobel Maver 'of the crymes of witchcraft, sorcerie, useing of charmes and inchantmentis, and otheris divilishe practices, offensive to God, skandell to the trew relgioun, and hurt of diverse our goode subjectis', but did not accuse her of making a pact with the Devil.[18] Similarly, the commission against three female witches (most likely Janet Pirie, Janet Stark and Helen Birrell) and one

[14] The expansion and editing of Larner *et al.*, *Source-Book* which was required to complete this research has been entitled the Scottish Witch-Hunt Data Base or SWHDB. The remainder of the references to specific cases in this article will use the SWHDB. The SWHDB is now available in electronic form. SWHDB (Macdonald, 2001). SWHDB, case 3034; James Kirkton, *A History of the Church of Scotland, 1660–1679* (Lewiston, NY, 1992), p. 108.

[15] SWHDB, case 2873. Sir George Mackenzie, *The Laws and Customs of Scotland in Matters Criminal* (Edinburgh, 1834), p. 98.

[16] SWHDB cases: Margaret Cuthbertson (3169); Agnes Kinsman (3171); Jonet Tailor (3175); Jonet Moodie (3174); Jonet Horne (3173); Christian Moodie (3172); Jonnet Henrysone (3170). These cases were discovered and the quotation taken from R. Bensen, 'South-West Fife and the Scottish Revolution: The Presbytery of Dunfermline, 1633–1652' (M.Litt. thesis, University of Edinburgh, 1978), App. 2, p. 266. NAS, Dunfermline kirk session, CH2/592/1, fos. 20–1.

[17] SWHDB, case 3218; J. E. Simpkins, *Examples of Printed Folklore concerning Fife* (London, 1914), p. 96.

[18] *RPC*, 2nd ser., i, p. 246.

male witch issued on 13 April 1626 contains the same phrase. It is only in some of the commissions granted after this that more explicit references to the Devil can be found. The commission to put Janet Dempster to trial, for instance, stated that Janet had confessed to 'the renunceing of hir baptisme, ressaveing of the devills mark, and geving of hir soule and bodie over to the devillis service'.[19] All of these commissions include the name of John Spottiswoode, archbishop of St Andrews, yet not all of the commissions signed by him include references to the Devil.[20]

III

Why this might be is difficult to ascertain. The simplest answer would be to suggest that the presence of the Devil was assumed in all of these cases, but noted in only a few. This, indeed, may be true. What is worth noting, however, is that while this presence may have always been assumed in the background, it was never the main focus of concern in either the commissions or the church court records themselves. The concern was not with demonic compact but the harm done to neighbours. The initial charges against Janet Dempster made before a church court centred on the harm she had done to a neighbour after she had been driven away when she had used a spinning wheel without receiving permission.[21] William Lamb claimed to have overheard Helen Birrell say 'ane muckle black [-haired] man come into her house with cloven foote and buckles upon them' and had stayed for supper with her and her family. Helen denied this statement and the claim that she had said she was this man's 'tenant', but Helen was never accused of being in compact with the Devil.[22]

Commissions included a variety of phrases, some of which made reference to the Devil. In 1622, in the midst of a significant hunt in Dunfermline presbytery, a commission was issued to put five women to trial in Aberdour as they had been arrested and examined on suspicion of witchcraft. After their arrest and careful examination by the bailies, the commission stated that they had all 'frelie and of thair awne accord' confessed to the murder and to speaking with the Devil, who seemingly had been with them when they committed the murder.[23] Commissions issued the next year, also for Dunfermline presbytery, stated that those named had already

[19] *RPC*, 2nd ser., i, p. 309.

[20] *RPC*, 2nd ser., i, p. 447. The commission against Helen Wilsoun also included oblique references to her being at meetings and 'conferences with the devill' and was signed by the archbishop. Similarly, commission against Margaret Henderson, 27 May 1627, *ibid.*, p. 607. The exception is the commission granted in June against Elspett Neilsoun and Annas Munk. The commission bore the archbishop's name, but was in the more traditional form: *ibid.*, p. 425. The commission for Katherine Chrystie, 17 Nov. 1627, made no mention of the Devil. It was signed by several people, including the archbishop. A difference here may have been the fact that Chrystie had yet to be imprisoned. *RPC*, 2nd ser., ii, p. 122.

[21] SWHDB, case 2373; J. G. Dalyell, *The Darker Superstitions of Scotland illustrated from history and practice* (Edinburgh, 1834), pp. 424–5.

[22] J. Campbell, *The Church and Parish of Kirkcaldy from the Earliest Times till 1843* (Kirkcaldy, 1904), pp. 167–8.

[23] *RPC*, xiii, pp. 49–50.

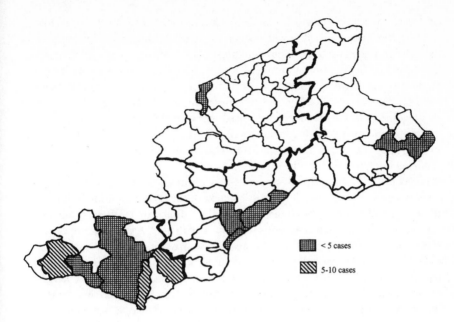

Witchcraft cases in Fife where references are made to the Devil, 1560–1648

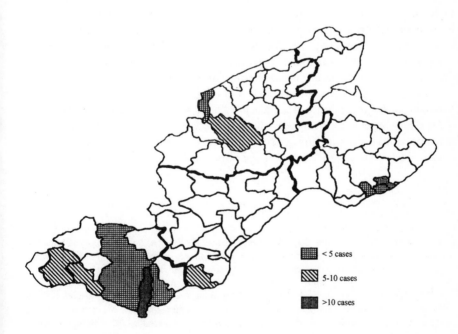

Witchcraft cases in Fife where references are made to the Devil, 1649–1710

confessed to 'sundrie devilish practices' and, in a commission dated 18 March 1623, to 'the cryme of witchcraft, conferring with the devil, and geiving over of thame seffis saule and body to him and his service'.[24] The next year, Janet Umphra, her sister Maisie Umphra, Alexander Clerk, Marjorie Rowand, Marion Stirk, and Janet Watt in Culross, along with Anna Smith in Torryburn, were accused as witches. The charges, as laid out in the commission of 19 February 1624, accused these women of 'witchcraft, sorcerie, useing of charmes, and consulting with the devill'.[25] Some of the privy council commissions issued in the witch-hunt which swept Cupar presbytery in 1661 and 1662 also contained references to the accused 'entering into paction with the divell' but again these references began in the middle of a hunt which was already under way.[26] Commissions were also issued against seven suspects in Torryburn in 1666. The text of the commission did not say that these women had already confessed, but did define witchcraft in terms of the renunciation of baptism and entering a pact with the Devil.[27] Reference to the Devil appears in many, but by no means all, commissions.

References to the Devil also appear in church court records. A turning point in the trial of Alison Coke in Kirkcaldy came after she confessed to having entered the Devil's service. While the time of this confession was carefully entered in the session record, the confession came after an extensive period of investigation into Alison's acts of malefice against her neighbours, an investigation which included Alison being warded in the church steeple. After the confession was made, the concern turned back to acts of malefice.[28] Agnes Wallace in Crail confessed in 1643 to having been in the Devil's service for forty-three years, having been 'witchit' by her mother.[29]

Robert Maxwell, who had previously been barred from communion because of ignorance, was brought before the session of Dunfermline in April 1649 and interrogated regarding 'some things that looks like witchcraft'. He confessed to having made a pact with the Devil. Maxwell named others as witches, including John Murdoch in Dunfermline, and Isobel Kellog in Dalgety who he claimed had been present at several meetings with the Devil. While this reference to Isobel was a cause for some concern, her being warded as a suspected witch also owed a great deal to her previous bad reputation, as well as the fact that suspects in Aberdour had also named her.[30] During the same year and in the same presbytery a vagabond named

---

[24] *RPC*, xiii, pp. 192–3.

[25] *RPC*, xiii, pp. 439–40.

[26] *RPC*, 3rd ser., i, pp. 90, 141–3, 154, 191.

[27] *RPC*, 3rd ser., ii, pp. 2, 192.

[28] Town Hall, Kirkcaldy, Kirkcaldy kirk session, 8 October 1633; Sir John Sinclair (ed.), 'Trial of William Coke and Alison Dick for Witchcraft, Extracted from the Minutes of the Kirk Session of Kirkcaldy, A.D. 1636', in *The Statistical Account of Scotland, 1791–1799*, vol. x: *Fife* (Wakefield, 1978), pp. 811–14.

[29] *The Diary of Mr John Lamont of Newton, 1649–1671*, ed. G. R. Kinloch (Edinburgh, 1830), p. 6.

[30] W. Ross, *Glimpses of Pastoral Work in the Covenanting Times: a Record of the Labours of Andrew Donaldson, A.M., Minister at Dalgetty, Fifeshire, 1644–1662* (Edinburgh, 1877), p. 194; Bensen, 'South-West Fife and the Scottish Revolution', App. 2, p. 270; NAS, Dunfermline kirk session, CH2/592/1, fos. 89, 90, 96; *Extracts from the Kirk-Session Records of Dunfermline, 1640–1689*, ed. E. Henderson (Edinburgh, 1865), p. 31.

William Crichton was accused as a witch. After being warded for five days, he confessed to being a witch and having made a pact with the Devil twenty-four years previously. He was burned several days later.[31] While the Devil was mentioned in these situations, each of these individuals was sought as a witch for specific reasons.

There are only a handful of cases in Fife where the Devil's role is more active, including making a specific pact with his followers and, in some cases, having sex with them. Grissell Gairdner, a widow, was executed for witchcraft in Newburgh, a parish in Cupar presbytery, in 1610. Among the charges against her were that she had consulted with the Devil, and committed murder by witchcraft.[32] During the major Inverkeithing witch-hunt which occurred in Dunfermline presbytery in 1649–50 various references to the Devil were made. The confessions of Margaret Martin, Katherine Grieve and Isobel Leitch which are included in the justiciary court records all referred to the Devil. Margaret Martin admitted to meeting the Devil who appeared in 'the likeness of ane gentle man' in Beatrix Thomson's house and giving herself over to the Devil's service by placing one hand on her head, the other on the sole of one foot, renouncing her baptism and receiving the Devil's mark. Katherine Grieve confessed to meeting the Devil at Margaret Blackburn's house and giving herself to his service. Katherine also stated that the Devil 'had copulation with her'. Isobel Leitch was asked directly if 'the devill had copulated with hir'.[33]

What is missing from these confessions is any indication of what evil deeds Katherine, Margaret and Beatrix did while they were in the service of Satan. Instead the concern of the questioners was with how many meetings each attended, who was at these meetings, and who the ringleaders or officers were. The ringleader was declared to be Margaret Henderson, Lady Pittadrow. Margaret Blackburn declared that one of the main reasons Lady Pittadrow called one of the meetings was to 'complaine to the devill' about the minister, Mr Walter Bruce.[34] The same year, in the presbytery of Kirkcaldy, commissions were issued against Janet Brown, Isobel Gairdner and Janet Thomson. Brown was accused of meeting the Devil, disguised as a man, while he was in the presence of the other two, with renouncing her baptism and receiving the Devil's mark on her right arm. Proof of this Devil's mark was ascertained in the following way: 'Mr James Wilson, minister of Dysart, in presence of Mr John Chalmers, minister at Auchterderran, thrust a long pin of wire into the head, and she was insensible to it.' All three were found guilty and executed the

---

[31] Bensen, 'South-West Fife', App. 2, p. 269; *Extracts from the Kirk-Session*, ed. Henderson, p. 27; NAS, Dunfermline presbytery, CH2/105/1, 51; NAS, Dunfermline kirk session, CH2/592/1, fo. 76; E. Henderson (ed.), *Annals of Dunfermline* (Glasgow, 1879), p. 317.

[32] Pitcairn (ed.), *Trials*, iii, pp. 95–8; A. Laing, *Lindores Abbey and its Burgh of Newburgh* (Edinburgh, 1876), pp. 219–22; NAS, justiciary court records, JC26/7/1. The record gives details such as the role her husband played and her age. I am indebted to Michael Wasser for this information.

[33] NAS, justiciary court records, JC26/13/5.

[34] NAS, justiciary court records, 10 July 1649, JC26/13/5. The confessions of Margaret Mairtine, Katharin Grieve, and Issobell Leitch.

same day.[35] Some days later, Isobel Bairdie was accused of drinking a toast to the Devil and pledging herself to him. She and two other unnamed individuals were convicted, strangled and burned at the stake.[36]

In Culross in 1675 four women, three of whom were widows, were accused as witches before the high court of justiciary: Katherine Sands, Isobel Inglis, Agnes Hendries, and Janet Hendries.[37] What makes this case interesting is the ordering of the details, the fact that they are all present, and the sequence: the giving of oneself over to the Devil's service from head to foot is followed by receiving the Devil's mark, which is followed by carnal copulation. Even the sexual act follows a stereotype: his 'nature' (i.e. penis) was cold, and several echoed Janet Hendries' comment that he 'used her after the manner of a beast'.[38] The meetings did not happen out in the field or in their homes (although other meetings did). The recent gatherings took place in the deserted West Kirk of Culross. As much as Katherine Sands, Isobel Inglis, Janet Hendries and Agnes Hendries all made these confessions, and then admitted to them in court prior to their execution at the gallows between Leith and Edinburgh on 29 July 1675, we clearly have here the elite stereotype. That the trial was held before the high court and the executions took place outside the burgh is important.

When we look beyond the stereotypical elements of the confession we begin to see the forces that might have been at play in this case. Katherine Sands was the daughter of a woman who had already 'suffered for the cryme of witchcraft'. She was suspected of poisoning her brother who had wrongfully taken all of the 'goods and gear' of her father, which were supposed to be divided equally among the children. It was this loss of her share of the inheritance which caused her to enter the Devil's service, after which she gave her brother a white drink which caused his illness and death. Although the timing of the drink is unclear, the fact that she was accused of entering the Devil's service thirty-four years previously suggests the quarrel had been a long one. Katherine would have been at the very least middle aged and probably considerably older. Isobel Inglis had entered the Devil's service because her fields were not as rich as her neighbours, a condition the Devil promised to rectify: 'he desired her to be of good cheer she would gett it also tymplie doen and with alse good furrows as her neighbours'. Janet Hendries was aided in a quarrel. Agnes Hendries was promised, after she complained that 'she had not wherewith to live,' that once she entered the Devil's service 'she should not want'.[39] The event that brought these women to notice was their

[35] The source of this remarkable information is H. Arnot (ed.), *A Collection and Abridgement of Celebrated Criminal Trials in Scotland from AD 1536 to 1784 with historical and Critical Remarks* (Edinburgh, 1885), pp. 401–3. Arnot claims to be quoting a manuscript which was in the possession of a Major Melville of Murdochcairnie.

[36] SWHDB, Bairdie, no. 2596. The unnamed witches are cases 2585 and 2586. The executions took place some time in Aug. or early Sept. Arnot, *Trials*, pp. 402–3.

[37] Sands was the only one married. NAS, justiciary court records, JC2/14, pp. 346–54; Simpkins, *Examples of Printed Folklore*, pp. 350–1.

[38] Simpkins, *Examples of Printed Folklore*, p. 351.

[39] *Ibid.*, pp. 350, 351.

Year	Presbytery	Parish	Source	Spells	Meetings	Murder	Service	Baptism renounced	Pact	Devil's mark	Sex	Other	Number of witches
1622	Dunfermline	Aberdour	com		✓	✓							5
1623	Dunfermline	Inverkeithing	com		✓		✓					✓	9
1624	Dunfermline	Culross	com	✓	✓							✓	6
1624	Dunfermline	Torryburn	com		✓	✓						✓	1
1626	Kirkcaldy	Dysart	com	✓	✓			✓					1
1626	Kirkcaldy	Wemyss	com				✓	✓	✓				1
1627	Kirkcaldy	Wemyss	com	✓									1
1661	Cupar	Collessie	com						✓				5
1661	Cupar	Newburgh	com					✓	✓				2
1666	Dunfermline	Torryburn	com					✓	✓				7
1610	Cupar	Newburgh	JC			✓	✓					✓	1
1649	Dunfermline	Inverkeithing	JC			✓	✓	✓	✓	✓	✓	✓	19
1675	Dunfermline	Culross	JC	✓				✓	✓	✓	✓	✓	4
1633	Kirkcaldy	Kirkcaldy	KS				✓						2
1643	Dunfermline	Dunfermline	KS		✓							✓	1
1649	Dunfermline	Dalgety	KS/Prs		✓								1
1649	Dunfermline	Dalgety	KS/Prs						✓			✓	1
1649	Dunfermline	Dunfermline	KS/Prs						✓				1
1704	St Andrews	Pittenweem	KS				✓		✓	✓			4
1704	Dunfermline	Torryburn	KS				✓		✓	✓		✓	1
1655[c]	St Andrews	St Monans	lit	✓					✓				1
1663	St Andrews	Anstruther	lit									✓	1
1665	Dunfermline	Culross	lit	✓								✓	1
1643	St Andrews	Crail	unk				✓						1
1649	Kirkcaldy	Burntisland	unk	✓				✓		✓			6

Abbreviations: com – commission; JC – Justiciary Court; KS – Kirk Session; Prs – Presbytery; lit – literary source; unk – unknown

Witchcraft accusations in Fife

assault on Robert Primrose while they were returning from one of their meetings at the West Kirk.

The last cases of suspected witchcraft in Fife contain fascinating references to the Devil. In 1704 Patrick Morton, the 16-year-old son of a smith in Pittenweem, became ill and accused Beatrix Laing of bewitching him. The hunt spread rapidly beyond Beatrix to include seven other individuals. Isobel Adam, Beatrix Laing, Nicolas Lawson, and Janet Cornfoot all 'confessed' to renouncing their baptism, to 'compact with the Devil', and with being at meetings with others and the Devil. Beatrix Laing, in her later complaint to the privy council, spoke of how she had come to make her confession:

> because she would not confess that she was a witch and in compact with the devill, [she] was tortured by keeping her awake without sleep for fyve days and nights together, and by continually pricking her with instruments in the shoulders, back, and thighs.

The confession to meeting the Devil was qualified. She had seen him only once upon the moor when he appeared in the shape of a black dog. Beatrix recognised it as the Devil because he could change his shape. Beatrix survived but one of the accused, Janet Cornfoot, was lynched by a mob on 30 January 1705.[40]

A more minor incident in Torryburn in 1704 blended traditional accusations with some of the details heard in Culross in 1675. The events began at a special meeting of the session to deal with the story that Jan Bizet had been 'molested by Satan'. On her walk home at night after having been drinking Jan Bizet was extremely disturbed, crying out, as Agnes Henderson remembered it, 'O God, O Christ there is Lily coming to take me and [hir] blue doublets O Mary Wilson keep me she is coming'.[41] After being imprisoned, Lillias Adie confessed to being a witch, indeed to having had a compact with the Devil 'since the second bury of witches in this place'. She claimed to have given herself over to the Devil, to have had carnal intercourse with him, and then added that his feet were cloven. She claimed to have been summoned by Grissel Anderson to a meeting one moonlight night where everyone clapped and honoured the Devil as their prince. Apart from Elspeth

---

[40] Beatrix Laing's petition to the privy council, 1 May 1705, in D. Cook, *Annals of Pittenweem: being notes and extracts from the Ancient Records of that burgh* (Anstruther, 1867), pp. 124–5. NAS, Pitten-weem kirk session, May 1704, CH2/833/3, fo. 29. St Andrews University Muniments, presbytery of St Andrews records, 14 June 1704, Ch2/msdeposit/23, vol. 4. Janet Cornfoot's lynching became the subject of a series of pamphlets: *A Just Reproof to the False Reports and Unjust Calumnies in the Foregoing Letters; A True and Full Relation of the Witches at Pittenweem to which is added ...;* and *An Answer of a Letter from a Gentleman in Fife to a Nobleman ...,* all in D. Webster (ed.), *A Collection of Rare and Curious Tracts on Witchcraft and the Second Sight; with an Original Essay on Witchcraft* (Edinburgh, 1820). Cf. E. J. Cowan and L. Henderson, 'The last of the witches? The survival of Scottish witch belief', Chapter 12 below.

[41] NAS, Torryburn kirk session, 20 June 1704, CH2/355/2. Others heard slightly different versions of the call. How much Jean Bizet drank was disputed, although it seems that those who stated she was drunk were probably close to the truth as the next day Jean was complaining 'of an sore head and in a sweat and she seemed not right'. This information is also excerpted in the witchcraft pamphlet *Minutes and Proceedings*, in Webster (ed.), *Rare Tracts*, pp. 129–46.

Williamson, she knew no one at the meeting.[42] In prison Adie adhered to her confession. When asked if the Devil had a sword, her reply was that she believed 'he durst not use a sword'. She had been angry with the Devil, who had promised many things which he had not delivered. She also accused Agnes Currie of being in attendance at the last meeting.[43]

When she was asked about the meeting, Elspeth Williamson admitted to having attended and noted her surprise that no psalms had been sung. She believed, but was not sure, that Mary Wilson had taken her to this meeting. One final comment of note: she claimed that when the Devil left she could not hear his footsteps on the stubble.[44] The accusations continued until Janet Whyte, Agnes Currie, Bessie Callander and Mary Carmichael had been added as suspected witches. Some of the accusations were of long standing – for example, the claim that Agnes Currie had bewitched a child who had died after baptism twenty-four years previously.[45] There were few real claims of malefice, and those there were centred on Agnes Currie. For all of the time spent in examining these women and the fact that Lillias Adie confessed and Elspeth Williamson did not deny she was a witch, nothing much came of this. Events ended in confusion after Lillias died in prison.

IV

The Devil was present in Fife witchcraft cases. The table illustrates the sources, parishes, and kinds of accusations involved. It is still surprising, given how historians have treated this topic, that he was absent from so many and when present seemed to be more a background character than an active participant. The Devil was assumed, but it does not seem that an effort to root him out was central to all of even the cases where he did appear. Part of this may be due to the nature of sources for Fife. There are few cases which appeared in justiciary court records. By contrast, we have many cases which appear in the records which came from the local community – burgh, kirk session and presbytery records. The primary concern in the community records was with the disruption the individual could cause through her begging or curses. The best evidence we have of this comes from the case of William Coke and Alison Dick, where a variety of sources have survived. Both were considered witches due to their troublesome behaviour before any concern for the Devil was expressed.

This minor role of the Devil stands in sharp contrast to the portrait we have been given of the Scottish witch-hunt. In certain areas of Scotland, for example

---

[42] NAS, Torryburn kirk session, 29 July 1704, CH2/355/2; *Minutes and Proceedings*, pp. 135–6.

[43] NAS, Torryburn kirk session, 31 July 1704, CH2/355/2.

[44] The latter is quoted from *Minutes and Proceedings*, p. 140. NAS, Torryburn kirk session, 19 Aug. 1704, CH2/355/2.

[45] NAS, Torryburn kirk session, 29 Aug. 1704, CH2/355/2, 76. *Minutes and Proceedings*, p. 142. Agnes Currie is listed along with several accused witches from Pittenweem as being released on a bond of caution: NAS, justiciary court records, JC26/D/245.

Haddington, the Devil and fear of the demonic pact may have been a more significant player than in Fife. Even should this prove to have been the case – and I would suggest for the moment that the question has not, outside of the North Berwick trials, been adequately addressed – we should take seriously Stuart Clark's recent observation that it 'is simply not the case that witchcraft theory caused "witch hunts"' but rather 'the reverse is much more likely to have been true'.[46] Whichever way we come at it, the Devil and belief in the demonic pact can no longer be used to explain the severity of the Scottish witch-hunt.

We are left with two important questions. The first arises from the scattered, puzzling references that are found in the few cases where an individual is asked to describe the Devil in some detail. While there are some details which fit our stereotype of Satan, for example the colour black and the feet described as being 'cloven', there are other details which do not fit. Where do they come from? The second question is simply, if it was not the Devil and the demonic pact that motivated the extensive witch-hunt in Fife, what was the reason for the concern? Why were people hunting witches?

The picture of the Devil presented by those accused of witchcraft in Fife contains a complex mixture of demonological and popular belief. The coven of witches who confessed to having met at the abandoned West Kirk at Culross described renouncing their baptism and the painful act of sex with the Devil. At the same time, Katherine Sands confessed to dead people attending their meetings, as well as a scene involving 'the devill dancing and playing and that the devill played to them on a pype and that frequentlie they had a blowe light when it was dark'.[47] The scene is reminiscent of that which Andrew Patrick claimed to have seen by the side of the loch – a gathering where there was dancing and revel; however, Patrick did not identify the man at the centre of the revel as Satan. When asked if the Devil had a sword Lillias Adie of Torryburn stated that she believed 'he durst not use a sword'. She also confessed that the Devil objected to her attending church, an objection which apparently did not prevent her from going.[48] Another strange comment was that of Elspeth Williamson, who remarked that she could not hear the Devil's footsteps on the stubble as he left. Early in the witch-hunt in Fife Alison Pearson in Byrehill confessed that she had been taken by 'ane lustie mane, with mony mene and wemen' to a mystical place where there was much piping and dancing and merriment.[49] The 'lustie mane' was not named as the Devil.

Instead of the details we would expect in a portrait of the great enemy of God and humanity, what we find are elements that in places are suggestive of a fairy or an elf. Elves did not use metal, hence would refrain from carrying a metal sword. They enjoyed revels of dancing and piping and could slip away from these quietly. One would expect that Satan would reward those who had sworn him service. Instead,

---

[46] S. Clark, *Thinking with Demons: the Idea of Witchcraft in Early Modern Europe* (Oxford, 1997), p. vii.

[47] NAS, justiciary court records, JC2/14, p. 350.

[48] NAS, Torryburn kirk session, 31 July 1704, CH2/355/2. *Minutes and Proceedings*, pp. 135–6.

[49] Pitcairn (ed.), *Trials*, i, pp. 162–5. Where precisely 'Byrehill' was is unclear. Arnot, *Trials*, p. 390.

as Isobel Inglis of Culross protested, the promise to give her goods as fine as those of her neighbours was never honoured. This sounds very much like the trick a fairy might play. This 'mingling of beliefs' was noted by J. A. MacCulloch, who described the parallels between fairy revels and the witches' sabbat. He suggested that 'the mingling of really separate beliefs was perhaps thus also brought about by the determination of the judges to find Satan's craft everywhere, quite as much as by the folk themselves and their attribution of similar things to different orders of beings'.[50] Another folklorist, Katharine Briggs, also noted that fairies loved dancing and revelling.[51] The Fife populace seems to have held on to these beliefs far longer than historians have assumed, blending them somewhat with the more elite ideas of the demonologists, yet never abandoning the traditional ideas regarding fairies. The historian Geoff Quaife has suggested that the Scottish populace

> readily accepted the concept of the pact, sexual intercourse between Devil and his followers and the link between ill-fame and diabolic alliance – concepts resisted by the peasantry in other parts of Europe.[52]

The evidence from Fife does not support this statement.

The absence of certain elite notions is also striking. There is only one reference in Fife to witches flying, and that comes, not from a confession, but from a literary source. There is no cannibalism and little evil done at these gatherings. Instead, there is merriment and revel, with a male figure playing the tune on his pipes. In a few confessions, the Devil may have had a cold 'nature', but he even here he does not appear as particularly evil or demonic.

The blending of the popular and elite traditions and the resilience of the popular tradition needs to be taken seriously. Indeed, it may be that the populace had a greater role in shaping the ideas which the Scottish elite held about witches than we have noted. Sir Walter Scott allowed some of his witches to claim their power, not from Satan, but from fairies.[53] Mr James Hutchison preached a sermon against witches in the midst of the hunt in Renfrewshire in 1697. While he mostly articulated elite ideas such as the demonic pact and carnal copulation, he made one remarkable comment:

> Again we would distinguish between ane act of Devilrie Ignorantly and surprizingly committed without any foregoing compact, and ane act of Devilrie that proceeds from a compact with the Devil: It may be suppon'd for clearing this That in a company of witches when a person falls among them accidentally and is surprized and they say 'up and away' or 'mount & flee' and he sayes that too and he flies with the rest to this or

---

[50] MacCulloch, 'Mingling of fairy and witch beliefs', 236, 242, 243.

[51] K. M. Briggs, *The Personnel of Fairyland: a Short Account of the Fairy People of Great Britain for Those who Tell Stories to Children* (Oxford, 1953), p. 47.

[52] Quaife, *Godly Zeal*, p. 59.

[53] M. C. Boatright, 'Witchcraft in the novels of Sir Walter Scott', *University of Texas Studies in English*, 13 (1933), 95–115, at p. 112. In the same paragraph he writes that Scott 'adhered to the traditions of his country. He followed the popular tradition more closely than the theological one. His witches were not all evil.'

that countrey and preys upon such a person or his goods and returns again, this person is not a witch, he speaks the word the rest speaks Inadvertently & is carried away with the rest.[54]

This sounds surprisingly like the belief that people may stumble into a fairy ring and be carried off with the fairies. The session of Kilmore cited Farquhar Ferguson in 1716 and charged her with using charms to help cure people who had been elf-shot.[55] The isle of Bute witnessed a witchcraft case in 1650 in which belief in fairies was prevalent.[56] The Revd Robert Kirk, the minister of Aberfoyle, wrote a book in which he described the fairies as beings with a real existence.[57] Popular culture proved remarkably resilient.

V

This of course leaves us with an important question. If the elite notion of the Devil did not permeate Fife culture and drive the witch-hunt, what did? Why were the church courts interested in pursuing witches? Why were the local nobility willing to serve on commissions to put witches to trial? Why under certain conditions was the populace willing to identify the local women considered to be witches? To state the obvious, all elements of society believed in the reality of witches and their power to harm or heal. Whether this power ultimately derived from Satan or from other sources was a question for academics to ponder. The average person feared the harm and disruption caused by witches. It was a significant incident when in Anstruther in 1701 Elizabeth Dick was turned away from the mill while she was begging. It was reported by several witnesses that the grain being ground in the mill turned red and remained red until one of the people who had turned Elizabeth away ran to her and gave her alms, at which point Elizabeth blessed the mill and all was returned to normal.[58] Such power was honoured and feared. When asked the populace could produce evidence of harm done by the village witches, harm which often went back many years. Generally speaking, however, they had to be asked and have some assurance that the authorities were going to take their complaints seriously. Pleas for evidence against Alison Dick in Kirkcaldy went unheeded in 1621. It was only

---

[54] James Hutchison, 'A sermon on witchcraft in 1697', ed. G. Neilson, *SHR*, 7 (1910), 390–9, at pp. 392–3.

[55] J. Gilmore, 'Witchcraft and the Church in Scotland' (Ph.D. thesis, University of Glasgow, 1948), p. 110.

[56] Gilmore, 'Witchcraft', p. 2. Gilmore quotes J. K. Hewison, *Bute in Olden Times*, regarding the case of Finwell Hudmen: 'she being bruted for a witch or (as the commone people call it) being with the fayryes'. Gilmore also cites a case from the parish of Kingarth where one man charged another with slander for saying that he was frequently in the company of the 'Fairfolk', p. 196.

[57] Robert Kirk, *An Essay of the nature and actions of the Subterranean (and, for the most part,) Invisible People, heeretofoir going under the Names of Elves, Faunes, and Fairies, or the lyke, among the Low-Country Scots* (Edinburgh, 1815; first pub. 1691).

[58] St Andrews Muniments, Anstruther kirk session, Ch2/625/2, 246. There is no reference to the Devil in this case. The session referred the matter to the presbytery.

several years later when she had been warded because of a scandalous shouting match with her husband William Coke that the evidence was produced.[59]

To understand the dynamics of witch-hunting, as Christina Larner reminded us, it is necessary to look not at what motivated the common people, but what motivated the elite. It was, after all, the elite who controlled the demand for and supply of witches.[60] If the elite's concern was not with the Devil, what was the reason for their interest in hunting witches? To understand this we must see the witch-hunt not in isolation, but as part of a far broader programme intended to control the thoughts, values and behaviours of the entire population. The witch-hunt needs to be seen as part of this broader programme, a programme which attacked everything from the celebration of Christmas to going to holy wells, from sexual behaviour to the use of charms to cure cattle and sheep.[61] During a five-year period from 1645 to 1650, the presbytery of Kirkcaldy not only pursed seven cases of witchcraft, but spent a great deal of time attempting to alter patterns of sexual behaviour, in particular around pre-marital sex but also surrounding adultery. The presbytery was also involved in shaping political thought, attempting to exclude from the sacrament of communion all those who had supported too vigorously the 'Engagement' which the church argued had been ungodly.[62] The church was attempting to build a godly society, and the burgesses, local lairds, judiciary and nobility were willing to go along with most elements of this programme. The old women accused of witchcraft were, in this sense, a threat to the building of this godly society. That threat was irrespective of any belief in demonic pacts or witches' sabbats or carnal copulation with his Satanic Majesty. The mere knowing of a charm to cure, even when the charms contained references to God, or were in Trinitarian form, was enough to make one a threat to this programme of building the godly society.[63]

Who was that shadowy man who danced in the middle of the crowd of women which Andrew Patrick saw by the side of the lake? Was he the Devil or a fairy, or a combination of both? Probably the latter, but the key point is that it did not really

---

[59] Town House, Kirkcaldy, Kirkcaldy kirk session, 13 Feb. 1621; Campbell, *The Church and Parish of Kirkcaldy*, pp. 166–7.

[60] Larner, *Enemies of God*, pp. 1, 22, 60.

[61] M. F. Graham, *The Uses of Reform: 'Godly Discipline' and Popular Behavior in Scotland and Beyond, 1560–1610* (New York, 1996); S. J. Davies, 'The courts and the Scottish legal system, 1600–1747: the case of Stirlingshire,' in V. A. C. Gatrell *et al.* (eds), *Crime and the Law: the Social History of Crime in Western Europe since 1500* (London, 1980).

[62] Macdonald, 'Threats to a godly society', pp. 324–33.

[63] Isobel Hevrie was brought before the session for knowing this charm:

Three bitter has the[e] bitten

Evil hart, evill eye, and evil Tongue

Almost three ply

But wyl be Father, Sone and Holy Ghost.

Campbell, *Church and Parish of Kirkcaldy*, p. 166. Clark, *Thinking with Demons*, p. 459, argues that there was as much hostility among intellectuals to white witches as to black ones. For more on charmers, see J. Miller, 'Devices and directions: folk healing aspects of witchcraft practice in seventeenth-century Scotland', Chapter 6 below.

matter. This is why no one bothered to ask questions about who he was, or whether Elspeth Seath had entered into a pact with him. It is possible, perhaps probable, that had the church officials been able to ward and watch her in the way they demanded, such questions would have been pursued. Still, she was a witch without these questions being asked, let alone answered. She was a witch, not because of a pact with the Devil, but because she was known as a witch by her neighbours, as someone who could heal or harm, and a troublesome neighbour. In the godly society which the church was trying to create and which other members of the elite supported, any powers to harm or heal belonged only to God and could be explained only by the church. To this enterprise, the Devil or a demonic pact were not required to make her an enemy or a threat; she was a threat by her very existence.

4

The Scottish witchcraft panic
of 1597

Julian Goodare

Philomathes: What thinke ye of these strange newes, which now onelie furnishes
purpose to al men at their meeting: I meane of these Witches?
Epistemon: Surelie they are wonderfull: And I think so cleare and plaine confessions in
that purpose, have never fallen out in anie age or cuntrey.[1]

When James VI published his book *Daemonologie* late in 1597, witchcraft was
'newes'. And no wonder, for James's book appeared just as one of Scotland's five
great witchcraft panics, that of 1597, was dying down. James had himself played a
major role in the panic – but it was not just about him. The previous national
panic, that of 1590–1, involved him intimately, but thanks to the persuasive revision of Jenny Wormald, even that is now being attributed less to him than before.
Dr Wormald's revision of accepted views on the king's involvement also extends to
Daemonologie itself and to 1597, and will be discussed in what follows.[2]

The leading scholar of the Scottish witch-hunt, Christina Larner, regarded the
panic of 1597 as the most difficult one to explain.[3] The problem is one of evidence.
The panic of 1590–1 generated a large amount of material, especially as far as concerned the king. For the seventeenth-century panics (1628–30, 1649, 1661–2), we
have a good idea of their overall shape. Local trials were held under commissions
of justiciary issued centrally, and the central government kept records of their
issue. In 1597, although commissions were issued centrally, no records were kept.
Surviving local records are difficult to use, and most have not survived. We want to
explain the panic, but even a simple reconstruction of events involves groping in
the dark. The effort must nevertheless be made, because the evidence we *do* have
throws flashes of light on the subject to show us a panic that spread rapidly across
Scotland, convulsing the local communities most intensely involved and causing
disturbance at the highest levels of government. It was indeed 'newes'.

---

[1] James VI, *Daemonologie*, in *MPW*, p. 1.

[2] J. Wormald, 'The witches, the Devil and the king', in T. Brotherstone and D. Ditchburn (eds), *Freedom and Authority: Scotland, c.1050–c.1650* (East Linton, 2000).

[3] Larner, *Enemies of God*, p. 70.

I

The panic had causes at several levels, and the relative influence of each is hard to determine. There had to be some basic background factors enabling trials to start. Both the populace and the elite had to believe in maleficent witchcraft, it had to be a crime triable in the courts, and the witchcraft beliefs had to be specific enough to allow courts to think that they could distinguish guilt from innocence in individual cases. Moving on from this background situation, which certainly existed in late sixteenth-century Scotland, various developments could make a panic more likely. The experience of social and political instability could bring home to people the immediacy of divine and demonic intervention in the world. Then witchcraft itself had to be publicised, to encourage people to see the threat to their ideals in the specific form of witches, rather than (for instance) Antichrist. One or two high-profile witchcraft trials might be enough for this. These trials might or might not themselves provide a further factor: a snowball of accusations, in which the witches were seen not as individuals but as members of a conspiracy. It was not enough to prosecute witches one at a time; they had to provide the names of accomplices.

Witchcraft was a religious and political crime, and in the 1590s Scottish religion and politics were in turmoil. The radical presbyterian movement had gained control of the church in 1592 after a long struggle, but differences between their ideals and those of king and courtiers became increasingly apparent. Co-operation between king and presbyterians broke down in 1596. The presbyterians demanded that James punish the dissident Catholic earls of Huntly, Errol, Angus and Crawford, while the king wanted to reintegrate them into the body politic. They also demanded that he dismiss the 'Octavians', eight exchequer commissioners with far-reaching powers and alleged Catholic tendencies. James countered by accusing a leading minister of treason. A spectacular showdown occurred on 17 December 1596, when the presbyterians tried to force the issue. There was a riot in Edinburgh against the Octavians; the king and council fled, but the presbyterians failed to rally noble support and the attempted coup collapsed within days. A royalist clampdown followed, and 1597 was the year in which the king sought to dictate a new settlement, with the beleaguered presbyterians determined to fight every step of the way.[4]

1597 was not just a year of political and religious disruption; it was also a year of famine. The period 1594–9 saw repeated harvest failures, and from time to time there was mass starvation.[5] Witches were not blamed directly for this, but it could well have increased social tensions in local communities, with resentment at begging. A feeling of the immediacy of divine – or diabolical – intervention in the

---

[4] A. R. MacDonald, *The Jacobean Kirk, 1567–1625: Sovereignty, Polity and Liturgy* (Aldershot, 1998), chs. 3–4; cf. Calderwood, *History*, v, and *CSP Scot.*, xii, *passim*.

[5] S. G. E. Lythe, *The Economy of Scotland in its European Setting, 1550–1625* (Edinburgh, 1960), pp. 20–1; A. J. S. Gibson and T. C. Smout, *Prices, Food and Wages in Scotland, 1550–1780* (Cambridge, 1995), pp. 167–8.

world could also have raised peasants' concerns about witchcraft. The elite, for whom famine threatened their income from rents, could have felt this too. The summer of 1597 also saw an outbreak of plague. Witch-hunting, by demonstrating a willingness to eliminate ungodliness, could be seen as an attempt to solicit God's favour at a time when the land stood much in need of it. The presbytery of St Andrews linked plague and famine with witch-hunting on 17 August 1597, when it ordered a public fast 'because of Goddis jugementis presentlie strykinge be pestilence and famine, as also of the discoverie of the gryt empyre of the deivill in this countrey be witchecraft'.[6]

The old theory that ergotism may have contributed to witchcraft accusations has recently been examined for possible Scottish relevance. Eating rye contaminated with the ergot fungus could induce hallucinations and convulsions that might be interpreted as demonic possession. Ian Whyte has pointed out that although rye was a rare crop in Scotland, large quantities were imported from the Baltic in famine years.[7] Only the most blinkered technological determinist could regard ergotism as a *general* explanation for witch-hunting in Scotland or anywhere else, but the famine of 1594–9 may have provided appropriate conditions. There is mention of the magistrates of Aberdeen importing rye and rye meal in 1596.[8] Difficulties arise, however, in relating the symptoms of ergotism to the actual witchcraft cases of 1597. Accusations that witches caused demonic possession are distinctive; 1597 produced no obvious cases.[9] Ergotism may have contributed to some cases, but the evidence is insufficient to say positively that it did.

Whatever the background stresses of famine, the immediate context of the panic was political and religious. The final months of 1596 provided an agonising experience of political instability. Moreover, it was not a matter of political parties competing vigorously but legitimately. None of the parties wanted to be embroiled in conflict; they believed in ideals of unity and harmony. The presbyterians felt guilty for defying the king: the king felt guilty for treating some of his subjects as enemies. They *sought* unity and harmony. Something on which they could all unite was likely to be seized on with relief. In the aftermath of December's attempted coup, that was witch-hunting.

A few witches had been tried in the Edinburgh justiciary court late in 1596. The most notable was Christian Stewart, whose confession to have bewitched Patrick Ruthven to death 'with ane blak clout' was heard, in apparently increasing detail,

---

[6] M. C. Smith, 'The Presbytery of St Andrews, 1586–1605: a Study and Annotated Edition of the Register of the Minutes of the Presbytery of St Andrews, Volume I' (Ph.D. thesis, University of St Andrews, 1986), p. 231.

[7] I. D. Whyte, 'Ergotism and witchcraft in Scotland', *Area*, 26 (1994), 89–90; see also K. Duncan, 'Was ergotism responsible for the Scottish witch hunts?', *Area*, 25 (1993), 30–6, and W. F. Boyd, 'Four and twenty blackbirds: more on ergotism, rye and witchcraft in Scotland', *Area*, 27 (1995), 77.

[8] Lythe, *Economy of Scotland*, p. 20.

[9] James's mention in *Daemonologie* of 'a younge lasse troubled uith spreits layde on her be uitchcraft' was probably written in 1591. He later amended the passage to remove a topical reference to the event 'even now': *MPW*, p. 165.

first by the ministers of Perth in August, then by a minister, bailie and physician in Edinburgh, and finally by King James in September. She was executed in November. She seems to have been an isolated case; details are incomplete, but there is no suggestion that she was asked about accomplices.[10] Stewart did not set the snowball rolling, but the interest generated by her case may have put ideas into the heads of some influential people.

There was probably no single snowball – at least not in the sense of a single witch to whom all subsequent cases could be traced back. Instead cases arose in various localities, convincing local elites that witchcraft was a conspiracy rather than an affair of isolated individuals. Once sensitised to the issue, they would pursue subsequent cases more vigorously and press for names of accomplices more often. Meanwhile news of their activities would spread, and elites in other localities would have an example to follow. The central authorities, too, would become more worried about witchcraft with each case that was brought to them. It is worth emphasising that all cases, at least initially, *were* brought to them. After Christian Stewart few trials were held centrally, but commissions of justiciary had to be issued by the crown. No specific central initiative launched the panic, but all that was necessary was to encourage, rather than discourage, witchcraft prosecutions by the local authorities. At times that encouragement was enthusiastic and compelling.

II

By far the most detailed information about the panic of 1597 comes from Aberdeenshire, where a remarkable dossier of trial records survives.[11] Concern about witchcraft arose in three separate Aberdeenshire localities in January and February. The initial investigations were by three different local authorities and the witches concerned were not linked to each other. However, it is quite possible that news of one prosecution was picked up by neighbouring authorities, encouraging them to act.

The earliest actual trials were in Slains, 15 miles north of Aberdeen. The local magnate, the earl of Errol (one of the Catholic earls), obtained a commission of justiciary that enabled his officials to execute several witches. In Dyce and Fintray, 5 miles to the north of the city, two kirk sessions began investigations that would eventually lead to the execution of a prominent local charmer, Isobel Strachan alias Scudder. And in the city itself, the magistrates obtained their own commission of justiciary to prosecute Janet Wishart, a burgess's wife with an evil reputation, and six of her relatives and associates. Wishart, like Strachan, attracted public interest

---

[10] Pitcairn (ed.), *Trials*, i, pp. 399–400. For another case that seems to have been isolated but prominent, that of Janet Garvie, see W. Fraser, *Memorials of the Earls of Haddington*, 2 vols (Edinburgh, 1889), ii, p. 69. The king's letter to the lord advocate ordering her prosecution (22 Nov. 1596) is endorsed 'His majesties warrand to persew the witche', indicating that only one witch was then in question.

[11] For what follows see J. Goodare, 'The Aberdeenshire witchcraft panic of 1597', *Northern Scotland*, 21 (2001), 17–37.

because her neighbours swarmed to accuse her of maleficent acts, and she was executed on 19 February. But neither Wishart nor Strachan were themselves interrogated, and prosecutions based on their reputation could extend no further than the associates credited to them by public opinion. Strachan's daughter was prosecuted but acquitted.

It was a few days after Wishart's execution that the snowball was set rolling. Her son Thomas Leys was interrogated, confessed to having made the demonic pact and attended a witches' sabbath, and named a number of women as having been present. Hauled in themselves and (like Leys) probably tortured, several of these women also confessed and named further names. The Aberdeen magistrates now panicked in earnest, and rushed back to Edinburgh to seek a further commission of justiciary – not to try named individuals this time, but to try all cases of witchcraft. A five-year general commission was granted on 4 March to the magistrates and sheriff depute of Aberdeen.

The newly-empowered commissioners spent the rest of the month interrogating and burning their way through the suspects generated by Leys. They then turned to the Lumphanan and Cromar area, 25 miles to the west, remembering that the previous national panic in 1590–1 had produced two prominent witches from that area. Margaret Bain, the sister of one of them, was a sitting target, a midwife with a magical reputation; interrogated, she too named further suspects. This was not enough for the commissioners, who summoned the local lairds and kirk sessions of half a dozen parishes in the area to provide yet more names. Some were distinctly reluctant, either providing no names or warning that their local charmers had nothing maleficent known against them. Nevertheless, this systematic trawl netted a number of witches in March and April. The commissioners also raked over the embers of the earlier prosecutions in Slains to obtain more names from that locality. A few further witches, either isolated individuals or small groups, were identified elsewhere in the sheriffdom by local elites who heard of the prosecutions, and the Aberdeen tolbooth saw a constant succession of trials.

By the end of May, the Aberdeenshire panic had burned itself out. Records are incomplete but at least twenty-seven people had been executed, and there had been one suicide and one death in prison. Eight people had been convicted of non-capital magical offences, and five had been acquitted. Thirty-four people had been named formally as witches and their fates are unknown; some had at least initial proceedings taken against them and some may even have been executed. A revival of interest in the autumn and winter would lead to four more prosecutions – three acquittals and one execution. This makes a total of at least eighty people caught up in the panic, thirty of whom died as a result of it.

III

The Aberdeenshire panic can open a window into events elsewhere that are otherwise obscure. In other parts of the country, we have *indications* that similar events were taking place, but little or no detailed information. When sources speak merely

of 'many witches burned' this should be regarded as evidence that trials similar
to those in Aberdeenshire were taking place, even if the detailed evidence on the
trials has disappeared. Two features of the Aberdeenshire panic might help to
identify the scale of prosecutions in other localities. Firstly, the earliest trials were
under individual commissions of justiciary, for the trial of specific, named witchcraft suspects. Once the trials started to snowball and further suspects were uncovered, a general commission was obtained. A general commission is thus a strong
sign of large-scale prosecutions. Secondly, witches who were interrogated were
likely to generate further names of suspects, while those prosecuted on the basis of
neighbours' information alone were likely to remain isolated cases. Evidence of
interrogations may also be evidence of large-scale prosecutions.

One of the problems when dealing with fragmentary information is that some
cases may represent background noise – witchcraft prosecutions that would have
happened even without the panic. But comparison with the next decade, when
there was no panic, suggests that such cases would be few. Christina Larner and her
research assistants found thirty-nine cases in 1600–9, an annual average of about
four. It is true that the present chapter explores local sources that Larner *et al.* did
not use, but even on the most drastic upward revision of their statistics the annual
background figure would remain a handful.[12] The Aberdeenshire evidence reveals
isolated witches as caught up in the panic, because news of witchcraft prosecutions
elsewhere encouraged local action against them.

Some isolated cases certainly look like the kind of thing that happened in normal years. The increase in such cases during the panic indicates that most of them
probably occurred only because witch-hunting was in the news elsewhere, but
there is no means of knowing which individual cases were prompted by such news.
Peebles presbytery, between February and May, investigated Janet Wallace for 'gew-
ing of drinkis and slaying of sum withe hir drinkis etc, and using of uther socereis
and inchanntmentis'. However, the family of a woman she was alleged to have
killed declined to pursue the charge, and the presbytery eventually concentrated on
prosecuting Wallace for slandering the reader at Peebles.[13]

The kirk session of South Leith, by contrast, had the general subject of witchcraft on its mind on 16 June and was not just responding to an individual complaint; two cases occurred on the same day. William Ford, one of the deacons,
was ordered to do penance for 'consulting with a warlow [i.e. warlock] in
Newcastell in England'. Archibald Tait had been 'consulting with Bessie Aikin

[12] Larner *et al.*, *Source-Book*, p. 239. In addition to the sources cited elsewhere in this chapter, the following records were examined, all in NAS: Ellon presbytery, 1597–1607, CH2/146/1; Dalkeith presbytery, 1582–1630, CH2/424/1; St Cuthbert's kirk session, 1595–1609, CH2/718/2; Galston kirk session
accounts, 1592–9, CH2/1335/1; Stirling Holy Rude kirk session, 1597–1614, CH2/1026/1; St Monance
kirk session, 1597–1617, CH2/1056/1; Haddington burgh court books, 1585–97, 1597–1603,
B30/10/6–7; Haddington burgh council minutes, 1581–1602, B30/13/2. No witches were found for
1597. This includes most and perhaps all of the kirk session and presbytery material in NAS. There may
be more witchcraft material in burgh records, in family papers, or in archives held locally.
[13] NAS, Peebles presbytery minutes, 1596–1624, CH2/295/1, fos. 5v., 6v.–7r., 9r.

suspected of witchcraft'.[14] Criminal proceedings against Aitken herself may have begun at this time, though her trial would come only in November. Another place where criminal prosecutions were then well under way was Elgin, surely inspired by recent witch-hunting in nearby Aberdeenshire. On 27 May, 'the minister producit the commissioun fra his majestie purchast aganis vitches and counsalaris with thame'.[15] This, evidently a general commission, may well indicate a major local panic.

Witch-hunting began in Fife in January, when the kirk session of Anstruther Wester began proceedings against Janet Fogow that led to her execution. That session heard five witchcraft cases in 1597, though in other years the number never exceeded two.[16] Witch-hunting was organised in the Pittenweem area by the courtier Colonel William Stewart, commendator of Pittenweem, in consultation with the presbytery of St Andrews. In June he had draft dittays against four witches, including Janet Fogow; they and perhaps others had been burned by 7 July.[17] One intense episode was reported by the English ambassador Robert Bowes. King James spent several days in St Andrews, to purge the university's presbyterians 'and for the trial and punishment of witches':

> The number of witches exceed; many are condemned and executed chiefly for their revolt from God and dedicating themselves and services to the Devil, by especial sacrament (as they term it) in receiving the Devil's mark set in their flesh and in secret part as it has been confessed by and seen in many and wherein many of several sorts are accused. They profess sundry fantastical feats to have been executed by them, all which shall (I think) be published, as I forbear to trouble you therewith.[18]

Another set of Fife witch-hunters, the bailies of Burntisland, panicked so badly that they wholly lost sight of justice. On 26 July, Janet Finlayson complained to the privy council that the bailies had tried her for witchcraft under a commission of justiciary, and the assize had acquitted her. Despite this, the bailies had ordered the burgh clerk not to 'delyver the proces of hir tryall and clengeing' and were planning a fresh trial. The bailies, who offered no defence, were ordered to desist.[19] Witch-hunting in Fife was not seriously checked, since on 4 August, six members of the presbytery of St Andrews were commissioned 'to examine the weimen of the paroche of Largo suspected of witchcraft'.[20] On 11, 14 and 17 August the magistrates of Kirkcaldy took cautions for the entry to trial of twenty-two women

---

[14] NAS, South Leith kirk session minutes, 1597–1610, CH2/716/1, fo. 1r.

[15] *Records of Elgin, 1234–1800*, 2 vols, eds W. Cramond and S. Ree (New Spalding Club, 1903–8), ii, p. 52.

[16] M. F. Graham, *The Uses of Reform: 'Godly Discipline' and Popular Behavior in Scotland and Beyond, 1560–1610* (Leiden, 1996), pp. 227, 304.

[17] Smith, 'Presbytery of St Andrews', pp. 221–4, 226.

[18] Bowes to Burghley, 13 July 1597, *CSP Scot.*, xiii, I, p. 56.

[19] *RPC*, v, pp. 405–6. James was in Falkland at the time, away from the council: Bowes to Burghley, 31 July 1597, *CSP Scot.*, xiii, I, p. 65. For another Burntisland case see W. Ross, *Aberdour and Inchcolme* (Edinburgh, 1885), pp. 343–4.

[20] Smith, 'Presbytery of St Andrews', p. 229.

and three men – a large-scale operation which, as we shall see, also spread to nearby Inverkeithing.[21]

Perthshire seems to have experienced large-scale witch-hunting. The prominent witch of late 1596, Christian Stewart, had been from Perth. The Chronicle of Perth noted: 'Ane great number of witshes brint, through all the partis of this realme in June 1597'.[22] In July 1597, the bailies of Perth were ordered to 'retene ane wiche unburnt' until the king could come.[23] If James meant to pardon the witch, the order would probably have said so. Presumably he wanted to interrogate her or him in person, as he had done with Christian Stewart and would do with others.

The chronicler Patrick Anderson wrote a brief but important account of the panic. Although he focused (as we shall see) on a witch from Fife, his paragraph on the subject was headed 'Sorcerie in Atholl'. His statement that 'speciallie in Atholl both of men and women ther was in May att one convention upon a hill in Atholl to the number of 2300 and the Devill amongst them' may be unique in the annals of Scottish witch-belief.[24] Atholl seems to have had a reputation for witchcraft.[25] However, it was more than simply a remote and uncanny Highland locale for Lowland stories, since a complaint to the privy council in March 1598 catches the echoes of a witch-hunt that the earl of Atholl had apparently been conducting for some time, using two imprisoned witches to identify others.[26]

IV

The single most important witch of 1597 was Margaret Aitken, the so-called great witch of Balwearie.[27] Balwearie in Fife had long associations with the supernatural. James V in 1539 had had a terrifying nightmare about Thomas Scott, son of its laird, who on his deathbed visited the king 'with a company of devils'.[28] Sir Michael

---

[21] Fife Council Archives, Glenrothes, Kirkcaldy burgh court book, 1595–97, fos. 129v.–132r. I am grateful to Dr Stuart Macdonald and his Scottish Witchcraft Data Base for alerting me to these cases.

[22] *The Chronicle of Perth, 1210–1668*, ed. J. Maidment (Maitland Club, 1831), p. 6.

[23] NAS, treasurer's accounts, 1596–7, E21/71, fo. 131r.

[24] Edinburgh University Library, Patrick Anderson, 'Chronicles of Scotland', 2 vols, Laing MSS, III.203, vol. ii, fo. 266v. All subsequent quotations from this folio.

[25] It had been the countess of Atholl (Margaret Fleming, sister of one of Mary queen of Scots' 'four Maries') who had used witchcraft in 1566 to cast the queen's labour pains on the baby's prospective wet-nurse: A. Fraser, *Mary Queen of Scots* (London, 1969), p. 321. In 1570, an elaborate golden gift was intercepted on its way to Queen Mary, with threatening heraldic symbolism, 'we suppone from the witches of Athole': Richard Bannatyne, *Memorials of Transactions in Scotland, 1569–1573*, ed. R. Pitcairn (Bannatyne Club, 1836), p. 61.

[26] *RPC*, v, p. 448.

[27] The term 'great witch' is interesting. Agnes Sampson, one of the North Berwick witches, had been described as a 'great witch' at the height of her revelations: Bowes to Burghley, 7 Dec. 1590, *CSP Scot.*, x, p. 430.

[28] John Knox, *History of the Reformation in Scotland*, 2 vols, ed. W. C. Dickinson (London, 1949), i, p. 29.

Scott of Balwearie, a thirteenth-century physician, had passed into folklore as a wizard.[29] Anderson's account of the panic of 1597 began as follows:

> Much about this tyme there was a great number of witches tryed to be in Scotland, as the lyke was never heard tell of in this realme; speciallie in Atholl both of men and women ther was in May att one convention upon a hill in Atholl to the number of 2300 and the Devill amongst them; a great witch of Balwearie told all this and said she knew them all weill eneugh And what marks the Devill hade given severallie to everie one of them.

Most of what we know about the great witch of Balwearie comes from Archbishop John Spottiswoode, who wrote an ecclesiastical history in the 1620s. In 1597 he was a parish minister in Midlothian, but already involved in national affairs.

> This summer there was a great business for the trial of witches. Amongst others one Margaret Atkin, being apprehended upon suspicion, and threatened with torture, did confess herself guilty. Being examined touching her associates in that trade, she named a few, and perceiving her delations find credit, made offer to detect all of that sort, and to purge the country of them, so she might have her life granted. For the reason of her knowledge, she said, 'That they had a secret mark all of that sort, in their eyes, whereby she could surely tell, how soon she looked upon any, whether they were witches or not:' and in this she was so readily believed, that for the space of three or four months she was carried from town to town to make discoveries in that kind. Many were brought in question by her delations, especially at Glasgow, where divers innocent women, through the credulity of the minister, Mr John Cowper, were condemned and put to death. In end she was found to be a mere deceiver (for the same persons that the one day she had declared guilty, the next day being presented in another habit she cleansed), and sent back to Fife, where first she was apprehended. At her trial she affirmed all to be false that she had confessed, either of herself or others, and persisted in this to her death; which made many forthink their too great forwardness that way, and moved the king to recall the commissions given out against such persons, discharging all proceedings against them, except in case of voluntary confession, till a solid order should be taken by the Estates touching the form that should be kept in their trial.[30]

The 'discharge of all proceedings', although not quite as Spottiswoode represented it, probably refers to a proclamation of 12 August (to be discussed shortly). The chronology thus suggests that Aitken was exposed about 1 August. When 'for the space of three or four months she was carried from town to town', this must have begun some time in April.

Aitken's success inspired imitators in her own locality. Several of those caught up in the large-scale Kirkcaldy witch-hunt were denounced by Agnes Ewing, 'trayare of witchcraft and sorcerie'. The magistrates of Kirkcaldy at one point loaned Ewing

[29] John Leslie, *Historie of Scotland*, 2 vols, eds E. G. Cody and W. Murison (Scottish Text Society, 1888–95), i, pp. 340–1; P. F. Tytler, *Lives of Scottish Worthies*, 3 vols (London, 1831–40), i, pp. 119–28.

[30] John Spottiswoode, *History of the Church of Scotland*, 3 vols, eds M. Napier and M. Russell (Spottiswoode Society, 1847–51), iii, pp. 66–7.

to their colleagues in Inverkeithing, making special arrangements to ensure her return. Ewing was still active on 17 August, despite the proclamation of the 12th.[31]

The Aitken affair was notable for subjecting witchcraft suspects to the water ordeal. No reference to the swimming of Scottish witches has yet been found for any other period, but the evidence for 1597 is clear. Anderson concluded his account: 'Ther was many of them tryed by sweiming in the water by binding of ther two thumbs and ther great toaes together for being thus casten in the water they fleeted ay above.' This is corroborated by James's *Daemonologie*, when he mentioned 'two good helpes' to the detection of witches. One was the search for the Devil's mark, which was to become a standard procedure in the Scottish witch-hunt.[32] The other was

> their fleeting on the water: for ... it appears that God hath appoynted (for a super-natural signe of the monstrous impietie of the Witches) that the water shal refuse to receive them in her bosom, that have shaken off them the sacred Water of Baptisme, and wilfullie refused the benefite thereof.[33]

These distinctive proceedings suggest that a special commission, using special procedures, was established to carry Aitken around the country. James's passage on the water ordeal indicates that he took an interest in the commission and approved of its activities. He may even have pressed later for its special procedures to be adopted by statute, as we shall see. But, as Spottiswoode's account makes clear, the trials ended abruptly when Aitken was exposed as a fraud.

V

The Aitken fiasco led to a proclamation marking a crucial stage in the hunt. It was issued in the king's name by the privy council at Falkland on 12 August. We do not know who took the initiative, or even who was present at the council that day. The king probably concurred in the order, or at least was involved in preliminary discussion of it. His presence at Falkland had led to the council convening there, but either just after the 12th or just before, he himself left for Stirling and then the west. The important things on the council's mind in Falkland were plague and the Catholic earls. Plague had broken out in Dunfermline and was spreading. Two of the Catholic earls, Angus and Errol, had visited the court at Falkland and pressed hard for restoration; the major decision taken there

---

[31] Fife Council Archives, Glenrothes, Kirkcaldy burgh court book, 1595–7, fos. 130r.–130v. A 'Marion Ewyne detector of witchcraft' was also mentioned at one point, who may be an error for Agnes or perhaps her sister.

[32] W. N. Neill, 'The professional pricker and his test for witchcraft', *SHR*, 19 (1922), 205–13; S. W. MacDonald, 'The Devil's mark and the witch-prickers of Scotland', *Journal of the Royal Society of Medicine*, 90 (1997), 507–11.

[33] James VI, *Daemonologie*, in *MPW*, p. 56. This remark probably dates from 1597, since it forms part of a long marginal addition to his original draft: *ibid.*, p. 165. It proved to be one of the few points that seventeenth-century writers cited from James's book: *ibid.*, p. 154.

was that a parliament should be proclaimed for December at which they would be restored.[34]

The proclamation expressed concern that 'grite danger may ensew to honest and famous personis gif commissionis grantit to particulair men, beiring particulairis aganis thame, or to ony nowmer of commissionaris conjunctlie and severallie (quhilk in effect gevis pouer to ane or tua of thame to proceid), sall stand and be authorized'. These commissions, to commissioners 'conjunctlie and severallie', were revoked. The proclamation invited their holders to apply for replacements, which would be granted 'to thame and sum baronis and ministeris unsuspect, to the noumer of three or foure conjunctlie at the fewest'.[35]

The direct effect of this can only have been modest. Most commissions of justiciary were granted for the trial of specific individuals, and the commissioners are unlikely to have dawdled in holding the trial, if only because they would not keep suspects in prison longer than they needed. Aberdeen received its first commission on 2 February and held trials under it between the 17th and 23rd. If this is typical, the only witchcraft suspects whose lives the proclamation could have saved were those for whom commissions had been issued in the previous three weeks, plus those who would have been tried under *general* commissions that were still active. In practice even general commissions usually came to a natural end; Aberdeen's, granted on 4 March, had largely done so by the end of May. But Aberdeen's was not one of those revoked, for it had not been issued 'conjunctlie and severallie' – and many general commissions were probably the same. The magistrates and sheriff depute of Aberdeen revived the prosecution of witches in October 1597 and again in 1599, using their existing commission.[36]

If the order was important, it was probably not for what it did directly, but for what it implied. Here it could carry more than one interpretation, even among those around the council table on 12 August. To some councillors, the Aitken fiasco probably marked the beginning of a new, more cautious approach. Preventing future injustice meant treating future requests for commissions differently. Rather than handing out commissions indiscriminately, these councillors wanted to ask questions, and refuse commissions where the answers were unsatisfactory. They were also perhaps going to make more effort to ensure that requests for commissions came before them, instead of being presented to the king via informal court channels that did not necessarily allow for expert scrutiny of the evidence presented. Spottiswoode remembered the order as 'discharging all proceedings … except in case of voluntary confession'; although wholly inaccurate as to the letter of the order, this may reflect something of the cautious spirit in which some councillors intended it.

[34] Bowes to Burghley, 15 Aug. 1597, *CSP Scot.*, xiii, I, pp. 72–3; *RPC*, v, p. 411; Calderwood, *History*, v, p. 655.

[35] *RPC*, v, pp. 409–10. For a discussion of Christina Larner's misleading interpretation of the order, see J. Goodare, 'The framework for Scottish witch-hunting in the 1590s', *SHR*, 81 (2002, forthcoming).

[36] Goodare, 'The Aberdeenshire witchcraft panic of 1597'.

However, to others the order could be a mere public-relations exercise. Those who were still panicking no doubt regretted the execution of innocent people in the Aitken affair, but they were not going to let that prevent them from pursuing the genuine witches who, they were convinced, were still at large. Some public response had to be made to the Aitken affair because the public had witnessed miscarriages of justice. Hence the recall of the existing commissions. But witch-hunting councillors must have noted that the effect of the order need be no more than to call in commissions issued to one or two people, replacing them with commissions issued to three people.

One of those who wanted to continue the prosecutions was the king. This was particularly important because he did not need the council's concurrence to do so; he could issue commissions of justiciary without them. Nor would he necessarily be bound by the order's requirement to name multiple commissioners. A general commission was issued to Sir Alexander Bruce of Airth as *sole* justice to try any witches in his lands. Its date is incomplete but it must have been issued after 29 July.[37] Was it also after 12 August? There is, at any rate, direct evidence that James was still promoting witch-hunting after the order. Three days after it, Bowes reported:

> The king has been lately pestered and in many ways troubled in the examination of the witches which swarm in exceeding number and (as is credibly reported) in many thousands. McKolme Anderson confesses that he and other witches practised to have drowned the king in his passage over the water at Dundee at the late general assembly of the church there [in May], and the life of the prince has been likewise sought by the witches, as is acknowledged by some of them.[38]

So the link between witchcraft and treason had resurfaced. The witches were following North Berwick precedent remarkably closely in aiming to *drown* the king, while the threat to the prince echoed the threat to James's marriage in 1590. This is one of the points at which the inadequacy of the source-material for 1597 is most striking. The absence of a pamphlet like *Newes from Scotland* (1591) is especially regrettable, as is the failure to publish the witches' confessions, promised in July. If his confession had survived, Malcolm Anderson might have been as prominent in the history of Scottish witchcraft as the witches of North Berwick. The evidence that we do have both for 1590–1 and for 1597, the reports by and to the English ambassador, is similar in tone for both episodes. We can say far less about 1597 than about 1590–1 because so much other evidence has disappeared. But we can recognise that it did once exist. 1597, in short, was another North Berwick – a major panic over treasonable witchcraft that was thought to be directed against the king personally. No wonder he was bothered.

On 5 September, one of Bowes's Edinburgh informants put the king's anti-witch concern at the head of a long list of news items:

---

[37] AD 1597, AR 31, i.e. between 29 July 1597 and 24 March 1598. W. Fraser, *The Elphinstone Family Book*, 2 vols (Edinburgh, 1897), ii, p. 136.

[38] Bowes to Burghley, 15 Aug. 1597, *CSP Scot.*, xiii, I, p. 73.

The king has his mind only bent on the examination and trial of sorcerers, men and women. Such a great number are delated that it is a wonder, and those not only of the meanest sort but also of the best. Hereat all estates are grieved and specially the church, affirming that the form of proceeding is neither conform to the law of God nor man.[39]

These reports contradict the impression given by Spottiswoode – that pressure for witch-hunting came from over-zealous ministers. Instead they show the king leading, and 'the church', or at least a vocal part of it, sceptical. The presbytery of St Andrews had still been endorsing witch-hunting on 17 August, when it had proclaimed the public fast referred to earlier; but on 1 September it ordered 'a supplicatioun to be maid to his majestie for repressing of the horable abuse by carying a witch about, and Mr Robert Wilichie ordanit to request magis[tratis] of Sanctandroes to stay the same thair'.[40] This almost suggests that the Aitken commission was still active, and indeed there is no positive information on its discharge. However, the Kirkcaldy magistrates were still using the services of Agnes Ewing, 'tryour of the wiches', on 17 August, and the St Andrews order could refer to this. It was not the last that would be heard of the 'horable abuse by carying a witch about'.

James was pursuing the subject of witchcraft in other ways too. The report of 5 September continued:

The king has written upon the 4th instant to four ministers on this side [of the Forth] whom he will to come to Falkland the 13th instant to preach in his presence upon divers texts of Holy Writ, as he has nominated to either of them touching the essential power of Satan either by permission or power of God. He has also written to 12 other ministers of Angus and Fife to be present that day to censure that doctrine and to reason the cause. The letters came here this morning which is like to engender a great grief in their hearts, affirming the king to be no high priest.[41]

James was probably seeking advice in order to put the finishing touches to his book *Daemonologie*. The title page bears the date '1597'; there is no direct evidence for a more precise publication date, but it has plausibly been argued that it was later in the year, not long before 16 March 1597/8, when a London printer registered an intention to print an English edition.[42] This also fits with the events of the autumn. James's book had been conceived, and written at least in part, as an immediate reaction to the witchcraft trials of 1590–1;[43] but its *publication* clearly represents a reaction to the trials of 1597. In it, witch-hunting has just been happening, it is 'newes'. The intention was to publish the witches' confessions at the same time.[44] The treatise itself has been discussed by several scholars, especially Stuart Clark,

[39] Advices from Scotland, 5 Sept. 1597, *CSP Scot.*, xiii, I, p. 78.

[40] Smith, 'Presbytery of St Andrews', p. 232.

[41] Advices from Scotland, 5 Sept. 1597, *CSP Scot.*, xiii, I, pp. 78–9. That witches were uppermost in James's mind is confirmed by Bowes to Burghley, 8 Sept. 1597, *ibid.*, p. 81.

[42] James VI, *Daemonologie*, in *MPW*, p. 177.

[43] R. Dunlap, 'King James and some witches: the date and text of the *Daemonologie*', *Philological Quarterly*, 54 (1975), 40–6.

[44] James VI, *Daemonologie*, in *MPW*, p. xx; Bowes to Burghley, 13 July 1597, *CSP Scot.*, xiii, I, p. 56.

and more recently Lawrence Normand and Gareth Roberts.[45] What matters here is simply its overall argument. Witches exist; they should be prosecuted by the lawful authorities; those who deny these points are badly astray, and perhaps actually in league with the witches. The immediate targets seem to have been those among the ministers, and indeed among 'all estates', who criticised the king's support for the prosecution of witches in the autumn of 1597.

Recently, however, Jenny Wormald has attempted to place a 'sceptical' construction on James's role during the 1597 panic, and even on *Daemonologie* itself.[46] She agrees that James had actively promoted the panic of 1590–1 (though persuasively setting his involvement in the context of initiatives by others); in 1597, however, the only role she has for James is that of sceptic, curbing others' excesses. She argues that in 1592, James had handed over responsibility for dealing with witchcraft to the church, indicating that the 'motivating force' for witchcraft trials was 'not a witch-hunting king, but the witch-haunted Kirk. Thus was the machinery for witch-hunting put into place; and four years later, it was used to the full in the next great outburst of persecution in 1596–7.' I have argued elsewhere that this is a fundamental misunderstanding of the 1592 order, which was only tangentially about witchcraft at all, contained no 'machinery' for witch-hunting, and was in any case never implemented. In 1597, as throughout the 1590s, the only 'machinery' available for witchcraft trials was commissions of justiciary issued by the crown, or trials in the Edinburgh court of justiciary.[47]

What of James himself in 1597? Dr Wormald dates 'the first signs of his concern at what was going on' to 14 April, when 'he quashed the proceedings against two suspected witches' in Aberdeenshire. But this refers to an order issued by the lords of council and session; such orders went out under its signet without crossing the king's desk, even though like most governmental orders they ran in the king's name.[48] There is no positive evidence that James ever heard of the episode. Dr Wormald's next evidence of James's 'scepticism' comes from the order of 12 August revoking outstanding commissions of justiciary. But we do not know that it was James's initiative; and even if it was, it was merely a necessary response to the Aitken fiasco. James probably interrogated Aitken, given his enthusiasm for interrogating witches in the summer and willingness to travel to do so. But he never claimed to have doubted her, or to have exposed her. This contrasts strikingly with

[45] S. Clark, 'King James's *Daemonologie*: witchcraft and kingship', in S. Anglo (ed.), *The Damned Art: Essays in the Literature of Witchcraft* (London, 1977); L. Normand and G. Roberts (eds), *Witchcraft in Early Modern Scotland: James VI's* Demonology *and the North Berwick Witches* (Exeter, 2000), pp. 327–52.

[46] Wormald, 'The witches, the Devil and the king', pp. 177–80. All quotations from Dr Wormald's paper are from this passage. I should stress that up to this point I regard her paper as persuasive and important.

[47] Goodare, 'Framework for Scottish witch-hunting'.

[48] *Spalding Misc.*, i, pp. 163–4; R. K. Hannay, 'The early history of the Scottish signet', in *The College of Justice: Essays by R. K. Hannay* (Stair Society, 1990), pp. 317–18.

his later enthusiasm for exposing frauds, and loudly claiming personal credit for discoveries like the Gunpowder Plot.[49]

Dr Wormald has difficulty explaining the evidence of James's *subsequent* witch-hunting initiatives, especially the report of 5 September. However, by quoting only the last sentence of the first passage from it quoted above – 'Hereat all estates are grieved and specially the church, affirming that the form of proceeding is neither conform to the law of God nor man' – she contrives to give the impression that churchmen were frustrated by James *preventing* them from hunting witches. Those who read the entire passage will see that this is the reverse of the truth. She continues by mentioning some of his anti-presbyterian moves (irrelevant to witch-hunting) and concludes triumphantly: 'The second great witch-hunt of the reign was fizzling out in the face of determined royal scepticism.' It is not clear that 'scepticism' is a helpful concept in the aftermath of the Aitken fiasco, since all those involved were convinced believers in witches; but it may be taken as shorthand for a view that prosecutions should proceed with caution and that panic measures were inappropriate. 'Scepticism' of this kind there probably was, but James did his best to discourage it.

Thus we come to Dr Wormald's interpretation of *Daemonologie*, the publication of which she argues convincingly was decided on at about this time. She makes little or no attempt to engage with James's arguments as set out in the book, perhaps realising that a 'sceptical' reading of his text would be impossible to construct. Instead she seems to argue that although he wrote it, he did not really believe what he had written:

> It was written partly for self-reassurance and partly as a signing-off by a man who still believed in witchcraft and demonic power, but who found it increasingly impossible to believe that the hundreds of women condemned in 1596–7 were all witches.... He was getting something out of his system.... The Preface tells us that his intention was to resolve doubting hearts. Perhaps the most doubting heart was that of the author.

Since Dr Wormald can produce virtually no warrant from James's text to support this interpretation, we are entitled to ask what evidence she has for James's doubts. *Daemonologie* is, she says, 'a very short book' (actually about 26,000 words, over twice the length of *The Trew Law of Free Monarchies*), and 'was done in a hurry'. She argues the latter point – her most substantial one – on two grounds. Firstly the fragments of the first draft are unusually free of corrections. But the king, and his adviser James Carmichael, made extensive revisions to the *second* draft.[50] In any case the first draft was probably written nearer to 1591 than to 1597 and cannot represent a 'signing-off'. Secondly the printed edition is notoriously inaccurate, supposedly showing that James was not interested in it. But he *chose* to revise the book and send it to the printer in 1597, although his even longer *Paraphrase upon the Revelation*, written in the 1580s, remained in manuscript until 1616. There

[49] J. Sharpe, *The Bewitching of Anne Gunter* (London, 1999), pp. 175–89; James I, 'A Discourse of the Powder-Treason', in his *Workes* (London, 1616), pp. 227–8.

[50] James VI, *Daemonologie*, in *MPW*, pp. 161–5.

could be all sorts of explanations for *Daemonologie*'s typographical shortcomings: most likely James was called away by other business in the week that he should have been checking proofs.[51] It seems implausible to use a book's poor state of production as evidence that the author did not really believe what he had written in it.

The idea that James had doubts about witch-hunting need not be ruled out entirely. Perhaps many other witch-hunters did too. However, in the absence of solid evidence, the idea must remain in the realm of speculation. The question of when and how James lost his enthusiasm for witch-hunting, turning instead to the exposure of fraudulent demoniacs, has been much debated. Probably, as Christina Larner and Stuart Clark concluded, his move to England had much to do with it. Dr Clark also pointed out a consistent quasi-empirical core to James's beliefs, and his keenness to interrogate witches personally in 1597 supports this.[52] This topic would repay further study. The conclusion that can be drawn here is that if James's supposed doubts in 1597 influenced his public behaviour at all it was to spur him into action to defend demonological orthodoxy – both in print, and by means of faggot and stake.

VI

So a new series of trials was launched in late August and September, by which the king attempted to rehabilitate witch-hunting. Although his views are clear, there is no need to pin all the responsibility on him: no doubt others supported him. Few details of these trials are known, and even their locations are doubtful, not being given by Bowes on 15 August or 8 September or his informant on 5 September. James himself flitted about to avoid the plague, being mentioned in Edinburgh, Falkland, Hamilton, Linlithgow, Perth and Stirling.

Stirlingshire was one area where there was undoubtedly a local panic at this time. On 7 September, Stirling presbytery commissioned certain ministers 'to try and examin thais women alreddie apprehendit and to be apprehendit heiraftir for wichcraft, and qwhat thay find, to report the samin to the presbyterie that thay may judge thairon befoir any of thame thoill ane assyss [i.e. undergo criminal trial]'. The investigation was large-scale enough to require bureaucracy: Elizabeth Hamilton was 'accusit of wichcraft and abusing of the pepill, as at lenth is sait doun in the Register thairof'. On 5 October the commissioners reported that Katherine Kello and Janet Crawford 'ar apprehendit for witchcraft with quhome thay have enterit in tryell as thair confessionis bearis in thame selfis in the Register thairof'.[53] As in Aberdeenshire, the use of confession evidence may well indicate that names of accomplices were being obtained. The 'Register' appears to have been a dossier of evidence for use

---

[51] He did not correct it in later editions either – those of 1603 (which he may not have seen before publication) and 1616. But if this tells us anything, it tells us about his attitude to the book at those dates, not in 1597.

[52] Larner, *Witchcraft*, p. 18.

[53] NAS, Stirling presbytery minutes, 1596–1604, CH2/722/3 (unfoliated), 7, 21 Sept., 5 Oct. 1597.

in a criminal court; possibly it was used to solicit a commission of justiciary, but it seems more likely that a commission had already been obtained and that the execution of Hamilton, Kello, Crawford and others was a foregone conclusion.

The king still wanted to interrogate witches personally, and took an active interest in the Stirlingshire panic. On 16 September he ordered the magistrates of Stirling to send an unnamed 'prickat wiche' to him at Linlithgow, 'that scho may be reddy thair that nycht at evin attending our cuming for hir tryell in that depositioun scho hes maid aganis Capitane Herring and his wyffe'.[54] So the Stirling authorities were using witch-pricking as well as extracting confessions – another indication of a large-scale panic. Patrick Heron and his wife Christian Reid had a bitter property dispute with Sir William Menteith of Kerse and his son, and the Menteiths were surely the people who had arrested the 'prickat wiche' and shaped her deposition to promote their interests.[55] On 19 October, Heron (who had prudently fled) was being prosecuted for witchcraft by the Menteiths and the lord advocate in a special session of the justiciary court. The case was continued to the next Stirlingshire justice ayre in response to a letter from the king, and disappears from the record.[56] The Menteiths worked together with the Bruces of Airth; William Bruce younger was their cautioner in the Heron dispute.[57] The witchcraft commission to Sir Alexander Bruce, mentioned above, probably dates from this period. The Stirlingshire panic seems to have been widespread.

It may have been the Heron case that prompted the court of justiciary in Edinburgh to resume a role in witchcraft trials. It had heard such cases late in 1596, but once panic set in, all cases had been tried locally under royal commission. The Edinburgh court did not generally hear many cases – under fifty were recorded for all crimes during 1597, and none at all between 20 August and 18 October.[58] But after Heron's case on 19 October, only two more other cases were heard before the court again had a witchcraft case, that of Janet Stewart, Christian Livingstone, Bessie Aitken and Christian Sadler on 12 November. All were convicted, though Aitken escaped execution through pregnancy.[59] They were folk healers from the Edinburgh area, and on 15 November, the presbytery of Edinburgh followed their conviction with an order 'that consulteris with witches salbe censured according to the actis of the generall assemblie'.[60]

---

[54] *Extracts from the Records of the Royal Burgh of Stirling, 1519–1666*, ed. R. Renwick (Glasgow, 1887), p. 86.

[55] *RPC*, v, pp. 218–20, 276–7. For more on how this was done see L. Yeoman, 'Hunting the rich witch in Scotland: high-status witchcraft suspects and their persecutors, 1590–1650', Chapter 7 below.

[56] Pitcairn (ed.), *Trials*, ii, pp. 23–5.

[57] *RPC*, v, p. 658.

[58] NAS, justiciary court, books of adjournal, 1596–1604, JC2/3, pp. 158–236. Some of these involved more than one person. I am grateful to Ms Lauren Martin for advice on the books of adjournal.

[59] NAS, justiciary court, books of adjournal, 1596–1604, JC2/3, pp. 224–9; Pitcairn (ed.), *Trials*, ii, pp. 25–9, 52–3. Bessie Aitken had been mentioned in South Leith in June.

[60] NAS, Edinburgh presbytery minutes, CH2/121/2 (unfoliated), 15 Nov. 1597.

Interest in witchcraft at a national level continued into November. On 28 November, Lord Ochiltree's commission as lieutenant and warden of the west march included witchcraft among the list of crimes he was empowered to prosecute – the first Border commission to do so.[61] But after so many executions, the supply of actual witches was probably dwindling. In Aberdeenshire, an attempted revival of witch-hunting in November led to one execution, that of Andrew Man; he named numerous further suspects, but a potential snowball of trials was halted abruptly when the first three to be prosecuted were all acquitted.[62] St Andrews kirk session in late October punished for slander a woman who had accused a neighbour of witchcraft.[63] Haddington presbytery had long been concerned about 'the dumme boy possessit' who 'gangis about dissaving the people and giving answeris by signes'. They never caught him, but in November they pounced on a consulter, not only with him, but with Janet Steel 'suspectit of witchecraft'. Steel was hauled in, but under interrogation turned out to be a charmer with nothing particularly demonic about her.[64] The end of the panic, as so often, was an anticlimax.

VII

There was, however, a coda, in the form of an act of parliament. Spottiswoode described the order of 12 August as 'discharging all proceedings ... till a solid order should be taken by the Estates touching the form that should be kept in their trial'. There was nothing in the order itself about this, but something may have been said informally, since it was decided to summon a parliament at the time of the order. That parliament met on 1 November, and on 16 December it passed an act on witchcraft. Through administrative error this act was never printed, and only the title is now known, 'Anent the forme of proces against witches'.[65] This was one of only three acts on witchcraft ever passed by the Scottish parliament, and an attempt must be made to reconstruct it, at least in outline.[66]

The act was mentioned in March 1598, when the general assembly included the following as one of its 'greives' to the king: 'To advyce with his majestie, if the carieing of profest witches from towne to towne, to try witchcraft in uthers, be laufull ordinar tryall of witchcraft, or nocht.' The king replied that 'be ane act of the last parliament, it is remittit to certaine of his hienes counsell, certaine ministers

---

[61] *RPC*, v, pp. 424–5; T. I. Rae, *The Administration of the Scottish Frontier, 1513–1603* (Edinburgh, 1966), p. 64.

[62] Goodare, 'The Aberdeenshire witchcraft panic of 1597'.

[63] *St Andrews Kirk Session Register, 1559–1600*, 2 vols, ed. D. H. Fleming (SHS, 1889–90), ii, p. 838.

[64] NAS, Haddington presbytery minutes, 1596–1608, CH2/185/2 (unfoliated), 12 Jan., 23 Nov., 7 Dec. 1597, 1 Feb., 8 Feb. 1598. For more on charmers, see J. Miller, 'Devices and directions: folk healing aspects of witchcraft practice in seventeenth-century Scotland', Chapter 6 below.

[65] *APS*, iv, p. 157. For the failure to record the act see J. Goodare, 'The Scottish parliamentary records, 1560–1603', *Historical Research*, 72 (1999), 244–67, at p. 264.

[66] The other acts were in 1563 and 1649: *APS*, ii, p. 539, c. 9; vi, II, p. 152, c. 44. There were also acts of parliament issuing commissions for individual witchcraft trials.

and advocates, to conclude upon a solid order anent tryall of witches, and to advyce whither the forsaid carieing of witches is permissive, or not'.[67] A slightly later, summary version of this reply added 'physicians' to the list of those who were to 'consult and report'.[68]

So the act set up a commission to make recommendations about what evidence should be received in witchcraft trials, in the aftermath of the Aitken affair. Presumably the commission never reported, since no more is heard of it – a common fate for such bodies. The interesting question is: which of the parties was in favour of 'carieing of profest witches from towne to towne'? The assembly's question echoed the earlier complaint from St Andrews presbytery against the 'horable abuse by carying a witch about', and it seems that they took a similar view. The phrasing of the assembly's question – is this 'laufull ordinar tryall'? – indicates that they favoured the answer 'No', since the 'ordinar' evidence in criminal trials for witchcraft came not from other witches like Aitken but from the suspect's own confession or witnesses to the crime. Had they been demanding that the evidence of other witches as informers should *additionally* be received, they would have asked not whether it was 'ordinar' but whether it was 'permissive'. Which was the word used in the king's reply, indicating that it was he who favoured the broader evidential categories that would legitimise Aitken's witch-detecting role. The other controversial aspect of the Aitken commission had been the swimming test, and in *Daemonologie*, James endorsed that too. Neither witch-detectors nor the swimming test established themselves in regular Scottish witch-hunting practice after 1597, probably because of the caution of the general assembly and its sympathisers.

The assembly was not, of course, against witch-hunting as such. It heard a complaint that civil magistrates were freeing convicted witches, and ordained that presbyteries should proceed with ecclesiastical censures against such magistrates.[69] There had recently been strife in Perth over something like this. On 28 November 1597, 'the sessione ordeinis the magistratis to travell with his majestie to obtene a commissione to execut Jonet Robertsone sorcerer quha long hes bene detenit in ward'.[70] Perhaps other local magistrates were hesitating too. The assembly's order was also part of a broader struggle in which the church sought to defend exclusive control over ecclesiastical censures, especially excommunication, against civil encroachment.[71] Its disagreements with civil authority in 1597 over witch-hunting may well have intensified the struggle on both sides.

---

[67] *Booke of the Universall Kirk: Acts and Proceedings of the General Assembly of the Kirk of Scotland,* 3 vols, ed. T. Thomson (Bannatyne Club, 1839–45), iii, pp. 937–8.

[68] John Row, *History of the Kirk of Scotland,* ed. D. Laing (Wodrow Society, 1842), p. 189.

[69] *Booke of the Universall Kirk,* iii, pp. 938–9.

[70] NAS, Perth kirk session minutes, 1597–1604, CH2/521/3, p. 5.

[71] J. Goodare, *State and Society in Early Modern Scotland* (Oxford, 1999), pp. 183–92.

VIII

Let us attempt an overall assessment of the panic. The first issue is the scale of the events involved. The most intense episodes of known witch-hunting were in Aberdeenshire (mainly March to May), Fife (May to August), Perthshire (June and July), the numerous places visited by the Aitken commission including Glasgow (April to July), and Stirlingshire (August to October). Of these five, there are incomplete figures for Aberdeenshire only: 80 known cases including 27 known executions. There were numerous further cases outside these areas, and much evidence is missing. The best guess that can be made at an overall figure is probably to multiply the Aberdeenshire figures by five and say cautiously that there may have been about 400 cases overall during 1597, mostly between March and September. Something under half of these are likely to have have resulted in execution. Although nothing can match the 660 cases of 1661–2, these figures make the panic of 1597 one of Scotland's largest.[72]

Witch-hunting was normally a consensual process on which the authorities agreed. That consensus broke down in 1597. The Aitken affair led to obvious governmental disagreement; the order of 12 August, which was probably intended by some councillors to curtail the prosecutions, was followed by a much-criticised push to rehabilitate witch-hunting in September. Who among the Scottish elite gained from the burnings, and who lost?

Spottiswoode implied that James was the hero of the Aitken affair, but James was the hero of his whole book. At the time, the king did not come well out of the business; if he had, he would have been the first to say so. Whatever people thought of his promotion of the Aitken commission while it was riding high, they were shocked by its collapse in August, and there was explicit criticism of James's role in September. When *Daemonologie* appeared in print, public praise for the learned royal author was conspicuous by its absence.

The dissident presbyterian ministers failed to grasp the opportunity that this presented to them. Some of them, notably in the radical-dominated presbytery of St Andrews, were among the ministers who criticised the king in September, but they were unable to capitalise on the royal discomfiture – presumably because many were known to have been zealous supporters of witch-hunting up to the moment when Aitken was exposed. The presbyterians David Calderwood and James Melville omitted any mention of the 1597 witchcraft panic, or even the publication of *Daemonologie*, from their contemporary histories. They had, to be sure, much else to write about for that period, but both found space for a lengthy account of the eclipse of 25 February 1598, and Melville had himself been active in the St Andrews prosecutions.[73] Their silence on the witch-hunt, a manifest work of

---

[72] B. P. Levack, 'The great Scottish witch-hunt of 1661–1662', *Journal of British Studies*, 20 (1980), 90–108, at p. 90; Larner, *Enemies of God*, p. 61.

[73] Calderwood, *History*, v, pp. 681–2; James Melville, *Autobiography and Diary*, ed. R. Pitcairn (Wodrow Society, 1843), pp. 438–9.

God if there ever was one, was surely deliberate; they were drawing a veil over an episode that embarrassed them. This would also fit with the use later made of the panic by Spottiswoode, once he became the presbyterians' arch-enemy, to blame the 'credulity' of certain ministers – by implication, those on the opposite side from him. John Cowper, minister of Glasgow, whom he named, had in the 1580s been actively presbyterian, even defying the king to his face.[74]

The most bitter public recriminations after the panic also centred on Glasgow. The presbytery of Glasgow in November threatened with the branks 'diverse per-sones within the toun and citie of Glasgw quha traducis and sclanderis unjustlie the ministerie of the said citie, as the authoris of puting to deathe the persones latlie execut for witchcraft within the said citie'. In February 1598 it made John Morrison do penance for having 'offendit God, his kirk and Mr Johnne Couper ane of the ministeris of Glasgw, for spreading of the infamous libell contenit in the deposi-tioun of umquhill Margaret Aiken ane notabill witche aganis the said Mr Johnne be sindrie copeis thairof in diverse partis of this cuntrey'.[75] The 'infamous libell' – another piece of missing evidence – thus circulated well beyond Glasgow. Morrison seems to have been from Kyle, connected with the Cunningham family.[76] The pres-bytery's line against him was not that the executions had been perfectly justified, but that they had not been the ministers' fault. Witch-hunting had backfired, and nobody wanted to take responsibility.

So the great witch-hunt of 1597 ended, with little or no credit gained by anyone involved. Even the Catholic earls, entrenched opponents of the presbyterians, had blood on their hands. The only possible gainers, and then only in the long term, were the councillors who had hoped to use the order of 12 August (which Arch-bishop Spottiswoode praised, even if he misrepresented its nature and authorship) to curtail witch-hunting. One of these councillors may well have been Alexander Seton, one of the Octavians, who later became earl of Dunfermline and chancellor of Scotland. He also became Spottiswoode's greatest rival, so it is not surprising that the archbishop gave him no credit.[77] Spottiswoode was no positive enthusiast for witch-hunting, but Seton definitely disapproved of it. In 1614 he marshalled his col-leagues on the council to exclude women's testimony from witchcraft trials – a move that would have reversed a personal initiative of the king in 1591, and would greatly have impeded future witch-hunting. Seton's move did not set the precedent he hoped; intense witch-hunting recurred in the late 1620s, and it would be a further

[74] J. Kirk, 'The Development of the Melvillian Movement in Late Sixteenth Century Scotland' (Ph.D. thesis, University of Edinburgh, 1972), pp. 594–5. Cowper's brother William, minister of Perth, also seems to have promoted witch-hunting right to the end.

[75] 'Extracts from the registers of the presbytery of Glasgow, 1592–1601', *Miscellany of the Maitland Club*, i (1833), p. 89.

[76] *RPC*, v, p. 689; cf. *RMS*, vi, no. 432. He was a 'servitor to the ladie Ricardtoun', unidentified but probably from this area too.

[77] M. Lee, 'King James's popish chancellor', in I. B. Cowan and D. Shaw (eds), *The Renaissance and Reformation in Scotland* (Edinburgh, 1983), pp. 174–7.

half-century before witchcraft panics were finally curtailed in Scotland.[78] But when he sought to inject procedural caution into witchcraft trials he surely had the panic of 1597 in mind. One significant legacy of the panic may have been that it took so long – three decades – before there was another one.

[78] 'The trial of Geillis Johnstone for witchcraft, 1614', eds M. Wasser and L. A. Yeoman, *SHS Miscellany*, xiii (forthcoming); M. Wasser, 'The privy council and the witches: the curtailment of witchcraft prosecutions in Scotland, 1597–1628', unpublished paper; B. P. Levack, 'The decline and end of Scottish witch-hunting', Chapter 10 below.

5

The Devil and the domestic: witchcraft, quarrels and women's work in Scotland[1]

Lauren Martin

[The Devil promised Janet Barker] that schoe sould be als trymelie cled as the best servand in Edinburgh, and that he wald geve hir ane red wylliecott or red kirtle, and that thairupoun scho condiscendit to be his servand for half ane yeir gif he wald keip promeis.... As also hes confessit in hir examinatioun that schoe hes had dyvers tymes carnall copulatioun with the devill both in hir awin littill chope, and in the said umquihile Jonet Cransoun hir hous, and had ado with [him in] hir naiket bed, quha was heavie abone hir lyk ane ox and nocht lyk ane uther man.

Trial of Janet Barker, Janet Cranston and Margaret Lauder,
24 December 1643, Edinburgh.[2]

Item, about seventeen yeiris or thairby ye haveing conceaved ane devilish evill will and malice against Helen Trumble in Kaikmuir hill, she being then fostering [i.e. wet-nursing] a bairne to William Scot in Dalkeith, because she being in use to buye butter and such lik wair from yow, went by yow to utheris, by reasone that she gott ill pen-nieworth and unconscionable weight from yow, quhairupon yow then, threatned hir that ear long she should gett hir leave from hir maister and a lash on the arse, and within tuelff houres thairefter the child that she wes fostering being at that tyme in good health according to your threatneing by your sorcerie and witchcraft took a sud-den and fearfull sickness of quhich it dyet within tuentie four hours thairefter and sua wes crewlie murdred by your sorcerie and witchcraft and conforme to your prediction the said Helen Trumble got hir leave.

Trial of Janet Cook, 10 September 1661, Dalkeith.[3]

These excerpts exemplify two types of evidence in Scottish witchcraft trials in the justiciary court at Edinburgh. The first concerns the witch's relationship to the Devil (in the form of a demonic pact); the second concerns harm caused by the witch to neighbours (usually following a dispute about work). Scholars have characterised these two types of evidence as arising from separate systems of belief – one from the

---

[1] Many thanks to Louise Yeoman for her help with my research.
[2] *SJC*, iii, p. 611; NAS, books of adjournal, justiciary court, JC2/8, fos. 347r.–348v.; cf. Larner *et al.*, *Source-Book*, no. 163.
[3] NAS, justiciary court processes, JC26/27/3, item 15, article 2; cf. JC2/10, fos. 34r.–41r., 43v.–49r.; Larner *et al.*, *Source-Book*, no. 402.

elite, and the other from the peasants.[4] Testimony about demonic pacts and quarrels followed by harm may, however, be seen as complementary sets of evidence. Both took shape from the ideology and practices of the domestic configurations of Scottish peasants.

I

'The domestic', as a term of analysis, describes the gendered, ideological and practical aspects of marriage and work.[5] It combines family, household, production and reproduction into one frame of reference. This chapter argues that 'the domestic' of early modern Scotland structured the cultural landscape of witchcraft beliefs in two ways. First, the demonic pact, a heterosexual, contract-like union between the witch and the Devil, was conceptually akin to Scottish marriage.[6] Marriage was the founding moment of a new household, inaugurating domestic relationships. Second, marriage, household formation and women's work – all aspects of the domestic – also structured the quarrels that often led to witchcraft accusations.[7] The association of the demonic with cultural understandings of 'the domestic' destabilised women's roles in marriage and work, demonising the day-to-day roles of women in early modern Scottish society.

My discussion of witchcraft and neighbourhood disputes may seem reminiscent of Alan Macfarlane's work on early modern witchcraft in Essex. Using the anthropological theory of functionalism, Macfarlane saw Essex witchcraft accusations as having arisen from the dynamics of refusal of charity and village tensions in a social climate where poverty and insecurity were rising. He found that the majority of

---

[4] Many scholars maintain that there was a distinction or conflict between popular and elite culture. I do not challenge this rich scholarship. For examples, see R. Muchembled, *Popular Culture and Elite Culture in France, 1400–1750* (Baton Rouge, La., 1985); B. Ankarloo and G. Henningsen (eds), *Early Modern European Witchcraft: Centres and Peripheries* (Oxford, 1991).

[5] The concept of 'the domestic', as used in this chapter, was drawn from peasant studies in anthropology and history and feminist reconfigurations of the notion of the 'household'. It is the practical and symbolic structuring of the household and family in the context of production and reproduction. For key texts see L. Tilly and J. Scott (eds), *Women, Work and Family* (New York, 1978); K. Young, C. Walkowitz and R. McCullagh, *Of Marriage and the Market: Women's Subordination in International Perspective* (London, 1981); W. Roseberry, 'The ideology of domestic production', *Labour, Capital, and Society*, 19 (1986); W. Roseberry, 'Issues and agendas: domestic modes, domesticated models', *Journal of Historical Sociology*, 1 (1988); E. Katz, 'Breaking the myth of harmony: theoretical and methodological guidelines to the study of rural third world households', *Review of Radical Political Economy*, 23 (1991); M. Kearney, *Reconceptualizing the Peasantry: Anthropology in Global Perspective* (Boulder, Colo., 1996).

[6] D. Purkiss, 'Sounds of silence: fairies and incest in Scottish witchcraft stories', in S. Clark (ed.), *Languages of Witchcraft: Narrative, Ideology and Meaning in Early Modern Culture* (London, 2001), pp. 81–9, points out that female witchcraft suspects' testimony about sex with the Devil or a male fairy highlights a transformative social experience common to women in early modern society. She does not specify marriage, but the implication is obvious.

[7] For a discussion of the neighbourhood dynamics of witchcraft accusation and belief, see R. Briggs, *Witches and Neighbors: The Social and Cultural Context of European Witchcraft* (New York, 1996).

witchcraft suspects in Essex were old, poor, usually widowed women.[8] There are two main differences in our findings: theoretical and evidentiary.

First, the social and cultural phenomenon of witchcraft is too complex to be reduced to a mechanistic 'function'. The search for the 'cause' of witchcraft accusations and prosecutions from some outside, 'rational' source (whether economic, pharmacological or social) assumes that witchcraft beliefs were not real, and that we post-Enlightenment historians have a corner on truth. Neighbours accused their neighbours of witchcraft, and courts of law prosecuted people for the crime of witchcraft, because they all believed in the reality of witches and the Devil. Witchcraft accusations and prosecutions should be seen in relation to a combination of both the difficulties surrounding practical social relations and broader cultural (and discursive) formations.[9]

Second, the main dynamic in Macfarlane's model, refusal of charity followed by perceived magical harm, presupposes an unequal economic relationship between accuser and accused. In Scottish trials, quarrels leading to witchcraft accusation were overwhelmingly between relative social equals, not between neighbours of higher and lower social status. Also, women accused of witchcraft in Scotland were not usually poor or marginal to their communities. The female witch was generally a wife or widow of middling peasant status, or sometimes the wife or widow of a craftsman, shopkeeper or burgess. She is presented in the trial records as vengeful and quarrelsome. While not usually the wife of a laird or aristocrat, the Scottish witch was not a marginal figure. She was usually a well-known, established member of her community. Her reputation for witchcraft often took decades to solidify.

Trial records do not show that the persons who denounced neighbours as witches did so based upon a perception of a demonic pact. Rather, the main basis of community denunciation was perception of magical harm. The demonic pact was later 'read' into neighbourhood disputes by ministers, magistrates and prosecutors. It is unclear to what extent local accusers believed in the demonic pact.

If the last twenty years of scholarship on witchcraft has taught us anything, it is that witchcraft trials had many different causes and that they were tied up within many different discourses – about religion, power, nature, women, God and

---

[8] A. Macfarlane, *Witchcraft in Tudor and Stuart England: a Regional and Comparative Study* (London, 1970). Macfarlane's work is often lumped together with the work of Keith Thomas, *Religion and the Decline of Magic*, first published in 1971. The two together are often referred to as the 'charity-refused' model, recently summarised as 'the hypothesis that most accusations of witchcraft arose from situations where the accused was refused charity by the accuser, who then felt guilt and attributed subsequent misfortune to the malice of the person refused'. J. Barry, 'Introduction: Keith Thomas and the problem of witchcraft', in J. Barry *et al.* (eds), *Witchcraft in Early Modern Europe: Studies in Culture and Belief* (Cambridge, 1996), pp. 8–9.

[9] This is not to advocate an uncritical cultural relativism or the absolute 'otherness' of early modern peoples. See Stuart Clark's introduction to *Languages of Witchcraft*, pp. 2–9, for a discussion of Caro Baroja and the contribution of anthropology to witchcraft studies. Also see S. Clark, *Thinking with Demons: the Idea of Witchcraft in Early Modern Europe* (Oxford, 1997), ch. 1, for a discussion of the epistemologies of witchcraft studies, and the need to view witchcraft beliefs in terms of their own linguistic and cultural structures.

authority.[10] This chapter traces one 'conceptual link between conditions and consequences', rather than searching for direct causes for witchcraft trials.[11] Neither marital problems nor work alone necessarily 'caused' people to accuse someone of witchcraft. Witchcraft was not merely an easy way to get rid of a troublesome neighbour, or to scapegoat an undesirable person. Rather, there were multiple conceptual links between marriage, work and witchcraft that encouraged accusers to see and feel witchcraft in their everyday quarrels. The consequences of quarrels, in turn, were seen and felt by some as evidence of powers from a demonic pact.

Recent feminist scholarship argues that witchcraft beliefs mirrored the cultural formations of women's everyday experiences.[12] This richly suggestive work examines connections between witchcraft beliefs and fantasies about the experiences of mothering and being mothered, the maternal body and to a lesser extent the experience of mothers as housewives. Scottish witchcraft beliefs, accusations and trials articulated some concerns about the biological and social aspects of motherhood, but the category of motherhood did not itself provide the overall structure for the many cultural formations of witchcraft. Rather, the trials show a broader relationship between witchcraft belief and both marriage and work – the broadest categories structuring life for women and men. Marriage and work included and affected ideas of 'motherhood' and the activities of women as mothers including childbirth and childcare. This variety of women's work was essential to production, consumption and exchange in the early modern Scottish economy.

II

Evidence for this chapter includes cases from my survey of witchcraft trial records from the court of justiciary in Edinburgh from the 1590s to the 1670s, some published witchcraft cases, demonological treatises and legal and anecdotal evidence on marriage and household formation. These are central, rather than local sources. They are not a representative sample of all types of witchcraft trials,[13] but they are the most detailed sources for cultural and social information about Scottish witchcraft. High Court records contain cases from panic years and non-panic years and from various locales in Scotland.

---

[10] R. Briggs, '"Many reasons why": witchcraft and the problem of multiple explanation', in Barry *et al.* (eds), *Witchcraft*.

[11] Clark, *Thinking with Demons*, p. 111.

[12] F. Dolan, *Dangerous Familiars: Representations of Domestic Crime in England, 1550–1700* (Ithaca, NY, 1994); L. Roper, *Oedipus and the Devil: Witchcraft, Sexuality and Religion in Early Modern Europe* (London, 1994); D. Willis, *Malevolent Nurture: Witch-Hunting and Maternal Power in Early Modern England* (Ithaca, NY, 1995); D. Purkiss, *The Witch in History: Early Modern and Twentieth-Century Representations* (London, 1996).

[13] The majority of witchcraft trials were conducted locally under a commission of justiciary, usually issued by the privy council. Trials might go to the high court if no local commission was available, or if someone requested it (the suspect, lawyers or local nobility). Cf. J. Goodare, 'Witch-hunting and the Scottish state', Chapter 8 below.

All of the trial records present problems of interpretation. Ministers, kirk session elders, bailies, sheriffs and other local experts on witchcraft shaped peasant testimony once witchcraft suspicion had shifted to an official denunciation to the authorities.[14] While specific interrogatories to suspects and accusers do not survive, it is clear that accusers were asked only a limited range of leading questions designed to satisfy the accepted legal elements of the crime of witchcraft. This shaping of evidence by learned and legal witchcraft belief affected the testimony of all witnesses, accusers and accused.[15] Confessions, a seemingly direct line to popular beliefs, are likewise murky. Suspected witches were jailed in poor conditions without proper food, warmth or clothing, often leading to despair, guilt, repentance, or emotional collapse – all of which were recorded and used as evidence.[16] Sleep deprivation ('waking') was also widely used to extract confessions. During the pre-trial incarceration and 'waking', ministers and other officials preached, exhorted and pressured suspects to confess to the right sorts of things.

III

How was the witch's relationship to the Devil conceptualised? With what other types of everyday relationships did it resonate? There are three early modern models that resemble demonic pacts: bonds of manrent, covenant theology and marriage. All three were central elements in Scottish life. Bonds of manrent and covenant theology, however, while clearly relevant to witchcraft, do not get to the essence of the demonic pact as a heterosexual contract. Marriage does.

Although the Scottish Witchcraft Act of 1563 did not mention the demonic pact, the Devil was central to witchcraft beliefs and witchcraft trials in Scotland. Roughly 75 per cent of the witchcraft trials in my survey recorded demonic references. Only 11 per cent clearly proceeded without demonic content. The remaining non-demonic cases did not record enough information to rule out the Devil. Roughly half of the male witchcraft cases were non-demonic – a much higher proportion than for female witchcraft.[17]

According to James VI, in *Daemonologie* (1597), the way to Satan was opened 'either by the great ignorance of the person he deales with, ioyned with an euill life,

---

[14] C. Holmes, 'Women: witnesses and witches', *Past and Present*, 140 (Aug. 1993), 45–78; C. Ginzburg, 'Witchcraft and popular piety: a Modenese trial of 1519', in his *Clues, Myths and the Historical Method* (Baltimore, Md., 1986).

[15] More than one hundred trial records made it clear that many witchcraft charges were formulaic. However, comparison of pre-trial witness statements with trial documents shows a divergence of concerns: peasant accusers emphasised malefice, the official trial emphasised demonic forces behind malefice.

[16] For example, Janet Cook, NAS, JC26/27/3, items 1–23; JC2/10, fos. 34r.–41r., 43r.–49v.; Larner *et al.*, *Source-Book*, no. 402.

[17] For the lesser role of the Devil in local cases, see S. Macdonald, 'In search of the Devil in Fife witchcraft cases, 1560–1705', Chapter 3 above.

or else by their carelesnes and contempt of God'.[18] After an initial temptation, the Devil enacted a formal pact in the following manner.

> [H]e first perswades them to addict themselues to his seruice: which being easely obteined, he then discouers what he is vnto them: makes them to renunce their God and *Baptisme* directlie, and giues them his marke vpon some secreit place of their bodie, which remaines soare vnhealed, while [i.e. until] his next meeting with them, and thereafter euer insensible, how soever it be nipped or pricked by any, as is dailie proued, to give them a proofe thereby, that as in that doing, hee could hurte or heale them; so all their ill and well doing thereafter, must depend vpon him.[19]

According to James and many trial texts, the Devil lured unsuspecting converts with promises of protection, vengeance against enemies and that they should never want.[20]

James also believed that witches attended secret meetings with the Devil and other witches for the purpose of harming God's people – a conspiracy.[21] Many High Court trials make reference to witches' meetings (covens or conventions), where anywhere from three to one hundred witches gathered to pay homage to the Devil or to plan and execute large-scale harm. But the Devil also had a personal, contractual relationship with each witch as well as being the leader of a confederacy of witches.

Pamphlet and trial evidence shows that the demonic pact was clearly part of Scottish witchcraft beliefs from at least as early as the 1590s and probably earlier.[22] The concept of a demonic pact took time to evolve and in early trials was often mingled with fairy lore. But the search for the Devil's mark, an indication of the pact, was a common pre-trial procedure throughout the whole of the witch-hunting period in Scotland.

Katherine Oswald's trial in 1629 was one of the first High Court cases to display a fully developed demonic pact – consent to join the Devil followed by sex and attendance of meetings. She allegedly went to the Devil because she had an evil will and a deadly malice 'aganist sindrie of his maiesteis guid subiectis'. She was accused of meeting with the Devil and other witches and bringing new converts. Alexander Hamilton, a confessed and later convicted witch, testified that Oswald had told him 'that scho was to meit that nycht uith the devill hir maister in ane den betuix Nydrie and Edmestoun'. According to Hamilton, he was invited to come along to the meeting and 'befoir the devill his depairtoir he had carnall copulatioun uith the said

---

[18] King James VI, *Daemonologie, in Forme of a Dialogue, Diuided into three Bookes*, ed. G. B. Harrison (New York, 1966), p. 32.

[19] *Daemonologie*, p. 33.

[20] *Daemonologie*, pp. 32–3. For example see Margaret Brysone, JC2/10, fos. 18r.–20v.; *Spalding Misc.*, i, p. 107. Cf. Larner, *Enemies of God*, p. 148.

[21] In *Daemonologie*, pp. 38–9, 43, James described practices surrounding witches' meetings.

[22] J. Wormald, 'The witches, the Devil and the King', in T. Brotherstone and D. Ditchburn (eds), *Freedom and Authority: Scotland, c.1050–c.1650* (East Linton, 2000). M. Wasser, 'Ambition and failure: Scotland's unknown witch hunt, 1568–1569', unpublished paper, has found evidence that a large-scale witch-hunt, using notions of the demonic pact, was attempted in the 1560s, but failed.

Katharene and had the use of hir body'. A minister and two tolbooth servants searched for and found a Devil's mark on Oswald's body while she was being held for trial.[23] By the time of the last big witch-hunt in Scotland (1661–2), sex with the Devil was recorded in standardised, formulaic language in trial records.[24]

According to Larner, 'The Demonic Pact initiated, in fact, a standard feudal relationship, reflecting standard assumptions about all significant human bonds in this period'. By this she meant entering into a relationship of service in exchange for 'certain economic benefits'.[25] Certainly, King James's version of the demonic pact as a relationship based on protection and revenge is suggestive of, but different from, the bond of manrent.[26] Bonds of manrent were written contracts that set out the relationship between feudal lords and their followers. The relationship between the two parties in a bond of manrent was ordered along lines of 'kindness' or kinship. Manrent documents typically invoked fictive kinship by using the terms father and son to describe the relationship.[27] Lynch characterises the relationship as a written and codified version of the link between a lord and his followers where 'protection was offered in exchange for homage'.[28] This relationship definitely resembles some aspects of the demonic pact. Both set up hierarchical relations between a superior and inferior characterised by fealty and homage.

Larner's assertion that the demonic pact was a 'standard feudal relationship' is no doubt partially true. But bonds of manrent enacted fictive, same-sex and cognatic 'kinship' (related by blood) – whereas the demonic pact involved heterosexual, affinal 'kinship' (related by marriage). Early modern human bonds were fundamentally both gendered and hierarchical. The demonic pact, like marriage, involved gendered notions of complementarity and subservience. Women were deemed naturally weaker than men. Bonds of manrent were hierarchical, but the power differential was of degree, not kind. The feudal lord was ranked higher because of wealth (military or landed) or status, not by 'nature'.

Covenant theology was the dominant religious idea in post-Reformation Scotland.[29] It was regularly preached from the pulpit, occasionally dramatised through grand, national covenants, and stretched to its military and political limits in the 1640s and 50s during the covenanting wars. Notions of covenant nuanced how people thought about contracts, relationships among people and relationships

[23] *SJC*, i, pp. 130–40; cf. NAS, JC2/6, fos. 303r.–310r.

[24] Larner, *Enemies of God*, pp. 129–30.

[25] Larner, *Enemies of God*, p. 148.

[26] J. Wormald, 'Bloodfeud, kindred and government in early modern Scotland', *Past and Present*, 87 (May 1980), 54–97; J. Wormald, *Lords and Men in Scotland: Bonds of Manrent, 1442–1603* (Edinburgh, 1985).

[27] Wormald, 'Bloodfeud', 72.

[28] M. Lynch, *Scotland: a New History* (London, 1991), p. 60.

[29] L. E. Schmidt, *Holy Fairs: Scottish Communions and American Revivals in the Early Modern Period* (Princeton, NJ, 1989); L. A. Yeoman, 'Heart-Work: Emotion, Empowerment and Authority in Covenanting Times' (Ph.D. thesis, University of St Andrews, 1991).

between people and higher powers. Witches' group activities could be seen as inversions of the people's covenant with God. Larner stated:

> The covenanted people were God's people, firmly bound to him in a special relationship by a special promise. The Demonic Pact was therefore, for the Scots, a particularly horrific inversion. The term 'covenant' was frequently used in the final indictments and the confessions as a synonym for the Pact.[30]

This passage may be slightly misleading, since in post-Reformation Scottish theology, the covenant between the elect and God had two faces – personal and national.[31] The personal relationship was the covenant of grace, an individual contract between God and members of his elect. The national covenant was akin to Old Testament notions of a covenanted people with a special relationship to God.[32] Similarly, the Devil had personal relationships with individual witches and was also the head of all witches. Witchcraft was the opposite of 'true' religion. Through renunciation of their baptisms, witches were to seal a new relationship with the Devil and to serve and worship a new, evil God-figure – the Devil.

The languages of bonding, covenanting and witchcraft were similar. No doubt both feudal and religious languages and experiences resonated strongly with witchcraft belief. But neither gets to the heart of the heterosexuality of the demonic pact; nor do bonds or covenants highlight the status of the partners within the demonic pact. Analogy to the marital relationship captures the missing element.

IV

In marriage, a man and woman were united in hierarchy by contract, consummated by sex.[33] Just as a woman's legal persona was subsumed within her husband's, a woman turned 'witch' was subsumed within the identity of her Devil-husband. A husband was deemed responsible for his wife's 'ill and well' being just as James VI

---

[30] Larner, *Enemies of God*, p. 172.

[31] In both, Christ was often referred to as the 'bridegroom' while the elected individual and the national church were seen as the 'bride' of Christ: Schmidt, *Holy Fairs*, pp. 120, 162–6. Yeoman describes a 'double covenant' theory of Protestant conversion – a 'transition from the state of despair and possible damnation (covenant of works) to the state of election (covenant of grace)': L. A. Yeoman, 'The Devil as doctor: witchcraft, Wodrow and the wider world', *Scottish Archives*, 1 (1995), 93–105, p. 94.

[32] J. Coffey, 'Political thought of the Scottish Covenanters', in J. R. Young (ed.), *Celtic Dimensions of the British Civil Wars* (Edinburgh, 1997); Yeoman, 'The Devil as doctor'.

[33] W. Coutts, 'Wife and widow: the evidence of testaments and marriage contracts, *c.*1600', in E. Ewan and M. M. Meikle (eds), *Women in Scotland, c.1100–c.1750* (East Linton, 1999); W. D. H. Sellar, 'Marriage, divorce and the forbidden degrees: canon law and Scots law', in W. N. Osborough (ed.), *Explorations in Law and History: Irish Legal History Society Discourses, 1988–1994* (Dublin, 1995); R. D. Ireland, 'Husband and wife: (a) post-Reformation canon law of marriage of the commissaries' courts, and (b) modern common and statute law', R. D. Ireland, 'Husband and wife: divorce, nullity of marriage and separation', and G. C. H. Paton, 'Husband and wife: property rights and relationships', in G. C. H. Paton (ed.), *An Introduction to Scottish Legal History* (Stair Society, 1958); L. Leneman, *Alienated Affections: the Scottish Experience of Divorce and Separation, 1684–1830* (Edinburgh, 1998), p. 3.

wrote for the Devil and his witches: 'all their ill and well doing thereafter, must depend vpon him'. The 'significant human bond' of marriage was not simply a 'standard feudal relationship'.

Civil and ecclesiastical law both governed marriage, although the ultimate legality and validity of marriage rested within civil law.[34] There were two types of marriage in early modern Scotland: regular and irregular. Regular marriage was public. It consisted of the proclamation of banns on three Sundays prior to marriage, promise or mutual consent to marry, a church solemnisation, and consummation through copulation.[35] Irregular marriage took place in secret. It occurred if promises in the present tense were exchanged or if promises in the future tense were followed by sex.

The demonic pact operated along the lines of the barest requirements of a legally binding marriage – irregular marriage. Irregular marriage, while subject to public censure, was binding so long as the parties were free to marry.[36] Sex following a promise to marry was viewed as constituting consent to marriage; as such it was a linchpin in the legal definition of the contract of marriage.[37] Similarly, a woman became a witch through the present or future consent to enter a demonic pact followed by sex. Such consent could be preceded, as it was in marriage, by a period of courtship. Margaret Lauder confessed that she met with the Devil several times before consenting to have sex and be his servant. At their first meeting 'he imbracet the said Margaret Lauder in his airmes at the drinking of the beir, and pat his airme about hir waist'. The Devil later appeared to her while she was collecting ale for a witches' gathering, and she refused his sexual advances. The Devil angrily knocked the ale out of her hands, whereupon she screamed and ran away. Eventually she consented to the Devil's advances, and he 'come and lay with hir eftir ane beistlie maner lyk a doig quhill hir bak was towardis him'.[38]

The demonic pact thus incorporated both the structure of irregular marriage – consent of both parties combined with sex – and the character of marriage in general (i.e. the expectations for both parties in a regular or irregular marriage). Irregular marriage and the demonic pact had the same contractual structures (consent and sex) and both were secret, but all three (irregular marriage, regular marriage and the demonic pact) enacted a heterosexual contractual union involving sex. What did this union entail?

---

[34] A. E. Anton, '"Handfasting" in Scotland', *SHR*, 37 (1958), 89–102, p. 94. For a discussion of the sacramental status of marriage in England see C. Peters, 'Gender, sacrament and ritual: the making and meaning of marriage in late medieval and early modern England', *Past and Present*, 169 (Nov. 2000), 63–96.

[35] R. Mitchison and L. Leneman, *Girls in Trouble: Sexuality and Social Control in Rural Scotland, 1660–1780* (Edinburgh, 1998); Leneman, *Alienated Affections*, p. 6.

[36] D. M. Walker, *A Legal History of Scotland*, vol. v: *the Seventeenth Century* (Edinburgh, 1996), p. 658; Anton, 'Handfasting', 93. 'For such irregular marriages [*per verba de praesenti* and *per verba de futuro subsequente copula*] to be valid, neither the proclamation of banns, nor the presence of a priest was necessary': Sellar, 'Marriage', p. 62.

[37] Sellar, 'Marriage', p. 62.

[38] *SJC*, iii, pp. 611–12.

Women lost their legal personae upon marriage (regular or irregular). The husband gained ownership of the wife's moveable property (*jus mariti*) and he gained administrative control over all of her heritable property (*jus administ-rationis*). The latter included land, rents and other unmoveable property rights.[39] However, women could alter their fate by creating a written marriage contract, a legally binding pre-nuptial property arrangement, that might grant them more control over and inheritance rights in the matrimonial property.[40] The husband also possessed rights over his wife's person.[41] Husbands were allowed to hit their wives, but a woman could seek a divorce if she could demonstrate 'extreme cruelty'.[42] Male dominance was supreme in theory, but not always in practice.[43]

Just as a husband gained rights over the person and goods of his wife in marriage, the Devil similarly gained special rights over his witches. The Devil had sexual access to the witch's body, dominion over the witch's actions in life and future rights to the witch's soul. Body symbolism in some confessed promises to the demonic pact reinforces the notion of the Devil receiving total control over the witch's body. For example, Christian Henderson testified that Helen Fraser told her 'to put ane hand to the croune of hir heid, and the other to the soile of hir fute, and so beteich quhat-evir wes betwein hir handis to the Dewill, and sche suld want nathing that sche wald wiss or desyir'.[44] Further, according to King James, the witch must promise, among other things, 'to do such thinges as he will require of them'.[45] The demonic pact was akin to marriage not only in structure, but also in the quality (or type) of relationship between the female and male parties.

The demonic pact, although structurally similar to the marriage contract, was fundamentally subversive of the marital relationship and the contract of marriage. In the demonic pact, the witch renounced not only her baptism, but also her marriage ties because of her adultery with the Devil. She took on a new master – the Devil.[46] Women as witches were outside the usual boundaries that policed women's moral and sexual behaviour – father, husband, brother, church and God. Julian Goodare writes about the female witch: 'her sexuality was out of control, since the authorities saw her as having transferred her sexual allegiance from men to the

---

[39] J. Mair, 'Marriage, Property and Law: an Uneasy Alliance' (Ph.D. thesis, University of Edinburgh, 1991), pp. 26–31.

[40] Coutts, 'Wife and widow', p. 180.

[41] Walker, *Legal History*, vii, p. 660.

[42] Leneman, *Alienated Affections*, p. 6.

[43] J. Finlay, 'Women and legal representation in early sixteenth-century Scotland', in Ewan and Meikle (eds), *Women in Scotland*.

[44] *Spalding Misc.*, i, p. 107.

[45] *Daemonologie*, p. 33. In trial records the Devil was not usually said to command specific acts, outside of worshipping him. Rather, he encouraged witches to perpetrate as much evil and harm as possible to thwart God and further the misery and suffering of humankind. Larner notes that storms plaguing James's return to Scotland with his Danish bride in 1590 'were attributed to witchcraft encouraged by the Devil because of his hostility to the godly union of Protestant princes': 'The crime of witchcraft in Scotland', in B. P. Levack (ed.), *Witchcraft in Scotland* (New York, 1992), p. 34.

[46] Dolan, *Dangerous Familiars*, chs. 1–2, on petty treason is particularly suggestive here.

Devil'.[47] In demonological and legal theory the witch, by making a pact with the Devil, was perceived to have subverted the only civil contract women were expected to make and uphold – marriage. This amounted to a secret betrayal of the domestic realm, as most women accused of witchcraft continued in their usual domestic duties and household arrangements after supposedly having made a pact with the Devil. But the betrayal also carried a resonance in the spiritual realm. In abandoning the sexual hierarchy of the domestic, the female witch was also abandoning God through the renunciation of her baptism that went along with sex in the formation of a demonic pact. Women as witches, by entering a demonic pact, set up an alternate, secret, 'anti-domestic' within the natural world. This set in motion a linked chain of sexual, social and spiritual betrayals and subversions of man and God.

If the demonic pact assumed that the witch was the female wife to the male Devil-husband, Scottish male witches (15–20 per cent) create a problem. In trial records of male witches, I found only one mention of sodomy.[48] Most cases involving male suspects did not refer to 'carnal dealings' with the Devil. Male witchcraft cases, rather, only recorded sex with another female witch or with a female spirit (interpreted by the prosecution as the Devil in female form), if at all. In cases where the male witch had 'carnal dealings' with a female witch, she seems to have been a mediator between the male witch and the Devil. This could be the case particularly with male witches who were husbands of female witches.[49]

The attempt to turn the Devil figure into a woman, while not common, is interesting for this discussion. Only two of the eighteen trials of male witches that were surveyed presented this strategy – Andrew Man (1597–8)[50] and Patrick Lowrie (1605).[51] Andrew confessed to meeting and having sex with the Queen of Elphen and Patrick supposedly learned his craft from a spirit woman named Helena McBurnie. Both presented some eccentric beliefs unique to their cases. None the less, the prosecution in both cases altered the details of their encounters with the preternatural to fit learned notions of the demonic pact as a specific kind of relationship with the Devil.

Andrew Man's case highlights the 'female mediator' strategy. He confessed to a sexual relationship with the Queen of Elphen spanning about thirty years. Although the prosecution regarded the Queen of Elphen as the Devil in the shape of a woman, it is clear in the trial record that, for Andrew, aside from being the source of a good time, she was also the access point for her male consort, Christsonday. Andrew described Christsonday as God's godson and regarded him as an

[47] J. Goodare, 'Women and the witch-hunt in Scotland', *Social History*, 23 (1998), 288–308, at p. 307.

[48] This was the trial of Michael Erskine, 2 April 1630. The charges were 'Certain points of witchcraft and filthy sodomy at length set down in his dittay'. He was found guilty. The court record gave no details of the accusations or explanation for the mention of sodomy. NAS, JC2/6, fo. 322r.; cf. Larner *et al.*, *Source-Book*, no. 149.

[49] Goodare, 'Women and the witch-hunt', 304; Larner, *Enemies of God*, p. 149.

[50] *Spalding Misc.*, i, pp. 117–25; Larner *et al.*, *Source-Book*, no. 2302.

[51] NAS, JC2/4, fo. 58r.; Pitcairn (ed.), *Trials*, ii, pp. 477–9; Larner *et al.*, *Source-Book*, no. 121.

angel. He said that the 'Quene of Elphen hes a grip of all the craft, bot Christsondy is the Gudeman, and hes all power under God'.[52] Through having heterosexual sex with the Queen of Elphen, Andrew received the power of Christsonday, her consort – a female mediating between two men, thereby maintaining the heterosexual structure of the demonic pact. The prosecution squeezed Andrew's preternatural encounter with elves and angels into its mould of the demonic pact.

Not all male witches' relationships to the Devil were mediated through females. Some confessed to pacts that were not structured like heterosexual marriages. John Neil (1637),[53] who was accused predominantly of magical healing, described a demonic pact that resembled a master–pupil relationship with the Devil. This type of relationship was typical in magical healing cases involving male suspects. In Alexander Hamilton's case, the demonic pact was sealed after he received 4 shillings sterling.[54] His demonic pact allowed rather more equal relations with the Devil than either the marriage or the master–pupil type of pact, although the Devil was still described as his master.

While male witches had a wider range of types of relationships with the Devil than did female witches, one can detect in records of male witchcraft trials a sort of crisis of representation. As Goodare remarks, a clear model never really emerged for how to conceptualise the male witch's relationship with the Devil.[55] Males were dealt with on an *ad hoc* basis. Male witches not mediated by a female figure seem aberrations from the norm of the heterosexual structure of the demonic pact. But even within this theoretical confusion, sexual relations between male witches and female witches or female spirits seem to emphasise the heterosexual nature of the demonic pact.

V

How were understandings of witch–Devil relationships related to local quarrels followed by magical harm? Marriage, aside from constituting a contractual relationship, was also the practical and ideological founding moment of a household.[56] Quarrels followed by harm arose from the practical, day-to-day experiences of households. The demonic pact did not form the basis of local witch labelling. Instead, the domestic arrangements of middling peasants structured the cultural content of witchcraft

[52] *Spalding Misc.*, i, pp. 120–1.

[53] NAS, JC2/7, fos. 1r.–2r.; *RPC*, 2nd ser., iii, pp. 400, 443, 448, 513, 541, 563, 584; Larner *et al.*, *Source-Book*, no. 152.

[54] NAS, JC2/6, fo. 315v.

[55] Goodare, 'Women and the witch-hunt', 304.

[56] This is borne out by the relatively late age of marriage in Scotland. Men usually waited to marry till they could afford to set up some sort of household. See R. A. Houston, 'Women in the economy and society of Scotland, 1500–1800', in R. A. Houston and I. D. Whyte (eds), *Scottish Society, 1500–1800* (Cambridge, 1989), p. 126; D. A. Symonds, *Weep Not for Me: Women, Ballads and Infanticide in Early Modern Scotland* (University Park, Pa., 1997), p. 99; I. D. Whyte and K. A. Whyte, 'Wed to the manse: the wives of Scottish ministers, *c*.1560–*c*.1800', in Ewan and Meikle (eds), *Women in Scotland*, p. 225.

accusations and community witchcraft beliefs. Local-level accusations converged with elite understandings of the demonic pact at the level of the domestic – marriage, household and community. Specifically local-level witchcraft accusations usually resulted from women's work within domestic configurations.

The domestic in early modern Scotland involved deeply ingrained hierarchical relationships: men over women, old over young, those who lived off surplus over those who physically worked the land. Farming practices and household organisation, while controlled by men, structured work for all members of peasant households. Men, as heads of households, were farmers, craftsmen, tradesmen, fishermen, millers and more. Women were responsible for some aspects of production as well as reproduction – feeding and clothing the household, tending the animals, harvesting crops, carrying peats and water, organising the children and servants and producing goods for exchange (including cloth and dairy products). Much of this work brought women out of their homes, into fields, villages and other people's homes.[57] Households, while usually headed by a married couple, supported and drew labour from their children and a variety of servants. Individual households were viable economic and social units only through intense, and often tense, links with other households, the larger community, landlords and state institutions. Witchcraft accusations demonstrate that women played a key role in maintaining, or sabotaging, those connections.

Witchcraft trial records shed light on fears and concerns about the dangers and uncertainties of everyday life – particularly that part of everyday life carried on by women. Minor losses of dairy products, crops and livestock, or the death of able-bodied family members could mean the difference between breaking even, sinking further into debt, or even falling into the ranks of the landless poor. In local witchcraft accusations, both the substance of the quarrels and the objects of magical harm were drawn from the arena of women's work. Quarrels about women's work and household duties were a major trigger for local witchcraft accusations. Roughly 80 per cent of Scottish witchcraft trial records in my survey contain evidence of some quarrelling; 53 per cent contain accusations of misfortune following quarrels and disputes related to domestic work. And in 36 per cent of female witchcraft cases, quarrels about work were the central axis of the trial. I found no male witchcraft trials where quarrelling was central.

This is not to say that *all* quarrels that led to witchcraft accusations were between women and about women. Men whose occupations brought them into contact with women, particularly millers, fishers and websters, could also be involved, though less frequently. Women often brought grain to be milled by male millers, sold fish caught by male fishermen, and sold thread to and bought cloth from male websters. Quarrels could thus arise at the borders between male and female spheres of work. Male work could also be threatened by witchcraft when a witch quarrelled

---

[57] For a fuller account of women's work, see Symonds, *Weep Not for Me*, ch. 4; Houston, 'Women'. For the economy see I. D. Whyte, *Scotland Before the Industrial Revolution: an Economic and Social History, c.1050–c.1750* (London, 1995).

with a man over prices or the quality of a product.[58] Also quarrels leading to witchcraft accusations between women and men could arise when a suspect quarrelled with the husband or brother of a woman with whom she was quarrelling.

The quarrels tended to be about aspects of female labour such as cloth production, dairying and healing. They occasionally involved the work of motherhood. Witchcraft suspects quarrelled with both men and women, and with people of lower, equal and higher social status. Detailed descriptions of quarrels show that married women and widows could be active in the control of their household land and in production, consumption and exchange of goods and services. Women's typical actions in these spheres could cause problems within their households and with their neighbours – problems that sometimes led to witchcraft accusations. Witchcraft trials, therefore, open a window into the daily lives of early modern Scottish women that is rivalled by few other documentary sources.

In 1597 Janet Wishart was accused of killing the daughter of a man who refused to sell her some wool.[59] Isobel Young in 1629 was accused of causing Cuthbert Simpson 'to misthryve and go bak in his estait' after he refused to exchange one web of cloth for four webs of cloth.[60] In the midst of the 1661 witch-hunt, Margaret Hutchison was accused of bewitching Beatrix Molewell's servant in revenge for a quarrel about putting her cloth where Beatrix usually put hers.[61] In 1661, Agnes Sandie, a dairy seller, accused Janet Cook of killing her dairy cow after causing it to give blood rather than milk. This apparently happened as the fulfilment of a curse Janet made to Agnes for selling curds and whey to her daughters without prior consent.[62] Isobel Young was accused of bewitching a millstone, the mill creek and the miller himself, after refusing to pay a milling fee she thought was too high.[63] Alison Jollie was tried and acquitted for witchcraft in 1596. She was accused of hiring a witch to intervene on her behalf in a dispute with Isobel Hepburn for 'the alledgeit redeming of an aker of land' that Alison had possessed for two years.[64]

Some women's work included small-scale magical remedies or even regular, recognised healing activities. In small-scale healing there was no mention of a fee, and cures were effected on their own livestock, fields and family members or close neighbours. Counter-magic can also be included in the small-scale category. This seems to be different from recognised healing practitioners who were denounced for witchcraft. In such cases healing was performed for a fee, the practitioner's territory was large and accusations concerned the act of healing itself and not quarrelling.

---

[58] See Isobel Young, 1629, *SJC*, i, pp. 96–120; Elizabeth Bathgate, 1634, NAS, JC2/7, fos. 148v., 154r., 160r.–167v.; Agnes Finnie, 1644, *SJC*, ii, pp. 627–43.

[59] *Spalding Misc.*, i, pp. 83–7; cf. Larner *et al.*, *Source-Book*, no. 2244.

[60] *SJC*, i, p. 109. For the whole trial see *SJC*, i, pp. 96–121. Cf. Larner *et al.*, *Source-Book*, no. 142.

[61] NAS, JC2/10, fo. 31v.; cf. Larner *et al.*, *Source-Book*, no. 401.

[62] NAS, justiciary processes, JC26/27/3, item 9, no. 1.

[63] *SJC*, i, pp. 97–100.

[64] NAS, JC2/3, fo. 135; cf. Pitcairn (ed.), *Trials*, ii, pp. 397–9; Larner *et al.*, *Source-Book*, no. 109.

Recognised healing practitioners form their own case-type; and male witches were more likely than female witches to be professional healers.[65] Both types of healing, paid and unpaid, should be seen as 'work'.

Although the reasons for quarrels were not always recorded in trial documents, the objects of magical harm usually were. Witches were thought to attack things, animals or people vital to the productive capacity of the household of the accuser. The actual participant in the quarrel was not always the one harmed by the witch. More often than not their cows, crops, spouses or children were bewitched – killed, destroyed or otherwise made to suffer. The substance of disputes leading to witchcraft accusations was not usually childbirth or childcare directly, although these were certainly aspects of women's work. Rather, the quarrellers' children and infants were objects of the witch's malice. Elizabeth Bathgate was accused of killing the infant child of George Sprott, a webster after they had a dispute about cloth. Elizabeth 'in ane gret spleane and anger thraitining to do hime ane evil turne'.[66] Elizabeth admitted to pinching the child and leaving a bruise. She was also accused of selling enchanted eggs to the Sprott household that caused the child's bruise to swell into the shape of a large goose egg. The child then pined away and died.[67] Suspected witches were frequently accused of casting mysterious, debilitating diseases on children and adults alike.

Women were largely responsible for the production of milk, butter and ale. It is not surprising, therefore, that these were thought to be particularly vulnerable to witchcraft.[68] Dairy cows were often targets of witchcraft malice, outnumbering other types of livestock in bewitchment cases. After a dispute with the witchcraft suspect, butter would not churn, milk would turn to blood, or cows, bulls and oxen might go mad and die. Ale would mysteriously go flat or turn bitter.[69]

The quarrels that women engaged in should be seen as verbal work. It was essential for household survival and economic security that women barter and haggle over prices, occasionally browbeat a competitor or friend into accepting a price or term of trade, and perhaps intimidate neighbours. This type of verbal work seems to have been so common that it was often used in witchcraft defence arguments to explain the suspect's aggressive behaviour. Isobel Young's violent verbal outburst to a man accompanying a messenger was explained as 'sum passionet speiches quilk

---

[65] For more on this, see J. Miller, 'Devices and directions: folk healing aspects of witchcraft practice in seventeenth-century Scotland', Chapter 6 below.

[66] NAS, JC2/7, fo. 160r., item 1.

[67] NAS, JC2/7, fos. 148v., 154r., 160r.–167v.; *RPC*, 2nd ser., v, pp. 176–7, 572, 593, 605–6; Larner *et al., Source-Book*, nos. 155–6.

[68] The notion that witches (or fairies) stole cows' milk and injured cows predated and outlived the period of active witch-hunting in Scotland: R. Hutton, *The Stations of the Sun: a History of the Ritual Year in Britain* (Oxford, 1996), p. 222.

[69] For example, Isobel Cockie, *Spalding Misc.*, i, pp. 110–16; Beigis Tod, NAS, JC2/4, fo. 221r.; NAS, 'Witchcraft Papers', JC40/2–3; Pitcairn (ed.), *Trials*, ii, pp. 542–4. For Janet Cook, see note 15 above. Cf. E. Ewan, '"For whatever ales ye": women as consumers and producers in late medieval Scottish towns', in Ewan and Meikle (eds), *Women in Scotland*.

mycht be usuale to wemen cited be messingeris'.[70] Likewise, healing and protective magic can be seen as verbal work of a different kind. Magical remedies involved learning and repeating words.

Thus physical and verbal work structured both the types of quarrels that resulted in witchcraft accusations and the objects of the witch's malice and revenge. Local witchcraft accusations revolved around the practical aspects of the domestic – production and consumption of goods, the day to day running of households, raising children and co-operating with neighbours. The quarrels that led to witchcraft accusations typically focused on the kinds of work usually done by women. Peasant witchcraft beliefs did not as directly incorporate the main kinds of work for which men were usually responsible – ploughing and sowing seed, heavy lifting, carting, and most crafts (such as tanning, fleshing or shoemaking).[71] Those aspects of male work that regularly interacted with female work, such as milling, fishing and weaving, seem to have been more likely subjects of quarrels leading to witchcraft and more susceptible to tampering by means of witchcraft. Witchcraft trials associated women and women's work with the Devil – thus demonising women, and their productive and social roles within early modern Scottish society and culture.

VI

When witchcraft was a crime, marriage and the labour of female heads of household structured how people thought about acts of malefice attributed to witches and women's relationships to the Devil. Accusations of witchcraft involving quarrels about women's work were the backbone of evidence used by prosecutors as proof of demonic witchcraft in the trial itself. The legal definition of witchcraft, involving a relationship to the Devil, bled outward to demonise those aspects of women's work that led to witchcraft accusations in the first place.

Without a confession the role of the Devil could only be inferred, because the witch's relationship with the Devil was, by definition, secret. Here quarrels followed by misfortune were an important piece of evidence that prosecutors used to infer the participation of the Devil, thereby proving that the accused was a witch, i.e. that she had entered into a demonic pact. Janet Cook's first trial in September 1661 illustrates this. Both a set of witness statements and a formal dittay survive.[72] In both, Helen Turnbull accused Janet of killing a baby she was wetnursing (thereby destroying her livelihood) in revenge for a quarrel about Janet's butter

---

[70] *SJC*, i, p. 101.

[71] For anecdotal evidence of smiths as having magical powers against witchcraft, see E. J. Cowan and L. Henderson, 'The last of the witches? The survival of Scottish witch belief', Chapter 12 below.

[72] NAS, JC26/27/3, item 12 is a list of statements taken at Dalkeith from Jan. to Aug. 1661. The articles are informally ordered, and in first person. They clearly reflect witness statements and have a flowing, oral style. NAS, JC27/26/3, item 15, although undated, contains the same allegations as the previous document, but the handwriting is more formal, witnesses are described as 'present', and the articles are in second person for use in court.

prices. The first document is rambling, conversational and confrontational. It records Helen's interview, accusation of Janet and Janet's responses. The first record of Helen's accusation mentions neither the Devil nor witchcraft. The second document compresses the quarrel about butter and the harm suffered by Helen, but specifically alleges that Janet killed the infant by her 'sorcery and witchcraft'. It seems clear that the prosecution inferred witchcraft and the Devil from Helen's tale of quarrels and harm.[73]

The association of the Devil with women, marriage and work in both the legal definition of witchcraft and in local quarrels indicates a profound unease with women in society. This does not mean that witch-hunting was a cynical mask for woman-hunting. Rather, it means that women, marriage and women's work were points of tension within the multiple conceptual relationships that made up witchcraft beliefs and trials. The conceptual links between witchcraft beliefs and the practice of witchcraft trials drew from and affected a broad cultural field in which women were central – namely the domestic (the conceptual binder of marriage, household, family and work).

Marriage as an institution was the legal and practical basis of household formation, and it placed women in a subordinate social position. The household organised social relations (marriage, child raising and service) and productive relations. Both men and women occupied central roles in the production of food, drink, cloth and other commodities for exchange and consumption. Within household production, women had some power. Households, however, were incomplete on their own. Each household, with husband, wife, children and servants, was intricately linked to other such units through ties of co-operation, dispute, exchange, mutual debt and circumstances of geography. Witchcraft beliefs destabilised how people viewed women within this domestic configuration; and witchcraft trials tore families, households, communities and lives apart.

The early modern fear of witches resonated with and was shaped by other, more naturalistic fears. The demonic pact and local quarrels demonstrate a profound unease about women in marriage, work and community relations. Scottish witchcraft beliefs were structured by, and in turn helped to structure, the way people thought about and (perhaps) feared women in work, position and power in their households and by extension in the social structure and economy of Scottish middling communities. Witch-hunting was not just an expression of mass panic or religious fanaticism, but was grounded in specific everyday relations and practices – notably marriage, labour and the running of households.

---

[73] NAS, JC26/27/3, item 12, article 6; item 15, article 2. The same pattern recurred throughout the documents from both of Janet's trials.

6

Devices and directions: folk healing aspects of witchcraft practice in seventeenth-century Scotland

Joyce Miller

In the seventeenth century, folk healers used a number of ingredients or devices – water, metal, animals, clothing, salt, fire – which they included in directions about healing rituals issued to their clients. Directions were the instructions about the use of certain devices, for example the manner in which the ritual was to be undertaken or the particular place to which they were to go. It is these 'devices and directions' and how they were used as folk healing aspects of witchcraft practice which will provide the main source of evidence in this chapter.

This book is an examination of the Scottish witch-hunt in context. This chapter concentrates on beliefs and practices of folk healing, or charming, rather than the witch-hunt itself or the prosecution of witches as such. Why were charmers sometimes prosecuted for witchcraft? On the other hand, why were there so few? Some of the procedural aspects of charming practice were latterly primarily associated with highland society, which may have given an impression that they were only part of highland culture. However, this chapter demonstrates that these practices were equally common to lowland society in early modern Scotland.[1]

Three interconnected strands will be explored. Firstly, the intrinsic differences between witches and charmers will be explained. Secondly, the general discourse of disease in early modern society in relation to both elite and popular cultural attitudes will be touched upon. And thirdly, detailed analysis of the charms themselves will demonstrate that they were not random or whimsical but were founded on belief and empiricism, or experience, in which both the charmer and the recipient participated.[2]

---

[1] Two communities from lowland Scotland were examined in this study; however, the term lowland is not used to imply or emphasise any cultural or social difference between highland and lowland Scotland.

[2] For a more general examination of charmers, charming and attitudes of seventeenth-century society in Scotland, see J. Miller, 'Cantrips and Carlins: Magic, Medicine and Society in the Presbyteries of Haddington and Stirling, 1600–1688' (Ph.D. thesis, University of Stirling, 1999).

I

The first question to address is: what was charming? Charming was one feature of witchcraft practice and belief, but not all charmers practised witchcraft nor did all witches practise charming. In some cases one person's charmer may have been another person's witch. However, under what circumstances the questionable practice of charming could become the crime of witchcraft is difficult to establish categorically.[3]

Witchcraft, sorcery and charming were all features of magic or preternatural power. Although magic had developed a negative meaning, this hostility increased as a result of witchcraft prosecution and theological developments, which stressed its irrationality and downplayed its cultural significance and relationship with religious belief.[4] Since all three were aspects of magic, charming was therefore related to, and in some cases part of, witchcraft practice and belief, yet it was not entirely the same. It shared many of the same physical and verbal actions – the words and deeds – of witchcraft, but it was usually equal to, and opposite from, witchcraft. Unlike witches, who were labelled by others, charmers knew who they were and would label themselves as such. There was also a difference between the perceived source of the power of the two groups and, very importantly, their intent. Witchcraft was demonic and malicious: charming was neither.

The authorities, and particularly the church, did attempt to include charming with the prosecution of witchcraft. In 1646 the General Assembly of the church attempted to extend the scope of the witchcraft act to include charmers:

> Because our addresses to the ordinar judge for punishment of charming, it is informed to us that the Acts of Parliament ar not expresslie against that sinne, which the rude and ignorant ar much addicted unto; may it therfor please your lordships that the Act of the 9 Parliament of Queen Marie made against witches and consulters be enlarged and extended to charmers, or that such other course be taken as that offence may be restrained and punished.[5]

Throughout the period of witchcraft prosecutions in Scotland, individuals were investigated and interrogated for practising charming. However, at local level, attitudes were varied. The two presbyteries that were examined closely demonstrate the variation in investigation and prosecution of witches and charmers that was seen in Scotland. The Haddington presbytery had a higher percentage of accusations of both witchcraft and charming – 83 per cent – compared to Stirling, which had only 17 per cent.[6] Given that the estimated population of Haddington was

---

[3] J. Gilmore, 'Witchcraft and the Church in Scotland subsequent to the Reformation' (Ph.D. thesis, University of Glasgow, 1948), pp. 101–2. Gilmore identified that it was a problem that the church acknowledged, but he did not offer any explanation for it.

[4] S. Clark, *Thinking with Demons: the Idea of Witchcraft in Early Modern Europe* (Oxford, 1997), pp. 214–16.

[5] *Records of the Commissions of the General Assemblies of the Church of Scotland, 1646–1647*, eds A. Mitchell and J. Christie (SHS, 1892), p. 123.

[6] Miller, 'Cantrips and Carlins', ch. 12.

approximately 1.75 times greater than Stirling this difference was quite remarkable.[7] Eighty-seven per cent of those who were accused of demonic witchcraft were from the Haddington presbytery, and only 13 per cent from the Stirling presbytery. The figures for accusations of charming, however, demonstrate the complete opposite: 56 per cent of those who were accused of charming came from the Stirling area, and 44 per cent from Haddington. This illustrates that local conditions and habits appear to have influenced both the rate, and type, of accusation that was processed through the church rather than any a national pattern.

The church punished the majority of charmers, but some were prosecuted for witchcraft if their charming actions were categorised as indicating demonic intervention. Local kirk sessions and presbyteries examined evidence both from accused charmers and their clients in order to ascertain whether or not the practice was demonic. But the church appeared to have difficulties in deciding what to do with them. In October 1630 the Dalkeith presbytery asked the synod of Lothian and Tweeddale for advice about charmers, those who consulted them and also those who had been slandered with no evidence of practice. The synod replied, 'those that are simple charmers and consulters suld be refered to thair [own] repentance'. As for those who had been slandered they thought nothing of them.[8] It would appear then that if the practice was believed to be demonic, then civil intervention would be required, if not it could be dealt with at local level by the church and the individual's own conscience. The whole area was clearly confusing. On some occasions the question of whether the practice was demonic or not, was decided by whether rituals had been used, and whether these involved the use of words and actions, either alone or in combination.

In the seventeenth century the kirk session, the lowest level of church committee, was an important force in social discipline. It could discuss a range of social and criminal misdemeanours, many of which it could discipline itself at local level. In some situations it would refer to the presbytery for advice, particularly if secular intervention was felt necessary, but many cases were dealt with at local level. The punishments that the kirk session could impose included monetary fines and public repentance, and appearance in sackcloth was commonly used to punish participation in charming. Excommunication, although still available, was used only rarely.[9]

During the early modern period one obvious distinction between witches and charmers was whether they caused harm or provided assistance. Put simply, the term charmer was used in Scotland to denote individuals who diagnosed and counteracted the effects of harmful witchcraft; gave healing advice that involved the use of words and rituals; helped locate lost goods; offered advice about love;

---

[7] M. Flinn, *Scottish Population History from the 17th Century to the 1930s* (Cambridge, 1977), p. 188. This calculation is based on the hearth and poll taxes of the 1690s.

[8] NAS, Dalkeith presbytery records, CH2/424/1.

[9] Cf. Miller, 'Cantrips and Carlins', esp. ch. 8. For a general discussion of the church and discipline see M. Graham, *The Uses of Reform: 'Godly Discipline' and Popular Behavior in Scotland and Beyond, 1560–1610* (Leiden, 1996).

and predicted the future.[10] Charmers, therefore, identified themselves as having special knowledge and skills and were known to their own communities and often to others. Although all of these aspects of charming practice were important, it is those related to healing that will be examined here as they demonstrate that it was based on a solid cultural tradition of belief and practice.

In 1631 Rosie Graham from Gargunnock told Margery Ker to

> gang to some of her neighbours houses and seek from them the thing that slew the mice [i.e. a cat] without speaking the proper name or suffering any other to speak the name of it, and after she had gotten it, she bad her put it thrice under her wambe about the cow [i.e. around the cow under its belly] and after the third time to fling it out the door. After that she bad her take the left foot shoe and put it thrice about the cow under her wambe in like manner and every time to give the cow one clap with the sole of it. Thereafter she bad her take the milk of [the] cow and put it out at ane hole of the house where yr was no light come in and cause keep it on the other side and take it to a march [i.e. boundary] burn[11] where she would mix some of it [i.e. the burn] with the milk and bring it home and put thrice therof in the cows lug. All of which she confessed she did and that she got the cat in William Swan's house.[12]

Margery's complaint appears to have been that although her sick cow was cured by the treatment recommended by Rosie Graham, some time later she lost another animal. Turning to the church, however, very likely in the hope of getting Rosie punished, appeared to backfire for Margery. It was she who was instructed to make public repentance in sackcloth as well as pay a monetary fine. The records are frustratingly silent about the fate of Rosie Graham, but on this occasion she may have escaped public censure.

Life in seventeenth-century Scotland was extremely difficult for the majority of people, and survival was often a struggle. Religious and political wars, famine and plague killed many,[13] but there were other, more immediate and personal, dangers. A fear of witchcraft and the power of witches themselves, to some extent encouraged by religion, existed at all levels of society.[14] This fear was evident in explanations

[10] The term charmer was used in Scotland, as opposed to the term 'cunning folk', which was more commonly used in England. Robin Briggs discusses the distinction between witches and cunning folk, or *devins* in France, in *Witches and Neighbours: the Social and Cultural Context of European Witchcraft* (London, 1996), pp. 122–6, 171–4, 277–81. Cf. J. Sharpe, *Instruments of Darkness: Witchcraft in England, 1550–1750* (London, 1996), esp. pp. 66–70, and K. Thomas, *Religion and the Decline of Magic: Studies in Popular Beliefs in Sixteenth and Seventeenth-Century England* (London, 1971), chs. 6–7.

[11] March burns were important in denoting the physical limits of communal space.

[12] SCA, Gargunnock kirk session records, CH2/1121/1.

[13] For an overview of social and economic conditions in seventeenth-century Scotland, see I. Whyte, *Scotland Before the Industrial Revolution: an Economic and Social History, c.1050–c.1750* (London, 1995), chs. 6–12; also T. C. Smout, *A History of the Scottish People, 1560–1830* (London, 1969), chs. 3, 5–8. For the religious and political troubles, see W. Makey, *The Church of the Covenant, 1637–1651* (Edinburgh, 1979), D. Stevenson, *The Scottish Revolution, 1637–1644: the Triumph of the Covenanters* (Newton Abbot, 1973), and D. Stevenson, *Revolution and Counter-Revolution in Scotland, 1644–1651* (London, 1977).

[14] W. Naphy and P. Roberts (eds), *Fear in Early Modern Society* (Manchester, 1997), esp. D. Gentilcore, 'The fear of disease and the disease of fear'.

about harm or damage experienced by people, such as the destruction of foodstuffs, loss of animals and personal illness or injury. Beigis Tod from Longniddry was accused in 1608 of casting an unknown sickness onto Alexander Fairlie. The boy 'vanischet away with vehement sweiting, and continuall burning at the heart, quhilk seiknes indurit with him the space of tua monethis, that nane luikit for his lyfe'.[15] Jean Craig from Tranent was accused of laying an illness on Beatrix Sandilands in 1649 which caused her to 'become mad and bereft of her naturall wit'.[16] These cases illustrate the perceived harmful effect of witchcraft, since both Tod and Craig were prosecuted for malicious witchcraft.

Yet this belief in and fear of witchcraft as a negative or destructive power also permitted its neutralising through the use of charming.[17] Charming included either counter magic, which could be used against an identified source of malefice, or protective magic, which was used in a more generalised beneficial manner. Society needed to believe that the power of witchcraft could be reversed. In 1608 Isobel Greirson from Prestonpans, was accused of casting an illness onto Robert Peddan which caused him to 'swoon and faint'. Peddan then remembered that he owed Greirson 9s 4d which he took to her and asked her three times to restore his health, saying: 'Gif ye haif done me ony wrang or hurt, repair the samin and restoir me to my health'.[18] Within 24 hours Peddan had recovered his health. In another case Elspeth Wood was accused by the Haddington kirk session in 1653 of causing George Forrest's cow to lose its milk by stealing a tether.[19] The milk was later restored when the tether was returned to Forrest. In the right circumstances, both parties understood that what had been harmed by witchcraft could be healed by charming.

But what was meant by the term charming and how did it differ from witchcraft? The term was included in the dittays against many of those accused of witchcraft. James Reid from Musselburgh was accused in 1603 of being a common sorcerer and charmer, and Isobel Bennet was accused of sorcery, witchcraft and charming in 1659.[20] However, there were also those who were classified simply as charmers, with no reference to the nefarious practices of witchcraft or sorcery. Janet Anderson from Stirling was accused of charming in 1617 and 1621.[21] She confessed that

---

[15] Pitcairn (ed.), *Trials*, ii, II, pp. 542–4.

[16] *SJC*, iii, p. 813.

[17] Briggs, *Witches and Neighbours*, pp. 180–3; Thomas, *Religion and the Decline of Magic*, ch. 7 and pp. 648–51. Cf. É. Pócs, *Between the Living and the Dead: a Perspective on Witches and Seers in the Early Modern Age* (Budapest, 1999), pp. 109–11.

[18] Pitcairn (ed.), *Trials* ii, II, pp. 523–6. The identification of the malefice and the subsequent interaction between the injured party and the malicious witch, as well as the state of the relationship between the two prior to the harm, were important characteristics of village witchcraft and culture. They permitted a process of comfort by pacifying any personal conflict and restoring neighbourly relations without involving state or ecclesiastical authorities. Cf. Briggs, *Witches and Neighbours*, pp. 180–5; Sharpe, *Instruments of Darkness*, p. 161.

[19] NAS, Haddington kirk session records, CH2/799/1.

[20] Pitcairn (ed.), *Trials* ii, II, p. 421; NAS, justiciary court records, JC26/26.

[21] *RPC*, 2nd ser., viii, p. 345.

she cured a child who had 'tane a brash [i.e. short burst] of seiknes thrugh ane ill ee' by charming the child's vest using her hands and a spoken verse. George Beir from Haddington was a seventh son,[22] and he told the session how he cured people of the cruells, also known as the king's evil or scrofula – a form of lymphatic tuberculosis – by using threads and a spoken charm.[23] He was told by the kirk session in 1646 that if he 'should be found practising the curing of the cruells heirefter that he should satisfy as a charmer'. These cases reveal that certain people and practices were perceived as being quite distinct from witches and witchcraft.

In contemporary terms, therefore, charming clearly had quite a different purpose from that of either witchcraft or sorcery. Charming was the antidote to witchcraft but could also be used to cure some natural diseases. Many of the rituals and practices were common to all three, but the intent, and the source of the power, of charming were very different. Like witchcraft and sorcery, charming used magical power but it was used to counteract witchcraft and sorcery. Unlike witchcraft and sorcery, the source of charming power was not, according to charmers, demonic. It was some other source, sometimes human or sometimes spiritual. On occasion these spirits may have been categorised by others as having been demonic in form, and even sometimes as the Devil himself, but not by the charmers themselves.

II

If charming was a form of magical healing practice then how did its practice relate to the wider context of health and disease? During this period access to the advice and care of professional medical practitioners was limited to the elite and those of their household.[24] For the majority of the population health advice came from other sources: another family member or a friend, or someone with some special knowledge or training such as a gardener or blacksmith, both of whom had special knowledge and expertise, or from some local charmer. Trained gardeners, like the monks who had tended medicinal gardens and plants, would have specialised

---

[22] It was believed that seventh sons or daughters were born with special powers and were able to heal by touch: Thomas, *Religion and the Decline of Magic*, pp. 237–9; W. Hand, 'The folk healer: calling and endowment', *Journal of the History of Medicine*, 26 (1971), 263–78.

[23] NAS, Haddington kirk session records, CH2/285/5. The term 'king's evil' was recorded in Scotland by the late sixteenth and early seventeenth century: see *Dictionary of the Older Scottish Tongue*. In 1633, during his visit to Edinburgh, Charles I was claimed to have touched about 100 people to cure this disease, as well as coins which were believed to have the same healing powers. J. G. Dalyell, *The Darker Superstitions of Scotland* (Glasgow, 1834), p. 62. There was also a well at Livingston in West Lothian, now not visible, which was known as the Rose Well. It was claimed that it derived its name from the practice of kings of Scotland using water from the well to touch people who were suffering from the rose or king's evil, before sunrise on New Year's Day: *Original Name Books of the Ordnance Survey*, 50 (1856), p. 15.

[24] Works covering the general history of medicine in Scotland include H. Dingwall, *Physicians, Surgeons and Apothecaries: Medical Practice in Seventeenth-Century Edinburgh* (East Linton, 1995), and D. Hamilton, *The Healers: a History of Medicine in Scotland* (Edinburgh, 1981). For England: L. M. Beier, *Sufferers and Healers: the Experience of Illness in Seventeenth-century England* (London, 1987).

knowledge about the effects of certain plants and herbs.[25] Blacksmiths worked in the mystical and mysterious elements of fire and metal and because of this special skill were consulted as healers.[26] The third option, someone known to have some knowledge of charming or magical healing, was not the only option available but was clearly an acceptable choice. The service offered by charmers was perhaps not so unusual when it is placed in the wider context of healers in general.

The diagnoses offered by charmers were based on the principle that diseases or misfortune were caused by bewitchment, which involved the transference of a negative or evil force through the use of sympathetic magic. The treatments they offered used the same principle.[27] People, animals or objects could be bewitched either deliberately or accidentally, but the rationale behind the charms was the removal of the disease – or more accurately the force or energy which caused it – by transfer onto someone or something else or its disposal elsewhere. Several charmers explained how they disposed carefully of intermediate objects, such as clothing, or hair and nail trimmings, which had belonged to the diseased person, in case the disease was transferred accidentally to someone else. Andrew Aiken told the Stirling presbytery in 1636 that 'ane part of the witchcraft went with the water and gif any passed over it, they wald gett skaith by it'.[28]

In contrast, according to contemporary elite medical theories, diseases were caused by an imbalance of the four humours, and the rationale which informed early modern medical treatment was the restoration of balance using purges to remove and tonics to restore. According to Galenic medical theory each individual symptom would be treated separately. Although on the surface it would appear that the different systems of medical advice had little in common, it is possible to argue that a philosophy of peace and balance informed both forms of treatment. Both groups appear to have believed that an external force had an internal effect, both physically and spiritually. Orthodox medical practitioners attempted to expel an unwelcome humoral disturbance followed by the administration of a restorative tonic, whereas those who believed that bewitching was the cause of illness

[25] In the seventeenth century the Faculty of Physicians and Surgeons of Glasgow was concerned about gardeners, whom they saw as unlicensed rivals to their monopoly and attempted to limit their practice. On 28 Jan. 1657 they ordered James Dowgall, a gardener, to 'abstain in all tyme heirafter from using & excercising any pairt of the airt of chirurgaiurie or prescribing of any medicamentis of physick'. Royal College of Physicians and Surgeons of Glasgow, Minute Book of the Faculty of Physicians and Surgeons, 1602–1688, 1/1/1.

[26] Blacksmiths had been associated with the Celtic smith-God Gobniu who was regarded as having mystical healing powers. Blacksmiths were also held in high regard because they worked metal into tools, weapons and armour. Cf. Thomas, *Religion and the Decline of Magic*, pp. 795–6; M. Beith, *Healing Threads: Traditional Medicines of the Highlands and Islands* (Edinburgh, 1995), pp. 99–100. For a blacksmith's treatment for depression, see Martin Martin, *A Description of the Western Islands of Scotland*, c.1695 (facsimile of 1st [1698] edition, Edinburgh, 1994), p. 183.

[27] For a discussion of the use of magic in healing, see Thomas, *Religion and the Decline of Magic*, chs. 7–9. W. Hand, 'Folk curing: the magical component', *Béaloideas*, 39–41 (1971–3), 140–56, discusses the disposal of objects used in healing; cf. W. Hand, *Magical Medicine* (Berkeley, Calif., 1980), pp. 18–23.

[28] SCA, Stirling presbytery records, CH2/722/5.

understood that some form of force had to be expelled before spiritual and physical balance could be restored. Both systems had their own internal logic, were firmly based on accepted principles and beliefs, were part of a shared popular and elite culture and, importantly, were legitimised by the rest of society who participated in their use.

Although some of the principles behind the treatments recommended by charmers may have shared something with orthodox medicine, the content and application were very different. Orthodox medical treatments were still firmly Galenic and Hippocratic in their approach and the emphasis was on purging or expelling using blood-letting, enemas, emetics, diuretics, expectorants and diaphoretics.[29] After being purged, the patient was restored by the administration of tonics. Most of the ingredients for these prescriptions were vegetable in origin although occasionally animal products would be used.

Charmers recognised the causes of those diseases which they felt they could treat and those they could not. Janet Anderson told the privy council that she could tell when someone was 'witchit' or 'blasted by an ill wind', but she stressed that she could not treat the gravel – stony deposits in the bladder or kidneys.[30] The gravel was one of the most serious and painful physical complaints recorded in the seventeenth century and although medical treatments were used the condition often required surgical intervention, something charmers did not do.[31] In general, treatments recommended by charmers did not include the same physical ingredients that were used in orthodox medicine. Ingredients or components recommended by charmers were important, but their power or perceived efficacy came from their ritual use as much as the ingredients themselves.

III

The recurrent motifs or features in the charming treatments that were analysed in this study may be categorised according to time, place and manner.[32] The ritual could be carried out at a particular time of day, week or year; at a particular place such as a boundary, crossroads, bridge or river; in a particular manner, perhaps in silence; or particular direction, moving sunwise, anti-sunwise or backwards. Further categorising motifs which were recorded included the use of words or spoken

---

[29] Dingwall, *Physicians*, p. 142.

[30] *RPC*, 2nd ser., viii, p. 345.

[31] Dingwall, *Physicians*, pp. 160, 154–5, 180–1; Hamilton, *Healers*, pp. 75–6. Peripatetic lithotomists or stone cutters often carried out surgical removal of gravel or the stone. Stirling Burgh Council, the kirk session and others contributed to the cost of operations on a number of occasions. For example they paid £12 'to the Highland doctor for the cutting of John Stewart, litster, his son of the stone' in 1697: *Extracts from the Records of the Burgh of Stirling, 1667–1752*, ed. R. Renwick (Glasgow, 1889), p. 84. Glasgow had such a problem with the condition that they paid Iver McNeill to be the town lithotomist in 1656: A. Duncan, *Memorials of the Faculty of Physicians and Surgeons of Glasgow, 1599–1850* (Glasgow, 1896), pp. 239, 245.

[32] Hand, 'Folk curing', p. 141.

charms; the use of a particular type of water, or at specific places; numbers; fire; the use of an object such as a shoe, nail, thread or belt; cutting of nails or hair; use of an animal; meal, usually oats but occasionally wheat. Although charmers did not use the polypharmacy of orthodox medicine they still employed a wide variety of motifs.

Detailed research in local sources from the presbyteries of Haddington and Stirling between 1603 and 1688 has revealed almost 100 references to some form of charming.[33] They have been examined for the use of ritual and words, either alone or in combination, or for the inclusion of other motifs. The use of a physical ritual was by far the most common feature, as nine out of ten treatments (92 per cent) included a reference to some form of ritual or routine.[34] Physical rituals by themselves featured in over half the total charms (54 per cent). Words were mentioned in 42 per cent of the charms. A third (38 per cent) used words and ritual together but in this sample, perhaps rather surprisingly, only 3 per cent used words by themselves.

IV

Andrew Youll, who tied a live toad around the neck of his sheep in 1646, told the church officials that he had not used any words along with his ritual. Nevertheless he was reprimanded by the Haddington kirk session and told that unless he stopped using the ritual he would be censured as a charmer. The Haddington presbytery decided that Adam Gillies and his wife were not witches because, although they had tied wheat and salt to their cows' ears, they had not used any words and had merely been carrying out, in the words of the church authorities, an 'ignorant superstition'.[35] To a large extent these physical rituals appear to have been excused as having carried out through simple ignorance rather than deliberate transgressions. The use of ritual alone appears to have been regarded by the church and judicial authorities as charming not witchcraft. In this case the rituals or charming might be seen to have been superstitious practice continued through ignorance rather than outright deliberate, demonic practice.

There was some concern, however, that rituals could be used to conjure supernatural spirits or powers and were therefore still very much antithetical to Christian practice.[36] As Clark points out, the term superstition had a number of applications or definitions that were used by the church. Firstly, superstition was used to define that which was opposite to accepted religious practice. Secondly, it was used to denounce certain practices and habits as valueless, either because they were carried out excessively or in the wrong manner. In its third version, superstition, or inappropriate worship, was associated with demonic worship.[37] In general, its use was

---

[33] Miller, 'Cantrips and Carlins', ch. 11.

[34] 8 per cent of the references to charming did not include any detail about specific aspects or features.

[35] NAS, Haddington presbytery records, CH2/185/5.

[36] Clark, *Thinking with Demons*, ch. 32.

[37] Clark, *Thinking with Demons*, esp. pp. 476–9.

perceived as due to ignorance and lack of understanding rather than active rejection of the authority of the church. In 1581, parliament passed an act making it illegal to visit wells and participate in pilgrimages.[38] In 1629 the privy council issued a similar proclamation.[39] In 1648 the Dunblane synod passed an ordinance which again urged the abandoning of 'superstitious wells and chapels whereunto people resort'.[40] It would appear, however, that the ordinary population did not respond immediately, or at all, to these proclamations. Despite the desire of the authorities to force the general populace to abandon these practices they continued to be important to many and so continued to be observed despite the threat of punishment. For those involved, an accusation of charming or 'ignorant superstition' was in many ways a better option than an accusation of witchcraft which might result in execution.

V

Rituals often used a physical object such as water, metal, animals, shoes, clothing, herbs, salt, eggs, wood or threads. Over two-thirds (67 per cent) of the rituals included some reference to one or more such objects. Other features included specific reference to movement, washing, cutting, the laying on of hands, times of the day, numbers, boundaries, restrictions and verbal requests.

The most common motif was water, mentioned in just under half the procedures (44 per cent). Water from wells was specified the most often (18 per cent); followed by south running water (10 per cent) and then sea water (1 per cent). In 15 per cent of the rituals the source or type of water was unspecified. Typically the water was used either as a drink or an ablution, and it was generally associated with other motifs such as a number, an item of clothing, a time of day or a place. Water may often have been the most important feature as it was usually mentioned first.

Steven Maltman from Gargunnock treated Janet Chrystie with a drink of south running water which he had charmed by the addition of a stone.[41] Andrew Aiken, also from the Stirling area, treated humans and animals with south running water.[42] Margaret Dickson from the Haddington district, washed John Sharp's child's vest, as well as the child itself, three times with south running water.[43] The importance of south running water may be connected with the Indo-European tradition of positive association with the right. The right side is aligned with light, day, good and movement to the right. When facing to the east the south is located on the right and so could be seen to have positive connotations.[44]

---

[38] *APS*, iii, p. 212.

[39] *RPC*, 2nd ser., iii, p. 241.

[40] *Register of the Diocesan Synod of Dunblane, 1662–1688*, ed. J. Wilson (Edinburgh, 1877), p. 263.

[41] SCA, Stirling presbytery records, CH2/722/5.

[42] SCA, Stirling presbytery records, CH2/722/5.

[43] NAS, Haddington presbytery records, CH2/185/5.

[44] E. Lyle, *Archaic Chaos* (Edinburgh, 1990), pp. 92–104.

The use of well water was also quite specific. Bessie Stevenson advised the wetting of mutches, or cloth hats, which were then to be put back on the sick person, and vests and other items of clothing could be used in the same manner.[45] Other accounts of rituals associated with wells describe visiting the well, taking some of the water and leaving a small token or votive offering – such as a penny, a small coin or even an iron nail – behind.[46] The wells that were mentioned appear to have been local 'holy' wells. The Protestant churchmen attempted to suppress visits or pilgrimages to 'holy' wells, which they felt represented pre-Reformation religious practice. Many of the wells, however, were not designated 'holy' from a purely Christian perspective. It is likely that many were pre-Christian in origin rather than simply pre-Reformation and were designated as being traditional due to local custom. However, since the church authorities perceived all forms of observance not controlled by the church as heretical it did not matter to them whether the well was pre-Christian or pre-Reformation.

VI

Washing a person, particularly if the illness was associated with a fever or sweating, may have been a sensible action designed either to bring down the person's temperature or to help them rest after a fever had broken. Janet Tailzeor from Stirling recommended washing only the hands and feet of a sick child in south running water in 1629.[47] Alternatively, the whole person could be washed. Andrew Aiken, already mentioned above, washed all of John Sibbald's body with south running water.[48] As well as its practical use, washing may have had an important symbolic meaning and may have implied a spiritual, as well as physical, cleansing.

Occasionally the laying-on of hands was mentioned along with washing. The use of touch again may have had spiritual connotations as it symbolised the perceived special power of the charmer. These people claimed that they were endowed with special or mystical powers, particular circumstances of birth or some physical ability or disability that distinguished them as different and special.[49] Perhaps God had chosen them for a purpose. The church and demonologists, however, had a problem with this explanation. Although pre-Reformation church practice certainly did not actively encourage rivals to priests, it was the Protestants who felt most threatened by them. They were reluctant to accept that God might have conferred special skills, therefore the source of the power must have been demonic. To claim this sort of justification was seen as idolatrous and against the first Commandment.[50] Witchcraft and demonology were difficult areas for all and charming was undoubtedly part of the whole topic.

[45] NAS, JC26/26.
[46] SCA, Stirling presbytery records, CH2/722/4.
[47] SCA, Stirling presbytery records, CH2/722/5.
[48] SCA, Stirling presbytery records, CH2/722/5.
[49] Hand, 'Folk healer'.
[50] Clark, *Thinking with Demons*, pp. 489–97.

Twenty-nine per cent of the rituals referred to a number, making it the second most frequent single motif. Numbers were always associated with some other motif or feature: threads, movement, water or objects. The number three was mentioned most although two, four, five, nine and eleven were also mentioned. Margaret Dickson told John Sharp to go round his house three times.[51] Agnes Anderson's remedy for mawturning (nausea) involved turning a child three times head over heels between barn doors or round an oak post.[52] Another charm to remove illness was recorded by Margaret Harvie. She told Margaret Milne's mother to remove three pieces of thatch from above the door of Isobel Keir's house as Isobel Keir was thought to be responsible for Margaret Milne's distress.[53] Andrew Aiken spoke a charm five times over the afflicted person.[54] John Sharp reported that he had been advised to go round his house nine times.[55]

The symbolism of numbers is a controversial area, but it is clear that numbers were an important feature of healing rituals although their specific meaning may be difficult to determine. All the numbers used may have had a particular significance but three is perhaps the easiest one to examine. The use of three, or triads, has obvious Christian overtones associated with the Trinity, but it is likely to have even older religious significance or origins. The division of the body, and also society, into a threefold structure separating the head, the middle and the lower parts was seen in many cultures.[56] The head or top was associated with mental thought and represented by priests and philosophers, the middle symbolised strength and was represented by soldiers and fighters, and the lower areas were associated with basic behaviours such as sex or appetite and represented by the common or lower orders.[57]

VII

The use of tethers, belts or threads was mentioned in 12 per cent of the treatments.[58] Bessie Stevenson from Stirling used a belt and two threads to diagnose heart fevers. She explained that one thread was placed on either side of a belt, which was then put

---

[51] NAS, Haddington presbytery records, CH2/185/5.

[52] NAS, Haddington presbytery records, CH2/185/6.

[53] NAS, JC26/26. Using something that belonged to another person either to harm or to remove the harmful charm was based on the principle of sympathetic magic and was common throughout central and western Europe. The 'analog injury' is discussed in Pócs, *Between the Living and the Dead*, p. 116.

[54] SCA, Stirling presbytery records, CH2/722/5.

[55] NAS, Haddington presbytery records, CH2/185/5. Margaret Dickson told the church authorities she had told Sharp to go round his house three times, he told them Dickson had said nine times.

[56] The motif of the number three is seen in a number of folk tales and ballads. The use of three knots to ensure favourable winds is recorded in Scandinavian folk tales as well as Scottish versions from Orkney, Shetland and Gaelic-speaking areas. In the *Odyssey* Odysseus was given a bag of winds to help him sail his ship home. Cf. 'The Three Knots', in A. Bruford and D. A. MacDonald (eds), *Scottish Traditional Tales* Edinburgh, 1994), pp. 391–5, 480.

[57] Lyle, *Archaic Chaos*, pp. 142–55.

[58] Thomas, *Religion and the Decline of Magic*, pp. 217–18, discusses the examination of girdles as a means to diagnose or assess a patient's health.

under the armholes of the sick person. The belt was left in place and if the person was diseased then the threads would move to one side.[59] James Mill reported that Margaret Dickson had told him he would be cured if he went through a piece of green yarn, although she told the kirk session that she had told him to wind it around the afflicted part.[60] George Beir, in order to treat scrofula, wound two black silk threads around the diseased part of the body.[61] In order to recover her senses, or cure her emotional distraction, Agnes Symson from Stirling, was restrained with tethers and left alone overnight at a local well.[62] George Forrest, mentioned earlier, had the milk restored to his cow once its tether had been returned.[63]

Tethers, belts or threads may have been used simply as intermediate physical objects, but they may also have symbolised another motif, that of movement – particularly an encircling or turning movement – which was also mentioned in 12 per cent of the rituals. Janet Anderson passed clothing around a pillar in order to charm it.[64] John Sharp was told to go round his house at midnight.[65] This also highlights another motif – a specific time of day, which was also mentioned in 12 per cent of occasions. Marjorie Wingate was reported to the kirk session of St Ninian's in Stirling for being at a well before sunrise in order to get water to heal her father.[66] Andrew Aiken told George Syme that he would be cured if he collected water before daybreak.[67] In these cases the instructions also stressed that the individuals were not to speak to anyone on their journeys.

The emphasis on midnight and dawn was expected but, surprisingly, in this sample there were not as many mentions of any specific days such as saints' days or other calendar festivals such as Beltane or Samhain as had been anticipated. Beltane (1 May) and Samhain or Halloween (31 October) were associated with visiting wells or carrying out other protective or healing rituals. Andrew Aiken did tell the presbytery that he had gone to Bothkennar on Beltane day to collect south running water, which he had sprinkled about the ground for the protection of his 'guids' or livestock over the next year. But he argued that this was not an unusual ritual, indicating that it was probably an accepted local practice.[68]

These special times of day or year also symbolised another device – boundaries – that accounted for 6 per cent of the motifs. Boundaries could be either physical or spiritual. A physical boundary could mark a private or domestic space such as a doorway, or a community limit such as a march stone or burn. The space within the boundary was known and safe, but beyond lay unknown, and possibly dangerous,

---

[59] NAS, JC26/26.

[60] NAS, Haddington presbytery records, CH2/185/5.

[61] NAS, Haddington presbytery records, CH2/185/5.

[62] SCA, Stirling presbytery records, CH2/722/7.

[63] SCA, Haddington kirk sessin records, CH2/799/1.

[64] *RPC*, 2nd ser., viii, p. 346.

[65] NAS, Haddington presbytery records, CH2/185/5.

[66] SCA, St Ninian's kirk session records, CH2/337/1.

[67] SCA, Stirling presbytery records, CH2/722/5.

[68] SCA, Stirling presbytery records, CH2/722/5.

territory. Rowan twigs, commonly placed above doorways, provided protection from unwelcome spirits for houses and their inhabitants. It was a march burn – water situated at the limit of the community space – that Margery Ker had been instructed to visit by Rosie Graham in order to get water to heal her cow.

On the other hand a boundary might be less temporal, such as the boundary between night and day or between different seasons. There were also boundaries between the physical world and the preternatural, or supernatural, world of fairies and other spirits. Dusk, dawn or midnight or the change from one season to another, were times of change but also vulnerability. Supernatural forces, perhaps in the form of non-corporeal spirits, were at their most powerful during these times and could cause damage to crops and animals. Early modern society may not have believed absolutely in the reality of some other world, but the possibility of its existence was undoubtedly acknowledged. The physical world, or middle-earth, was neither heaven nor hell but somewhere else. The intangible other worlds of heaven, hell and purgatory were concepts recognised by society and given legitimacy by the church. Therefore the existence of a fairy realm was possible. Like heaven and hell, the other world of fairyland, or elfane, had both tangible and intangible forms. Like heaven and hell it also usually had no exact location although its entrance or portal was known to exist. Sometimes, but not always, it was under or over a hill. This other world was also a place where time and space existed in different planes and, although it could not be seen, it was believed that the effects of the other world could be felt in this world.

VIII

A variety of animals were used in healing rituals. Cats and toads were both mentioned in Haddington and Stirling, and the use of other animals was recorded elsewhere. Martin Martin, in his account of his tour of the Western Isles during the seventeenth century, mentioned the use of girdles made of seal skin to cure sciatica.[69] Other sources refer to the use of hens and cockerels. Black cocks were often buried at the site of an epileptic's first fit or seizure so that the falling sickness, as it was termed, would be transferred to the bird.[70] The use of a live toad buried outside the threshold of an afflicted person's house or tied about the neck of sheep was likely to reflect this same belief in disease as an entity which could be transferred elsewhere or onto some other being. The use of animals in medicine was not confined to charmers. Although used in a different manner animals or, rather, animal products, were also recommended by orthodox medical practitioners. Their prescriptions included such varied ingredients as animal skin or fat and faeces or even boiled frogs.[71]

---

[69] Martin, *Description of the Western Islands*, p. 136.
[70] Beith, *Healing Threads*, p. 169.
[71] NLS, MS 548, Reverend John Landess's journal, 1660–1705.

Heat, salt and iron, well-recognised motifs associated with protection against, or removal of, spirits such as fairies or the dead, were included in 4 per cent of the rituals. Isobel Bennet from Stirling used a horseshoe to frighten the 'good neighbours' or the fairies,[72] and Andrew Aiken burned clothing worn by the sick person because the illness that he was trying to help was caused by 'an evill minde be the fairie folk [which] must be helpit be fyre'.[73] A similar understanding may have informed the practice of putting a nail on the chest of a corpse, which was done by Agnes Bennet from Pencaitland in 1651. Bennet told the kirk session that the nail would keep the spirit of her dead sister from coming back.[74] This practice suggests that if there was not a real fear of the other or spirit world, there was at least an awareness of its potential danger.

IX

The remedies offered by charmers in the seventeenth century were as varied as the treatments prescribed by orthodox medicine, but both were founded on logical principles and experience. The treatments displayed a consistency of technique, belief and participation, which show that charmers and society had a solid cultural foundation for understanding the causes of disease and the efficacy of their healing practices. Knowledge and skill in charming was both passed on through generations and gained through empiricism, but the knowledge was neither arbitrary nor chaotic. The charms were founded on both cultural and religious or spiritual traditions; their similarity with pre-Reformation practice was certainly marked although their principles and origins are likely to have been even older. This does not imply that charming was simply an alternative religious belief system recognised by a small section of the population. On the contrary most of society practised and understood an amalgamation of beliefs. It was the organised church itself, not society, which incorporated certain beliefs and rituals for its own purposes and rejected others. The pre-Reformation church accepted pleas to saints or pilgrimages to holy sites to help relieve suffering, but the Protestant church removed these elements of worship or ritual as being too Catholic in meaning. It has been suggested that the Protestant church in Scotland caused a change in attitude towards the causes and cures of disease. The church wanted sufferers to turn to the comfort of prayer and personal contemplation and responsibility, rather than using charms or magic.[75] The goal was to achieve an ideal godly state, but it is clear from the records that many of the ordinary members of the population were slower in abandoning a system which they had followed for generations and which provided comfort, hope and control. In the absence of access to professional healers and in the wider context of witchcraft belief, the practice of charming was mainstream, rather than alternative, medicine.

---

[72] NAS, JC26/26.
[73] SCA, Stirling presbytery records, CH2/722/5.
[74] NAS, Pencaitland kirk session records, CH2/296/1.
[75] Graham, *Uses of Reform*, p. 308.

Witchcraft practice in seventeenth-century Scotland was complex and mystifying, both for the ecclesiastical and secular authorities and the population at large. Charming – or folk healing – was only one aspect of witchcraft, but it was an extremely important one as it provided both spiritual and practical comfort. It provided society with a means to counter the threat of malicious witchcraft. Charming also demonstrates that contemporary definitions of witchcraft practice, in its broadest sense, were not fixed solely in demonic terms, but were at times fluid and dynamic. Indeed charming continued to be practised long after the church and the law had decided that witchcraft was no longer a threat.

7

Hunting the rich witch in Scotland: high-status witchcraft suspects and their persecutors, 1590–1650

Louise Yeoman

Alan Macfarlane's pioneering study of the witch-hunt in Essex produced a profile of the typical witch as a woman aged 50–70, poorer than her neighbours who in a climate of socio-economic change were less willing to give her alms. Her cursing when alms were refused was characterised as witchcraft.[1] This is an important insight, but it covers only one pattern of witch-hunting. Christina Larner, comparing the Scottish situation with Macfarlane's study, put Scottish witches 'slightly further up the stratification scale' than the English ones who were at 'the bottom of the heap' – and, as she also pointed out, some Scottish witches were of higher status still. The subject of high-status witchcraft suspects has received little attention. Larner identified 192 Scottish witches whose social status was known. Of these she classed 16 as nobility, 2 as lairds and 14 as burgesses. Many of these high-status people were women.[2] When witch-hunters targeted women of substantial means, what does their choice of victim tell us? Can we learn anything about the women themselves, their antagonists and the nature of witch-hunting from studying some of these cases?

High-status cases were prominent in the political witch-hunts of the fourteenth century which claimed such victims as Walter, bishop of Litchfield, Guichard, bishop of Troyes, Count Robert of Artois, and of course every Templar Philip of France could get his hands on. The main case of a high-status woman is that of Dame Alice Kytler.[3] She found herself accused of witchcraft when her younger children wanted to break a will that favoured the children of a first marriage. This theme of envy over inheritance and money will recur in this chapter as we examine propertied Scotswomen of the late sixteenth and early seventeenth century who found themselves accused of witchcraft, in a fashion which women of their class and status would not normally expect.

---

[1] A. Macfarlane, *Witchcraft in Tudor and Stuart England* (London, 1970).

[2] Larner, *Enemies of God*, pp. 89, 91.

[3] J. B. Russell, *Witchcraft in the Middle Ages* (London, 1972), pp. 189, 194.

I

Let us take Euphame MacCalzean as our first example. Her father was Thomas MacCalzean of Cliftonhall, a prominent and wealthy Edinburgh advocate. She was married to Patrick Moscrop, the son of one of her father's friends, and a man prominent enough to sit in as justice depute on a number of cases in 1590. Both families were worth thousands of scots pounds each.[4] So rich and prominent an heiress was Euphame that Patrick even agreed to take her name MacCalzean. This couple were worth a great deal of money. In the will of Patrick's mother Katherine Littill, she left them sums amounting to 3,400 merks, a lot of money in 1584. However, she left her daughter Katherine and her spouse a mere 560 merks, and who was Katherine Moscrop's spouse? David Seton, bailie of Tranent, who in 1590 initiated the North Berwick witch-hunt in his own house with the torture of his own servant Geillis Duncan. Who was one of the most prominent witches Geillis named? Euphame MacCalzean.[5]

The North Berwick hunt soon snowballed to involve spectacular accusations of treason. However, if we look away from the blinding fascination of this, then more light emerges. Most of the malefices alleged against Euphame related to her extended family. She was accused of attempting to cause the death by magic of her own and David Seton's father-in-law, the advocate John Moscrop. Her original sabbath convention was supposed to have been held for obtaining 'the wrack of David Seton and his guids'. She had allegedly tried to kill her own husband, Seton's brother-in-law, with whom her marriage had apparently never gone smoothly. She was supposed to have killed her husband's sister's son (a nephew of David Seton and Katherine Moscrop) and her uncle Henry MacCalzean's daughter Lilias.[6]

This last point is crucial, because Euphame had a property dispute with her uncle over the lands of Cliftonhall themselves.[7] His relations to his niece may have been tense for long-standing reasons. Euphame had been born illegitimate and had been legitimised by her father in 1558, thus effectively preventing Henry from snapping up her father's rich inheritance, in the way he was able to do with the unlegitimated child of another of the MacCalzean brothers, William.[8] Euphame was all that had stood between Mr Henry and a very large inheritance – and perhaps he also had his eye on her escheat, worth 5,000 merks in 1592. She had to go to court against other members of her family to protect her lands. Her son and heir had died, leaving her with three co-heiress daughters, and her attempts at matchmaking for them proved

---

[4] NAS, commissariot of Edinburgh, testament of Thomas MacCalzean, CC8/8/11, fo. 86v.; testament of John Moscrop, CC8/8/3 (6 Feb. 1601, unfoliated volume); testament of Clement Litill, CC8/8/11, fo. 365v.; C. P. Finlayson, *Clement Litill and his Library* (Edinburgh Bibliographical Society, 1980), pp. 6–7, 13. Patrick Moscrop as justice depute: personal communication from Dr Michael Wasser.

[5] Pitcairn (ed.), *Trials*, i, pp. 247–8; NAS, will of Katherine Litill, CC8/8/14, fo. 179.

[6] Pitcairn (ed.), *Trials*, i, pp. 247–8.

[7] Pitcairn (ed.), *Trials*, i, pp. 247–8.

[8] *RMS*, iv, nos. 1313, 1558; *Register of the Privy Seal of Scotland (Registrum Secreti Sigilli Regum Scotorum)*, 8 vols, eds M. Livingstone *et al.* (Edinburgh, 1908–), viii, no. 2112.

to be controversial. She was accused of bewitching Mary, the sister of royal favourite James Sandilands of Slamannan, and Mary's intended husband Joseph Douglas of Pumfraston. She had allegedly been trying to frustrate this match, and pushing one of her own daughters as a match for Pumfraston instead. It would be Sandilands who eventually obtained the escheat of her lands.[9]

The family feud aspects of this major Scottish witchcraft case are striking. David Seton's personal accusations against his sister-in-law, that she was trying to wreck his goods and gear and slay their rich father-in-law, were pregnant enough, but even stronger evidence survives. Geillis Duncan, the maidservant at the bottom of it all, the first to be interrogated under torture, 'as she would answer to her God', when about to be executed on the Castlehill of Edinburgh, swore that the deceased Euphame and her co-accused Barbara Napier were innocent, that what she had said about them was 'bot all leisings [i.e. lies]', and that she was 'caussit and persuaded by the tua David Setons in Tranent [father and son] and otheris' to make the accusations.[10] So vital was Seton's part that one can describe a major dimension of this famous case as Seton vs MacCalzean with a lot of innocent bystanders thrown in, and some very important sharks, such as Sandilands, circling the carnage, hunting for escheats.

II

Perhaps it is necessary to put the North Berwick case study in a wider context. The 1590–1 panic was not the first major panic in Scotland – there had been a large hunt in 1568–9.[11] But it was one of the very few witch-hunts in Scotland in which members of the nobility were accused, and members of the gentry were convicted and executed. There were previous cases in which high-status men and women were accused (such as the trial and execution of the Lord Lyon King-at Arms in 1568), but they are not so well documented.[12] From 1590 onwards, it is possible to get a clearer picture of the hunting of rich witches.

Convictions for witchcraft can be identified with reasonable confidence. If someone convicted of witchcraft had any money then they were escheated. Their moveable estate fell to the crown, which usually granted it (for a fee) to a royal favourite, or an official involved in the prosecution, or a member of the accused's family. These cases appear in the privy seal register of escheats. In conjunction with Larner's *Source-Book*, the register of escheats can be used to identify high-status witches. The register of escheats was interrupted for ten years in 1650 by the Cromwellian invasion, so this chapter will look at witchcraft cases involving gentlewomen between the North Berwick panic and the battle of Dunbar. During the

    [9] Pitcairn (ed.), *Trials*, i, p. 252.

    [10] NAS, justiciary court processes, 4 Dec. 1591, JC26/2/20; cf. L. Normand and G. Roberts (eds), *Witchcraft in Early Modern Scotland: James VI's Demonology and the North Berwick Witches* (Exeter, 2000), p. 198.

    [11] NAS, Airlie Muniments, GD16/25/4.

    [12] Balfour, *Historical Works*, i, p. 345.

period 1590–1600, covering the panics of 1590–1 and 1597, no gentlewomen apart from Barbara and Euphame are known to have been convicted and the only other women of social status to be escheated were two wives or relics of burgesses.[13] During the period 1622–32, covering the 1628 panic, four burgesses' wives or relics were escheated. During the period 1640–50, covering the small panic of 1643–4 and the large one of 1649–50, again there were four burgesses' wives escheated. After 1600, therefore, no gentlewomen were escheated.[14] So Larner's assertion that high-status witchcraft accusations were rare can be confirmed and amplified: accusations were rare, and convictions in this period non-existent.[15]

Reasonably comprehensive information can also be gathered on accusations against high-status women that did *not* lead to convictions. It is unlikely that there were any unknown trials and acquittals, because the court case itself would have received enough contemporary attention. But accusing a high-status person of any crime was a risky action and it is likely that some accusations were rapidly dropped, leaving no traces in the written record. Yet any accusation against a member of the elite that was pursued seriously enough *would* leave a good deal of documentation, even if it was dropped before it came to court. The suspect might well succeed in complaining to the privy council, or a contemporary chronicler might note the case. Most of the remainder of this chapter will be concerned with four accusations of this kind – the only ones that are known for the first half of the seventeenth century.[16] Helen Arnot, Lady Manderston, and Jean Home, Lady Samuelston, were both accused by Arnot's husband, George Home of Manderston, in 1629–30; Marie Cunningham, relict of John Erskine of Chapelland, was accused by James Kennoway, burgh clerk of Culross, in 1644; and Margaret Henderson, Lady Pittadro, was accused by Walter Bruce, minister of Inverkeithing, in 1649.

Apart from these cases, the escheats yield no women above the burgess class convicted of witchcraft. It is highly likely that the burgess cases follow similar dynamics to those of their social superiors which are explored below. Bob Scribner touches on this phenomenon in cases such as that of Ursula Fladin, wife of a linen weaver, pointing out how it revealed 'a complex power game being fought out within a community around an accusation of sorcery'. Witches of greater than marginal status had property and families with reputations to uphold. Such women and such families were willing to fight their accusers and they often succeeded. Scribner dealing with women similar to the burgess-class accused of the Scottish escheats notes

---

[13] NAS, privy seal, PS1/61–70; privy seal minute book, PS6/3; Larner *et al.*, *Source-Book*. Before 1590, not only is there generally less documentation on the background to witchcraft trials, but the privy seal minute books do not generally identify witchcraft cases, so comprehensive information on convictions is harder to gather.

[14] NAS, privy seal, PS1/112–16; privy seal minute book, PS6/4.

[15] Larner, *Enemies of God*, p. 89.

[16] The Erskine of Dun poisoning case is omitted. The sisters Helen, Isobel and Annas Erskine were accused of consulting a witch, not of being witches. The primary accusation against them was of being art and part to murder. Pitcairn (ed.), *Trials*, iii, pp. 267–9.

that 'the accusation of witchcraft was introduced at a late stage as part of a judicial contest and did not always compel assent on the part of the authorities'.[17] This pattern bears interesting similarities to the cases explored below, where pre-existing feuds between non-marginal individuals in a community issued into witch accusations but rarely succeeded in convincing a court to convict.

When we look at the higher-status Scottish cases, a pattern starts to emerge. In the majority of cases the women were mothers of sole female heiresses. In two cases the women themselves were sole heiresses. In the cases of Lady Manderston and Lady Pittadro these were well dowered women with tochers of thousands of merks. Perhaps, as Carol Karlsen's research on New England indicates, tensions over female inheritance could lead to witchcraft accusations. This may be for the reasons that Karlsen indicates – that propertied women were functioning in a male sphere and excited male envy. This would explain the accusations against those who were themselves heiresses. However, as Karlsen also notes, mothers of heiresses were also accused. All these women were 'aberrations in a society with an inheritance system designed to keep property in the hands of men'. There were many female heiresses and mothers of heiresses in Scotland, yet only a very few of them were ever pursued this way. What made one heiress more likely to be accused than another? Karlsen suggests that the major determining factors were 'disagreeable personalities' and the way in which the women's behaviour was understood socially.[18] Some of the answer, however, may lie with the witch-hunters as much as with the women themselves. Witch-hunters too may be constructing their own social and psychological dramas.

Karlsen has suggested that 'to presume that in lodging their complaints accusers exploited the witchcraft belief system for sinister ends overlooks the enormous power of religious convictions and cultural ideology to shape social behaviour'.[19] She points out that witchcraft was one of several explanatory systems for natural and social misfortunes. However, given that 'witchcraft beliefs constituted one of *several* explanatory systems' (italics mine), then the question arises: why did the witch-hunters choose this particular explanation in preference to others such as providence or ill-fortune? The case of Isobel Young in Dunbar, tried for witchcraft in 1629, shows how other explanations could be found for the misfortunes which were often attributed to witchcraft. Isobel's defence counsel offered all sorts of explanations for the misfortunes which her alleged victims had suffered: commonsense reasons, medical reasons, moral reasons and providential reasons; why mills failed to work; how people died of 'hydropsie' or froze to death; why people failed in business because they were 'deboschit'; why cursing was not cursing but merely the natural behaviour of an 'irritat and choleric woman'; and even that the

---

[17] R. Scribner, 'Witchcraft and judgement in Reformation Germany', *History Today*, 40:4 (April 1990), 12–19, at p. 15.

[18] C. Karlsen, *The Devil in the Shape of a Woman* (New York, 1987), pp. 83, 101, 117.

[19] Karlsen, *The Devil in the Shape of a Woman*, p. 133.

decay of someone's estate might have been occasioned by 'the secret judgement of God, for it is notourlie knawn that he tuk upone him to be father to ane barne gotten by his awin father in adulterie'. Perhaps the best explanation was that someone's face had broken out because she had drunk 'the pourings of ane auld ail barrel'.[20]

Whilst this might simply be a good lawyer finding reason after reason why his client was innocent, his explanations had to have at least a veneer of plausibility and they show the diversity of explanations available to an early modern Scot confronted with a disaster. Even more interesting were the responses of some of the witnesses. When asked to give their oaths as to whether Isobel had caused their misfortunes by her witchcraft, several witnesses refused this explanation. Some said that they simply did not know or would not take it upon their souls that she caused their losses, but at least one directly invoked providence. Cuthbert Simson said of his 'misthryving' and financial losses which reduced him to poverty that he 'taks the samyn fra God for his sins'.[21] Isobel was cleared of a number of the charges but was found guilty of others – but even here only by a 'plurality of vottis', so the explanations of her lawyer may well have had some effect.[22] This case gives an example of how other explanations were available for misfortune. It was not always necessary to find a witch to blame things on.

III

One of the main mechanisms allowing wealthy women to be accused of witchcraft was a pre-existing feud with someone who had privileged access to confessing witches. These cases differ from the New England ones examined by Karlsen. These Scotswomen not only had enemies, but they had the bad luck to have enemies who could wield influence in the key initial stages of a witch-hunt.

The definition of the witch-hunter needs to be clarified here. It does not include the many Scots gentlemen who dutifully took commissions to investigate witchcraft cases in the same way that they took commissions to investigate slaughter, broken men and theft – 'our justices in that part' as the privy council commissions call them. It focuses on those among them, and among their necessary apparatus of bailies, clerks and ministers, who had actively promoted the initial phase of the witch-hunt. This was the local agitation which first led to depositions being presented to the privy council asking for a commission to be appointed with powers to prosecute, condemn and execute a witch. These were the local men whose credibility was enough to turn gossip into action, and to direct the action in the way that they chose.

The initial stage, when the witch was arrested, was vital, because this was when the witch was 'watched' and her confession extracted. Stuart Macdonald's recent

---

[20] NAS, books of adjournal, JC2/6, fos. 265–70.
[21] NAS, books of adjournal, JC2/6, fo. 275v.
[22] NAS, books of adjournal, JC2/6, fo. 276v.

study of the Fife witch-hunt indicates that when the crucial step of isolating and 'watching' the witch could not be taken due to lack of will-power or resources, then acquittal almost automatically followed.[23] By contrast, if that step *was* taken, then an influential man on the spot was in an ideal position to direct the interrogation in the direction he wanted it to go – to get the initial witch to name the names that came to his mind.

Let us examine four men who had feuds with accused women and who participated in these vital early stages. They were a laird, a bailie, a clerk of local courts and a minister. We have already met Bailie David Seton, and to him we can add George Home of Manderston, James Kennoway, clerk to the regality courts of Kincardine and formerly burgh clerk of Culross, and (briefly) Mr Walter Bruce, minister of Inverkeithing. Accused witches are often supposed to have been quarrelsome people – but were the most active witch-hunters quarrelsome people too? Let us look at the nature of some of these quarrels.

Helen Arnot, the daughter of Sir John Arnot of Birswick, lord provost of Edinburgh, was at first glance a strange target for a witchcraft accusation. She was a powerfully-connected godly lady of some repute, the daughter of a remarkably rich man, worth over £20,000 at his death.[24] She had however been unlucky in her marriage to George Home of Manderston. In 1620 she had been forced to obtain a decreet of adherence against her husband.[25] Manderston's ill-treatment of his wife may have had something to do with the fact that her fabulously rich father had left him absolutely nothing in his will in 1616. Manderston indeed was his principal debtor, owing the old man the enormous sum of 14,000 merks.[26] In December 1629 things got worse. A confessing warlock, Alexander Hamilton, accused Lady Manderston of having tried to murder her husband by witchcraft. And this was a confessing warlock who happened to have been detected by Manderston's exertions.[27]

Manderston had also been involved in irregularities in the taking down of Hamilton's deposition. He had spoken to the prisoner whilst he was in the process of having his deposition taken. The information concerning this conference emerged about a month later in January 1630 from James Mowat, the writer of Hamilton's deposition. Mowat had previously perjured himself before the privy council whilst trying to accuse someone else of writing the deposition which accused Lady Manderston. He said he had 'forgadderit' with Home to tell him that Alexander Hamilton had spoken things 'concerning him'. Home rewarded him for

[23] S. Macdonald, 'Threats to a Godly Society: The Witch-Hunt in Fife, Scotland, 1560–1710' (Ph.D. thesis, University of Guelph, 1997). Cf. S. Macdonald, *The Witches of Fife: Witch-Hunting in a Scottish Shire, 1560–1710* (East Linton, 2001, forthcoming).

[24] NAS, commissariot of Edinburgh, 20 Jan. 1616, testament of Sir John Arnot of Birswick, CC8/8/49.

[25] J. B. Paul (ed.), *The Scots Peerage*, 9 vols (Edinburgh, 1904–14), ix, p. 72; *SJC*, i, p. 147.

[26] NAS, commissariot of Edinburgh, 20 Jan. 1616, testament of Sir John Arnot of Birswick, CC8/8/49.

[27] *RPC*, 2nd ser., iii, p. 397; *SJC*, i, p. 147.

this information with money. Another notary, Patrick Abernethy, told how he had been sent to fetch ale and had come back to see 'James Mowatt writing and Hamilton's lips going'.[28] So Mowat took the deposition alone with the prisoner after speaking with Home of Manderston and taking money from him. The result was the accusation of Manderston's wife, Helen Arnot. In June 1630, after the witchcraft accusations, their relationship had deteriorated to the point where the council felt it necessary to force Manderston to give an obligation under pain of £1,000 to Helen, 'her men, tenants and servants', that he would not molest or harm them.[29] In the same month his wife was suing him to recover her conjunct-fee lands and he was ordered to produce writs which he was withholding from her. By November there were divorce proceedings.[30]

This does not exactly cast Manderston in the role of husband protecting his wife from witchcraft charges which is generously assigned to him by the editor of the relevant privy council volume.[31] Probably what happened was that Manderston arranged to get his wife incriminated – and then incurred the wrath of her powerful relatives. So he recanted and aided her defence, leading to the case being dropped.[32] Hamilton the warlock denied all knowledge and said that he had got the information from John Neill in Tweedmouth – another warlock produced by Manderston's investigations.[33]

When John Neill was taken in for questioning he accused another of Manderston's female relatives: his cousin Janet Home, Lady Samuelston, heiress and only daughter of his uncle, William Home of Whitlaw.[34] A high-powered commission was established to look into her alleged witchcraft, including the lord advocate, the clerk register and the bishop of Dunblane – and it exonerated her.[35] Had something happened between Janet and Manderston which might have led to him prompting John Neill to make that accusation?

Janet later (in 1631) told a very interesting tale to the privy council about her cousin's behaviour. The events which she spoke of happened 'about a year ago, before her marriage' (i.e. at the beginning of 1630). She was influenced by Manderston to make an assignation to his son of a tack of teinds upon condition that the assignation should be kept by herself undelivered, but Manderston came to her house in Berwick and in her absence meddled with the said tack so that she was disappointed of her rent and all means to settle her accounts. She craved the council's protection for herself and her husband. If Janet's account is true, then her cousin had been swindling her out of money at the time before her marriage when she had no husband to protect her from his activities. This financial deceit happened at the

[28] *RPC*, 2nd ser., iii, p. 398.
[29] *RPC*, 2nd ser., iii, p. 582.
[30] *RPC*, 2nd ser., iii, pp. 560, 578, 554.
[31] *RPC*, 2nd ser., iv, pp. xli–ii.
[32] *RPC*, 2nd ser., iii, pp. 361, 378, 397–400.
[33] *RPC*, 2nd ser., iii, p. 443.
[34] Paul (ed.), *Scots Peerage*, iii, p. 285; *RPC*, 2nd ser., iii, 563.
[35] *RPC*, 2nd ser., iii, pp. xli–xlii.

same time as Manderston developed his enthusiasm for witch-hunting. Perhaps the witchcraft accusation was designed to help undermine Janet's credibility as a witness in any potential legal case against Manderston. Or perhaps Manderston had a guilty conscience which led him to believe that those he had wronged were revenging themselves on him by witchcraft.

One clue might lie in Manderston's attitude to his indebtedness. He was so deeply in debt that he had to punctuate his witch-hunting with repeated requests to the privy council for protection from his creditors so that he could continue his investigations – an exceptional plea but an effective one which allowed to him to escape arrest by his creditors over an entire year. He very likely had other enemies and financial problems too. He explained at one point to the council that 'he hes other actions before the lords of session'. In one of his supplications to the council for protection from arrest for debt, he complained of some of his creditors who were specially known to be his 'malitious unfriends' and accused them of being accomplices with John Neill the warlock, so that the matter was one 'concerning not only his life and estate but the glory of God and the King's pleasure'.[36] Manderston was not only indebted but trying to tar his creditors with the brush of witchcraft. Whilst large debts were a common feature of seventeenth-century Scottish life, accusing your creditors of witchcraft was not. Manderston's indebtedness somehow became more than a personal matter. It was also a public matter concerning the 'the glory of God and the King's pleasure'.

Manderston thus comes across as a self-important, quarrelsome figure with bad relations to his peers. His debts had become not only a matter of personal survival, but a matter for the supernatural. He showed little sign of awareness that his problems might have something to do with his own financial management. A providential explanation would have necessitated his repentance to God for the sins which had brought this affliction upon him. Witchcraft by contrast allowed him to blame his problems on others. Furthermore it allowed him to present himself not as a wretched sinner who deserved what he got but as a saviour of those around him – the protector of society from the scourge of witchcraft. Perhaps the key to his use of witchcraft as an explanation for his debts was an unwillingness to take responsibility for his own unhappy circumstances.

Let us return for a moment to our original witch-hunter: David Seton, nemesis of Euphame MacCalzean. We have already discussed Euphame's more advantageous financial position, but the accusations which Seton's witch-hunting generated reveal that he not only had feuds with Euphame and the schoolmaster John Fian but also with a much more important man, his equal and rival in the local elite: John Cockburn in Woodheid. Donald Robeson confessed that 'John Cockburn commanded him to work the destruction of Seton's goods and gear and promised him 50 punds for the doing of it'.[37] Less than two years afterwards, Seton killed Cockburn

---

[36] *RPC*, 2nd ser., iii, pp. 554, 677.
[37] NAS, justiciary processes, JC26/2/19.

and was escheated (29 June 1593). He was escheated a second time for an unpaid debt the next month.[38]

Seton, then, was quarrelsome, indebted and obsessed with the idea that people were trying to 'wrak his goods and gear'. His financial losses, like Manderston's, were being caused by a demonic agency. Seton, too, showed himself to be unusually vigilant and active in the matter of witch-hunting – serving the public and protecting his masters Lord Seton and the king. In the arguments against jurors to sit on the case of Barbara Napier, Seton was described in the objections to his brother sitting upon the assize as having 'instructed thame quha ar to be usit as witnesses' and as being 'the principall informer of the witches, inventar of thair persuit, bringer in of the witches, suborner, luiker for ane reward'.[39] He and Manderston sound similar in their quarrelsomeness and indebtedness, and in their zealous pursuit of witches as an answer to their problems. Again there was a touch of grandiosity here – what was good for Seton and Manderston was to them a matter of the public good. Their enemies were the enemies of the commonweal.[40]

IV

The pattern becomes clearer when we look at another high-profile witchcraft case. Marie Cunningham, the elderly widow of John Erskine of Chapelland, was the mother of three co-heiresses, one of whom, Janet, was accused with her in Culross in 1644.[41] She complained that her persecution was due solely to the 'haitrent' of James Kennoway, writer to the signet and clerk of the town.[42] Like Barbara and Euphame she was able to avail herself of excellent legal counsel with the result that her case had to be referred to the lord advocate. A local court which attempted to try her on a privy council commission found itself embarrassed by the arguments of her counsel Mr David Williamson, 'quhilks could not be answered by the procurator fiscall who had no skill of law'. The court also felt unable to try her because of the 'contingencie of manie of the judges to the said Marie', so the case was moved to the higher court where unfortunately no further records survive for the case.[43] High-profile cases sometimes became too hot to handle locally because tensions

---

[38] NAS, privy seal, PS1/65, fos. 171v., 197.

[39] NAS, justiciary processes, JC6/3, May 1591. The description comes after a return to discussing the Seton case for which John Seton was desired to be barred from the assize.

[40] The lower-status North Berwick witches to whom Seton had access confessed that he was the victim of a special convention held for the 'wrak of his goods and gear' at Foulstruther. The other victims for whom special conventions were held were of exalted status: Lady Jean Kennedy, the earl of Angus and the king himself. Seton may implicitly have been claiming such status in everyday life. Normand and Roberts (eds), *Witchcraft in Early Modern Scotland*, pp. 148–9.

[41] Her daughters were Janet, Marie, Margaret, Catherine, Christian and Magdalene and niece Anna Gordon: *RMS*, ix, no. 866; *RPC*, 2nd ser., viii, p. 37.

[42] *RPC*, 2nd ser., viii, pp. 37–9.

[43] *RPC*, 2nd ser., viii, p. 37.

were roused and many of those called upon to try the accused were closely connected by blood and other ties.[44]

In this case we know more about James Kennoway, the witch-hunter, than we
do about Marie Cunningham. We do not know precisely why he picked on her
but as she had the money to hire a top Edinburgh lawyer, then she certainly must
have had an escheat worth having, if nothing else. Kennoway had close business
connections with influential members of the local elite, notably Edward Bruce, earl
of Kincardine, whose bailie he seems to have been.[45] His excellent connections,
however, were not enough to save him from being imprisoned for debt for five
years as the result of an extended wrangle over the debts of one of his fellow-
burgesses Alexander Blaw, in a case concerning a ship called the *John* of Culross.[46]
The complicated legal wrangle dragged on even after Kennoway's death.

In the meantime, released from the tolbooth of Edinburgh, Kennoway returned
to witch-hunting. In 1662 and 1666 he was involved in the processes against
eighteen witches in Culross and Torryburn.[47] His correspondence reveals an
intense wrangle concerning the 1666 witch-hunt: his attempt to deprive the family
of Agnes Brown, one of the witches, of her estate. In particular, this meant the
500–merk dwelling house in Bilbow which she had formerly occupied.[48] The other
witches executed in the hunt were too poor to warrant his attention as they had
only 'kirk alms' to exist on and left only 'their own brats of clothes and some
sundrie trashie plenisching in their housis'.[49] Agnes was Kennoway's only hope of
recouping some of his expenses for his involvement in the hunt. There is no
evidence of a pre-existing feud in this case, but Kennoway's description of her as a
'bastard gotten in adulterie', combined with her wealth, perhaps explains why she
was targeted in the first place.[50]

The contest with her relatives opens a window into Kennoway's character. He
lamented and itemised in cash his expenditure of time, money and effort 'exhorting'
witches to confess, organising for them to be watched and writing their depositions.
Helping with the execution of seven witches had been a time-consuming and

---

[44] Margaret Wallace, NAS, privy seal, PS1/94, fo. 13r., was tried in Edinburgh not her native Glasgow.
Lady Pittadro was moved to Edinburgh, not tried in her native Inverkeithing, presumably for similar
reasons. She would have been closely related to her judges – see below. Being tried in the higher court
gave a better chance of acquittal. On one occasion a case was deliberately tried in a lower court with a
sympathetic lord of regality. 'The trial of Geillis Johnston for witchcraft, 1614', eds M. Wasser and L. A.
Yeoman, *SHS Miscellany*, xiii (forthcoming).

[45] He bought out Kincardine's part ownership of a ship: NAS, Johnston of Sands, GD300/36. Kennoway's notebook, 1667, mentions sums of money collected from Kincardine's courts: NAS, Bruce of
Kinross, GD29/1434.

[46] NAS, decreet of admiralty court, 1 Feb. 1649, Johnston of Sands, GD300/36; other related documents, GD300/88. NAS, Kennoway to his son, 28 June 1660, Bruce of Kinross, GD29/1957/1; same to
same, 8 Aug. 1660, GD29/1957/5.

[47] NAS, Bruce of Kinross, GD29/1957/22.

[48] NAS, Bruce of Kinross, GD29/1957/17.

[49] NAS, Bruce of Kinross, GD29/1957/10, GD29/1957/17.

[50] NAS, Bruce of Kinross, GD29/1957/23.

expensive business.[51] He passionately believed that he deserved the escheat more than her family. Consequently he was prepared to attempt to discredit her relatives to the earl of Kincardine. He enlisted his son, a servant to Sir William Bruce of Balcaskie, to speak to the earl and to obtain the escheat.[52] He described himself in his petition to Kincardine as 'being confident that your Lordship would rather allow him who is your servant and clerk to persew that benefit' as opposed to Agnes Brown's heir 'that cumbersome fellow in Dunfermling called Mores who hes been often fashing and trubling your lordship'.[53] He spent several letters over the space of two years going over this to his son, busily instructing him how to obtain the escheat. Among other things he warned his son to pretend that the escheat was worth half of its real value and to do everything as privately as possible.[54] The Kennoways obtained the escheat in 1666 but had to fight to hold on to it against Agnes's heirs.[55] Kennoway senior emerges from his letters as a self-righteous, quarrelsome man who was as quick to damn his enemies as any scolding witch. What shines through is his strong, almost grandiose sense of entitlement to someone else's inheritance and the aggressive and devious methods he employed.

Kennoway's writings also provide a fascinating glimpse into his own concept of the sacredness of magistracy. On 28 June 1660, overjoyed by the Restoration and hoping to get out of jail, Kennoway wrote to his son. He discoursed about his son's duties to his master and lady (Sir William Bruce of Balcaskie and his wife): 'not to serve them in a carnall fear bot in love proceeding from the fear of God'. He himself was in jail 'due to the powar of Satan and malice of man' but confident that 'God shall revenge all my grief and grudge and all the injurie and oppression that I have suffered'. He went on to wish that there

> shall not be a memorial of any member of that wicked commonwealth who baselie betrayed and with bloodie hands murdered, murdered the sacred person of the Lord's anoynted, their supreme sovereign lord and master King Charles the first and who so cruelly and mercilessly with hellish hatred persecuted thir ten years bygan the sacred person of the Lord's anoynted our present gracious and sacred sovereign King Charles the second whom God hath in his mercy after a wonderfull manner established upon the throne of his father.

Kennoway then moved into an even more elevated rhetorical and poetical strain in writing of Charles II:

> As he is now called Charles the great it shalbe, before the end of sixty thrie that greater three times he shalbe. God increase his graces in his royall heart for I am sure he is highly beloved of the Lord God, for the King put not his trust in chariots nor horses nor in the arms of fleshe bot his sacred majestie did stronglie trust in the living God

---

51 NAS, Bruce of Kinross, GD29/1957/17.

52 NAS, Bruce of Kinross, GD29/1957/10, GD29/1957/25.

53 NAS, Bruce of Kinross, GD29/1957/16–17; Kennoway's petition, 9 Mar. 1668, GD29/1957/39.

54 NAS, Bruce of Kinross, GD29/1957/16–20, GD29/1958/30–1.

55 NAS, privy seal, English register, escheat of Agnes Brown indweller in Torry granted to James Kennoway servitor to Sir William Bruce of Balcaskie, Nov. 1666, PS2/3, fo. 29.

his maker and saviour. O gratious and sacred sovereign Jehovah Jirie is thy God and wer and ay shal be, thou hast made him thy resting cod, Jehovah jirie is thy God and wes and ay shal be.[56]

Kennoway was certainly a believer in the sacred nature of magistracy and this may tie in to Stuart Clark's suggestion that successfully arresting witches demonstrated the divine protection and sanctity of the magistrate's office through his inviolability to witches. This point was dwelt on at length by James VI and I in his *Daemonologie*.[57] Such beliefs may have been a godsend to unstable, debt-ridden or ill-famed magistrates, like Manderston, Kennoway and Seton. Successfully arresting witches would demonstrate that God approved of them and protected them, even if no-one else did. Manderston and Seton cast themselves as protecting other magistrates as well as themselves: detecting witches for the 'glory of God and the King's pleasure' or to protect Lord Seton and the king. Kennoway expressed exaggerated deference to sacred royal paternal authority and a conviction that the 'powar of Satan' was implicated in his personal troubles. Hunting the witches, the 'bad mothers', protected the fathers – the founts of sacred authority, the very founts from which Seton and co. derived their authority.

V

Our final case comes from Fife in 1649. Margaret Henderson, Lady Pittadro, must have been the highest-status victim of all, with the possible exception of Euphame. She was a sister of Henderson of Fordell, a prominent local laird, and had a clutch of sisters married into the most prominent neighbouring families.[58] She herself came to her husband William Echline of Pittadro with a tocher of 4,000 merks and a marriage contract signed by the earl of Mar, no less, when she was married in 1597.[59] None the less, the marriage was unfortunate, Echline ran up huge debts and had lost his lands for debt by 1615.[60] By 1623 he was dead and his son and heir Henry was fighting as a soldier in Flanders: the last trace which records show of him. The mention was in a sasine purchasing land for her daughter Grizell, his sister.[61]

The issue of female inheritance thus surfaces again. And twenty-six years later, in 1649, Henry and Grizell's mother Margaret found herself accused of witchcraft by the minister of Inverkeithing, Walter Bruce. He was the son of Bruce of Kincavil, a member of the same landed elite as herself. Bruce was the key figure in a virulent witch-hunt that broke out in Inverkeithing in 1649. A confessing witch deponed

[56] NAS, Bruce of Kinross, GD29/1957/1.

[57] S. Clark, 'King James's *Daemonologie*: witchcraft and kingship', in S. Anglo (ed.), *The Damned Art: Essays in the Literature of Witchcraft* (London, 1977).

[58] NAS, Henderson of Fordell, GD172/237, her marriage contract.

[59] NAS, Henderson of Fordell, GD172/237, GD172/1464, discharge by Margaret and her sisters, Euphame, Elspeth and Barbara.

[60] NAS, register of sasines, RS31/17, fo. 321r., sasine to Euphame Dickson.

[61] NAS, Henderson of Fordell, GD172/114, sasine to Grizel Echline.

before him that Lady Pittadro had raised the Devil 'that she might complain to the Devil upon Mr Walter Bruce for buying of the house whilk he is in and whilk she would haiff had to her good son and that the said Lady Pittadro was the cause of all his trouble'.[62] So he had trumped Lady Pittadro in buying a house which she wanted for her son-in-law and presumably her daughter too.

So what was Walter Bruce's trouble? In 1650, just after the witch-hunting panic of 1649, he was deposed by the presbytery of Dunfermline for 'gross neglects of the special duties of his ministry'. He was also part-owner of a ship – commercial activity unbecoming to a minister. He was 'indiscreet in his language in sermons', saying that 'the spirit of godliness in thir times was ane salt humour arysing fra the melt, trubling the stomach and ascending to the head whilk made a cracking of the brain'.[63]

Whatever he was neglecting it was not hunting witches, because in July 1649 he had had at least twenty-three accused – among them the wives of the magistrates of Inverkeithing, whom, according to his complaint to the estates of parliament, 'the magistrates refused to apprehend'.[64] By applying to parliament, Bruce succeeded in getting a commission to those members of the burgh who evidently supported his views that their fellow burgesses were married to witches, an action which cannot have failed to split the small burgh down the middle. No doubt this contributed to the readiness of his parishioners to complain about him to the presbytery, and we need to see the accusations against him in the light of that.

Bruce was not a convinced covenanter; he conformed to episcopacy at the Restoration. But he was clearly a convinced witch-hunter. There are no obvious signs that Bruce was in debt, but his commercial activities were regarded as a scandal in a man of the cloth. There may have been debts which we do not know about in the absence of the burgh records. He was deposed, but his most prominent victim, Lady Pittadro, died of natural causes or committed suicide in the tolbooth of Edinburgh where she had been transferred to await trial.[65]

VI

The kind of witch-hunters who pursued their social equals are an enlightening group. Of the four men discussed in this chapter, all were of a quarrelsome disposition. Three had heavy debt or business problems, while the fourth was carrying out illicit commercial activity from which his profession should have barred him. Two were closely related to their victims by blood or marriage, and all four seem to have been particularly zealous. The accusations all came in panic years – 1590, 1629–30, 1644, 1649 – and in such years women were accused who did not fit the usual suspect profile for a witch.[66] A handful of unusual cases hardly makes a satisfying

---

[62] NAS, justiciary court processes, JC26/13/5, bundle B.

[63] H. Scott (ed.), *Fasti Ecclesiae Scoticanae*, 7 vols (2nd edn, Edinburgh, 1915–), v, p. 43.

[64] NAS, justiciary court processes, JC26/13/5, bundle B; *APS*, vi, II, p. 510.

[65] Balfour, *Historical Works*, iii, pp. 43–7.

[66] Karlsen, *The Devil in the Shape of a Woman*, p. 6.

sample, and indicates an area where there may be more work to be done. Still, let us attempt some hypotheses.

We may be looking at the personality profile of a certain type of witch-hunter: quarrelsome, indebted men of some status who did not wish to take responsibility for their own misfortunes. They perhaps felt the need to prove themselves to higher authority in order to compensate for and to cancel out their own personality flaws. These men felt that their enemies must also be public enemies. When they came into conflicts with their female peers such men might be quicker than others to label them witches. Men had few ways of getting rid of female social equals who were not their own wives; violence against other people's women was very much disapproved of and punished. A long-running conflict with a woman, on whom her foe was in no position to take revenge, might rankle for years before finally, under the right circumstances, generating witchcraft accusations.

Perhaps echoing Lyndal Roper here, these men were in a way setting up their own personal dramas or fantasies with them at the centre. Roper argues that 'the fantasy of witch-hood is created in a project of collaboration between the questioner and accused', and that the whole dramatic process of interrogation and confession could provide a 'theatrical opportunity' for the accused to recount and restage emotional conflicts from her life.[67] Witch-hunting too could set up a drama, with the zealous witch-hunter at the centre of the universe saving his community from the forces of ultimate evil. Just as a witch had to 'select' the elements which made up her confession, so the witch-hunter had first of all to select witchcraft as the explanation for his troubles (in preference to other available explanations) and then to select the questions which he asked confessing witches, the names which he mentioned to them and the troubles for which he blamed them. It is also possible that witch-hunters were playing out conflicts in their lives – creating their own narratives either in collaboration with others or in their own correspondence. So David Seton rose from obscure small-town magistrate to the hero of *Newes from Scotland*. So George Home of Manderston, erring husband and hopeless debtor, obtained a glowing testimonial from Charles I. And so James Kennoway was able to rationalise his sense of entitlement to the house of Agnes Brown.[68]

Modern super-hero movies and computer games offer ordinary people a chance to 'save the universe' against enemies with unnatural powers. In a society which believed that supernatural beings could actually give human beings special powers for evil, witch-hunters had a chance to play out this fantasy for real. Only they could preserve the kingdom, or their home town, from Satanic attack. Through witchcraft accusations, half-fantasised, half-based on real slights, they could actually for a moment hold the centre stage which they thought they deserved and which their ineptitude or anti-social behaviour usually denied them.

[67] L. Roper, *Oedipus and the Devil: Witchcraft, Sexuality and Religion in Early Modern Europe* (London, 1994), pp. 227, 230–1.

[68] Pitcairn (ed.), *Trials*, i, p. 247; *RPC*, 2nd ser., iii, p. 381; NAS, Bruce of Kinross, GD29/1957/16–20.

In a situation where most people in the community are fearful or uneasy, due to storms, famine, war or change of government, then the paranoid member of the community can suddenly start to look like a true prophet. Maybe everyone *is* out to get them – especially witches. Working his way up to his prey, by starting on lower-class women who could be forced to incriminate her, a zealous witch-hunter could secure proof that his own hated female foe was actually a witch. In doing so, he could imagine himself reaping the applause and admiration of a grateful community who would finally recognise his true worth and her wickedness – a very satisfactory drama. In the course of a witch-hunting panic he would leap from Clark Kent to Superman.

But then the bubble would burst. A characteristic of a panic is that it burns itself out as less and less credible accusations are made – taking the credibility of the accusers with it. Probably, judging by their troubled careers, they then fell back into greater ignominy than they had been in before. Of the seven high-status women who were accused, only two were successfully convicted and executed, and none after 1600. On the whole, they were protected by status, connections and the wealth to hire good lawyers. Assizes and commissions were reluctant to proceed against them. Witchcraft came to be seen as a lower-class crime in a way that it had not been in the Middle Ages.

So if the hunting of these rich witches was the last resort of a paranoid scoundrel, it was not a particularly successful one. It is a measure of the powerful forces driving the witch-hunters that they made their accusations in the teeth of the odds against success. This perhaps lends weight to Karlsen's contention that such witch-hunting was not merely a cynical ploy, that the protagonists genuinely did believe, for culturally-determined reasons, that their female foes were assuredly witches. It would explain why they took the gamble of making accusations that were so unlikely to succeed. It tells us a great deal about them and how they played out their inner uncertainties on a public stage.

8

Witch-hunting
and the Scottish state

Julian Goodare

Haveing issued furth a comissioun to yow against certane persons accused of the cryme of witchcraft, and being desireous that thair tryell may not be informall but upon sume well grounded evidentes, wee thought fitt heirby to recommend to your speciall care that, notwithstanding any confessiouns emitted by the parties befor the ecclesiasticall judge, you would appoint tuo or on[e] at least of your number to repare to the parties with some of the ministers befor whom they formerly confest, and cause them renew thair confessioun in thair presence.

Earl of Loudoun, chancellor, 12 April 1650.[1]

God Allmighti send a gud tryell of all the wichtis, and send them a hotte fyre to burne them with.

Countess of Eglinton, 8 May 1650.[2]

Witch-hunting was an affair of state, and it could preoccupy the highest in the land. In April 1650, the chancellor of Scotland took time off from dealing with anti-covenanting uprisings, delicate negotiations with the exiled Charles II and deteriorating relations with Cromwell, to write a long letter to some local commissioners who were about to try three Berwickshire witches. One of Scotland's five great witchcraft panics, that of 1649, was dying away; Loudoun realised that its 350-odd accusations and trials had not all reached a high standard of judicial impartiality. In urging that the forthcoming trial 'may not be informall but upon sume well grounded evidentes' he hoped to prevent further miscarriages of justice. But not everyone shared his concern. The countess of Eglinton, consumed by righteous zeal, felt that a 'gud tryell' for witchcraft could have only one outcome: execution.

In their different ways, both these quotations show us a witch-hunt orchestrated, or at least supervised, at a very high level. This will not surprise readers of Christina Larner, whose work remains the essential starting-point for an understanding of the

[1] John, earl of Loudoun, chancellor of Scotland, to George Home of Kimergem and others, 12 April 1650, HMC, *Fourteenth Report, Appendix, Part III* (London, 1894), pp. 109–10.
[2] Mary, countess of Eglinton, to Alexander, earl of Eglinton, 8 May 1650, W. Fraser, *Memorials of the Montgomeries, Earls of Eglinton*, 2 vols (Edinburgh, 1859), i, p. 296.

Scottish witch-hunt. Although she was well aware of local and community concerns about witchcraft, and indeed devoted more of her book to community perspectives than to any other single topic, Larner took an ultimately top-down, social-control view of witch-hunting. Much recent research on witch-hunting elsewhere in Europe, however, takes a bottom-up view, stressing the local angle, and the pressure for prosecution from the witches' neighbours. Some of this work has explicitly taken issue with Larner's interpretation.[3] Yet the Scottish witch-hunt occurred in a period when the state was developing rapidly and seeking to exert its authority, and when that state's claim to godly legitimacy was particularly prominent. Can such a state still have a role in witch-hunting?

I

The governmental institutions responsible for witch-hunting were those of the criminal justice system. The general procedure for prosecution of crimes can be divided into five stages. The first stage was the occurrence of an unsanctioned and deviant act, the recognition that this act should be classed as a crime, and the identification of a suspect. With witchcraft, this first stage was usually more interesting, and certainly more complicated, than with other capital crimes like murder – so much so that a great deal of what has been written on witch-hunting has been about what witchcraft was thought to be and how witches were identified and labelled. For the present purposes, however, we need to concentrate on the other stages.

In the second stage, the community would decide that justice required the suspect to receive a criminal trial. This decision would be focused on, and probably led by, an aggrieved individual, such as a surviving relative in murder cases. It was conventional for the victim of a crime to act as the prosecutor in court. Off he would go, therefore, to the nearest court with jurisdiction over the crime concerned, to make his complaint and demand a trial.

The third stage was thus a decision by those responsible for that court whether to hold a criminal trial. This decision was made nominally by the court's judge, though probably in practice by the clerk to the court. It might be accompanied by an order to arrest the suspect – an order carried out by the court's officer or officers. The decision to hold a trial was based on prima facie evidence that a crime had been committed and that there was a case against the suspect. The fourth stage would be the trial itself, at which the judge presided, prosecution and defence put their cases, and the decision on guilt or innocence was made by an assize of local men who were expected to be familiar with the facts. If they convicted the accused,

---

[3] Notably R. Briggs, *Witches and Neighbours: the Social and Cultural Context of European Witchcraft* (London, 1996); R. Briggs, '"Many reasons why": witchcraft and the problem of multiple explanation' and B. P. Levack, 'State-building and witch hunting in early modern Europe', both in J. Barry *et al.* (ed.), *Witchcraft in Early Modern Europe: Studies in Culture and Belief* (Cambridge, 1996).

sentence would be passed by the judge; to the extent that he had discretion in his decision, the passing of sentence represents a fifth stage.[4]

A prosecution thus faced a series of hurdles, and could fall at any one. In the first stage, people might not agree that an unsanctioned act was criminal at all, or might have no idea about a suspect. In the second stage, arguments about a particular suspect's culpability might stop short of a consensus demanding a trial. Suspected witches and their relatives can sometimes be seen trying to persuade their neighbours not to take a case to court;[5] we mainly know about the times when they failed, but they must often have succeeded. In the third stage, the clerk to the court might tell the aggrieved neighbours to go away because their prima facie case was too weak; this would not be recorded, and only rarely do we have evidence of such cases. At the fourth and fifth stages, the assize might acquit, or the judge might impose an unusually lenient sentence.

This chapter will pay particular attention to the neglected third stage – the decision on whether to hold a criminal trial. This was the crucial point at which the formal machinery of justice was activated. The fourth and fifth stages were often formalities. The third stage was also the point at which *central* government became involved; from quite early on in the Scottish witch-hunt, the decision to hold a criminal trial was made centrally. And – to anticipate – the third stage was also the point at which witch-hunting would ultimately be halted for good.

In witchcraft cases, however, the decision to hold a criminal trial was *not* the point at which governmental authorities first became involved with a case. In most cases the church had already begun. The local courts of the church, newly created since the Reformation, were very much organs of government; indeed they were some of the most powerful organs that many people experienced. They also fitted neatly into an existing structure of civil authority.[6] Before a witch was tried by a criminal court, she or he had usually been identified by the kirk session, and had often been arrested and interrogated (typically with deprivation of sleep) to obtain a confession. The kirk session might also have collected depositions from aggrieved neighbours, or have searched the suspect for the witch's mark. The kirk session, or its superior court the presbytery, is found in the background to many witchcraft cases; but it was not a criminal court and so had to seek the co-operation of the civil authorities. This brings us back to the question of who authorised trials for witchcraft.

II

Before the Reformation of 1560, the normal authorities for punishment of witches were the church courts. Trials were rare, but a high-powered witchcraft trial was

---

[4] J. I. Smith, 'Criminal procedure', in Lord Normand (ed.), *An Introduction to Scottish Legal History* (Stair Society, 1958); I. D. Willock, *The Origins and Development of the Jury in Scotland* (Stair Society, 1966), pp. 143–57.

[5] BL, Alloa witchcraft cases, Egerton MS 2,879, fo. 7v.; J. Gilmore, 'Witchcraft and the Church in Scotland subsequent to the Reformation' (University of Glasgow, Ph.D. thesis, 1948), p. 241.

[6] J. Goodare, *State and Society in Early Modern Scotland* (Oxford, 1999), pp. 172–8.

authorised in *c.*1542 by commission from the archbishop of St Andrews.[7] Nominally, church courts could not impose a death sentence, and the condemned prisoner was supposed to be 'relaxed' to the secular authorities for execution. But the real responsibility was seen to lie with the church.[8]

The authority of the church courts largely ceased in 1560 as a result of an act of the Reformation Parliament, leading to a period of judicial confusion.[9] Jurisdiction over witchcraft was probably as confused as anything. The burgh court of Stirling seems to have thought itself competent to try witchcraft in 1562.[10] It is possible that secular courts had possessed some kind of common-law jurisdiction on the subject even before then. The surviving proclamation for the justice ayre of Jedburgh in 1510 inquired about many crimes, including 'gif thair be ony wichecraift or sossary wsyt in the realme'.[11] Evidence is scant, but there are at any rate no direct references to secular witchcraft trials before the Reformation.

Along with the Reformation came the well-known statute of 1563, bringing witchcraft within the jurisdiction of the secular criminal courts. Early modern Scotland possessed an intricate patchwork of such courts. The statute enjoined enforcement by 'the justice, schireffis, stewartis, baillies, lordis of regaliteis and ryalteis, thair deputis, and uther ordinar jugeis competent within this realme having powar to execute the samin'.[12] The term 'the justice' was crucial, since all other items on the list consisted of local courts with at best a minor role in the witch-hunt. 'The justice' was primarily a shorthand term for the *justice depute*, a middle-ranking official or officials exercising powers nominally delegated from the sinecure post of justice general, and answerable in practice to the justice clerk, an officer of state. The court held in Edinburgh by the justice depute or deputes can be referred to as the 'justiciary court', while noting that before 1672 it was not a body continuously in session, but an official or officials continuously in existence with powers to convene a court to try cases whenever required. The statute's term 'the justice' also encompassed *justice ayres* – periodic travelling courts that visited the localities with similar powers – and *commissions of justiciary* – royal commissions to private individuals, normally to convene an *ad hoc* court to hear a single case.

As for the local criminal courts, the sheriff courts were most important, and the statute named them second after 'the justice'. Burgh courts (unless, like some major burghs, they possessed shrieval powers) were not included; nor apparently were

---

[7] *St Andrews Formulare, 1513–1546,* 2 vols, eds G. Donaldson and C. Macrae (Stair Society, 1942–4), ii, no. 438.

[8] For a leading example see John Knox, *History of the Reformation in Scotland,* ed. W. C. Dickinson, 2 vols (London, 1949), i, p. 74; ii, pp. 244–5. Cf. H. Kamen, *The Spanish Inquisition: an Historical Revision* (London, 1997), pp. 202–3.

[9] D. B. Smith, 'The spiritual jurisdiction, 1560–1564', *Records of the Scottish Church History Society,* 25 (1993–95), pp. 1–18.

[10] *Extracts from the Records of the Royal Burgh of Stirling,* 2 vols, ed. R. Renwick (Scottish Burgh Records Society, 1887–89), i, p. 80.

[11] Pitcairn (ed.), *Trials,* i, I, p. 66*.

[12] *APS,* ii, p. 539, c. 9.

baron courts (unless the unusual phrase 'lordis of ryalteis' was meant to indicate them), private local courts which did not have jurisdiction over other major crimes. Regality courts were private local courts with extensive powers that will require further attention. For many purposes, however, it is sufficient to group local courts together. Unlike the justiciary court, justice ayres or commissions of justiciary, none of them were directly answerable to the crown. And in practice none of them played a significant role in witch-hunting. They did try witches sometimes, as we shall see, but the great majority of witchcraft trials were authorised centrally.

The structure of central criminal justice shifted during the early adult years of James VI, after about 1585. Justice ayres were used in one early witch-hunt in 1568;[13] but they were in decline, and by about 1590 were hardly ever held. Commissions of justiciary grew rapidly, and would soon come to dominate the witch-hunt. They were normally issued in response to a request by the would-be commissioners, who arrived at court with a story about a recent local crime and why they were the most appropriate people to punish it. Such commissioners would normally be lairds, or perhaps magistrates of royal burghs, the recognised rulers of Scottish localities. Commissions were administratively convenient, and demand for them was high.[14]

Commissions were issued in the name of the king. Before James VI's departure for England in 1603, the process might well require him to sign something, but he could not inform himself about the details of each case, and in practice the responsibility lay largely with his advisers. With whose advice, then, would he act? He could take advice either from trusted leading noblemen – a traditional pattern of kingship – or from the gentlemen of his chamber – a similar pattern since they were mostly relatives of noblemen – or from his privy council – a body which, unlike the nobles, contained members with legal expertise. Whether commissions of justiciary were obtained wholly through informal lobbying, or whether they also received formal consideration by the council, was a crucial question under James VI (and not just for witch-hunting). There were frequent complaints of partiality, and the privy council often resented what it saw as the chamber's undue influence in facilitating the issue of commissions.[15]

There were two types of commission of justiciary: quarter seal and signet commissions. Quarter seal commissions, a rare and old-fashioned type, were issued by chancery. They seem to have been authorised by the monarch, in the form of a 'signature' (a personally-signed order).[16] Chancery was a pen-pushing department

---

[13] M. Wasser, 'Ambition and failure: Scotland's unknown witch-hunt, 1568–1569', unpublished paper.

[14] J. Goodare, *The Government of Scotland, 1560–1625* (Oxford, forthcoming), ch. 9.

[15] Goodare, *Government*, ch. 9.

[16] A. L. Murray, 'The Scottish chancery in the fourteenth and fifteenth centuries', in K. Fianu and D. J. Guth (eds), *Écrit et Pouvoir dans les Chancelleries Médiévales: Espace Français, Espace Anglais* (Louvain-la-Neuve, 1997), pp. 143–9; cf. Scottish Record Office, *Guide to the National Archives of Scotland* (Edinburgh, 1996), p. 87. The quarter seal was a version of the great seal. I am grateful to Dr Athol Murray for advice on these issues. At least one commission (from April 1568) survives under what appears

rather than a decision-making centre, and the decision to issue a quarter seal commission was thus made through informal lobbying of the monarch. Signet commissions were more common. They too *could* be obtained through informal lobbying, but the signet was the seal always used by the privy council, and it is a fair conjecture that signet commissions were usually authorised by the council. They were also signed by the king, a practice denoting not that he had made the decision personally, nor even that he had read the document, but that he had taken his councillors' advice. After 1603, the council issued signet commissions without recourse to the king, and since it did not *receive* the power to do so in 1603 (though its powers were upgraded in certain other ways) it probably had the power to do so before that date as well.[17]

Although commissions were always issued centrally, neither type is well documented in central records before mid-1608, when a register of signet commissions was established.[18] As for quarter seal commissions, chancery could note them in its responde books, but these existed to keep track of court fines and forfeitures, neither of which could be expected from the conviction of the average witch. So before 1608 it is easy to find commissions for which there is no central record.[19]

Both types of commission were in use within months of the passage of the witchcraft statute. In October 1563, the earl of Moray received a commission under the quarter seal to try several serious crimes including witchcraft ('artem magicam') in the northern sheriffdoms.[20] But when in December 1563 the general assembly of the church was informed of some witches, it went to the privy council. The most natural thing for the council to do would have been to issue a commission of justiciary under the signet.[21]

Most commissions of justiciary were for the trial of named individuals, but there were also some *general* commissions to try all cases of the crime within a locality (usually within a specified time limit). Such commissions could facilitate mass prosecutions, and may have been more common during periods of panic. On 2 February 1597, during the early stages of the national witchcraft panic of that year, the magistrates of Aberdeen received a commission to try five named people. Once one of them started to name further suspects, panic set in. On 4 March a general royal commission 'for haulding of justice courtis upon all persones delatit and suspect of witchcraft within the diocie and syrefdome of Abirdene, for the space of

---

to be the seal of the justice general: NAS, Airlie muniments, GD16/25/4; cf. J. H. Stevenson and M. Wood, *Scottish Heraldic Seals*, vol. i: *Public Seals* (Glasgow, 1940), p. 43.

[17] *RPC*, vi, pp. 558–60.

[18] NAS, register of commissions, 1607–16, PC7/1. There is one stray case from 24 Sept. 1607, but all the others are mid-1608 onwards.

[19] A number are identified in J. Goodare, 'The Scottish witchcraft panic of 1597', Chapter 4 above.

[20] *Exchequer Rolls of Scotland*, xix, p. 518.

[21] *Booke of the Universall Kirk: Acts and Proceedings of the General Assembly of the Kirk of Scotland*, 3 vols, ed. T. Thomson (Bannatyne Club, 1839–45), i, p. 44. No action by the council is recorded.

fyve yeris' was issued. The sheriff depute and burgh magistrates were the joint commissioners; local authorities themselves normally sought a commission rather than
proceeding independently.[22]

The privy council in the late 1590s gradually established monopoly control over
the issue of commissions of justiciary. Let us recall that the 1563 statute envisaged
trials (1) in the central justiciary court, (2) in justice ayres, (3) by commission of
justiciary under the quarter seal, (4) by commission of justiciary under the signet,
and (5) in local courts. The central justiciary court (1) was supervised by a privy
councillor, the justice clerk; the council could readily order that trials be held in it.
By 1590, we have seen that justice ayres (2) were already on the way out. In the
course of the 1580s, quarter seal commissions (3) seem effectively to have been
extinguished.[23] The issue has been complicated in the past by claims that a 'standing commission' or 'general commissions' existed between 1591 and 1597, but
these have been shown to be illusory.[24]

The question about signet commissions (4) was whether they required council
approval, or whether the petitioner seeking a commission could approach the king
through other channels, notably his gentlemen of the chamber. The council in the
late 1580s and 1590s regularly tried to stop James signing things it had not seen
(and not just commissions of justiciary: grants of money were also of deep concern). In 1598 the council emerged largely victorious, through a political settlement
in which leading gentlemen of the chamber were admitted to the council.[25] James
then consolidated the council's position by taking himself off to Westminster in
1603. Even after that he was just as much king of Scotland as he had ever been, and
still *could* sign commissions in response to an informal, personal approach.[26] But
from 1598 onwards, he normally deferred to the council.[27]

The triumphant privy council also began in 1598 to assert its supremacy over
presbyteries in questions of disputed jurisdiction. Several offences were both ecclesiastical and statutory: adultery, Catholicism and witchcraft. The council increasingly
intervened to discharge presbyteries from excommunicating people for such

---

[22] *Spalding Misc.*, i, pp. 83, 109–10; cf. J. Goodare, 'The Aberdeenshire witchcraft panic of 1597',
Northern Scotland, 21 (2001), 17–37.

[23] NAS, index to responde books, E1/14, unfoliated, *passim*.

[24] J. Goodare, 'The framework for Scottish witch-hunting in the 1590s', *SHR*, 81 (2002, forthcoming).

[25] Goodare, *Government*, ch. 6.

[26] After 1603 one had to be extremely well connected at court to bypass the normal channels. The
earl of Sutherland was; his brother, Sir Robert Gordon, was a gentleman of the bedchamber. Sutherland
asked him to 'sie if ye can get ane commissione from his majestie to put ane nomber of witches to ane
assise': Sutherland to Gordon, 23 Feb. 1615, W. Fraser, *The Sutherland Book*, 3 vols (Edinburgh, 1892),
ii, pp. 116–17.

[27] There are problems with the sources here. The privy council register is missing for the period Feb.
1603 to Aug. 1606, and surviving notes of council business for this period omit minor decisions: *RPC*,
vii, p. 232. And before about 1610 the privy council often did not minute its minor decisions. Thus a
signet commission on witchcraft was granted in Perth on 28 June 1602 to John Grant of Freuchie and
colleagues: W. Fraser, *The Chiefs of Grant*, 3 vols (Edinburgh, 1883), iii, pp. 198–9. The privy council
met there on that day, but did not record the commission: *RPC*, vi, p. 398.

offences. A witchcraft case in 1609 proved a crucial test case, and by 1610 presbyterian assertiveness had been curbed.[28]

That left only local civil courts (5) as potential rivals to the council. Although most of their sixteenth-century records have been lost, enough material survives to indicate that they never tried many witchcraft cases. This is particularly clear for burgh courts, the records of which survive in fair numbers; no significant concentrations of witchcraft trials have ever been found in them. The clause in the 1563 act enjoining them to prosecute witches may never have taken effect. Certainly by 1597, the Aberdeen case quoted earlier shows that a local sheriff depute and burgh magistrates – possessors of the two main types of local court – did not regard themselves as empowered to try witches. They were keen to do so but had to get a commission of justiciary.

Some sheriff courts may have tried a few witchcraft cases up to the early seventeenth century. Sir John Skene in 1597 was still aware that the 1563 statute required sheriffs to try witchcraft.[29] In 1606 and 1608, the sheriff court of Aberdeen may have regarded itself as competent to do so, though only preliminary proceedings are recorded and perhaps a commission would eventually have been sought.[30] When in 1606 the sheriff depute of Berwick intended to try Isobel Falconer for witchcraft, she petitioned the council claiming that 'this is a verie heich cryme, in the tryall quhairof thair wald be [i.e. ought to be] men of judgment, learning, gude conscience, and experience', qualities lacking in the sheriff depute and his proposed assizers. She could have strengthened her case by complaining that they also lacked a commission, but she did not.[31] But although caution is advisable in the face of evidential silences, there seem to be no later references to autonomous trials in sheriff or burgh courts. By the Restoration period any idea that local courts could try witchcraft – or had ever done so – had been lost to view. Sir George Mackenzie, who was sensitive to jurisdictional encroachments and who glossed the 1563 act as requiring local courts only to arrest suspects and concur in punishments, wrote: 'Nor find I any instances wherein these Inferior Courts have tryed this Crime.'[32]

What of regality courts, some of which had extensive theoretical powers? These were private courts held by landlords who had been granted the exclusive right to try serious crimes within their estates. Few of their records survive. However, witchcraft was not explicitly mentioned in regalities' charters, and they do not in practice seem often to have dealt with it. The earl of Atholl, possessor of an extensive regality, was doing so in March 1598, when the privy council intervened to

---

[28] Goodare, *State and Society*, pp. 186–92.

[29] Sir John Skene, *De Verborum Significatione* (Edinburgh, 1597), s.v. schireff.

[30] *Records of the Sheriff Court of Aberdeenshire*, 3 vols, ed. D. Littlejohn (New Spalding Club, 1904–8), ii, pp. 86, 140.

[31] *RPC*, vii, pp. 238–9. Falconer's enemies seem finally to have caught up with her in 1624: *RPC*, xiii, pp. 460–1.

[32] Sir George Mackenzie of Rosehaugh, *The Laws and Customes of Scotland in Matters Criminal* (Edinburgh, 1678), pp. 89–90.

order him to liberate some of those he had arrested.[33] The council was not quick
enough to stop what it regarded as an illegal trial in Brechin, apparently in the
regality court, in 1608.[34] But these cases seem to be exceptional. Throughout the
panics of the 1640s, the regality court book of Falkirk was silent on the subject
of witchcraft.[35] The regality of Dalkeith experienced intense witch-hunting in the
seventeenth century, normally through the issue of a commission of justiciary to
the regality's bailie. Clearly he was not thought competent to act without a commission.[36] The same applies to sheriff deputes and burgh magistrates, many of
whom received commissions.[37]

After about 1610 at least, then, there are likely to have been few autonomous
local trials – except in some remote regions. In Argyll, the earl was also justice general and later heritable justiciar, and the council agreed to respect his rights.[38]
Other remote local satraps might exercise untrammelled power. In 1617 the mar-
quis of Huntly sent his cousin, John Gordon of Buckie, sheriff-depute of Inverness,
to Sutherland and 'willit him to doe justice' on a witch there. Huntly did not sound
as if he was seeking a commission, nor is there any evidence that Gordon held
one.[39] But the overwhelming bulk of the evidence indicates that seekers of commissions routinely looked to the privy council.

III

How did the council use its monopoly position? In the period 1598–1625 it was
dominated by several people with a cautious approach to witch-hunting – the earls
of Dunfermline and Mar, Sir Thomas Hamilton (later earl of Melrose), and Archbishop John Spottiswoode. Dunfermline even tried unsuccessfully to reverse the
order of 1591 that had treated witchcraft as a *crimen exceptum* by allowing women
witnesses. Michael Wasser, who has examined their attitudes in some detail, argues
that they were scarred by the excesses of the panic of 1597.[40] In 1611 the sources
become fuller, and we begin to get a regular supply of recorded council decisions
on commissions of justiciary. The first was to issue a commission to the bishop of
Moray and four local lairds to try Marion Taylor and Marjorie Montgomerie. They
had already been examined by the bishop and by the presbytery of Elgin, who

[33] *RPC*, v, p. 448.

[34] *RPC*, xiv, p. 605.

[35] *Court Book of the Barony and Regality of Falkirk and Callendar*, vol. i: *1638–1656*, ed. D. M. Hunter
(Stair Society, 1991).

[36] E.g. *RPC*, 2nd ser., ii, p. 596. This case also shows the regality co-operating with the church courts,
since the witch's confession and other pre-trial depositions had been taken before the presbytery. For
one highly unusual case in a regality court, see 'The trial of Geillis Johnstone for witchcraft, 1614', eds
M. Wasser and L. A. Yeoman, *SHS Miscellany*, xiii (forthcoming).

[37] E.g. *RPC*, 2nd ser., i, pp. 456, 500.

[38] HMC, *Sixth Report, Appendix* (London, 1877), p. 624.

[39] Huntly to Sir Robert Gordon, 17 Aug. 1617, Fraser, *Sutherland*, ii, p. 132; cf. *RPC*, x, p. 2.

[40] M. Wasser, 'The privy council and the witches: the curtailment of witchcraft prosecutions in
Scotland, 1597–1628', unpublished paper. Cf. Goodare, 'The Scottish witchcraft panic of 1597'.

presented a 'certificate' of the interrogation to the council; it was noted that their guilt had clearly appeared to the 'said judges'. The subsequent trial can have been only a formality.[41]

Thus the privy council was in effect conducting the trial itself. Formally it was carrying out a preliminary examination of the evidence – but its decision was the one that determined the suspect's fate. The council demanded that the prosecution's evidence be placed on the table, and scrutinised it carefully. If the prosecution failed to prove its case, the commission would be refused and the suspect would go free. If the case was proven, a commission would be issued, with the understanding that conviction and execution would follow. And conviction and execution did usually follow; as we shall see, there was an extremely low acquittal rate. The suspects who were going to be acquitted were in effect acquitted by the council itself refusing to grant the commission.

The council's careful consideration of individual cases emerges in the variety of decisions that it made. Many cases must have been straightforward, and the council duly issued the commissions. But it had alternative courses of action open to it. In 1612 the council was 'suirlie informit' that five people were 'suspect and guyltie of the divilishe cryme of wytchecraft', which looks like a request for a trial commission. But the council granted a commission merely to *arrest* and *interrogate* the suspects. Later, when a report of the interrogation came in, a commission was issued – but for the trial of only three of them.[42] In another such case, depositions from neighbours seem to have been thought insufficient for the issue of a commission without further investigation.[43] In the 1640s, several commissions were issued that provided for the commissioners to hold the trial, but to report back to the council before passing sentence.[44]

The council could also decide to issue a commission, but to restrict it to a lesser crime. Some of these began in the locality as witchcraft cases but were downgraded by the council. The kirk session and magistrates of Perth brought criminal proceedings against Isobel Haldane and Margaret Hornscleuch in 1623, and Haldane's deposition survives to show that they regarded her crime as 'wischcraft'. However, the commission that was issued for their trial described them as 'suspect and guyltie of useing of charmes and abuseing of our subjectis with utheris practizis offensive to God, sclanderous to the trew religioun and hurtfull to our goode subjectis'. Witnesses' testimony and their own confessions bore witness to their 'unlawfull and divilishe practizes'. The word 'witchcraft' was carefully omitted from the commission, which was issued 'provyding that the punischement to be inflicted upoun thame extend not to lyff nor member'.[45]

---

[41] *RPC*, ix, p. 191.
[42] *RPC*, ix, p. 500; x, pp. 4–5.
[43] *RPC*, ix, pp. 387–8.
[44] *RPC*, 2nd ser., viii, pp. 12, 18, 41.
[45] NAS, register of commissions, PC7/2, fos. 222r.–v.; *RPC*, xiii, p. 270; 2nd ser., viii, p. 352.

Another option for the council was to order a case to be tried before the justiciary court in Edinburgh. This provided a fair chance that the witch would be convicted, but removed the responsibility from the local elite seeking the commission. This decision seems often to have been taken because the council perceived a strong but not overwhelming prima facie case against the suspect, and did not trust the local witch-hunters to hold the kind of trial in which the evidence on both sides would be heard. The justiciary court had an assize of local men, but it was convened by a justice depute, the prosecution was led by the lord advocate or his representative, and advocates could be assigned to the defence.[46] The result was a higher acquittal rate than for local trials – 30 per cent as against 4 per cent.[47]

A further filtering mechanism existed between 1624 and 1638. All informations on witchcraft were first to be presented to the bishop of the diocese, who would consider them in consultation with some of his ministers before reporting to the council. The initial order described recent practice:

> Sindre commissionis hes bene soght from the lordis of secreit counsall against personis suspect of witchcraft thir yearis bygane, and that upoun some dittaes and information is given in aganis the said suspect personis, quhairthrow the saidis lordis hes bene verie oft troubled be the importunitie of these who soght the saidis commissionis, and who constantlie affermed that all the dittaes and informationis given in aganis the said suspect personis wer trew.[48]

The involvement of bishops was a centralising measure, since Scottish bishops were very much central government's agents in the localities. Preliminary episcopal processing is noted in numerous cases, and probably occurred in many more.[49] In one 1627 case the council made out a commission but because the presbytery's investigation 'hes not bene so legallie and ordourlie done as the circomstanceis of the bussynes required', sent it to the bishop to investigate further before releasing it to the commissioners.[50] This did not make the bishop's concurrence to a prosecution essential. In 1629, Katherine Oswald's defence lawyers alleged that 'the said dittay [i.e. indictment] was presentit to my lord bishope of St Androis … quhais authoritie was socht to purches ane commissioun fra the counsall to certane judges for the pannellis tryell. His lordship refuiset to interpone his authoritie thairto.' But this refusal may help to explain why she was being tried in the justiciary court. After a ten-week investigation by the kirk session, the council had granted a commission to John Wauchope of Niddrie only to *arrest* Oswald; he had probably expected to *try* her.[51]

---

[46] See the introductions to *SJC*. I am grateful to Ms Lauren Martin for discussion of the role of the justiciary court, and for suggestions that have helped me clarify the conceptualisation of central and local authority.

[47] Calculated from the 'High Court' and 'Privy Council/Acts of Parliament' categories of Larner *et al.*, *Source-Book*, p. 237, table 2, omitting cases listed as 'Unknown'.

[48] *RPC*, xiii, p. 620.

[49] E.g. *RPC*, 2nd ser., i, pp. 309, 425–6, 447–8, 453, 607.

[50] *RPC*, 2nd ser., i, pp. 586, 600.

[51] *SJC*, i, pp. 138–9; *RPC*, 2nd ser., iii, pp. 206, 278, 290, 293. She was however executed: Larner *et al.*, *Source-Book*, no. 144.

Several decisions to issue commissions in 1626 show a similarity of phrasing, to the effect that the accused had been long time suspected guilty of the crimes of witchcraft, sorcery, using of charms, enchantments and other devilish practices.[52] Such standardisation may indicate that the councillors were not considering individual cases carefully. This was a period of upheaval in council procedures, as the political system adjusted itself to the accession of Charles I and his active fiscal, administrative and military demands.[53] Perhaps this routinisation contributed to the gradual escalation of witchcraft cases into a full-scale panic in 1628–30.[54]

But the 1628–30 panic does not represent a surrender to local demand by the council. On the contrary, the council's interest revived and even increased; they were clearly promoting the hunt actively. At its height, councillors are even found interrogating witchcraft suspects themselves. In January 1629, several councillors were commissioned to examine Isobel Young, then a prisoner in the Edinburgh tolbooth, 'and to report her depositiouns' to the council. They evidently got what they wanted, since a trial – and conviction – in the central justiciary court followed.[55] In November 1629, three councillors were commissioned to examine John Hogg and Margaret Nicolson, his spouse, to confront them with accusers, and 'after tryell' to imprison them or liberate them. Two weeks later they were freed.[56] Clearly this could happen in only a small minority of cases – but the fact that it happened at all tells us a lot about how councillors approached witchcraft cases. Most cases were no doubt routine and straightforward, but they did still look at each one. Those that were sent for trial were those that the council decided, after examining the evidence, really were straightforward. The fact that there were far more such cases during the panic, and that the commissions were duly granted, shows that the local elites and the privy council were *both* caught up in the panic.

Local witch-hunters thus learned that it was the council, rather than the commission judges and their local assizes, who needed to be persuaded of witches' guilt. If successful before the council, they could get to *be* the commission judges and select their own assizes. The privy council records often mention dossiers of prosecution evidence having been produced, and sometimes we see the dossiers being assembled. The magistrates and presbytery of Dumfries sought to prosecute several witches in 1650. Before seeking a commission from the authorities they sought advice from at least two lawyers about how to present their case and about the 'custome of the justice court'. In one case they were advised that the first article was 'verie considerable' but that 'the rest of the threats conteaned in the 2, 3 and 4 articles have not so necessarye ane cohesion with thair effects, althogh they be verie

---

[52] *RPC*, 2nd ser., i, pp. 246, 258, 275, 586.

[53] M. Lee, *The Road to Revolution: Scotland under Charles I, 1625–1637* (Urbana, Ill., 1985), ch. 1.

[54] Though in other cases individual concern continued, e.g. *RPC*, 2nd ser., i, pp. 469, 500.

[55] *RPC*, 2nd ser., iii, p. 4; *SJC*, i, p. 96.

[56] *RPC*, 2nd ser., iii, pp. 345, 358–9.

great presumptions'.[57] With lawyers already involved, it is easy to see the discussions before the privy council as being the real trial. Sometimes these discussions could be protracted. Lawyers acting for the magistrates of Aberdeen spent a frustrating summer in 1669 negotiating with the council for a commission to try some witchcraft suspects. The evidence was inadequate and the council, 'scrupulus in the thing beyond all measser', would not permit the torture that would allow the extraction of more. By this date, the central authorities were generally reining in local witch-hunting. The council eventually granted the commission, but insisted that John Preston, one of the justice deputes, should be conjoined with the magistrates in it.[58] However, Preston was later described as 'one inclined to burn too many for witches', and it seems that the witch-hunters got their way.[59]

It was at this time that Sir George Mackenzie expressed a low opinion of the council's practical powers when faced with attested confession documents. 'Albeit their confessions are sent to, and advised by the Council before such Commissions be granted, yet the Council cannot know how these confessions were emitted, nor all the circumstances which are necessary and cannot be known at a distance'.[60] But this assumed a higher standard of procedural rigour than had ever been normal before. A pre-trial confession before kirk session or presbytery had usually been quite acceptable.

Those who have argued that Scottish witch-hunting was a bottom-up process, with the initiative resting solely with the localities, have thus missed half the story. Witch-hunting was as much a top-down process as it was a bottom-up one. It is in fact wrong to see these two alternatives as mutually exclusive: rather we should recognise the harmonious co-operation between kirk session identifying witches and privy council authorising trials. Both shared the same general goal: to identify and punish witches in order to purge the land of ungodliness. When the privy council was considering whether to grant a commission of justiciary, it sifted through a good deal of evidence collected in the early stages of the investigation, usually by the kirk session. That evidence was produced willingly by the session, but it was ultimately produced because the council demanded it.

The real decision as to a witch's guilt or innocence was thus being made at the council board, rather than in the subsequent local justice court. The council kept records only of commissions that were granted, but other requests for commissions are known to have been refused because the council felt the evidence to be inadequate. The presbytery of Lanark in 1642 had the support of three prominent lairds and an earl in its bid for a commission to execute Marion MacQuhat, and submit-

---

[57] 'Unpublished witchcraft trials', ed. A. E. Truckell, *Transactions of the Dumfriesshire and Galloway Natural History and Antiquarian Society*, 3rd ser., 51 (1975), 48–58, at p. 54.

[58] *Aberdeen Council Letters*, 6 vols, ed. L. B. Taylor (London, 1942–61), iv, pp. 393–5, 399–403, 407–9, 412, 415, 417–19. For the commission see *RPC*, 3rd ser., iii, p. 45.

[59] Sir John Lauder of Fountainhall, *Historical Notices of Scotish Affairs*, 2 vols, ed. D. Laing (Bannatyne Club, 1848), i, p. 189.

[60] Mackenzie, *Laws Criminal*, p. 88.

ted a good deal of evidence; but the council determined that 'the pointes contained in her proces can no wayes demerit deathe'.[61] The local commission of justiciary was not a blank cheque; it was supervised carefully by the central authorities.

How far, in the absence of the accused witch, could the council's decision approximate to a criminal trial? A trial without the accused would later be regarded as the height of injustice. However, the very fact that the accused was considered innocent until proven guilty meant that it was normal practice in criminal trials to place the onus on the prosecution to prove its case beyond reasonable doubt. If that were done successfully, direct counter-evidence and counter-arguments by the defence were redundant and could lead only to perjury.[62] For the privy council, which was officially conducting only a preliminary hearing, the presence of the accused was even less necessary. Its role in witchcraft cases was analogous to the role it played in some prosecutions for treason, conducting a highly inquisitorial preliminary investigation that was experienced by those on the receiving end virtually as an actual trial.[63] And with treason, even the actual criminal trial could be held without the accused's presence.

These conclusions apply not only to the privy council, but to parliament itself, which emerged in 1649–50, and again in 1661, as an authority issuing numerous commissions for witchcraft trials.[64] One might not have expected parliament to give detailed consideration to individual cases, but in fact there does usually seem to have been a check of presbyteries' paperwork. Like the council, parliament was happy to endorse cases in which this was in order. In one 1649 case, parliament granted a commission of justiciary 'for burning of Agnes Hunter and others', noting that confessions had been obtained and that the presbytery of Haddington 'have found the samen sufficient for sutting [i.e. requesting] a commission according to law'.[65] A month later, parliament showed that it could be discriminating. One commission was granted for 'doeing justice wpon thrie witches whoise depositiouns', subscribed by members of the presbytery of Haddington, 'wer read in audience of parliament and found to be ane ground for granting ane commission'. Another deposition was read from the parish of Eyemouth; commission was granted 'for trying the same and to report'.[66] These cases were recorded together, so the difference in the second one is likely to have been deliberate. Even when parliament seems from its own minutes to have processed witches in large batches, it did in fact pay attention to individual cases. On one occasion when a commission

---

[61] *Selections from the Registers of the Presbytery of Lanark, 1623–1709*, ed. J. Robertson (Abbotsford Club, 1839), pp. 20, 22, 24–31. For further such cases see Mackenzie, *Laws Criminal*, p. 518; Wasser, 'Privy council'.

[62] D. Hume, *Commentaries on the Law of Scotland Respecting Crimes*, 2 vols (Edinburgh, 1844), ii, pp. 269–71, 297.

[63] Knox, *History*, ii, pp. 93–9; Goodare, *Government*, ch. 6.

[64] Larner *et al.*, *Source-Book*, pp. 151–7.

[65] *APS*, vi, II, pp. 732–3.

[66] *APS*, vi, II, p. 420, c. 101.

was noted for the trial of 'certaine persouns', Sir James Balfour wrote that thirty commissions were issued – and that 'ther depositions wer publickly read in face of parliament, before the housse wold wotte to the presidents subscribing of the acte for the clerke issewing of thesse commissions'.[67] This implies that some more summary procedure had been proposed and rejected.

The committee of estates, parliament's executive body, also issued many commissions in 1649. It was responsible for the case of Bessie Graham, when George Sinclair noted that 'a commission was granted upon more slender grounds, than any which had been granted before', and that evidence of guilt was *subsequently* found. The evidence consisted of the minister, who was the witch-hunt leader, and his servant and the kirk officer (enough to 'make a legal proof'), overhearing her in her cell conversing with the Devil. This was judicial laxity, but Sinclair thought that it was *unusual* laxity.[68]

In the later stages, the central authorities tightened their grip further. Instead of issuing a commission of justiciary to members of the local elite, the council could send the justice deputes out to hold special justice courts in the locality concerned.[69] This seems to have been welcomed by local witch-hunters, even though it further eroded local autonomy. The presbytery of Dunfermline, engulfed in the panic of 1649, petitioned parliament asking either that a justice depute should be sent to the locality, or that a 'standing commissione' should be granted to some local gentlemen to hold courts. If these requests were refused, and commissions were granted only for individual trials, the presbytery asked that at least they should have them gratis, 'lest throw the want of monie this work which the Lord hes so miraculuslie begunne and so wiselie heirtofore caried on perish in o[u]r hand'.[70] Far from wanting total control, the panic-stricken local elite wanted central help. And when the central authorities were also panicking, that help was usually forthcoming.

IV

The central authorities' volatility and readiness to panic is evident in the unusually *national* nature of the Scottish witch-hunt. Recent researchers have seen European witch-hunting as a community business, with neighbourhood quarrels and discourses generating a demand for witchcraft trials to which the central authorities merely responded. In a sense this was true of Scotland as well. There could never have been witch-hunts without neighbourhood quarrels to start the process off. But what of the great national panics of 1590–1, 1597, 1628–30, 1649 and 1661–2? Why did

---

[67] Balfour, *Historical Works*, iii, p. 437. He dated this as 20 July; it probably refers to the commissions minuted as being authorised on 19 July: *APS*, vi, II, p. 490, c. 249.

[68] George Sinclair, *Satans Invisible World Discovered* (Edinburgh, 1871), relation 15; Larner *et al.*, *Source-Book*, no. 2172.

[69] E.g. *RPC*, 3rd ser., i, pp. 11–12.

[70] *APS*, vi, II, p. 735.

about 60 per cent of all Scottish witchcraft trials occur during these five short bursts?[71] Why do we see the authorities up and down the country suddenly spring into action in the battle against Satan, simultaneously prosecuting their local witches?

These questions cannot be answered fully here. Each panic had unique elements, and further research is required. But the general pattern of periodic national panics in itself calls for comment; if there was a different explanation on offer for each one, we might still demand to know why they all look so similar.[72] It is worth while trying to sketch some common patterns in the panics.

The panics were not deliberately planned. Privy councillors did not sit round the council board and say to one another: It's time to cast off restraint and to plunge into a frenzy of accusations. Even if they had said it, the clerk would not have minuted it. Panics are not decreed, they *arise*. For most of the panics, there was no concrete central initiative.[73] Instead, cases began to occur in which the initial witch or witches named accomplices and was believed. Soon witchcraft would be transformed from the problem of individual witches with a known reputation into the problem of a ramified underground conspiracy. Everywhere one looked, one saw not just individual witches, but witches with numbers of accomplices. It was to deal with the frightening threat of secret, conspiratorial witchcraft that the authorities took the initiatives that we recognise as due to panic.

For witch-hunting to take off, both central and local authorities had to panic. The local authorities were in the front line, in touch with the common people and able to generate fresh suspects. Central authorities provided essential support by granting the trial commissions without which the local authorities could not act – and by shifting readily towards group commissions. One of the notable features of the early stages of the 1628–30 panic was the growing number of commissions to try, not just individual witches, but groups.[74] These could be for named groups, or *general* commissions to try all cases of witchcraft within a specified area and time-limit. General commissions could be seen as central abdication of responsibility, enabling trials to be held locally with no preliminary central scrutiny. More research is needed on general commissions – when and to whom were they granted? – but they were surely natural things for a panic-stricken council to issue to panic-stricken local elites. Before about 1662, both central and local authorities shared a common approach to the problem of witchcraft.

During the panics the central authorities saw the witchcraft problem as a national one, even though a 'national' panic was in some ways a patchwork of near-

---

[71] J. K. Swales and H. V. McLachlan, 'Witchcraft and the status of women: a comment', *British Journal of Sociology*, 30 (1979), 349–57, at p. 351. This figure omits the 1590s, for which data are less complete, and so is probably an underestimate.

[72] Cf. H. C. E. Midelfort, *Witch Hunting in South-Western Germany, 1562–1684* (Stanford, Calif., 1972), p. 121.

[73] The exception was the panic of 1590–1, which was orchestrated by the king to the extent that it involved treason.

[74] E.g. *RPC*, 2nd ser., ii, pp. 353, 469–70, 489.

simultaneous local ones. In a typical panic month, witch-hunting might occur simultaneously in about half a dozen parishes. Scotland had about a thousand parishes, of which about eight hundred were in the Lowlands (the Highlands were largely left out, not being integrated into the administrative structure of the state). This gives a rough figure of one per cent of the Scottish parishes each month. But next month it would tend to be a different 1 per cent. A panic might last between ten and twenty months, scattering bursts of witch-hunting widely across Lowland Scotland. The point is that as local panics flared up in further areas, they received equal support from the centre. If the panic arose first in Fife, privy councillors did not perceive a problem of witchcraft conspiracy in Fife and individual witches in Berwickshire. They responded just as readily to Berwickshire authorities' requests for group commissions, and may even (though the kind of evidence that would report this does not survive) have encouraged such requests.

Various other networks and institutions could help to spread panics. The general assembly of the church met regularly in the 1590s; its surviving minutes show no direct decision to promote witch-hunting nationally, but informal encouragement is possible. In 1593 the presbytery of Glasgow decided that 'anent the impietie of the witches and thair lait conspiracie, the samin be proponit in the nixt generall assemblie to be set furth in print, that the samin may be divulgat and maid notorious to the haill inhabitantis in this cuntrey'.[75] This may well indicate an interest in the recent pamphlet *Newes from Scotland*, the author of which was probably James Carmichael, minister of Haddington.[76] Leading ministers could range widely in search of witches. When the ministers of Edinburgh are found interrogating witches in Dalkeith, this seems routine, although it was well outside their formal jurisdiction.[77] The general assembly regularly encouraged witch-hunting in the 1640s. In 1649, the commission of the general assembly co-ordinated presbyteries in their pursuit of 'fugitive witches'. It also reminded presbyteries of the importance of hunting witches, and urged them when seeking commissions of justiciary to recommend names of commissioners.[78] There was no assembly at the time of the Restoration in 1661, but the launch of the witchcraft panic was accompanied by frantic ecclesiastical networking over the church settlement.[79] Oral information about witchcraft would have spread like wildfire through these networks. Finally, there were probably networks of news that had less to do with the authorities. In England, quite humble folk were not only interested in the public affairs of the day, but had means of acquiring news and passing it on. Before the days of a periodical

[75] 'Extracts from the registers of the presbytery of Glasgow, 1592–1601', *Miscellany of the Maitland Club*, i (1833), p. 59.

[76] R. Dunlap, 'King James and some witches: the date and text of the *Daemonologie*', *Philological Quarterly*, 54 (1975), 40–8, at p. 45.

[77] *RPC*, 2nd ser., ii, pp. 410, 442.

[78] *Records of the Commissions of the General Assemblies of the Church of Scotland*, 3 vols, eds A. F. Mitchell and J. Christie (SHS, 1892–1909), ii, pp. 307, 329, 337; cf. Gilmore, 'Witchcraft and the Church', pp. 65–72.

[79] J. Buckroyd, *Church and State in Scotland, 1660–1681* (Edinburgh, 1980), ch. 3.

press, a high proportion of what passed for news was information about witchcraft, prodigies and portents.[80]

V

Witch-hunting in Scotland was a remarkably centralised governmental operation. Apart from the prosecution of treason and of sedition ('leasing-making'), it is hard to think of any use of the criminal law that was so firmly controlled at the highest levels of government. After 1598, hardly any witches were executed except as a result of a deliberate decision by the central authorities.

Moreover, the local authorities welcomed this. Scotland was a unitary state, in which local authorities, even though drawn from indigenous elites, were not wholly separate from the central government.[81] Kirk sessions, burgh magistrates and sheriff deputes do not seem to have been worried by having to seek permission from the privy council to execute witches. They were content to accept a supporting role, identifying witches and conducting preliminary investigations of guilt; they did not seek to control the key decision on who was actually guilty. As the occasional local requests for privy council guidance indicate, they respected the council and trusted its judgment.[82] They were pleased to be gatekeepers at the preliminary stages – the privy council did not have local witch-finding agents directly under its command – but it is the harmony with which local witch-hunters blended into a central structure that is most striking. Witch-hunting powerfully aided governmental centralisation.

Witch-hunting also required that different local authorities co-operate. The minister and elders were often in the front line, at least in rural parishes, but they could not prosecute witches alone. Before anyone could set off for Edinburgh in search of a commission, the leading local lairds – often sheriff deputes or justices of the peace – had to be brought in.[83] Probably some witches escaped prosecution when the local consensus broke down. In Kilwinning in 1649, it was a 'special providence' that Bessie Graham was successfully prosecuted, for the parish's leading laird refused to co-operate, 'professing he thought all that was proven on her were but clatters'.[84] This case also indicates that reluctance to prosecute witches could occur in the localities as well as at the centre.

---

[80] A. Fox, 'Rumour, news and popular political opinion in Elizabethan and early Stuart England', *Historical Journal*, 40 (1997), 597–620; C. J. Sommerville, *The News Revolution in England: Cultural Dynamics of Daily Information* (Oxford, 1996), p. 20.

[81] 'Reliance upon local authorities does not … in any way detract from the unitary character of a state as long as those local authorities derive their authority from the central organs of the state and recognize their ultimate subordination to them.' B. P. Levack, *The Formation of the British State: England, Scotland and the Union, 1603–1707* (Oxford, 1987), p. 17.

[82] E.g. *RPC*, 2nd ser., viii, p. 236.

[83] Detailed local research might show that some of these men were themselves also elders in the kirk session. But it seems unlikely that the prestigious county gentry to whom commissions were so often granted would routinely be working parish elders.

[84] Sinclair, *Satans Invisible World Discovered*, relation 15.

Witchcraft trials spearheaded the state's move towards public prosecution. Before the late sixteenth century, crimes had been interpersonal and had largely been pursued by and through aggrieved private prosecutors. Now the lord advocate began to act as a public prosecutor, and after 1587, could prosecute alone even if the aggrieved party was unwilling to act. Most other crimes were still prosecuted jointly by both. With witchcraft, however, prosecutions in the court of justiciary were normally led by the lord advocate alone, even if there were aggrieved parties.[85] This happened in the localities too. Witchcraft trials under a commission of justiciary do not seem to have required a separate private prosecutor, and the commissioners seem to have combined the roles of judge and prosecutor – making these trials distinctively inquisitorial.[86] Witchcraft, although it was a hidden crime, was also an unusually *public* crime.

Both local and central authorities thus came to act inquisitorially, seeking out witches rather than merely responding to complaints from the witches' neighbours. The kirk session, which identified so many witches, was a fully inquisitorial body. There was no jury, and the minister and elders combined the roles of prosecutor and judge. They might claim to be providing a service to the community, but their primary role was coercive, stamping out ungodliness wherever it could be found. The essential nature of the crime of witchcraft was its ungodliness, not malefice against neighbours. This ungodliness was so fundamental that it did not even require a specific pact with the Devil.[87]

Nevertheless, the process of witch-hunting legitimised the state because such a large proportion of the witches – almost half – did have a reputation for witchcraft among their neighbours. The execution of these people may not have been universally welcomed; some of them were primarily known as folk healers, even if they had got into trouble for using their powers to harm. But there was at least a credible rationale to it. And this legitimising process, involving both central and local organs of government, culminated in a spectacular event – a trial and public execution by burning. The event often involved a hundred-odd people directly as witnesses, officials and members of the assize. Those people all learned something about the kind of behaviour that the authorities were not prepared to tolerate. Potential witches learned it; their relatives learned it; other members of the elite learned it. Since most of the hundred people had contributed to the witch's fate, they were learning by participation about how the state could seek out and punish the most deadly enemies of society.

Stuart Clark has commented on the importance of ceremony and majesty in conducting witchcraft trials. The judge possessed charisma through his office.[88] Such charisma was probably not a central feature of the average trial by commission of

---

[85] E.g. *SJC*, i, pp. 210–13.

[86] For a case where an aggrieved individual existed but was not a prosecutor, see *Spalding Misc.*, i, pp. 138–40.

[87] S. Macdonald, 'In search of the Devil in Fife witchcraft cases, 1560–1705', Chapter 3 above.

[88] S. Clark, *Thinking with Demons: the Idea of Witchcraft in Early Modern Europe* (Oxford, 1997), ch. 39.

justiciary, conducted by a temporary and often obviously amateur judge. The charismatic element, which must have impressed local elites seeking commissions, was the discussion at the council, involving an array of leading politicians who had to be approached via avenues of procedurally-conscious, fee-demanding bureaucrats. In the extant accounts for the trial and execution of witches, the expense of obtaining a commission often stands out as the largest single element.[89]

European scholars have generally found that large, stable states tended to discourage witch-hunting. The mass burnings took place in the fragmented princely states of the Holy Roman Empire, not in the core of France. Where there were appeal procedures, these tended to restrain the enthusiasm of local witch-hunters. There might be panic in a local community but not in the *parlement* of Paris.[90] But here, as with most other generalisations one can make about the European witch-hunt, there is room for exceptions. Just as there were small and decentralised states that did not hunt witches, there were larger and more centralised ones that did do so. The electorate of Bavaria, a state of comparable size to Scotland, hunted witches seriously over a long period with a good deal of central input. Bavaria's witch-hunting was less intense than some of the small states of nearby Franconia – but Bamberg and Eichstätt were more intense than just about anywhere in Europe. Other small states of the region, such as Ansbach and Regensburg, had very little witch-hunting.[91]

So the generalisation that small states hunted witches more intensely is just that – a generalisation. What we really need here are comparative studies of states of similar size, to show why they hunted witches so differently and to bring out factors other than size. Here Scotland, as a medium-sized state, forms a fascinating case study of centralised witch-hunting. Perhaps the unusual pattern of repeated national panics may indicate that Scotland was a relatively unstable state. Perhaps, too, witch-hunting tended to occur in a state that was *seeking* stability, not in one that *was* stable.[92]

The central authorities in Scotland were mercurial, sometimes triggering panic-stricken witch-hunts and sometimes slamming on the brakes. Local authorities panicked more rarely because they treated witch-hunting as part of their broad responsibility for moral discipline. If one kirk session was panicking but the next was not, this might lead the panic to spread – but would it not be equally likely that the second kirk session would calm the first down? The privy council had no neighbouring body to exercise a soothing influence on it. A rough calculation of local panics suggests that there would be, on average, something less than one panic per Lowland parish during the entire period of the witch-hunts. This average conceals

[89] Gilmore, 'Witchcraft and the Church', p. 427.

[90] B. P. Levack, *The Witch-Hunt in Early Modern Europe* (2nd edn, London, 1995), pp. 192–9, 231–2; cf. Levack, 'State building and Witch hunting', p. 99.

[91] W. Behringer, *Witchcraft Persecutions in Bavaria*, trans. J. C. Grayson and D. Lederer (Cambridge, 1997).

[92] Cf. T. K. Rabb, *The Struggle for Stability in Early Modern Europe* (London, 1974).

much variation – many parishes never hunted witches, while others did so repeat-
edly – but the difference between local and central concern is apparent. The central
authorities panicked five times, more than all but the most assiduous localities.

This erratic pattern hindered, rather than helping, the legitimising process. The
collapse of panics like those of 1597 and 1661–2 was a serious setback for all
involved, for it was evident that miscarriages of justice had occurred. It is not clear
whether the panics involved a precipitate decline in judicial impartiality, but there
was probably some relaxation. In the aftermath, the authorities would seek to
tighten up their procedures once more.

VI

This leads on to the question of how witch-hunts stopped. This cannot be dealt
with at length here;[93] but it is bound up with the nature of the state's involvement
with witchcraft. Did the central authorities, who had done so much to promote
and sustain witch-hunting, now take a conscious decision to put an end to it? If so,
when and how? If not, what does this tell us about the state's role?

The question of how witch-hunts stopped can be divided into three: how particular panics ended; how conditions changed so that panics could never recur; and
how the more persistent individual trials ceased. Individual trials were likely to per-
sist for as long as witchcraft remained a statutory crime, since popular witch-belief
continued and would occasionally attract support from local authorities. With the
abolition of the privy council in 1708, central supervision was removed and some
local courts seem to have acted autonomously. The last known execution, apparently carried out by the sheriff court of Sutherland, was in 1727, nine years before
the witchcraft act was repealed. Without repeal, such cases could have continued.[94]

The first question, on the ending of the last national panic, has been convincingly
answered by Brian Levack. He argues that the 1661–2 panic, 'like any other, required
not only adequate judicial machinery to bring witches to trial but a fear of witchcraft among influential members of society and a commitment by the ruling elite,
especially those who exercised secular power, to activate that machinery'. And it was
that same elite – and particularly those in charge of the central judicial machinery,
the court of justiciary and the privy council – who ended the hunt in the spring of
1662 by acquitting a number of suspects, curtailing powers of arrest and torture,
imprisoning two witch-prickers, and simply declining to authorise further trials.[95]

How then did conditions change so that panics like that of 1661–2 could never
recur? The 1662 initiatives did not close the door permanently on witch-hunting.

---

[93] For a fuller account see B. P. Levack, 'The decline and end of Scottish witch-hunting', Chapter 10
below.

[94] Cf. E. J. Cowan and L. Henderson, 'The last of the witches? The survival of Scottish witch-belief',
Chapter 12 below.

[95] B. P. Levack, 'The great Scottish witch-hunt of 1661–1662', *Journal of British Studies*, 20 (1980),
90–108, at pp. 97, 102–7.

The beginnings of a sixth national panic occurred in 1677–9, with outbreaks of multiple cases in different parts of the country.[96] Witch-pricking was still occurring in 1677.[97] Perhaps these happened despite the privy council, rather than because of it. But the council was still so far from wanting to put witch-hunting behind it that it even granted a one-year *general* commission in 1666, to try all cases of 'witchcraft and incest' in Orkney and Shetland. Nor did this commission specify, as some did, that 'voluntar confessions' were required.[98]

The privy council could occasionally display *more* interest in witchcraft trials than the local elite. Barbara Drummond was arrested on suspicion of witchcraft late in 1664, and the usual selection of the local elite received a commission of justiciary. Imprisoned first in Edinburgh, then in Stirling and her local Dunblane, her trial was long delayed either by the repeated failure of the commissioners to constitute a quorum of five, or by the non-appearance of her accusers. Her periodic petitions to the council produced, not her liberation, but increasingly peremptory orders to the commissioners to do justice. Their indifference continued, however, and in May 1667 the council finally ordered that she was to be freed – on finding caution to stand trial when summoned.[99] Drummond's two-and-a-half-year ordeal does not look like the product of local zeal. It is more reminiscent of the councillors conducting interrogations in person during the 1628–30 panic. In another significant case, in 1650, some witchcraft commissioners in Peebles referred the case of Isobel Alexander back to the privy council for advice, since she had retracted her initial confessions. Reluctant to acquit, they suggested a compromise, to have her 'remitted … to a more exact tryall to the paroch wher she lived formerly'. Yet retraction of a confession must have been common. Committed local witch-hunters would have ignored it and proceeded with Alexander's 'tryall and executioune' as they had been authorised.[100] Doubts thus arose in the localities, not just at the centre.

The imposition of procedural rigour in the aftermath of the 1661–2 panic was not entirely new. Initiatives to impose procedural rigour had marked the end of every panic from 1597 onwards.[101] The aftermath of the 1628–30 hunt produced more than one such initiative. The council in 1630 censured a local trial clerk who had been issuing false extracts from the trial record in order to promote a further trial. In 1632 it stopped a witch-pricker, declaring after interrogating him that 'his knowledge in this mater hes onelie beene conjecturall and most unlawfullie used'. It also reprimanded the baron-bailie of Broughton and minister of Leith, who had tortured Helen Hamilton 'without power or commissioun'.[102] The panic of 1649

---

[96] Black, *Calendar*, pp. 77–9; Larner *et al.*, *Source-Book*, pp. 42–4, 145–7, 221–3.

[97] Sir John Lauder of Fountainhall, *Historical Notices of Scotish Affairs*, 2 vols, ed. D. Laing (Bannatyne Club, 1848), i, pp. 145–6.

[98] *RPC*, 3rd ser., ii, pp. 136, 193. 'Voluntar confessions' may have meant that a confession extracted under torture was repeated without torture.

[99] *RPC*, 3rd ser., i, pp. 635, 637; ii, pp. 55–6, 172, 252–3, 283.

[100] *RPC*, 2nd ser., viii, p. 236.

[101] For 1597, see Goodare, 'The Scottish witchcraft panic of 1597'.

[102] *RPC*, 2nd ser., iii, pp. 450–1; iv, pp. 427, 432–3, 436–7.

was followed by Chancellor Loudoun's letter of 1650 with which this chapter began. All these initiatives show the central authorities trying to be cautious, and searching – perhaps awkwardly – for a compromise that would prevent obvious injustice while still allowing the guilty to be convicted.

What eventually sank witch-hunting in the courts was a growing feeling that there could be no such compromise in cases of witchcraft, because it was impossible to distinguish guilt from innocence using the kind of evidence usually available. This was not 'scepticism' about the existence of witchcraft, but it *was* scepticism about whether individual witches could be identified with confidence. In the seventeenth century, as today, a criminal prosecution required that guilt be proven beyond reasonable doubt; if doubt remained, the court must acquit.

The Restoration judges Sir George Mackenzie and Sir John Lauder had sown the seeds of such doubt assiduously. Their contribution, and especially Mackenzie's, is important and well known.[103] But it is to the period after the Glorious Revolution of 1689 that we must look for an unambiguous statement of this kind of scepticism – a statement that witchcraft can *never* be proven beyond reasonable doubt. In 1697, the leading politician and confidant of King William, James Johnstone, wrote:

> So as to witches: that there may be such I have noe doubt, nor never had, it is a matter of fact that I was never judge of. But the parliaments of France and other judicatories who are perswaded of the being of witches never try them nou because of the experience they have had that its impossible to distinguish possession from nature in disorder, and they chuse rather to let the guilty escape than to punish the innocent. If indeed there be malifics, they punish those malifics according to the laws and the nature of them, without respect to the principalls whence they proceed.[104]

This is the genuine voice of scepticism – not indeed about the existence of witches, but about the possibility of identifying them. Johnstone also narrowed down the field of witches' activities, focusing on demonic possession (the notorious Paisley trials of the time involved this). His indifference to 'the principalls whence they [malefices] proceed' indicated lack of interest in the demonic pact, and he cannot have thought of witchcraft as a conspiracy. Johnstone, like Mackenzie and Lauder, did not want to hunt witches; unlike them, he had coherent reasons for never doing so.

Johnstone's view was that of a politician. Lawyers had to acknowledge witchcraft as a crime for as long as the statute against it was in force, but politicians could choose which crimes to emphasise and promote – and which to downgrade. Johnstone could write as he did because his king and friend did not require divine legitimation. In this he differed from Mackenzie, who strenuously promoted the divine right of

---

[103] [Sir George Mackenzie,] *Pleadings in some Remarkable Cases before the Supreme Courts of Scotland, since the year 1661* (Edinburgh, 1673), ch. 16; Mackenzie, *Laws Criminal*, part 1, ch. 10; Sir John Lauder of Fountainhall, *Historical Notices of Scotish Affairs*, 2 vols, ed. D. Laing (Bannatyne Club, 1848), i, pp. 143–7, 163–4.

[104] Johnstone to Lord Polwarth, 1 April 1697, HMC, *Fourteenth Report, Appendix, Part III* (London, 1894), p. 132.

Charles II and James VII.[105] Mackenzie zealously persecuted the covenanters who challenged these kings in the name of their own divinely-legitimated system of theocratic government – a system that William's regime rejected as firmly as it did the divine right of kings. Mackenzie's identification of the enemies of his regime as covenanters probably helped him not to panic in the face of demands for witch-hunting in 1677–8.

All witchcraft prosecutions after 1662 went against the dominant trend. But the Restoration regime could have reversed the trend, because it still sought godly legitimacy. It happened not to identify its enemies as witches between 1662 and 1689, but it could have done. Any accommodation between the government and the covenanters would have opened the way to renewed prosecution of the ideological offence on which both could agree: witchcraft. Here the Revolution regime of 1689 onwards was different. Although it reached an accommodation with the covenanters, it introduced a degree of religious toleration. It hardly laid claim to godly legitimacy at all, distancing itself firmly from demands for religious persecution. Under the Revolution regime it was possible to say, for the first time, that the state would never again seek to eliminate witches as the enemies of God.[106] Until 1689, the Scottish state's aspiration to godliness meant that witch-hunting was always possible and often severe.

[105] Sir George Mackenzie, *Jus Regium: or the Just and Solid Foundation of Monarchy in General, and More Especially of the Monarchy of Scotland* (Edinburgh, 1684).

[106] For more on the approach of the Revolution regime see M. Wasser, 'The western witch-hunt of 1697–1700: the last major witch-hunt in Scotland', Chapter 9 below. Cf. Goodare, *State and Society*, pp. 317–18.

9

The western witch-hunt
of 1697–1700: the last major
witch-hunt in Scotland

Michael Wasser

So as to witches that there may be such I have noe doubt, nor never had, it is a matter of fact that I was never judge of. But the parliaments of France and other judicatories who are perswaded of the being of witches never try them nou because of the experience they have had that *its impossible to distinguish possession from nature in disorder*, and they chuse rather to let the guilty escape than to punish the innocent.[1]

From 1697 to 1700 the Renfrewshire region witnessed a significant upsurge in witchcraft accusations and prosecutions. In 1697 twenty-five witches were indicted in connection with the bewitching of a young girl, Christian Shaw of Bargarran.[2] In 1699 twenty-four other witches were indicted for a series of crimes focusing on two other young female demoniacs.[3] There were also many people accused but not indicted. These two mass prosecutions were connected by the ongoing attempts of a number of ministers and laymen to convict suspected witches. They took place within a context of moral panic, economic crisis and political instability. Taken together they represent a major regional witch-hunt, the last to occur in Scotland, or indeed in the English-speaking world.

---

[1] Mr James Johnstone to Lord Polwarth, 1 April 1697, HMC, *The Manuscripts of the Duke of Rox-burghe*, ed. W. Fraser (London, 1894), p. 132. Emphasis added.

[2] NAS, high court of justiciary, circuit court minute book, JC10/4, second pagination, pp. 1–2. There were actually 26 names, but one of these appears to be a repetition. The title 'circuit court minute book' is a misnomer as this trial had nothing to do with the circuit courts. The trial was based on a commission of justiciary issued by the privy council. There are three separate records contained in this volume. The first is the 1677 Maxwell of Pollok witchcraft trial, the second, which is cited here, is the Bargarran trial, and the third contains precognitions of witnesses from April 1699. The first two documents are separately paginated. Since the first paginated trial is not used here, no further effort will be made to distinguish between them. The third, which will be used below, is unfoliated.

[3] NAS, high court of justiciary, process papers, JC26/81/9. It can also be found in Edinburgh University Library, Laing MS II, 89/210–20. The old HMC designation is Laing MS II 89/135. The people named in 1699 were entirely different from those named in 1697 with the possible exception of Annabell Reid. There was a woman of this name in each document, but the 1699 indictment makes no reference to a previous involvement in the Christian Shaw case.

I

The conditions for a major witch-hunt were ideal, as many different factors coalesced. The possession cases provided spectacular examples of the Devil at work; the spreading news of the afflictions of the young girls focused public attention upon their plight, both in the region and amongst the political and legal elite in Edinburgh. There was a general climate of moral panic in the country in which religion itself seemed to be under assault. This was allied with a series of economic and political crises. There were also numerous credible witch suspects to seize, examine and try. These were women and men with local reputations as witches who were named by the demoniacs as their 'tormentors'. Many of them were also suspected of killing or harming their neighbours with their magic. The unifying factor behind all these conditions was God's providence. God would reward those who did his will and punish those who did not. God's will was clear: 'thou shalt not suffer a witch to live'.[4] To purge the country of its sins and return it to prosperity, the witches must die.

With both demand and supply high, one would have expected a large consumption of witches to result. However, in the end, the hunt was not very successful. Only seven witches were tried and executed in 1697, and in 1700 everyone who had been indicted in 1699 was released without trial.[5] Why did this happen? There were a number of countervailing influences acting to neutralise the witch-hunt, some of them more important than others. The least important were the practical factors. Trying and executing witches was expensive, and the country was poor. The kin and friends of the accused resisted the process. The Scots had to be sensitive to the disapproval of public opinion in England. These problems could have been – and were – overcome by a sufficient display of will.

More decisive were systematic doubts assailing many Scots themselves, doubts that undercut their will to proceed with trials and executions. These doubts focused on the reliability of the evidence used in the trials. Were the witnesses credible? Were the phenomena really diabolical in origin or was there a natural explanation? What about the possibility of fraud and delusion? These doubts were being expressed within the context of the scientific revolution – the attempt to understand physical phenomena through observation and theory. Eventually the accusations were rejected 'throw defect of probatione'.[6] The experience of these years proved decisive; never again were the Scottish authorities willing to issue multiple indictments or pursue a large-scale witch-hunt.

---

[4] James Hutchison preached a sermon on this text during the Bargarran trial. See G. Neilson (ed.), 'A sermon on witchcraft in 1697', *SHR*, 7 (1910), 390–9 , cited and interpreted in Larner, *Enemies of God*, pp. 163–5.

[5] NAS, high court of justiciary, books of adjournal, new ser., JC3/1, pp. 87–9. Larner, *et al.*, *Source-Book*, pp. 46–8, says that these witches were acquitted. This is a mistake.

[6] NAS, high court of justiciary, books of adjournal, JC3/1, pp. 88–9.

II

The witch-hunt had its origins in August 1696, when an 11-year-old girl named Christian Shaw began to display bizarre symptoms which continued until the end of March 1697.[7] She developed mysterious pains in her side, her body became stiff, she would go into a swoon, become insensible to outside stimulus, and fight and talk with invisible tormentors. Her symptoms developed slowly over a number of months, leaving her for a while, and then returning in even worse forms. In November 1696 she began to vomit up objects from her mouth – balls of hair, straw, pins and hot coals.

About this time her dialogues with her 'tormentors' took on a religious dimension – she identified them as witches, discussed scripture with them, extolled God, decried the Devil, called on them to repent and offered to make peace with them. Sometimes when she tried to name them or tell her parents or others what was happening she would lose her voice and be tormented with pain. At one point she began to try to run away; she moved so quickly that her feet seemed not to touch the ground, yet she was always caught before she left the house. Gradually she let it be known that she faced two imminent dangers. She could either become a witch herself, or the witches who were tormenting her would drown her, making it look like suicide.[8]

Christian's symptoms have recently been analysed in the *Scottish Medical Journal* and a tentative psychiatric diagnosis of '300.11 Conversion disorder' has been suggested.[9] Contemporaries also turned initially to medicine for an explanation. Christian was the daughter of a laird, John Shaw of Bargarran, and her parents were able to obtain the best treatment for her. In September a physician and apothecary from Paisley were brought to see her, and after this Christian was twice taken to Glasgow to be seen by Dr Matthew Brisbane, a prominent physician. The first trip appeared to result in a cure; the second, in November 1696, established that she was beyond medical aid.[10] Christian's family had to turn to other explanations and other cures.

---

[7] I have drawn primarily on Sir Francis Grant, Lord Cullen, *Sadducismus Debellatus, or a True Narrative of the Sorceries and Witchcrafts Exercised by the Devil and his Instruments Upon Mrs. Christian Shaw, Daughter of Mr John Shaw of Bargarran* (London, 1698) for the Christian Shaw case. This was published anonymously, but is credited to Grant by D. Wing *et al.*, *Short Title Catalogue … 1641–1700*, 3 vols (2nd edn, New York, 1994), i, p. 687, and by I. Adam, *Witch Hunt: the Great Scottish Witchcraft Trials of 1697* (London, 1978), p. 246, where a number of other contemporary printed accounts of the case are listed.

[8] Grant, *Sadducismus Debellatus*, pp. 1–38. Dr Hugh McLachlan has recently argued that the Bargarran narrative was similar in many ways to the Salem witchcraft narrative written in 1692 by the Rev. Deodat Lawson, and that therefore it is not to be trusted as a 'true narrative'. Hugh McLachlan, 'The Bewitchment of Christian Shaw', <http://swhn.gcl.ac.uk/shaw.html>, 11 Nov. 2000. However, for our purposes, it is only important that contemporaries, including the privy councillors who issued the commission to examine and try the witches, the prosecutor who tried them, and the jurors who convicted them, did give the narrative credence.

[9] S. W. McDonald *et al.*, 'The Bargarran witchcraft trial: a psychiatric reassessment', *Scottish Medical Journal*, 41 (1996), 152–8, especially p. 157. Conversion disorder is the modern term for what used to be called hysteria. I want to thank Dr Rachel Trockman for helping me on this point.

[10] Grant, *Sadducismus Debellatus*, pp. 2–4, 41–2.

The obvious alternative was that Christian was being possessed and tormented by witches. Possession of young females was by now a familiar tale in the annals of European witchcraft: it was a common occurrence in England and had formed a central part of the Salem witch trials in 1692.[11] From the beginning, the parish minister was helping the family. When it was concluded that the afflictions were of diabolical origin, the presbytery set up a weekly fast and prayer meeting at the Bargarran residence, and this culminated on 11 February 1697 with a public fast and prayers in Erskine church.[12] Christian's father also turned to the law. He asked the sheriff depute of Renfrew to imprison suspected witches named by his daughter, and this gave her some relief.[13] But her fits continued and an appeal to a higher power was made. John Shaw and the presbytery approached the privy council, asking it to appoint a commission to try the witches. Along with the request was sent a 'journal' of Christian's sufferings, attested by many of the local gentry.[14] On 19 January 1697 the council issued a commission to investigate the affair, and the road to the stake began for seven witches.[15]

Christian Shaw had initially named only two people. One was Katherine Campbell, a servant in the Bargarran household whom Christian had accused of theft; the other was Agnes Naismith, 'an old ignorant Woman, of a Malicious Disposition, addicted to Threatenings'.[16] As time passed, Christian named more people and some of those questioned by the commission of inquiry also named names. When the privy council issued its trial commission in March 1697, twenty-five people were inserted in it. Seven more suspected witches were described or their initials or names given in the narrative who were clearly not among those formally accused. One woman was named at the end of the trial, and two of the 1699 witches had earlier been accused by Christian Shaw but were not included in the 1697 documents. This gives a total of thirty-five accused witches, the names of thirty of whom are known: ten men and twenty women. In the course of the trial, which extended from 18 March to 19 May 1697, the witches were reduced to seven, all of whom were convicted and executed: three were men and four were women.[17]

---

[11] J. Sharpe, *Instruments of Darkness: Witchcraft in England, 1550–1750* (London, 1996), ch. 8; P. Boyer and S. Nissenbaum, *Salem Possessed: the Social Origins of Witchcraft* (London, 1974), especially pp. 1–21. Possession assumed greater importance in the latter stages of the European witch-hunt.

[12] Grant, *Sadducismus Debellatus*, pp. 12, 26.

[13] Traditionally, imprisoning a witch was supposed to deprive her of her power: Sharpe, *Instruments of Darkness*, pp. 155–6. One of the proofs alleged in favour of the diabolical nature of the crimes was that Christian 'was not Tormented by any of the Criminals after their Imprisonment'. Grant, *Sadducismus Debellatus*, p. 47.

[14] Grant, *Sadducismus Debellatus*, pp. 10, 22–3, 45.

[15] NAS, privy council, acta, PC1/51, p. 93.

[16] Grant, *Sadducismus Debellatus*, p. 1.

[17] *Ibid.*, pp. 1–38; NAS, privy council, acta, PC1/51, pp. 136–9; NAS, high court of justiciary, circuit court minute book, JC10/4, pp. 1–81. This is a relatively high percentage of men. Brian Levack gives three reasons why the percentage of men might rise, two of which apply partially to this case. One reason is that heresy was involved – in this hunt, there was a fear of atheism. Another reason was that the hunt was out of control. This was not true here, but the feelings of crisis were quite acute. B. P. Levack, *The Witch-Hunt in Early Modern Europe* (2nd edn, London, 1995), pp. 135–6.

III

Christian's fits and the trial of the witches were occurring against a backdrop of moral, economic and political crisis in Scotland. In the wake of the Glorious Revolution, Scotland saw a restoration of the presbyterian polity of the kirk, but the diehard presbyterians who returned to power were disappointed at the low moral tone and lack of religious enthusiasm of many of their compatriots. This escalated to a feeling of crisis with the publication of John Toland's *Christianity Not Mysterious* in 1696. A series of harvest failures during 1695–9 ushered in the famines of King William's 'seven ill years'. War with France decreased Scottish trade, and the failure of the Company of Scotland and its Darien scheme during 1695–1700 drained the country of resources. The Revolution Settlement also saw an upsurge of political instability in Scotland, exacerbated by economic crisis. The abolition of the lords of the articles left parliament difficult to control. Factionalism and lack of sufficient places for ambitious politicians meant infighting and indecision on the privy council. There were policy conflicts between King William and his subjects on ecclesiastical and economic issues. The Glencoe massacre and its subsequent inquiry eroded the moral legitimacy of the government.[18]

Witch-hunts tend to thrive most during periods of crisis, and Scotland in the late 1690s was suffering from multiple crises. Brian Levack identifies the 'mood of the entire community' as a precondition for witch-hunting and mentions the public discussion of witches and witchcraft, famine, religious crises, political crises and war as contributing factors.[19] During the Bargarran case and for a number of years thereafter these crises found specific expression in the Renfrewshire region. For example, 6 December 1696 saw the beginning of a French invasion scare that continued for a number of months.[20] This was not just a physical threat; the French represented the great Antichrist, the Roman Catholic church. As the Bargarran witches were being tried, taxes and troops were being levied in the west to repel the expected invaders.[21] The Bargarran witchcraft narrative contains references to beggars coming to the house, and this must be seen against the backdrop of an ongoing famine and the privy council's attempts to control food prices.[22] In 1698 the privy council itself was remodelled one month after it had promised to reopen investigations against witches in Renfrewshire.[23] Most striking of all was an 'exchange' that passed between

---

[18] Toland's book argued that Christianity could be seen as a purely rational religion, devoid of mysteries. It touched off the great Deist controversy that continued well into the eighteenth century. Its immediate impact on Scotland is shown in W. L. Mathieson, *Scotland and the Union: a History of Scotland from 1695 to 1747* (Glasgow, 1905), pp. 219–22. See also R. E. Sullivan, *John Toland and the Deist Controversy* (Cambridge, Mass., 1982). For politics, see P. W. J. Riley, *King William and the Scottish Politicians* (Edinburgh, 1979). A useful overview is provided by M. Lynch, *Scotland: a New History* (London, 1991), pp. 300–10.

[19] Levack, *The Witch-Hunt in Early Modern Europe*, pp. 161, 163–7.

[20] NAS, privy council, acta, PC1/51, p. 43.

[21] *Ibid.*, pp. 159 et seq.

[22] *Ibid.*, pp. 489–92, 517–18.

[23] *Ibid.*, pp. 476, 480–3.

Christian Shaw and Satan, which linked her own bewitchment to the moral and political crises associated with kirk polity:

> Art thou not the filthy Devil, for as brave as thou art with thy Silver and Gold Lace? Wouldst thou have me renounce my Baptism?…Dost thou say my Baptism will do me no good, because thou alledgest he was not a sufficient Minister that baptized me? thou art a Liar, I'll be content to dye ere I renounce my Baptism.[24]

Christian Shaw had been born circa 1686 in the last years of the episcopal church. She was probably baptised by an episcopal minister, but raised under a presbyterian regime.[25] In this exchange she reflected the moral crisis produced by the religious conflicts of the seventeenth century. The episcopalian–presbyterian contest was transmuted in Christian's mind into a temptation from the Devil, and it found its ultimate expression in accusations against the witches.

It was the question of morality that provided the link between witch-hunting and crises in the material world. To the pious presbyterian, what happened in this world was a complex interaction between God's providence and man's obedience. To simplify, if man ignored God's word, then disaster would follow; if he obeyed, then life would run smoothly. As one historian has observed, 'Throughout the crisis the Church attributed the famine to the sins and backslidings of the nation, and as a cure, recommended fast days!'[26] The fast held for Christian Shaw by her presbytery on 11 February 1697 fell between two national fasts for the sins of the nation proclaimed on 12 December 1696 and 15 April 1697.[27]

Witchcraft was not the only object of the moral cleansing desired by the kirk. In 1695 the old law against blasphemy was reaffirmed by parliament and in the autumn of 1696 a campaign was launched against blasphemers. It began with the conviction of John Fraser before the privy council in October, but the council could not impose the death penalty. Therefore the next victim, Thomas Aikenhead, was remitted to the justice court for trial on 10 November. He was convicted on 24 December and on 8 January 1697 he was hanged.[28] Other actions against moral offences included proclamations against profanity, commissions to try women for infanticide, and acts against Catholic priests.[29] Nor were witches the only scapegoats: on 20 April 1697 the Quakers in Edinburgh appealed for protection because people were attacking them.[30] However, it is witches who interest us here. Logically, if pursuit of witches

---

[24] Grant, *Sadducismus Debellatus*, pp. 28–9.

[25] Adam, *Witch Hunt*, pp. 93–4.

[26] W. Ferguson, *Scotland, 1689 to the Present* (New York, 1968), p. 79.

[27] NAS, privy council, acta, PC1/51, pp. 64–5, 176–8.

[28] M. Hunter, '"Aikenhead the atheist": the context and consequences of articulate irreligion in the late seventeenth century', in M. Hunter and D. Wootton (eds), *Atheism from the Reformation to the Enlightenment* (Oxford, 1992); Mathieson, *Scotland and the Union*, pp. 219–22. The link between the Aikenhead and Bargarran cases goes back as far as Macaulay in 1855 and is also drawn in I. Bostridge, *Witchcraft and its Transformations, c.1650–c.1750* (Oxford, 1997), pp. 24–31.

[29] NAS, privy council, acta, PC1/51, pp. 154, 186–8, 337–42, 407–9, 513–15.

[30] *Ibid.*, pp. 183–4.

was part of a wider moral campaign throughout Scotland, then it should not have been confined to the Bargarran case alone. And indeed, it was not.

IV

A concern with witches and witchcraft was evident throughout the period 1697–1700. The commission that tried the Bargarran witches had been empowered to conduct further investigations and lay further charges against other suspected witches.[31] On 4 October 1698 we learn that many suspected witches had been imprisoned in the Renfrew tolbooth, apparently for some time since they were in 'a starving condition'.[32] Francis Grant of Cullen, the Bargarran prosecutor, published a book on the case in 1698 in which, after lamenting the prevalence of witchcraft, he declared: 'But good things are hoped of our Magistrates, who have already so happily begun'.[33] Indeed, during 1698 and 1699 there was cause to believe that witchcraft prosecutions would extend beyond the west and result in a full-scale national hunt, the first since the early 1660s. On 1 March 1698, a commission was issued to try two witches in the stewartry of Kirkcudbright. On 18 July 1699 a commission was issued against twelve witches in Ross-shire.[34] But this was as far as it went. The most serious efforts and the largest number of witches remained confined to the west.

One of the problems hampering the pursuit of witches was money. In the economic crisis of the late 1690s money was scarce, and the privy council did not control the purse strings – it only made recommendations to the treasury. Two months after the trial, the prosecutors in the Bargarran case were still petitioning to be paid. Money problems also hampered the resumption of the trials. The starving witches referred to above were the object of a letter from the sheriff depute of Renfrew to the lord advocate: their prosecutors were threatening to abandon the pursuit, and the sheriff depute threatened to transfer the witches to the Edinburgh tolbooth. The privy councillors promised action: keep the witches until November, they asked, and we will provide a commission for their trial and recommend that the treasury pay their expenses. However in November King William reorganised the privy council and nothing was done about a commission to try the witches.[35] None the less, where a sufficient will exists, problems such as lack of money and political instability can be overcome. In March of 1699 responsibility for the trial of the western witches shifted from the privy council to the justice court, and trial preparations began to move forward.[36] The source of this will was religious

---

[31] *Ibid.*, p. 139.

[32] *Ibid.*, p. 476. These witches may have been left over from the Bargarran trial or they may have been new suspects.

[33] Grant, *Sadducismus Debellatus*, p. v.

[34] NAS, privy council, acta, PC1/51, pp. 386–9; *ibid.*, PC1/52, pp. 7–9.

[35] *Ibid.*, PC1/51, pp. 250–1, 476, 480–3, 519.

[36] NAS, high court of justiciary, books of adjournal, JC2/19, pp. 829–30. The last entry in the privy council records concerning the western witches was on 12 Jan. 1699 (NAS, privy council, acta, PC1/51, p. 519); the first entry in the justice court records was on 27 March 1699.

conviction. To better understand it, we need to look at some of the people involved in the trials.

V

Everyone committed to trying the witches was a pious presbyterian determined to see God's will done. This does not mean that presbyterians were always witch-hunters, nor that episcopalians were not; one of Scotland's major witch-hunts (1628–30) came at a time of episcopalian dominance and some early-seventeenth century bishops were enthusiastic witch-hunters.[37] However, in the late 1690s most people in power (both lay and clerical) were presbyterian, and two aspects of presbyterian religiosity lent themselves to a belief in witches. One was belief in a personal covenant with God, which facilitated belief in its opposite, the pact with the Devil. The other was the psychological experience of conversion, which involved resisting the temptations of the Devil. This enabled presbyterians to envision how others could succumb to those same temptations.[38]

Francis Grant of Cullen was one example of a man whose religious convictions led him to prosecute witches. Grant was a lawyer and writer, knowledgeable in the law and in ancient and natural philosophy. He later became a judge as Lord Cullen. A young man at the time of the Bargarran case, and the most junior of the prosecutors, he none the less did most of the actual pleading.[39] Learned lawyers and judges were among those most sceptical of the evidence presented in witchcraft cases, but in Grant this appears to have been countered by his equally strong religiosity. He was praised by Robert Wodrow as 'a man of great piety and devotion, wonderfully serious in prayer and hearing the word'. He refused to accept fees from clergymen, he strongly supported the laws against profanity, and in the wake of the Bargarran affair he and a few other lawyers founded a prayer society and a society for correspondence for religious purposes. Grant also published a book on the Bargarran case, in which he strongly defended not only the trial itself but the pursuit of witches in general.[40] This book and Grant's arguments will be considered at greater length below.

[37] Larner, *Enemies of God*, pp. 61, 72–3. George Gledstanes, archbishop of St Andrews, used the synod of Fife, where he was constant moderator, to pursue witches within his diocese: C. Baxter (ed.), *Ecclesiastical Records: Selections from the Minutes of the Synod of Fife, 1611–1637* (Edinburgh, 1837), pp. 61, 71, 75, 76, 79.

[38] L. Yeoman, 'Archie's invisible worlds discovered: spirituality, madness and Johnston of Wariston's family', *Records of the Scottish Church History Society*, 27 (1997), 156–86, and L. Yeoman, 'Heart-work: Emotion, Empowerment and Authority in Covenanting Times' (Ph.D. thesis, University of St Andrews, 1991). I want to thank Dr Yeoman for her help in understanding the nature of presbyterian religious experience. Any mistakes or misunderstandings are of course my own. See also Bostridge, *Witchcraft and its Transformations*, pp. 21–37.

[39] NAS, privy council, acta, PC1/51, p. 138; NAS, high court of justiciary, circuit court minute book, JC10/4, pp. 63, 74.

[40] Robert Wodrow, *Analecta*, 4 vols, ed. M. Leishman (Maitland Club, 1842–3), iii, p. 282, quoted in *DNB*, viii, pp. 385–6. For the attitude of lawyers and judges, see Levack, *Witch-Hunt*, pp. 236–9, A. Soman, 'Decriminalizing witchcraft: does the French experience furnish a European model?', *Criminal*

Sir John Maxwell of Pollok was another pious layman who strongly supported the pursuit of witches. The trial of witches in 1677 for bewitching his father was one of the most famous in Scottish history. At the Revolution he was nominated to the privy council and in 1696 he became a lord of the treasury. One contemporary described him as 'a very honest gentleman, of no extraordinary reach, zealous for the *Divine Right of Presbytery*, which hurries him often to do hard things to men of less confined principles, thinking it *doing God good service*'.[41]

It was not only men, but women as well to whom he was willing to do 'hard things'. Maxwell was one of the most important links between the 1697 and 1699–1700 prosecutions in the west. On the first day of the Bargarran commission he took the leading role, but was displaced at later sittings by more senior colleagues.[42] He was, however, the most assiduous of all the commissioners in his attendance. On 1 March 1698 he was one of those appointed to try two witches in Kirkcudbright, showing his continuing commitment to a moral campaign against witches.[43] In February of 1699 he was appointed justice clerk, and this appears to have been the precipitating factor behind the sudden enthusiasm in the justice court for trying witches.[44] The justice court consisted of a justice general, the justice clerk, and a number of lords of justiciary chosen from the lords of session. On 27 March 1699, less than two months after Maxwell took office, the court recommended that the lord advocate prepare indictments against the western witches. From 19 to 22 April the authorities heard and recorded testimony from ninety-one witnesses at Paisley and Glasgow, and on 29 April a formal indictment was drawn up against twenty-four witches.[45]

That Maxwell was the moving force behind these actions is further shown by his ties with the other determined witch-hunters, the ministers of the synod of Glasgow. A full analysis of the ministers is beyond the scope of this chapter – there were upwards of twenty-seven ministers involved in the 1697 and 1699–1700 investigations. A brief account, however, will show how important they were. Grant named fourteen ministers among the principal witnesses in the Bargarran case and many of these men appeared again in 1699.[46] The most important of these were Mr James Brisbane, minister of Kilcaholm, and Mr Neil Gillies, minister of the Tron in

Justice History, 10 (1989), 1–22, and the quote from James Johnstone at the beginning of this chapter, which is discussed at greater length below. The book is Grant, *Sadducismus Debellatus*.

[41] John Macky, *Memoirs of the Secret Services of John Macky, Esq.*, p. 226, quoted in G. Brunton and D. Haig, *An Historical Account of the Senators of the College of Justice* (Edinburgh, 1836), pp. 470–1.

[42] NAS, high court of justiciary, circuit court minute book, JC10/4, pp. 1, 7, 13, 15, 17, 18, 33, 58. Maxwell was the first president of the commission. The presidency then switched to Sir John Hamilton, Lord Halcraig, a lord of session, and when he left, to Alexander Stewart, Lord Blantyre, a local magnate and kinsman of the Shaws.

[43] NAS, privy council, acta, PC1/51, pp. 386–9.

[44] NAS, high court of justiciary, books of adjournal, JC2/19, pp. 827–9.

[45] *Ibid.*, pp. 829–30; NAS, high court of justiciary, circuit ourt minute book, JC10/4 (unfoliated); NAS, high court of justiciary, process papers, JC26/81/9.

[46] Grant, *Sadducismus Debellatus*, pp. 37–8.

Glasgow. Brisbane was named second among the Bargarran witnesses and first among the witnesses in 1699.[47] His little treatise concerning the witch's mark was included among the Bargarran trial records.[48] In 1699 the synod of Glasgow formed a witchcraft committee, and Brisbane attended it twice. Gillies, who was one of the Bargarran witnesses, attended every meeting of the 1699 committee.[49]

Maxwell was clearly the ministers' contact among the secular authorities. In January 1697 the initial appeal of the presbytery and the Shaw family had gone to him.[50] On 6 April 1699 the synod of Glasgow wrote to ask him to take steps to secure the persons of the witches, who were inclined to flee. They expressed their confidence in him and gave their promise that those involved in so good a work 'will not want their reward'. On 15 November 1699 the synod's witchcraft committee wrote to Maxwell again asking for help.[51]

On the surface, everything seemed to point to a successful trial, either in 1699 or 1700. The climate of moral panic, while it lacked the immediacy of a French invasion threat, was still there, as was the poor economy. In Sir John Maxwell, there was a man in authority who was willing to push things forward, in the ministers there were people who could shape opinion and co-ordinate accusations and evidence, witnesses existed in plenty, and there were two demoniacs as against one in the Bargarran case. Yet this was all for naught. Instead of a trial, the case endured one delay after another until finally, on 6 March 1700, the justice court dismissed the case without any trial, freeing the indicted witches.[52] The reason given for the delays was the poor quality of the evidence, and presumably it was the same for the dismissal. However this begs the question: why was the evidence considered defective, especially when it was similar in nature to that used in the Bargarran case? This question will be addressed in three stages. First we will consider the debate over witches and witchcraft that had been ongoing in Britain since the Restoration, then we will look at the evidence itself, and then we will examine the mounting doubts that consumed those responsible for the trial.

VI

It is beyond the scope of this chapter to analyse the witchcraft literature of Britain as a whole.[53] Instead, a selection of pertinent works will be examined, and the

---

[47] NAS, high court of justiciary, circuit court minute book, JC10/4, pp. 38–9, and *ibid.*, unfoliated.

[48] *Ibid.*, pp. 61–2.

[49] NLS, Wodrow MSS, Wod. quarto LXXIII, fos. 181r.–188r. I want to thank Dr Louise Yeoman for bringing my attention to this document.

[50] Adam, *Witch Hunt*, p. 43.

[51] NLS, Wodrow MSS, Wod. quarto LXXIII, fos. 179r, 187v.–188r.

[52] NAS, high court of justiciary, books of adjournal, JC3/1, pp. 88–9.

[53] W. Notestein, *A History of Witchcraft in England from 1558 to 1718* (New York, 1911), still has the best overview of the literary debate on witchcraft, although it is confined to England. Bostridge, *Witchcraft and its Transformations*, covers our period and advances the thesis that political purposes were paramount in the witchcraft literature. Bostridge, however, is concerned with beliefs rather than trials and so has a different perspective from the one presented here.

themes restricted to what is necessary for the argument. Four points need to be made: that the literature was truly British in its scope; that the purpose of the 'pro-witchcraft' literature was religious in nature; that it was increasingly concerned with 'proving' witchcraft as a physical phenomenon; and that it was designed to combat doubts concerning witches and witchcraft.

Three books will be used to establish these points. The first was the most important work on witchcraft written in Britain after the Restoration: Joseph Glanvill's *Saducismus Triumphatus*, published in 1681.[54] The second is *Satan's Invisible World Discovered*, written by George Sinclair and published in Edinburgh in 1685.[55] The third book we have already seen – Francis Grant's *Sadducismus Debellatus*, published in London in 1698. It demonstrates how the themes explored in the previous two books were influencing the minds and actions of those responsible for prosecuting witches in Scotland.

Each of these books had a British perspective. Glanvill's book contains twenty-eight witchcraft stories of which twenty-two were English, five were Irish, and one was Scottish – the 1677 Maxwell of Pollok case. Sinclair, too, did not confine himself to one country. Of his thirty-six stories, ten were English. Indeed, Sinclair borrowed heavily from Glanvill, in format and arguments as well as content. Grant's book was published in London, showing that a story restricted to Scotland could find an English audience. In fact, Grant published two editions, one in Edinburgh and one in London.[56] What this meant was that the western witch-hunt was being played out on a British stage, which in its turn was influencing the hunt. Sir John Maxwell himself was an example of this. The Maxwell of Pollok case was told in Glanvill, it formed the first tale in Sinclair, and Grant referred to the case in his arguments while Maxwell himself was on the bench.[57]

All three books shared a common purpose: to demonstrate the reality of God and the immortality of the soul by proving the existence of witches, the Devil and the spirit world. The enemy here was not the witches themselves but the spirit of 'atheism' that seemed to have settled on the land. Glanvill put his case clearly: 'Atheism is begun in Saducism: And those that dare not bluntly say, There is NO GOD, content themselves (for a fair step and Introduction) to deny there are

---

[54] There were a number of earlier editions, but Glanvill's work matured with his fourth, posthumous version, edited by Henry More: Joseph Glanvill, *Saducismus Triumphatus: or a Full and Plain Evidence Concerning Witches and Apparitions: In Two Parts. The First Treating of their Possibility, the Second of their Real Existence* (London, 1681). There were no significant changes after this. The book consulted for this chapter is a 1966 reprint of the 1689 edition: Joseph Glanvill, *Saducismus Triumphatus: or a Full and Plain Evidence Concerning Witches and Apparitions ... with an introduction by Coleman O. Parsons* (Gainesville, FL, 1966).

[55] George Sinclair, *Satan's Invisible World Discovered (1685) ... a Facsimile Reproduction with an Introduction by Coleman O. Parsons* (Gainesville, FL, 1969).

[56] The Edinburgh edition had a different title: *A True Narrative of the Sufferings and Relief of a Young Girl* (Edinburgh, 1698).

[57] Glanvill, *Saducismus Triumphatus*, pp. 463–69; Sinclair, *Satan's Invisible World*, pp. 1–18; Grant, *Sadducismus Debellatus*, p. 54.

SPIRITS or WITCHES.'[58] 'Sadducism' was the disbelief in a spirit world. Sinclair
followed Glanvill in this as in other things, noting that his book 'relates to one of
the *Out-works of Religion*, which the bold, and too much daring Infidelity of some
have assaultd'.[59] Grant's title, *Sadducismus Debellatus*, echoed Glanvill's, and in his
preface he lamented that 'there was never before any Society or Collective Body of
Atheists till these dreggs of time'.[60]

The spirit behind the pro-witchcraft literature was the same as that behind the
moral panic that sparked the western witch-hunt. As mentioned above, the panic
began with the publication of John Toland's *Christianity not Mysterious* in 1696.
Toland had been a student at the university of Glasgow, and the kirk saw his book
as symptomatic of a materialistic spirit tending towards atheism throughout the
British Isles. Aikenhead's execution for blasphemy was the most newsworthy result
of the moral campaign.[61] Grant deliberately used it in his narrative, noting that
Aikenhead had denied the existence of spirits and a Devil who tormented sinners,
but died repentant.[62]

However, it was one thing to support a belief in God by encouraging a belief in
witches, it was another thing to believe so much in a particular witch and her deeds
as to be willing to execute her. Yet if one could not believe in particular witches, then
might not one's doubts spread insidiously until they ended in atheism? It was this
link between the general and the particular that inspired the format of Glanvill's
book: a combination of philosophical reasoning, religious purpose, and individual
stories demonstrating the reality of specific instances of witchcraft and the supernatural. The point of the stories was to prove the existence of witchcraft by docu-
menting specific cases through the use of trustworthy evidence – trustworthy both
as to the people testifying and the internal logic and consistency of the testimony
itself. Sinclair followed the same format, but his work was much more heavily biased
towards stories of witchcraft and the supernatural: 'My purpose is only by some few
collections to prove the existence of Devils, Spirits, Witches, and Apparitions.'[63]
Grant saw his own book as being in this same tradition: 'The following narrative, as
to the truth of the matter of Fact, is the best attested piece of History of this kind,
that has occurr'd in many Ages: the most of the matters therein represented having
gained the assent of private Sceptics; and been prov'd before publick Judges.'[64]

This method of proving witchcraft was allied to contemporary natural philosophy, which we call science; both emphasised the empirical basis of knowledge.[65]

---

[58] Glanvill, *Saducismus Triumphatus*, p. 62.

[59] Sinclair, *Satan's Invisible World*, p. xv.

[60] Grant, *Sadducismus Debellatus*, p. v.

[61] Mathieson, *Scotland and the Union*, pp. 219–22; Bostridge, *Witchcraft and its Transformations*,
pp. 24–31.

[62] Grant, *Sadducismus Debellatus*, p. iv.

[63] Sinclair, *Satan's Invisible World*, p. xv.

[64] Grant, *Sadducismus Debellatus*, p. i.

[65] The literature on the history of science is immense and the various debates, while they are pertinent to the topic, are beyond the scope of this chapter. I have found the following book to be the most

Glanvill was a respected member of the Royal Society and the author of a book on the philosophy of science.[66] His insistence that the true scientist must avoid dogmatising and keep an open mind regarding phenomena was deployed in favour of witchcraft stories. He conceded the arguments of critics, acknowledging that there were many frauds and mistakes regarding testimony, there was coercion, and confessions could be the work of melancholy, deluded women. But, he argued, invalidating individual cases did not invalidate the phenomenon, and he presented the stories in his book as facts that could be relied on. Sinclair also came from a scientific background. He was a professor of philosophy and mathematics, wrote a treatise on 'Hydrostaticks', and devised experiments and engineering works. The philosophy behind his stories was adopted from Glanvill.[67]

Grant used this empirical, scientific approach both at the Bargarran trial and in his book. His preface summarised the valid reasons for doubting witchcraft stories, including 'the difficulty in conceiving the Manner or Philosophy, of some Operations and Appearances'. He then continued: 'But they are Men of weak Souls, and destitute of cleer thoughts; who deny all, because they have discovered Error in some; or condemn all Facts as false, because they know not how they came to exist'.[68] To satisfy people's doubts, he deployed scientific speculation to explain the mysterious effects of the witches. How could Christian Shaw be tormented by invisible witches that others could not see? 'Satan's Natural Knowledge, and Acquired Experience makes him perfect in the Opticks and Limning: Besides that, as a spirit, he excels in Strength and Agility; whereby he may easily Bewitch the eyes of others'.[69] He used the same reasoning to show how Christian could hear things that others could not: 'the same way as a sound directed through a speaking Trumpet reaches the Ears to which it is aimed without dispersing it self towards those that are not in a streight line betwixt 'em'.[70]

It must be noted, however, that the scientific reasoning was mixed with religious reasoning and that both served the same purpose: to combat doubts concerning the reality of witches and witchcraft. Thus arguments concerning the physical existence of witchcraft – which Grant called 'the matter of Fact' – were interspersed with arguments taken from the Bible or concerning God's providence. In the preface, after discoursing on the facts and philosophy behind witchcraft, he asserted that 'Providence designs those eminent occurrences rather for our Practical Instruction then for a Subject of notional Speculation'. In his arguments during the trial, he claimed that 'God in his ordinary Providence' prevented the witch from doing further harm

---

helpful and thought-provoking: B. Shapiro, *Probability and Certainty in Seventeenth Century England* (Princeton, NJ, 1983). It traces a shift in perceptions of knowledge through various disciplines including law and science, and has a chapter on witchcraft.

  66 *DNB*, vii, pp. 1287–8.
  67 *DNB*, xviii, pp. 293–4; Sinclair, *Satan's Invisible World*, pp. v–vii.
  68 Grant, *Sadducismus Debellatus*, p. i.
  69 *Ibid.*, p. 57.
  70 *Ibid.*, pp. iii–iv.

after she was imprisoned. In explaining how witches could be transported through the air, he drew upon the hurricane that appeared in the book of Job.[71]

The world-view espoused by Grant and other pro-witchcraft authors was one in which religion and science formed a unified whole, but even more importantly, God and the Devil continued to intervene in the world. To be sure, they did so through the manipulation of the natural world, but behind the seemingly random or weird events associated with witchcraft there lay a great purpose. God was manifesting his will, either directly, or by letting the Devil tempt mankind. And part of God's will was that his ordinances should be obeyed, including 'thou shalt not suffer a witch to live'. By showing witchcraft to be a 'matter of Fact' pro-witchcraft writers were doing God's work by combating people of the opposite persuasion, people whose doubts extended along a spectrum from disbelief in witchcraft to disbelief in God.

VII

While Grant is an obvious exception, most witchcraft writers and readers were remote from the real-life drama of the trials. They were not responsible for the lives of their fellow human beings. An examination of the evidence used in the 1697–1700 witch-hunt brings us into a different world. People testified to things that could result in the death of their neighbours; other people had to assess this testimony and pass judgment. *Sadducismus Debellatus* acts as a bridge between the two worlds: written and edited by the Bargarran prosecutor, it set out in great (but selective) detail the evidence and the arguments used to convict the witches.

When Grant made his speech to the jury he defined three types of evidence that the jurors had to consider. The first was evidence concerning the 'extraordinariness of the Crimes'; that is to say that the facts constituted witchcraft. The second was 'The Probability of concurring Circumstances' – circumstantial evidence establishing that the people on trial were the witches responsible for these crimes. The third was direct testimony by Christian Shaw and by some of the original twenty-five indicted witches – but not by the seven on trial – showing that those seven were guilty.[72] We will add a second classification system, consisting of four categories, to aid in our analysis. The first category is evidence that was 'supernatural' in itself. This is to say, that either it could not by its nature be corroborated by others – such as Christian's invisible tormentors – or the relationship between the evidence and its object required a supernatural intermediary, such as the witches' mark that all witches were supposed to bear. The second category is confessions, the third is reputation, and the last is witness testimony. The first category overlaps with the other three.

---

[71] *Ibid.*, pp. i, iii, 53.
[72] *Ibid.*, p. 47.

The evidence all pertained to the seven witches who were actually tried. They were accused of the murder of a minister and several children in addition to Christian's bewitchment. The supernatural nature of the crimes was proven by a combination of supernatural evidence, confessions and witness testimony. Christian testified as to her afflictions, five of the original twenty-five witches made confessions that were used at the trial, and there were also independent witnesses. For example, a minister testified that when he tried to restrain Christian from going up a flight of stairs 'he found a sensible weight, besides her own Strength drawing her from him'. Grant put his strongest emphasis on concurrences between Christian's testimony and that of other witnesses: 'When she complained, that her Tormenters had bitten and scratched her; the marks of the Nails and Teeth were seen upon her skin, with Blood and Spittle'. The testimony of Dr Brisbane that Christian's 'throwing out' of pins and other items from her mouth did not 'proceed from a Natural Cause' was also influential.[73]

The prominence of supernatural evidence in proving the supernatural nature of the crime should not be surprising, but it was also prominent in identifying the witches and linking them to the crimes laid against them. Most, but not all, had previous reputations as witches. All of the accused, however, had 'insensible marks', failed to shed tears, and provoked fits in Christian Shaw when they approached her. Some unique particulars were given regarding each witch. For example, it was found that after a ball of hair held by Katherine Campbell was burnt, Christian no longer threw up hairballs. Once again, supernatural evidence (the link between Katherine Campbell's hairball and Christian's affliction) was established by witness testimony. Grant argued that this evidence was enough to convict of itself, but if the jurors still had doubts, then the testimony of the 'confessants' should tip the balance.[74]

Six people gave direct testimony concerning the witchcraft and the identity of the witches: Christian Shaw herself, and five witches. These were the most controversial witnesses, and Grant expended his greatest effort persuading the jurors that they were to be believed. Some (including Christian) were under age, Christian, for whatever reason, was disturbed in her mind, and the five witches were suspect due to their bad character. The judges gave a 'nota' on these witnesses saying that something else would have to concur with their testimony to justify a conviction. Grant argued that this had happened: that the weight of the circumstantial evidence and direct testimony combined was such that the jurors had to convict. 'For it may as reasonably be imagined, that the most Regular and Curious Scheme had emerged from the fortuitous concourse of Atoms roving without Rule, as that so many Indications should *concenter* against each of these prisoners, and yet they remain Innocent of Witchcraft'.[75] The jurors agreed; they took six hours to consider the case, and then brought in guilty verdicts.[76]

---

[73] *Ibid.*, pp. 47–9.

[74] *Ibid.*, pp. 49–50.

[75] *Ibid.*, p. 51.

[76] *Ibid.*, pp. 50–2. In Scotland a jury could convict or acquit by majority vote. Six of the witches were convicted unanimously, and one by a majority of unspecified size. NAS, high court of justiciary, circuit court minute book, JC10/4, pp. 58–9.

When we turn to the 1699 evidence, we find only minor variations from that of 1697. To be sure, the sources are different. The Bargarran evidence has been taken from Grant's speech to the jury and thus is logically chosen and arranged to be convincing, while that of 1699 comes from the depositions and the indictment itself, and is therefore undigested. None the less the types of evidence are the same as in the Bargarran case. The tales, accusations and symptoms of the two demoniacs, Margaret Laird and Margaret Murdoch, were strikingly similar to those of Christian Shaw. There was supernatural evidence such as the witches' mark, and corroborating witness testimony. All twenty-four suspects were reputed to be witches, seven had been named by a previous 'confessing witch', and one confessed himself. The variations were those of degree. There appears to be less supernatural evidence, with only four people bearing the witches' mark. Only one of the witches confessed and implicated others. There was much more testimony concerning maleficium – the use of magic to harm one's neighbours.[77] This last may be an illusion of the sources: it may have been edited out of the Bargarran case as unconvincing.[78] None the less, there appears to have been sufficient evidence to warrant at least a few convictions. But it was never put to the test. The people responsible for the trial were losing confidence in this evidence. The doubts that Glanvill, Grant and other authors had wished to allay were growing instead.

VIII

Ideally, a discussion of the doubts entertained regarding witchcraft evidence would involve a systematic study of all the privy councillors, lords of justiciary, lawyers and ministers who were involved in the trials. Not only is this beyond the scope of this chapter, but most of these individuals did not leave statements regarding witchcraft. What we can do is show in a general way that doubts existed, grew and contributed to the abandonment of the trials. As part of this process, it is important to conceptualise 'doubt' as existing along a spectrum of beliefs. What was occurring was not a contest between true believers and complete sceptics, but between people with different degrees of doubt, who chose to emphasise different things.[79]

---

[77] NAS, high court of justiciary, process papers, JC26/81/9; *ibid.*, circuit court minute book, JC10/4, unfoliated; NLS, Wodrow MSS, Wod. folio XXVIII, v. 2, no. 73, fos. 167r.–174r.

[78] The great jurist Sir George Mackenzie gave his opinion that threatenings followed by misfortune, which was how maleficium was usually proven, was not very convincing. Sir George Mackenzie, *The Laws and Customs of Scotland in Matters Criminal* (2nd edn, Edinburgh, 1699), pp. 48–9.

[79] For example, Christina Larner has analysed two witchcraft tracts from 1697 (*Witch-Craft Proven*) and 1705 (*The Tryal of Witchcraft*). Both are 'pro-witchcraft' but the 1705 tract is much more cautious than that from 1697. Yet even with regard to the 1697 tract, Larner writes that although the author was expounding a traditional view of witchcraft, he was 'very worried about the physical possibility of many aspects of it'. C. Larner, 'Two late Scottish witchcraft tracts', in S. Anglo (ed.), *The Damned Art: Essays on the Literature of Witchcraft* (London, 1977), p. 234.

Doubt concerning the reliability of evidence was not new in Scottish witchcraft cases: it had surfaced during the Maxwell of Pollok case in 1677.[80] In the 1697–1700 hunt, doubts existed during the Bargarran trial itself. During the first two months of the trial, the number of witches at the bar fluctuated back and forth between twenty and seven, before settling on the latter.[81] In the middle of this process James Hutchison, minister of Killellan, directly addressed the question of doubt in a sermon: 'Will God command things impossible? Let us not say then it is impossible for us to know the intrigues of Satan, Why hath God said thou shalt not suffer a witch to live?'[82] This probably aided in securing the conviction and execution of seven witches, but it did not banish doubt entirely. The remaining witches were bound over for further proceedings on 28 May 1697, but nothing was heard concerning them again. The commissioners recommended proceedings against another witch, Mary Morison, but she was never tried either.[83] So the Bargarran commission, which could have purged the west of witches, stalled after its initial convictions. The steadfast denials of the seven who were burned may help to account for this, and for the fact that the witches who confessed were never tried or executed.[84]

A final notice concerning the Bargarran case comes from John Bell, who was a young minister in the Glasgow area during the Bargarran trial. In his tract, *The Tryal of Witchcraft*, published in 1705, he condemned the 'credulity' of the clergy and Glasgow professors at the time. Bell's tract was the last serious demonological work in Scotland, yet in retrospect, he felt that more doubt and caution should have been displayed towards the evidence in the case.[85]

When we turn to the 1699 depositions, we find more explicit, contemporary, evidence of doubts. On 1 May 1699 John Anderson, depute-clerk to the privy council, wrote to the earl of Findlater that 'I have bein in the west countrey precognosceing witneses agt witches, I think to little purpose.'[86] At least one person responsible for hearing the witchcraft evidence was not convinced by it, and while a depute-clerk did not have power, he did have influence, and might represent the thinking of others.

More extensive evidence of doubts comes from the records of the synod of Glasgow's witchcraft committee, which exist from July to November 1699. The committee faced a serious problem. On the one hand, witches were continuing their

---

[80] R. L. Harris, 'Janet Douglas and the witches of Pollock: the background of scepticism in Scotland in the 1670s', in S. R. McKenna (ed.), *Selected Essays on Scottish Language and Literature: a Festschrift in Honor of Allan H. MacLaine* (Lewiston, NY, 1992). I would like to thank Dr Louise Yeoman for this reference.

[81] NAS, high court of justiciary, circuit court minute book, JC10/4, pp. 1, 6, 7, 13, 15, 17, 18.

[82] Neilson (ed.), 'A sermon on witchcraft', p. 398.

[83] NAS, high court of justiciary, circuit court minute book, JC10/4, pp. 60–1. She was eventually included among the 1699 witches, and shared their dismissal in 1700. NAS, high court of justiciary, process papers, JC26/81/9 and *ibid.*, books of adjournal, JC3/1, pp. 87–8.

[84] Adam, *Witch Hunt*, pp. 204–12.

[85] Larner, 'Two late Scottish witchcraft tracts', pp. 228, 231–2.

[86] *Seafield Correspondence, 1685–1708*, ed. J. Grant (SHS, 1912), p. 264.

diabolical assault on Christian society so that the indictments needed to be supplemented and expanded. On the other hand, the ministers were forced to acknowledge that the evidence collected in April 1699 was not sufficient to convict, and that more evidence was needed. On 5 July the committee drafted a series of recommendations that addressed both issues and called for more investigations against new and old witchcrafts. Some of the April indictments should be revised and made more 'extensive'. Some of the proofs already gathered might be thought 'lame': if so witnesses should 'be gotten to prove the same more clearly & fullie'. The ministers claimed that at the April interviews, many of the witnesses were intimidated by the kin of the accused witches, and wanted them to be interviewed again under oath and in a non-threatening environment. The opposite treatment was recommended for the witches themselves: they should be imprisoned until trial and ministers should 'have accesse to deall with them to bring them to a confessione'. The 'governement' was called upon to publicise 'to the world' that the sufferings of the demoniacs were 'diabolical & preternatural'. Finally a suggestion was made that witch-prickers be on hand at the upcoming trial to find the insensible mark.[87]

The same problems were confronted in later sittings of the committee on 4 October, 24 October, and 14 and 15 November.[88] But the committee must have realised that it was fighting a losing battle. On 15 November it asked for and received a postponement of the circuit court.[89] This elucidates the justice court's comment that delays were due to 'defect of probatione'.[90] Even more tellingly, the committee recommended that the circuit court be abandoned altogether and be replaced by a privy council commission consisting of local gentlemen, as in 1697. Sir George Mackenzie, who was the foremost Scottish expert on criminal law, had acknowledged that it was easier to convict a witch before a local commission and for that very reason recommended that trials take place before the justice court or its circuits.[91] But the council had promised a commission in the past and then reneged. The ministers' request must therefore be seen as an act of desperation. They cannot have been surprised when the justice court dismissed the case, and no commission was forthcoming.

Unfortunately there are no statements from anyone involved in the 1699–1700 prosecutions that address the question of why the evidence was not convincing. To grapple with this important but elusive issue we must turn to indirect evidence, the best of which comes from Sir George Mackenzie and James Johnstone, each of whom wrote concerning the difficulty of distinguishing between natural and supernatural phenomena.

In his chapter on witchcraft Mackenzie was torn between two imperatives: the need to protect the innocent, and the necessity of punishing the enemies of God.

---

[87] NLS, Wodrow MSS, Wod. quarto LXXIII, fos. 182v.–183r.

[88] *Ibid.*, fos. 183v.–188r.

[89] *Ibid.*, fos. 183v.–184r, 186v.–187r.; NAS, high court of justiciary, books of adjournal, JC3/1, p. 29.

[90] NAS, high court of justiciary, books of adjournal, JC3/1, pp. 88–9.

[91] Mackenzie, *Laws and Customs of Scotland*, pp. 46–7.

Mackenzie was a judge during the 1661–2 witch-hunt and saw numerous examples of women unjustly executed.[92] In addition to problems like credulity, torture and melancholy women making false confessions, Mackenzie addressed the philosophical problem of how to distinguish between natural and supernatural causes. While acknowledging that in the past, many natural effects such as magnetism were looked upon as magical, he expressed confidence that now 'Learning hath sufficiently illuminat the world, so as to distinguish betwixt these two.'[93] None the less he warned that the utmost caution must be exercised in any witchcraft trial: 'And I condemn next to the Witches themselves, those cruel and too forward Judges, who burn persons by thousands as guilty of this Crime'.[94]

Mackenzie wrote in the 1670s. On 1 April 1697 James Johnstone expressed a more radical opinion in a letter to Lord Polwarth, the Lord Chancellor of Scotland; part of it is quoted at the top of this chapter.[95] Johnstone was the former Scottish Secretary, recently dismissed. The context of his letter was political but its subject-matter spoke to Scotland's moral panic, including witches. After stating his own belief in their existence he described how continental jurisdictions had given up prosecutions, not because of unbelief, but because 'its impossible to distinguish possession from nature in disorder'. In other words, the type of 'disorder' experienced by Christian Shaw and other witchcraft victims could proceed from either natural or supernatural causes. Foreign 'judicatories' had decided that it was impossible to distinguish one from the other and so ceased to prosecute the crime. What is most striking about the letter is the way in which it united politics, religion, law and natural philosophy. Johnstone addressed the Aikenhead trial as well as witches, and questioned its wisdom: 'every thing that is lawfull is not expedient'. Aikenhead's execution seriously damaged the presbyterians in English public opinion: 'they could not have given themselves a greater blow'. The implication was that prosecuting witches was also inexpedient.

It would appear that by the 1690s the elite politicians, lawyers and clergy who possessed the power to conduct witch-hunts had reached a delicate psychological balance between doubt and trust in witchcraft evidence. Some, such as Johnstone, clearly desired no more prosecutions. Others, such as the minister James Brisbane, clearly did. For most, we have no direct evidence, but indirect evidence suggests a shifting spectrum of opinion. In this state of balance it is possible that small changes in the degree of moral panic and the reliability of the evidence from 1697 to 1699 would have been sufficient to swing the balance of opinion among the judges and privy councillors to the side of caution, with the result that the push for a trial was abandoned in 1700.

---

[92] Mackenzie, *Laws and Customs of Scotland*, pp. 45–6. See also B. P. Levack, 'The great Scottish witch-hunt of 1661–1662', *Journal of British Studies*, 20 (1980), 90–108, at pp. 104, 106–8; Larner, *Enemies of God*, pp. 77, 186–90.

[93] Mackenzie, *Laws and Customs of Scotland*, p. 44.

[94] *Ibid.*, p. 45.

[95] Johnstone to Polwarth, 1 April 1697, HMC, *The Manuscripts of the Duke of Roxburghe*, p. 132. The letter is also analysed in Bostridge, *Witchcraft and its Transformations*, pp. 30–1.

Eventually doubts and caution reached such a level that trials were no longer possible in Scotland.[96] That stage had not yet been reached; many still continued willing to prosecute, and while 1700 marked the end of large-scale prosecutions in Scotland, individual trials continued for a while. Therefore, it is appropriate to give the last word to the eventual losers. On 2 August 1700 the kirk gave, as one of its reasons for a national fast, 'our slighting and misimproveing the purity and plenty of Gospell ordinances'.[97] The commandment 'Thou shalt not suffer a witch to live' was not being treated with its former respect.

[96] B. P. Levack, 'The decline and end of Scottish witch-hunting', Chapter 10 below. The last trial and execution was in 1727: E. J. Cowan and L. Henderson, 'The last of the witches? The survival of Scottish witch belief', Chapter 12 below.

[97] NAS, privy council, acta, PC1/52, p. 135.

10

The decline and end
of Scottish witch-hunting

Brian P. Levack

I

During the late seventeenth and early eighteenth centuries, prosecutions and executions for witchcraft in Scotland declined in number and eventually came to an end. The decline was marked by a reduction in the number of trials, a rise in the number of acquittals, and a drop in the execution-rate. The decline began in the early 1660s in the wake of the most intense witch-hunt the country had ever experienced, but it took more than fifty years for the trials to end altogether. The decline did not follow a linear path. After the hunt of 1661–2, which was the last national hunt, there were brief local panics in 1678 in East Lothian and again in 1697 at Paisley. The overall trend, however, was unmistakable. The witch-hunts that occurred after 1662 claimed far fewer lives than those of the 1590s or of the mid-seventeenth century, and the number of individual prosecutions was gradually reduced to a trickle. The last executions recorded in the central records of the country took place in 1706, while the last trial, one of questionable legality, occurred in 1727, a mere nine years before the British parliament repealed the Scottish witchcraft law of 1563. The British statute of 1736 officially determined that witchcraft in Scotland, as well as in England, was no longer a crime.

The main purpose of this essay is to account for this decline in the number of Scottish witchcraft prosecutions and executions after 1662. In so doing it will establish the extent to which the decline of Scottish witch-hunting conformed to a broader European pattern. This type of investigation has yet to become a central concern of witchcraft scholars. Historians of witchcraft have traditionally given much more thought to the question of why the trials began than why they came to an end. We have only a few surveys of the process throughout Europe[1] and a handful of local and national studies exploring the issue.[2]

---

[1] A. Soman, 'Decriminalizing witchcraft: does the French experience furnish a European model?', *Criminal Justice History*, 10 (1989), 1–22; B. P. Levack, 'The decline and end of witchcraft prosecutions', in S. Clark and B. Ankarloo (eds), *Witchcraft and Magic in Europe: the Eighteenth and Nineteenth Centuries* (London, 1999).

[2] R. Mandrou, *Magistrats et sorciers en France au XVIIe siècle* (Paris, 1968); H. Kneubühler, *Die*

Until recently, most of the scholars who addressed this question, usually in passing, attributed the decline in one way or another to the emergence of modern rationalism, the rise of science, or an even vaguer dispelling of ignorance and 'superstition'.[3] This interpretation arose during the Enlightenment, and it became the backbone of late nineteenth- and early twentieth-century liberal and Whig historiography. Historians writing in this tradition focused mainly on the content of published witchcraft treatises and the theological and philosophical controversies to which those treatises contributed. They assumed that the decline of witchcraft prosecutions had been caused by a decline in the witch-beliefs of the educated classes and therefore made little distinction between the two developments. The little that has been written on the decline of Scottish witchcraft conforms to this pattern.[4] The end of the trials thus became synonymous with the enlightened rejection of the demonological ideas that had provided the intellectual foundations of witch-hunting. Only recently have alternative approaches to the decline and end of European witchcraft prosecutions, based on either changes in judicial administration or economic and social factors, begun to take its place.[5]

An explanation of the decline of European witchcraft prosecutions in philosophical terms is highly problematic. The main problem is that the expression of sceptical ideas, especially those that denied the possibility of the crime of witchcraft, either had little impact among the intellectual elite or took place after witchcraft prosecutions had already begun to wane. There were, to be sure, sceptical voices throughout the entire period of witch-hunting, the most famous in the sixteenth century being those of Johann Weyer and Reginald Scot. These men did not, however, undermine the prosecutions. Not only did their ideas experience a cool reception in intellectual

---

Überwindung von Hexenwahn und Hexenprozess (Diessenhofen, 1977); J. C. V. Johansen, 'Witchcraft, sin and repentance: the decline of Danish witchcraft trials,' *Acta Ethnographica*, 37 (1991/2), 413–23; *Das Ende der Hexenverfolgungen*, ed. S. Lorenz and D. R. Bauer (Stuttgart, 1995); J. Klaits, 'Witchcraft trials and absolute monarchy in France,' in R. Golden (ed.), *Church, State and Society under the Bourbon Kings of France* (Lawrence, KS ,1982); E. W. Monter, *Witchcraft in France and Switzerland: the Borderlands during the Reformation* (Ithaca, NY, 1976), pp. 37–41; A. Soman, 'The parlement of Paris and the great witch hunt (1565–1640)', *Sixteenth Century Journal*, 9 (1978), 31–44; G. Henningsen, *The Witches' Advocate: Basque Witchcraft and the Spanish Inquisition, 1609–1614* (Reno, Nev., 1980); J. Sharpe, *Instruments of Darkness: Witchcraft in England, 1550–1750* (London, 1996), ch. 9.

[3] See for example W. E. H. Lecky, *The History of the Influence of the Spirit of Rationalism in Europe* (London, 1910), ch. 1.

[4] Larner, *Enemies of God*, pp. 78–9: 'Between 1680 and 1735 witch-belief disappeared almost without comment from the cognitive map of the ruling class'. Even if we exclude the ministry from this class, there is no evidence of such a disappearance. On the persistence of Scottish witch-beliefs and their association with a distinctive Scottish culture after the union of 1707 see I. Bostridge, 'Witchcraft repealed,' in J. Barry *et al.* (eds), *Witchcraft in Early Modern Europe: Studes in Culture and Belief* (Cambridge, 1996).

[5] The first national study of the decline of prosecutions, Mandrou, *Magistrats et Sorciers*, focuses on the new jurisprudence of French judges, but this jurisprudence is viewed as part of a broader intellectual change. K. Thomas, *Religion and the Decline of Magic: Studies in Popular Beliefs in Sixteenth and Seventeenth-Century England* (London, 1971), chs. 20–2, identifies social and economic changes in the decline of English witchcraft prosecutions but gives equal weight to changes in mental attitudes.

circles and elicit some vigorous responses,[6] but their scepticism itself was of a limited nature. Neither Weyer nor Scot, for example, took the extreme position that witchcraft was an impossible crime.[7] A group of late seventeenth- and early eighteenth-century sceptics, which included the Dutch Cartesian minister Balthasar Bekker and the Saxon jurist Christian Thomasius, came much closer to that radical position, but their scepticism emerged at a time when most Western European countries had already begun to end the trials. The views of Bekker and Thomasius, moreover, took even longer to be disseminated among the judges, magistrates and clergy who actually controlled the prosecutions. It will never be clear exactly when European ruling elites lost their belief in witchcraft, but we can be confident that very few of them did so until the trials were almost completely over.[8]

The problem of explaining the decline of witchcraft prosecutions in terms of a rejection of learned witch-beliefs becomes insurmountable when we focus on Scotland. There are few countries in Europe in which a philosophical or intellectual opposition to witch-hunting had a weaker voice or commanded less widespread support than in Scotland. To put the matter in its simplest terms, Scotland did not have any counterparts of either Weyer and Scot in the late sixteenth century or of Bekker and Thomasius a century later. Scotland did have its critics of witch-hunting, most notably the jurist Sir George Mackenzie, but Mackenzie refused in any way to lend support even to Weyer's philosophical position. Among Scottish judges, magistrates and clergy there was not even a hint of the argument that witchcraft was an impossible crime until long after decriminalisation, which took place in 1736. Mackenzie, both in his defence of the accused witch Maevia and in his summary of Scots criminal law, took pains to establish the existence of witches, even if those witches did not appear to be as numerous as many contemporaries claimed.[9] The furthest Mackenzie would go in challenging contemporary witch-beliefs was to deny the possibility of witches' flight and their metamorphosis into animals – issues with which orthodox demonologists were themselves uncomfortable.[10] The same reluctance to challenge the intellectual foundation of witch-hunting can be seen in the vigorous defence of the Paisley witches mounted

---

[6] E. W. Monter, 'Law, medicine and the acceptance of witchcraft, 1560–1680', in E. W. Monter (ed.), *European Witchcraft* (New York, 1969).

[7] Scot insisted in good Calvinist fashion that the age of miracles had passed and that a sovereign God would not permit human beings to exercise supernatural power, but he did not include the 'working of wonders by supernatural means' in his summary of the 'absurd and impossible crimes' attributed to witches. Reginald Scot, *The Discoverie of Witchcraft*, ed. M. Summers (London, 1930), pp. 7, 18–20, 89. Scot included these 'wonders' among the alleged crimes of witches that witch-hunters could not prove to be true. *Discoverie*, p. 19.

[8] For a full discussion of this problem see Levack, 'Decline and end of witchcraft prosecutions', pp. 33–40.

[9] Sir George Mackenzie of Rosehaugh, *The Laws and Customes of Scotland in Matters Criminal* (Edinburgh, 1678), pp. 80–108. Mackenzie's chapter on witchcraft is reproduced in *The History of the Witches of Renfrewshire* (Paisley, 1877), pp. 5–37, under the title of 'A treatise on witchcraft'.

[10] [Sir George Mackenzie,] *Pleadings in some Remarkable Cases before the Supreme Courts of Scotland, since the year 1661* (Edinburgh, 1673), pp. 185, 192.

by the advocate James Robertson in 1697. Robertson made a strong case for the innocence of his clients, but he never challenged the firm witch-beliefs of the prosecuting advocates, James Stewart and Francis Grant.[11] Even in 1730, three years after the last Scottish witch trial, the jurist William Forbes, in his authoritative summary of Scots criminal law, insisted upon the reality of witchcraft.[12]

The decline of Scottish witchcraft prosecutions, therefore, took place within the context of a general belief in the reality of the crime. This persistence of learned belief forces us to consider alternative explanations for the reduction in the number of prosecutions and executions. In particular it encourages us to take a legal approach, to focus on the judicial process itself and the concerns of the judges, lawyers and magistrates who were responsible for the operation of the judicial machinery. In the most general terms it encourages us to study the growth of a judicial rather than a philosophical scepticism, an outlook that does not question the reality of witchcraft but which does question whether specific individuals, and ultimately whether *any* individuals, could be proved guilty of this crime at law. Judicial scepticism in its various forms, especially the insistence on following due process in proceeding against witches, has been shown to have been highly instrumental in reducing the number of trials and executions in Spain after 1614, northern France after 1624, Würzburg after 1629, England after 1646, Italy after 1655, Sweden after 1676, New England after 1692, and Hungary after 1750. It was also instrumental in reducing the intensity of Scottish witch-hunting after 1662.

II

The episode which gave rise to this demand for legal caution was the great Scottish witch-hunt of 1661–2. That hunt was so large, involving a total of 664 named witches in four counties, and the death toll so great, that it almost inevitably called attention to the procedural irregularities that characterised it. The abuses identified specifically in the records of the privy council were the unauthorised arrest of suspects, the torture and pricking of suspects without proper warrant, and the use of other illegal means to extract confessions. The determination of the central government to prevent these abuses from recurring, which found expression in a proclamation of April 1662, marks the turning point in the entire history of Scottish witch-hunting.[13]

The impact of the witch-hunt of 1661–2 on the way in which subsequent witchcraft prosecutions were handled in Scotland can be seen in three different ways. First, after 1662 there was a significant increase in the number of trials that were conducted, or more closely supervised, by central judicial authorities, a development

[11] NAS, JC10/4, fos. 63–81. For more on this case see M. Wasser, 'The western witch-hunt of 1697–1700: the last major witch-hunt in Scotland', Chapter 9 above.

[12] W. Forbes, *Institutions of the Laws of Scotland* (Edinburgh, 1730), p. 32. 'Nothing seems plainer to me than that there may be, and have been witches, and that perhaps such are now actually existing'.

[13] *RPC*, 3rd ser., i, p. 198.

that resulted in a higher number of acquittals. Second, as a result of this increased control from the centre, there was a reduction in the incidence of judicial torture and the more frequent dismissal of cases in which it had been used illegally. Finally, in all witchcraft trials there was a more careful weighing of the evidence and greater adherence to strict standards of judicial proof. Taken together, these three developments go a long way towards explaining the reduction in the number of convictions and executions. They also explain, in an indirect way, the reduction in the number of trials.

The first and most important of these changes concerns the role of central governmental authorities in the trial of witches. In Scotland, as in virtually all countries in Europe, the main pressure to prosecute witches came from local communities. This is not to say that central governments did not from time to time initiate or at least encourage witch-hunts. Certainly they had done so in Scotland in 1590, just as they had in Bavaria in 1587 and at Køge in Denmark in 1612. But for the most part central governments were responding to requests from local authorities either to have the witches tried in the central courts or to give those same local authorities permission to try the witches in their own communities. At that point central judicial officials could either facilitate or impede the success of the trials. This meant that the intensity of witch-hunting in a particular area depended to a great extent upon the way in which the central government responded to these local initiatives.

Prior to 1662 the Scottish government had not followed a consistent policy regarding witch-hunting. King James VI himself had encouraged, if he had not actually inspired, many of the prosecutions in 1590–1, but during the large witch-hunt of 1597 the privy council had taken steps to reduce the intensity of witch-hunting. In that year noblemen and local officials, operating under commissions of justiciary to apprehend and try any persons suspected of witchcraft, had used their judicial power to settle personal disputes, thereby placing 'honnest and famous personis' in great danger. In order to prevent these abuses from recurring, the council revoked the commissions that had been granted to those men and required that any local authorities who wished to prosecute witches petition the council for new commissions, which would include at least three or four members operating conjointly.[14] After this time the council reviewed all requests for commissions of justiciary on a case-by-case basis, and this practice contributed to a significant decline in the total number of witchcraft trials during the next thirty years.

Over the long term, however, the practice of requiring conciliar approval of all justiciary commissions to conduct local witchcraft trials did not keep witch-hunting under control. At four critical junctures in the seventeenth century – 1628, 1643, 1649 and 1661 – major hunts took place. There were two main reasons for these breakdowns in the system. The first was that the government from time to time granted commissions of justiciary without carefully considering whether a local trial was warranted or whether due process had been followed in the arrest

---

[14] *RPC,* v, pp. 409–10.

and interrogation of the accused. Especially during the periods of intense prosecution, it issued them almost routinely in response to local requests.

Once these commissions were granted, there was little likelihood that the witches would be spared. The commissioners entrusted with the local trials of these witches were almost always legally untrained local lairds, magistrates or elders of the parish, rather than lawyers or justice deputes from Edinburgh. These men, according to Mackenzie, were 'not exactly acquaint with the nature of this crime'.[15] They also were in most cases the same men who had already interrogated the accused witches, gathered evidence of their guilt and sent a petition to Edinburgh requesting the trials. In these cases the trials, which were conducted by juries, did little more than confirm the suspicions of the community. Until the late seventeenth century witches tried on the basis of these commissions, unlike those tried in Edinburgh, did not have access to counsel.[16] It should come as no surprise that in more than 90 per cent of all the trials conducted by local commissioners the accused were convicted and executed.[17] As Mackenzie wrote in 1678, 'I have observed that scarce any who were accused before a Countrey Assize of Neighbours did escape that trial'.[18]

The second reason for the recurrence of large witch-hunts after 1597 was that from time to time the government actually encouraged the local discovery of witches. The intense witch-hunts that began in 1628, 1649 and 1661 formed part of broader governmental initiatives to punish crime, especially crimes of a religious nature, the goal being to establish Scotland as a godly state. Thus in 1628 the privy council instructed specially appointed commissioners to collect charges against people for more than seventy different crimes, with witchcraft close to the top of the list.[19] In 1649, the year in which King Charles I was executed and Scotland faced the prospect of renewed military conflict with England, the council conducted nothing less than a moral crusade against a variety of moral crimes, including adultery and witchcraft. In 1661, shortly after the Restoration of Charles II, the prosecution of witches took on a more political colour, as it became associated with a campaign waged by victorious royalists against rebellious Covenanters. In all these cases the central government catered to, if it did not take steps to stimulate, local demand for prosecution. At the same time local pressures to prosecute, often inspired or reinforced by religious fervour, intensified.

After 1662 this episodic pattern of recurrent witch-hunts, fuelled either by the neglect of the council or by its religious zeal, came to an end, leading to the decline in prosecutions that ended in 1727. Central judicial authorities, especially the

---

[15] Mackenzie, *Laws Criminal*, p. 88.

[16] *Ibid.* 'Nor have the pannels any to plead for them and to take notice who are led as witnesses; so that many who are admitted are *testes inhabiles*, and suspect.'

[17] Larner *et al.*, *Source-Book*, p. 237. These calculations are based on those cases whose outcomes are known. They include commissions granted by parliament as well as the council.

[18] Mackenzie, *Laws Criminal*, p. 88.

[19] *RPC*, 2nd ser., ii, pp. 437–8.

council and the lord advocate but also the judges of the justiciary court in Edinburgh, succeeded in imposing effective checks on local witch-hunting. They did this in three different ways. First, they reduced the number of conciliar or parliamentary commissions while at the same time taking steps to funnel local cases into the justiciary court at Edinburgh. Whereas more than 1,150 witches had been tried by conciliar or parliamentary commissions of justiciary before 1662, the total number of such cases heard between 1662 and 1727 dropped to 97. These trials still resulted in a high percentage of executions, at least among those trials whose outcomes are known (23 out of 24 cases), but the dramatic reduction in the number of trials goes a long way towards accounting for the overall pattern of decline. By contrast, the percentage of cases that were heard before the justiciary court (officially established as the High Court of Justiciary in 1672) increased after 1662, and more than two-thirds of those cases resulted in acquittals.[20] In some cases the justices deliberately denied requests for a local trial and ordered the cases to be heard in the justiciary court.[21]

This policy of reducing the number of trials conducted by local magistrates reflected a broader effort of the Scottish government in the late seventeenth century to centralise and rationalise the criminal justice system. This meant first of all insisting that all trials, especially those of witchcraft, be conducted by properly constituted authority. This was the import of the council's order of April 1662 and its frequent reiteration after that date. The government's policy became evident in 1674, for example, when the judges of the justiciary court dropped the charges against the accused witch Margaret Clerk after it was discovered that justices of the peace from Banff had brought her to trial. At that point the judges made it clear that 'no inferior judge, much less justices of the peace, were competent to the crime of witchcraft'.[22] Only central justices or those who were properly commissioned by them could bring witches to trial. Sir George Mackenzie, who was the lord advocate from 1677 to 1686, became the most vocal proponent of this policy. In 1680, for example, he secured the acquittal of the accused witch Bessie Gibb, mainly on the grounds that the magistrates and the bailie of the burgh of Bo'ness, who had originally proceeded against her, were not competent to try her.[23] Mackenzie's position on this question conformed to his broader objective to take criminal trials out of the hands of 'country-men' who did not have legal training and to entrust the entire process, including the determination of guilt, to professional lawyers and judges.[24]

The second means by which central authorities restrained the excesses of local witch-hunting was through the successful implementation of an effective circuit court system after 1671. This system, the heir to the medieval justice ayres and the Scottish counterpart to the English assizes, had been proposed from time to time

---

[20] There were 133 cases in all. Of those whose outcomes are known, only 24 witches were executed, while 58 were acquitted. Larner *et al.*, *Source-Book*, *passim*.

[21] NLS, MS 643, fo. 85; *A True and Full Relation of the Witches at Pittenweem* (Edinburgh, 1704), p. 12.

[22] NAS, JC2/14, fo. 181.

[23] NAS, JC2/15, fo. 103.

[24] Mackenzie, *Laws Criminal*, pp. 89–90.

in the sixteenth and seventeenth centuries, especially as part of the legal reforms of 1587, but the plan had never really got off the ground.[25] Only during the Cromwellian occupation of the 1650s did the circuit courts operate as intended. After 1671, these courts began to function in a regular fashion, and an increasingly large number of witchcraft cases were brought before them. These local trials, presided over by judges from Edinburgh, yielded far more acquittals than those in which local commissioners acted as judges. Between 1671 and 1709 only two witches are known to have been executed by circuit courts.[26]

The third step that the council took was to exercise tighter control over those witchcraft trials conducted by conciliar commissions. One of the main problems with these commissions before 1662 was that there was no central involvement in, or supervision of, the actual trial. In a number of commissions after 1662, however, the council insisted that a justice-depute from Edinburgh be included among the commissioners, thereby guaranteeing the presence of central authority at the trial.[27] Another tactic was to insist on conciliar review of the commissioners' sentences. The privy council did this in a commission granted to the Aberdeen burgh council in February 1669, and it followed a similar course of action in a commission granted in 1699 to try nine accused witches from Ross-shire. In this last instance the council appointed a special committee to decide whether the sentences of the commission should be carried out. As a result of this action, two witches who had confessed were given non-capital punishments, and the others were set at liberty.[28] This review of the commissioners' sentences is reminiscent of the way in which Continental countries, most notably France, Sweden and Russia, instituted the practice of submitting all sentences in witchcraft cases to appellate review. Scotland did not have an appellate structure of judicial administration, but this review of sentences by an *ad hoc* committee served the same purpose. It appears to have had the desired effect, since the trials did not result in executions.

III

The second change in the conduct of witchcraft trials after 1662 was the reduction in the use of torture. Torture played a central role in the prosecution and conviction of witches in many European countries. Its use allowed magistrates and prosecutors to secure the confessions that were necessary for conviction when witnesses were not forthcoming, and it also allowed them to obtain the names of alleged accomplices. By the same token the critiques of torture that developed throughout Europe in the seventeenth century played a vital role in reducing the number of convictions and executions. A group of early seventeenth-century treatises condemning the

---

[25] One effort to operate the system occurred in 1628. *The Earl of Stirling's Original Register of Royal Letters*, 2 vols, ed. C. Rogers (Edinburgh, 1885), ii, p. 377.

[26] Larner *et al.*, *Source-Book*, pp. 58–60.

[27] See for example *RPC*, 3rd ser., iii, p. 45.

[28] R. Chambers, *Domestic Annals of Scotland*, 3 vols (Edinburgh, 1861), iii, p. 216.

procedure, the most influential being that of the German Jesuit Friedrich Spee, was followed by the more comprehensive and systematic works of Augustin Nicolas, Michael Sassen and Christian Thomasius in the late seventeenth and early eighteenth centuries.[29] Scottish writers did not produce any formal treatises of this sort, but they did formulate a critique of the use of torture in witchcraft cases, and that critique played a crucial role in the decline of Scottish witchcraft prosecutions.

The essence of this Scottish critique was not that torture was *ipso facto* wrong or illegal but that it was being applied without proper authority. The law of torture in Scotland was that it could be administered only when specifically warranted by the council or parliament. In that regard it was essentially the same as the law of torture in England, which also prohibited the use of torture without the approval of the council. (The same law was also in force in Sweden, where the right to torture formed part of the royal prerogative.) There was therefore a striking difference between the Scottish law of torture and that which was in force in countries that followed a fully inquisitorial system of justice. In those countries torture could be applied by judges when sufficient circumstantial evidence, usually the testimony of one witness or the equivalent in circumstantial evidence, created a presumption of guilt.

The requirement that Scottish judicial authorities receive permission from the council or parliament to torture a suspected criminal was not adhered to in witchcraft cases. Of the thirty-nine torture warrants issued between 1590 and 1689 (when torture was restricted by the Claim of Right), only two involved cases of witchcraft.[30] Yet there is an abundance of evidence that torture was regularly applied in witchcraft cases. Not surprisingly it was almost always administered by local authorities, usually shortly after the arrest of the witch.[31] In many cases the torture was applied under the guise of pricking the witch for the Devil's mark, an investigatory procedure intended to produce sufficient presumption of guilt in order to request an indictment. Pricking a witch with large pins, known as the brods, could and did force the victim to confess just as readily as if she had been deprived of sleep or subjected to the more brutal torture of the boots.[32]

---

[29] [F. Spee,] *Cautio Criminalis* (Rinteln, 1631); A. Nicolas, *Si la Torture est un moyen seur a vérifier les crimes sécrets: dissertation morale et juridique* (Amsterdam, 1682); M. J. Sassen, *De usu et abusu torturae* (1697; other editions appeared in 1726 and 1735); C. Thomasius, *De Tortura ex fori Christianorum proscribenda* (Halle, 1705), *De origine ac progressu processus inquisitorii contra sagas* (Halle, 1712) and *Über di Hexenprozesse*, ed. R. Lieberwirth (Weimar, 1986).

[30] A total of 34 Scottish warrants for the years 1590–1689 appear in *RPC*. An additional five warrants were granted by Parliament: *APS*, iv, p. 108; v, pp. 396, 706; vi, II, p. 390 ('any uther forme of probatioun'); ix, pp. 30b, 102a, 191b. Torture was threatened against Baillie of Jerviswood: ix, p. 58.

[31] Lord Royston observed, 'Most of the poor creatures are tortured by their keepers'. NLS, Advocates' MS 25.3.15., fo. 60. See also Mackenzie, *Pleadings*, p. 196.

[32] Pricking was frequently identified with torture in the records. In 1661 Margaret Carvie and Barbara Horninam of Falkland appealed to the council, claiming they had endured 'a great deal of torture by one who takes upon the trial of witches by pricking'. Chambers, *Domestic Annals*, ii, p. 279. See also W. Stephen, *The History of Inverkeithing and Rosyth* (Aberdeen, 1921), p. 437; W. Ross, *Aberdour and Inchcolme* (Edinburgh, 1885), p. 331. In 1678 the council declared that inferior judges 'might not use any torture, by pricking, or by withholding them from sleep'. John Lauder,

Prior to 1662 the council had made only sporadic efforts to prosecute local authorities for administering torture without the required warrant in witchcraft cases.[33] The turning point came in the wake of the great witch-hunt of 1661–2. During that panic the Council noted that 'pricking, watching, keiping of them from sleip and other torture' had been responsible for the execution of innocent persons.[34] Shortly thereafter the council issued its proclamation prohibiting the use of torture in witchcraft cases without its specific permission. This prohibition was also included in some of the justiciary commissions granted during the next few years.[35]

The council's prohibition of torture in witchcraft cases was not completely successful. Reports of illegal torture continued to reach the council, especially during the East Lothian trials of 1678. In September of that year Katherine Liddell of Prestonpans, who had been arrested and imprisoned for witchcraft, petitioned the council to take action against those who 'did most cruelly and barbarously torment and torture' her 'by pricking of pines in severall parts of her body to the great effusion of her blood and whereby her skein is raised and her body highly swelled and she is in danger of her life'. Liddell herself was set free, while one of her tormentors, the pricker David Cowan, was imprisoned 'for presuming to torture or prick any person without warrant from the Council'.[36] Even this action failed to put an end to the practice. In 1680 five witches whose confessions were shown to have been the product of 'several types of torture' were set at liberty.[37] There is evidence that local authorities continued to administer torture illegally into the early eighteenth century, even after the British parliament passed a statute prohibiting the use of torture in all cases in Scotland.[38] During the famous witch-hunt at Pittenweem in 1704 one of the accused, Janet Cornfoot, swore that 'the minister did beat her severely until she confessed'.[39] Nevertheless, the prohibition by the council did help to reduce the frequency with which torture was applied and thus the number of convictions and executions in witchcraft cases.

The person who had recommended the release of the five witches of 1680 was Sir George Mackenzie, acting in his capacity as lord advocate. Mackenzie's primary concern in making this recommendation was the conduct of judicial business by

---

Lord Fountainhall, *Decisions of the Lords of the Council and Session, 1678–1712*, 2 vols (Edinburgh, 1759–61), i, p. 16.

[33] See for example the action taken against the tutor and minister of Calder in Nov. 1644. *RPC*, 2nd ser., viii, p. 37.

[34] *RPC*, 3rd ser., ii, pp. 188–9.

[35] *RPC*, 3rd ser., ii, pp. 192–3, 614; v, p. 171.

[36] *RPC*, 3rd ser., vi, p. 13. For the legal arguments in the prosecution of Liddell's tormentors, see the case of Liddell v. Rutherford in Fountainhall, *Decisions*, i, pp. 15–16; Black, *Calendar*, p. 79.

[37] NAS, JC2/15, fo. 159.

[38] 7 Anne, c. 21, par. viii.

[39] Letter from Mr Miller, 19 Nov. 1704, Folger Shakespeare Library, MS x.d. 436 (58). The minister of the parish was Patrick Cowper. Miller also reported that 'ministers have used a great deal of barbarous severities to extort confessions from those unhappie creatures'.

men who were not competent to do so. It was not torture as such to which 'Bluidy' Mackenzie, the persecutor of Covenanters, objected: he defended his own use of the practice in treason trials on the basis of reason of state and claimed that its use was sanctioned by the law of nations.[40] But he insisted that its use be restricted to the council and the judges of the justiciary court, a policy similar to that of the *parlement* of Paris proclaimed in 1624.[41] Only in this way could the procedure be used properly. It is noteworthy that even while recommending the use of a new instrument of torture in 1684, the thumbkins, the council insisted that any use of the device should be 'by their order'.[42]

A conflict between the burgh council of Aberdeen and the privy council provides us with the best illustration of the late seventeenth-century policy of the council regarding torture and also how it was connected to the issue of granting commissions of justiciary. In May 1669 the Aberdeen council apprehended three suspected witches on the basis of common fame and evidence that they had committed various malefices. The burgh council then wrote to the privy council requesting a commission of justiciary which would include the 'power of torture in the ordinary maner in lyk cases'.[43] The privy council responded that it would not grant the commission unless the burgesses submitted a confession of the witches and that under no circumstances would they grant them a warrant to put the witches to the torture. The burgesses responded by claiming that they needed a commission forthwith, since otherwise the witches, being old and kept in prison at the expense of the town, would likely die 'without trial or confession'. They offered to submit a statement of a presumption against the witches upon which a commission could be granted, and renewed their request for the power to torture, 'which it hath been the ordinary way of former commissions without something whairof they will not confess'.[44]

On 11 June the Aberdeen council reported that they were still waiting for a commission and that the council had indicated that it would not grant such a warrant to the Aberdeen magistrates alone, insisting that they be joined by 'some able persons'. The burgesses protested that they were as trustworthy and had carried themselves as legally and deliberately as any magistrates of any burgh in the kingdom.[45] Only when the Aberdeen council offered to pay the expenses of a justice depute from Edinburgh, John Preston, to travel north and sit with the Aberdeen magistrates, did the council relent and grant the commission on 15 July.[46] The

---

[40] Sir George Mackenzie, *A Vindication of the Government of Scotland during the Reign of Charles II* (Edinburgh, 1691); 'A Discourse on the Four First Chapters of the Digest', BL, Sloane MS 3828, fo. 127.

[41] Mackenzie, *Laws Criminal*, p. 543. At no time during this period did the council recognise the right of the justices to administer torture. On the parlement of Paris see Soman, 'Decriminalizing witchcraft', 1–10.

[42] *RPC*, 3rd ser., ix, p. 66.

[43] *Aberdeen Council Letters*, 6 vols, ed. L. B. Taylor (London, 1942–61), iv, pp. 393–4.

[44] *Ibid.*, p. 394.

[45] *Ibid.*, p. 398.

[46] *RPC*, 3rd ser., iii, p. 45. Preston had to be present. For the Aberdeen council's discussion of the suitability of Preston see *Aberdeen Council Letters*, iv, p. 403. For the inclusion of Preston in a later commission see *RPC*, 3rd ser., v, p. 171.

outcome of the trial of the three witches, together with a fourth who was named in the commission, is not known, although it was noted in the records of the council in August 1670 that several witches had been executed at Aberdeen on an unspecified date.[47]

This long jurisdictional conflict between Aberdeen and the council illustrates three important developments. First, the council after 1662 was determined not to grant torture warrants to local magistrates and was not at all receptive to the transparently false claim of the burgesses that such warrants had been granted on a regular basis in the past.[48] Second, the council had been reluctant even to grant the commission, on the apparent ground that they did not trust the magistrates to conduct a fair trial. Only after adding a justice depute from Edinburgh did they grant the commission, with specific instructions to conduct the trial according to the laws of the realm.[49] Third, even though the Aberdeen council did not receive permission to torture the accused, they apparently did secure the witches' eventual conviction and execution. Since the verdict was determined by a jury of local Aberdonians, that result should not surprise us. All in all, the episode reveals that the council, and in particular the lord advocate and justice clerk, were making a conscious effort to control the local prosecution of witches, even if in this case they did not prevent the witches from perishing.

IV

A third major reason for the decline in the number of convictions and executions in witchcraft cases was the greater care with which evidence was evaluated at witchcraft trials and the adherence of judges to increasingly rigorous evidentiary standards. In Scotland this development was closely associated with the greater participation of lawyers in witchcraft trials. Although Scottish criminal trials were similar to those in England in that the outcome was decided by lay juries, they differed from English trials in that the accused had a right to defence counsel. Representation consisted mainly in the submission of written pleadings by an advocate on behalf of the accused. In these pleadings the advocate would challenge the relevance of particular pieces of evidence to the libel, which is the proposition stating the reasons for the accused's guilt. This process, which resembled Continental European criminal procedure more than that of England, resulted in often long exchanges between the prosecutors and the defence lawyers. These debates on relevancy took place before the evidence was presented to the jury, and the judge's decision on these points of law could effectively lead to acquittals.

Until the late seventeenth century, very few Scottish witches could afford the cost of legal representation, and those who could usually were tried in the justiciary

---

[47] *RPC*, 3rd ser., iii, pp. 211–12.

[48] The burgh council certainly could not have been referring to its most recent commission, 25 Feb. 1669, which specifically prohibited it from using torture: *RPC*, 3rd ser., ii, p. 614.

[49] *RPC*, 3rd ser., iii, p. 45.

court in Edinburgh. Towards the end of this period, however, advocates represented witches more frequently and even appeared in some of the local cases heard
by commissioners of justiciary, such as in the trial of the Paisley witches in 1697.[50]
Lawyers could have a dramatic impact on the course of a witchcraft trial. They
could raise doubts regarding the supernatural causes of alleged *maleficia* and
impeach the credibility of witnesses who might not have been allowed to testify in
the trial of ordinary crimes. They could point out the insufficiency of the evidence,
especially when it was hearsay, and the irrelevancy of the evidence to the libel. They
could identify procedural irregularities upon which the judges would discontinue
proceedings or have the trial moved to Edinburgh, such as when the advocate for
Margaret Clerk showed the High Court of Justiciary in 1674 that the justices of the
peace in the sheriffdom of Banff had proceeded summarily and illegally against her
and had behaved most partially and unjustly.[51] In an earlier case David Williamson,
who represented the accused witch Mary Cunningham, succeeded in having the
case moved to Edinburgh when he showed that the procurator fiscal who prosecuted her in Culross, a man 'who had no skill of law,' could not answer his
defence.[52] Finally, lawyers could influence the jury to bring in acquittals. It is not
surprising, therefore, that the growing number of acquittals during the late seventeenth century coincided with the greater frequency of legal representation.

The more careful evaluation of evidence in witchcraft trials can be seen, first and
foremost, in a growing reluctance of lawyers and judges to accept confessions, traditionally regarded as the queen of proofs, as sufficient proof of guilt. In the East
Lothian trials of 1678 the judges released a group of witches who were about to
implicate 'sundry gentlewomen and others of fashion', attributing their confessions
to 'malice, or melancholy, or the Devil's deception'.[53] In his summary of Scottish
criminal law Mackenzie, who was responsible for a large number of acquittals in
such cases, argued that confessions to witchcraft (or any other crime) were valid
evidence only if such confessions were in no way extorted, if they contained nothing that was impossible or improbable, and if the person confessing was neither
melancholic nor suicidal.[54]

A second and even more frequent expression of the new judicial scepticism
was the argument of lawyers that events attributed to supernatural agency might
have had natural causes. This argument was particularly relevant to charges of

---

[50] *Witches of Renfrewshire*, p. 142.

[51] NAS, JC2/14, fos. 181–2. The lawyers objected that the indictment was pretended; that justices of
the peace had no authority to proceed against a person for witchcraft; that witnesses had not been
examined in the presence of the panel or assize; that neither an informer nor procurator fiscal had
pressed charges against her; and that she had not been given a list of the assize and witnesses.

[52] *RPC*, 2nd ser., viii, p. 37. This was in 1644. For a detailed account of this case see L. Yeoman, 'Hunting the rich witch in Scotland: high-status witchcraft suspects and their persecutors, 1590–1650', Chapter 7 above.

[53] Larner, *Enemies of God*, p. 117.

[54] Mackenzie, *Laws Criminal*, pp. 86–7; Larner, *Enemies of God*, p. 177.

maleficium, according to which it was claimed that witches had inflicted harm by supernatural, i.e., diabolical, means. The sceptical response to such allegations, frequently adopted when lawyers defended witches against such charges, was that the misfortune had natural causes, and that in order to convict a person of the crime, the possibility of natural causation had to be ruled out. The burden of proof was on the prosecution; all that was necessary to secure acquittal was evidence that natural causation was *possible*. In a number of trials in Scotland in the late 1620s, advocates for the witches had gone to great lengths to prove that malefices might not have been the product of supernatural intervention.[55] Later in the century Mackenzie, in defending the witch Maevia, argued that his client could not be proved to have caused her neighbour's madness, since 'distraction was a very natural disease'. The distraction, moreover, could have been caused by fear, of which Maevia was only the occasion, not the cause.[56] A similar argument regarding natural causation was made by James Robertson, the advocate for the seven Paisley witches accused of causing the demonic possession of Christian Shaw in 1697.[57]

Robertson was unable to bring about his clients' acquittal in this trial. Perhaps the speech of the prosecutor to the jury, threatening them that if they should acquit the witches they would be 'accessory to all the blasphemies, apostacies, murders, tortures and seductions, etc., whereof those enemies of heaven and earth shall hereafter be guilty when they gett out', frightened them into returning a guilty verdict.[58] Robertson had succeeded, however, in raising serious doubts about the possibility of actually proving the crime of witchcraft at law. The same doubts were expressed by the former Scottish secretary of state James Johnstone, right after the Paisley trials. 'The parliaments of France and other judicatories who are persuaded of the being of witches,' wrote Johnstone, 'never try them now because of the experience they have had that it's impossible to distinguish possession from nature in disorder'.[59] By 1704, when another case of possession led to local demands to prosecute a cluster of alleged witches at Pittenweem, the arguments of the French *parlementaires* and James Robertson seem to have prevailed. The council refused in this case to authorise a local trial.

V

The fact that seven of the Paisley witches were executed even after their counsel had presented a compelling defence reveals that the scepticism of lawyers and judges regarding the guilt of witches could not by itself bring an end to witchcraft executions in a country where guilt or innocence was still ultimately determined by lay

---

[55] Larner, *Enemies of God*, p. 178.
[56] Mackenzie, *Pleadings*, pp.187–8; Mackenzie, *Laws Criminal*, pp. 92–5.
[57] NAS, JC10/4, Pt. II, pp. 18–32.
[58] *Ibid.*, p. 81.
[59] *The Manuscripts of the Duke of Roxburghe*, HMC, Fourteenth Report, Appendix III (London, 1894), p. 132.

juries. The same was true in England, where during the late seventeenth century judges had not always been able to prevent the conviction and in some cases the execution of witches whom they believed were innocent. In both countries entrusting the determination of guilt or innocence to juries guaranteed that the decline of witchcraft prosecutions would proceed more gradually than in those countries where judges exercised more immediate control over the judicial process.[60] In the long run, however, the scepticism of Scottish lawyers, judges and advocates prevailed. Not only the convictions and the executions but even the trials themselves came to an end. The decline in the number of prosecutions can most reasonably be attributed to the difficulty local communities had securing commissions of justiciary and to the rising frequency of acquittals and dismissals. As George Nicholson of Aberdeen wrote in 1669, if the council did not support the burgh council's efforts to prosecute, the burgh would be much less likely to administer justice or petition the council for new commissions in the future.[61]

Even when the government stopped authorising local prosecutions and when local magistrates stopped asking them to do so, pressure from the local community, especially from the clergy, continued. Under these circumstances towns and villages that wished to take action against witches had three options. The first was to become reconciled to the fact that witches would now be able to live among them and to give up any hope of removing them. This is the decision that villagers and townspeople throughout Europe ultimately made, although not until the nineteenth and even the twentieth centuries in some parts of Europe. The second was to lynch the suspected witches. This of course had always been an option when the cost of proceeding against witches was too high, when the government refused to authorise a trial, or when an accused witch was acquitted. It became an even more viable option in the eighteenth century, when the number of acquittals and dismissals rose. Perhaps the most notorious witch-lynching in Scotland took place at Pittenweem in 1705, after two noblemen commissioned by the privy council dismissed charges of witchcraft that had been levelled against five women. The local community responded by pelting one of those witches, Janet Cornfoot, with stones and then crushing her to death, under heavy weights. At that time the government brought murder charges against her assailants.[62]

The third option was to encourage *local* officials to take unauthorised action against the witches. This seems to be what happened in the very last recorded witchcraft prosecution in Scotland, at Dornoch in 1727, when a sheriff-depute of Sutherland proceeded against two women, a mother and daughter, for witchcraft. The daughter escaped, but the mother, who had been accused among other things

[60] This was especially true in France. See Levack, 'Decline and end of witchcraft prosecutions', p. 57. For England see J. A. Sharpe, 'Witch-hunting and witch historiography: some Anglo-Scottish comparisons', Chapter 11 below.

[61] *Aberdeen Council Letters*, iv, pp. 406–7.

[62] NLS, MS 643, fos. 86–7. The witches had been released on bond and handed over to the commissioners. Another witch accused at Pittenweem, Thomas Brown, died in prison.

of riding her daughter after she had been transformed into a pony, suffered death by being burned in a barrel of pitch. In this case the sheriff-depute was not acting on the basis of any legal authority, nor is it clear whether he was observing due process. It is even uncertain whether the mother was convicted in court or whether she was lynched after the trial. When witchcraft prosecutions took this form it is difficult to make a distinction between a trial and a lynching. Whatever we may call it, it was clearly a procedure that was initiated and executed entirely by the residents of that village, and it received no support whatsoever from the central government.[63] Witch-hunting in Scotland, even in its last gasp, remained a local affair which the central government tried to control, regulate and eventually eliminate, but not always with complete success.

[63] Larner, *Enemies of God*, p. 78; E. Burt (ed.), *Letters from the North of Scotland*, 2 vols (Edinburgh, 1876), i, pp. 242–3. For more on this case and the Pittenweem one see E. J. Cowan and L. Henderson, 'The last of the witches? The survival of Scottish witch belief', Chapter 12 below.

11

Witch-hunting and witch historiography: some Anglo-Scottish comparisons

James Sharpe

I

The period of witch-hunting in Scotland was a remarkable one. Scotland, or perhaps more accurately Lowland Scotland, was an area of relatively intensive persecution, experiencing witch-hunts which were more severe than those of most other European states.[1] And, more particularly, as observers from at least Sir Walter Scott onwards have commented,[2] witch persecution in Scotland was far heavier than that experienced by its southern neighbour. Calculating both population levels and totals of convicted witches for the early modern period are imprecise exercises: but it is generally accepted that Scotland, with a population rising from about a quarter of England's to about a third over the relevant period, executed over twice as many witches, probably more than a thousand to probably less than 500, suggesting that witch executions per head of population in Scotland may have run at ten times the English level.[3] And, whereas witch persecution in England was usually a localised and spasmodic exercise involving accusations against individual women, or at most very small groups, the Scottish persecutions came in great waves: the endemic, if ill documented, trials of 1590–1 and 1597, the mass trials of 1628–30, the trials around 1649, and perhaps the greatest wave of persecution in Scotland of all, that of 1661–2. The contrast between the two national styles was signalled neatly by Robert Baillie, who, towards the end of the Cromwellian occupation of Scotland in 1659, commented that 'There is much witcherie up and downe our land, though the English be but too spareing to try it'.[4]

It would thus appear that a comparison between English and Scottish witch-hunting would be a rewarding activity. But, as in any exercise in comparative history

---

[1] B. P. Levack, *The Witch-Hunt in Early Modern Europe* (2nd edn, London, 1995), table 1, p. 23.

[2] Sir Walter Scott, *Letters on Demonology and Witchcraft* (London, 1884), p. 228.

[3] For Scottish execution totals, Larner, *Enemies of God*, p. 63; for England, J. Sharpe, *Instruments of Darkness: Witchcraft in England, 1550–1750* (London, 1996), p. 125.

[4] Cited in B. P. Levack, 'The great Scottish witch-hunt of 1661–1662', *Journal of British Studies*, 20 (1980), 90–108, at p. 93.

our starting-point must be an analysis of comparative historiography. The impression is that it was the Scottish hunts which first attracted sustained scholarly attention: in Sir Walter Scott's *Letters on Demonology and Witchcraft*, first published in 1830, and also in major contributions by those two other adornments of Edinburgh Society, Sir John Graham Dalyell and Charles Kirkpatrick Sharpe, as well as a lengthy later essay by Francis Legge.[5] Yet this nineteenth-century work was not matched in the early twentieth: George F. Black's 1938 listing of Scottish cases, to take the main example, although an essential starting-point for later researchers, contained little by way of sustained analysis of the materials catalogued, although it should be noted that Black, probably uniquely among students of the witch-hunts, did attempt to recreate something of the reality of the phenomenon by testing a pair of thumbscrews on himself.[6] There were no Scottish equivalents of that trio of pioneers into English witchcraft history, Wallace Notestein, George L. Kittredge and Cecil L'Estrange Ewen.[7] But with more recent works a parallel occurs. In the early 1970s, the publication of two books, by Alan Macfarlane and Keith Thomas, not only established a new paradigm for understanding early modern witchcraft accusations, but also effectively stopped scholarly research into witchcraft in Tudor and Stuart England for a quarter century.[8] In 1981, the publication of Christina Larner's *Enemies of God* similarly not only reminded all witchcraft scholars of the importance of the Scottish witch-hunts, but also provided a model of the subject which has gone unchallenged. It is necessary to remind ourselves of the main thrusts of these two interpretations of national witchcraft experiences.

The work of Macfarlane and Thomas, although recently subjected to reassessment, retains a fundamental importance.[9] It opened up the possibility of studying witchcraft 'from below', from the point of view of the peasant rather than the judge or the learned demonologist, it located witchcraft accusations firmly in the world of village tensions and interpersonal disputes, and it related the ebb and flow of accusations to socio-economic change. Both authors considered the interface between anthropological and historical approaches to witchcraft, while Macfarlane's work

---

[5] Scott, *Letters*; J. G. Dalyell, *The Darker Superstitions of Scotland* (Edinburgh, 1834); C. K. Sharpe, *A Historical Account of the Belief in Witchcraft in Scotland* (Glasgow, 1884); F. Legge, 'Witchcraft in Scotland', *The Scottish Review* (Oct. 1891), 257–88.

[6] Black, *Calendar*: the incident with the thumbscrews is recounted at p. 16, n. 41.

[7] W. Notestein, *A History of Witchcraft in England from 1558 to 1718* (Washington, DC, 1911); G. L. Kittredge, *Witchcraft in Old and New England* (Cambridge, Mass., 1929); C. L'E. Ewen, *Witch Hunting and Witch Trials: the Indictments for Witchcraft from the Records of 1373 Assizes held for the Home Circuit A.D. 1559–1737* (London, 1929); C. L'E. Ewen, *Witchcraft and Demonianism: a concise Account derived from Sworn Depositions and Confessions obtained in the Courts of England and Wales* (London, 1933).

[8] A. D. J. Macfarlane, *Witchcraft in Tudor and Stuart England: a Regional and Comparative Study* (London, 1970); K. Thomas, *Religion and the Decline of Magic: Studies in Popular Beliefs in Sixteenth and Seventeenth-Century England* (London, 1971).

[9] For Macfarlane, see the 'Introduction' by James Sharpe to the reissue of *Witchcraft in Tudor and Stuart England* (London, 1999); for Thomas, see J. Barry, 'Introduction: Keith Thomas and the problem of witchcraft', in J. Barry *et al.* (eds), *Witchcraft in Early Modern Europe: Studies in Culture and Belief* (Cambridge, 1996).

on Essex was a superb example of a detailed regional study based on a close analysis of court archives. Perhaps most relevantly for our purposes, Macfarlane and
Thomas, to some extent following earlier writers,[10] claimed that English witchcraft
was different. Unlike an imagined monolithic 'continental' witchcraft, English
witchcraft accusations were devoid of demonic input, did not involve accounts of
the sabbat, and were the outcome of peasant disputes and peasant fears of *maleficium* rather than the consequence of ruling class initiatives.

Larner's account of Scottish witchcraft described a radically different situation.
Larner had previously reviewed *Religion and the Decline of Magic* in the *Scottish
Historical Review*, where she cast doubt on the value of the neighbourly tensions
approach to witchcraft accusations, emphasised the need to study the legal system
in relation to witchcraft, and argued that there were aspects of witchcraft history
which needed to be studied by those with a knowledge of scholastic philosophy
rather than anthropology: news from Scotland indeed.[11] These themes were developed in *Enemies of God*. While remaining sensitive to the social history approaches
signposted by Macfarlane and Thomas, she presented what was essentially a refor-
mulated and reinvigorated version of witchcraft 'from above', an interpretation
owing much to the conceptual clarity which her work as a sociologist had given her.
'Witch-hunting', she assured the reader on the first page of *Enemies of God*, 'was an
activity fostered by the ruling class'.[12] To Larner, the rise of witch persecutions was
linked to state formation in the early modern period, and, in particular, the formation of the godly state, connected as this was to what she described as 'the emergence of Christianity as a political ideology'.[13] Peasant worries may have led to
initial accusations, but what made witch-hunts in the strict sense of the term possible was the emergence of the godly commonwealth: it was this, as Larner put it
strikingly, which made the witch 'a transfigured creature who began her career in
the farmyard as an enemy of her neighbour, and ended it in the court as a public
person, an enemy of God and the godly society'.[14]

It was this insistence on the importance of the impact of the godly state which
lay at the centre of Larner's interpretation of Scottish witchcraft. 'If there was one
idea which dominated all others in seventeenth-century Scotland', she wrote, 'it
was that of the godly state in which it was the duty of the secular arm to impose the
will of God upon the people'.[15] Or, as she remarked of Europe more generally:

> From the late fifteenth century, the evangelization of the populace coincided with the
> development of what can loosely be termed nation states. Nation states could not
> depend on the old ties to bind their people to them. Like all new regimes they
> demanded both ideological conformity and moral cleansing. Ideological conformity

[10] E.g. Kittredge, *Witchcraft in Old and New England*, pp. 24–5.
[11] *SHR*, 50 (1971), 168–71.
[12] Larner, *Enemies of God*, p. 1.
[13] *Ibid.*, p. 194.
[14] *Ibid.*, p. 5.
[15] *Ibid.*, p. 5.

in the sixteenth century meant overt adherence to the form of Christianity preferred within the region concerned.[16]

If the rise of witch-hunting was the outcome of the emergence of the godly state, so its fall was connected with the chronological point at which 'the establishment of the kingdom of God ceased to be a political objective and was replaced by the pursuit of liberty, the defence of property, the belief in progress, enlightenment, patriotism and other secular alternatives'.[17]

II

So we have two radically opposed focal points for English and Scottish witch-hunting: a standard interpretation of the English situation, admittedly somewhat contested of late, which stresses the importance of peasant fears and village tensions; and a view of Scottish witchcraft which emphasises the impact of officialdom and official ideology in the form of the godly state, resting not on an anthropological approach but rather, to quote Larner again, essentially on 'themes of political sociology: power, ideology, and legitimation'.[18] What we must do, it seems, is to challenge these two powerful interpretations, and consider how the very peculiarities embedded in each of them might help inform our reassessment of the other.

Let us begin at the bottom, with the peasantry. Larner emphasised that a peasant society was one of the prerequisites of the European witch-hunts. Yet she rejected an English-style village tensions model, partly because of her emphasis on the role of the godly state and its ideology, but also because she felt that the model was not relevant to the Scottish situation due to the static nature of the Scottish rural economy: 'The social and economic structure', she wrote, 'was relatively unchanged for a period a great deal longer at both ends than that covered by the witch persecution, relative, that is to say, to England and parts of the continent', while she also stated that 'at no point prior to or during our period did any important change occur'.[19] Larner also noted, in contrast to the English situation, the relevant absence of the type of research into Scottish social and economic history which would have helped illuminate the issue. Twenty years on, such research has progressed, although conclusions are still uncertain. Thus Ian Whyte, in a review of recent literature on the subject, commented on

one of the biggest gaps in our knowledge of early-modern Scotland, and, at the same time, one of the greatest unsolved problems relating to the society and economy of the period. This can be summarised in one basic question: what was happening in

[16] Larner, *Witchcraft*, p. 124.
[17] *Ibid.*, p. 90.
[18] Larner, *Enemies of God*, p. 193.
[19] *Ibid.*, pp. 41, 48.

agriculture and rural society in the decades between the Reformation and the outbreak of Revolution in 1638.[20]

But if the situation remains uncertain, it seems clear that Scottish agriculture in the late sixteenth and seventeenth centuries was not as static as the existing secondary literature may have led Larner to believe in 1981. Whyte, indeed, argued that 'the early seventeenth century now appears as a period of significant rural transformation rather than one of stagnation, involving a more positive response to population growth than has previously been accepted'.[21] And it was, of course, the most commercialised areas – the Lothians and Fife – which experienced the heaviest witch-hunting. Even after due allowance is made for political and religious contexts very different from those obtaining in England, detailed community studies might well demonstrate patterns of socio-economic change on a village level which would have to be built in to any revised model of Scottish witchcraft.

III

If Larner might have downgraded the importance of socio-economic change, one of her major contributions to witchcraft history was the centrality she afforded to the fact that the overwhelming majority of those accused of being witches were women. This point had certainly been neglected by Alan Macfarlane and Keith Thomas, although it should be remembered that Macfarlane's discussion of the problem did raise a number of themes to which subsequent writers have returned.[22] But if Larner emphasised the centrality of gender issues, she also sensed their inherent complications. 'There were periods in 1649 and 1661', she wrote, 'when no mature woman in Fife or East Lothian can have felt free from the fear of accusation'.[23] Yet it was normally not *any* woman who was accused, but, as in England, poor ones. Dalyell, for example, recorded a case in 1678 which led to the burning of nine women as witches, in the course of which the court chose to ignore the allegations of the accused against 'sundry gentlewomen and others of fashion'.[24] And even among the ungentle and the unfashionable, it was usually women of a particular type who featured in at least the initial accusations: for Larner, 'the essential individual personality trait does seem to have been that of a ready, sharp and angry tongue. The witch had the Scottish female quality of smeddum: spirit,

[20] I. D. Whyte, 'Poverty or prosperity? Rural society in lowland Scotland in the late sixteenth and early seventeenth centuries', *Scottish Economic and Social History*, 18 (1998), 19–32, at p. 19.

[21] *Ibid.*, p. 29.

[22] Notably in his comments on how witchcraft accusations might be connected to the workings of a female social sphere where women's social position power operated: Macfarlane, *Witchcraft in Tudor and Stuart England*, p. 161.

[23] Larner, *Enemies of God*, p. 197.

[24] Dalyell, *Darker Superstitions of Scotland*, pp. 670–1. For more on this aspect see L. Yeoman, 'Hunting the rich witch in Scotland: high-status witchcraft suspects and their persecutors, 1590–1650', Chapter 7 above.

and refusal to be put down, quarrelsomeness'.[25] Larner noted, however, that about a fifth of those accused of witchcraft were men, and that witchcraft was therefore 'not sex-specific but it was sex-related'.[26] Thus Larner presented a complex and in some ways perhaps contradictory interpretation of the view that the witch-hunts were the product of the victimisation of women, thus causing disappointment to the more thoroughgoing proponents of this viewpoint, such as Anne Barstow.[27]

Since Larner wrote, of course, the connection between women and witchcraft has assumed a central importance in studies dealing with England, while one of the most recent publications on Scottish witchcraft, by Julian Goodare, returns to this problem.[28] Yet the exact nature of the connection remains one of the most contentious issues in witchcraft history. Some writers have adhered to the straightforward proposition that witch-hunting was woman-hunting, and have related the phenomenon to other aspects of male mistreatment of women.[29] Alternatively, close study of not just those accused of witchcraft but also of their accusers, those witnessing against them, and their supposed victims has demonstrated that women were very prominent as accusers of other women as witches. This would suggest that witchcraft accusations reflected tensions in the domestic sphere, arising particularly when domestic space was transgressed by a woman suspected of being a witch, or when a child was thought to have been harmed by witchcraft.[30] This has, of course, been met by the counter argument that as with any other political system, for patriarchy to operate it had to convince the majority of those it ruled, and hence divided women by persuading most of them to conform.[31] Modern psychiatric theory has been adduced to argue that the witch figure, normally being portrayed as an older woman, was a representation of the bad or malevolent mother,[32] while another line of interpretation has centred on male medical opinion on and broader cultural attitudes to the female body.[33]

---

[25] Larner, *Enemies of God*, p. 97.

[26] *Ibid.*, p. 92.

[27] A. L. Barstow, *Witchcraze: a New History of the European Witch Hunts* (San Francisco, Calif., 1994), pp. 7–8, where Larner is castigated for turning away from the 'theory of persecution by gender, which she, more than anyone, had validated', to 'broader, and presumably more important questions of the craze, questions about Christianity as a political ideology, about crises in law and order – that is, the more traditional political questions'.

[28] J. Goodare, 'Women and the witch-hunt in Scotland', *Social History*, 23 (1998), 288–308.

[29] E.g. M. Hester, *Lewd Women and Wicked Witches: a Study of the Dynamics of Male Domination* (London, 1992).

[30] J. A. Sharpe, 'Women and witchcraft in seventeenth-century England: some northern evidence', *Continuity and Change*, 6 (1991), 179–99; R. Briggs, 'Women as victims? Witches, judges and the community', *French History*, 5 (1991), 438–50; L. Roper, *Oedipus and the Devil: Witchcraft, Sexuality and Religion in Early Modern Europe* (London, 1994), ch. 9.

[31] A point noted by Goodare, 'Women and the witch-hunt', 289.

[32] This argument is advanced in D. Willis, *Malevolent Nurture: Witch-Hunting and Maternal Power in Early Modern England* (Ithaca, NY, 1995).

[33] This is one of many themes developed in D. Purkiss, *The Witch in History: Early Modern and Twentieth-Century Representations* (London, 1996). For the relationship between motherhood and the

IV

If the exact nature of the significance of the gender aspects of witchcraft accusations remains contentious, even less certainty surrounds witch-hunting's supposed links with state formation. Obviously, this connection had a very personal embodiment in Scotland in the form of James VI. Many rulers may have been worried about witchcraft, but few of them personally presided over trials, and even fewer wrote works of demonology. According to *Newes from Scotland*, when the North Berwick witches asked the devil 'why he did beare such hatred to the king', he replied 'by reason the king is the greatest enemie he had in the world'.[34] As Stuart Clark has reminded us, 'the devil, of course, *was* disorder, the first rebellious subject who tried to bring chaos to heaven and succeeded in bringing it to man'.[35] It is axiomatic (if we may set aside the view that James's interest in witch-hunting arose from his difficult relationship with Mary queen of Scots and a tendency to see Elizabeth I as a surrogate mother)[36] that James's interest in witchcraft was closely connected with his views on divine right monarchy.[37] Yet it is also axiomatic that James's interest in witch-hunting diminished later in his life, especially after 1603, while it is also widely known that the Scottish privy council, alarmed by continuing witch-hunting, attempted to curb prosecutions in 1597.[38]

The Scottish state was relatively unformed in the reign of James VI, despite gradual movement towards what contemporaries would have considered to be a modern state system. As Larner put it, 'it is an understatement to say that Scotland was not a fully bureaucratised society in this period',[39] and, more particularly, the Scottish legal system was fragmented and decentralised.[40] It was, in fact, the essentially decentralised nature of many Scottish trials, by commissions issued from Edinburgh, which is striking, and which was by 1677 attracting adverse comment from Sir George Mackenzie.[41] Such factors have recently led Brian Levack to suggest that state formation, on any simplistic understanding of the term, cannot be seen as a central cause of the Scottish hunts, and stresses the 'essentially local dynamics of Scottish

---

domestic sphere in Scottish witchcraft, see L. Martin, 'The Devil and the domestic: witchcraft, quarrels and women's work in Scotland', Chapter 5 above.

[34] *Newes from Scotland* (London, 1591), Sig. B2.

[35] S. Clark, 'King James's *Daemonologie*: witchcraft and kingship', in S. Anglo (ed.), *The Damned Art: Essays in the Literature of Witchcraft* (London, 1977), p. 175.

[36] A proposition put forward in Willis, *Malevolent Nurture*, ch. 4.

[37] Clark, 'King James's *Daemonologie*': cf. C. Larner, 'James VI and I and witchcraft', in A. G. R. Smith (ed.), *The Reign of James VI and I* (London, 1973).

[38] Cf. J. Goodare, 'The Scottish witchcraft panic of 1597', Chapter 4 above.

[39] Larner, *Enemies of God*, p. 37.

[40] For a preliminary survey see S. J. Davies, 'The courts and the Scottish legal system, 1600–1747: the case of Stirlingshire', in V. A. C. Gatrell *et al.* (eds), *Crime and the Law: the Social History of Crime in Western Europe since 1500* (London, 1980).

[41] Sir George Mackenzie of Rosehaugh, *The Laws and Customs of Scotland in Matters Criminal* (Edinburgh, 1678), p. 88.

witchcraft prosecutions'.[42] What we have, perhaps, is the worst of both worlds: a situation where the government was keen on deploying the rhetoric of the godly state and the threat witchcraft offered to it, a rhetoric which seems to have been widely accepted and internalised, with a legal system which frequently devolved trials down onto a very local level, and into the hands of local lairds and clergymen who were unlikely to have a sophisticated attitude to the problem of proof in witchcraft trials. State formation's relevance to Scottish witch-hunting probably rests in the essentially formative and transitional phase which the Scottish state was experiencing in the later sixteenth and seventeenth centuries.[43]

Discussing state formation in the English context is a complex matter. In many ways England lacked the attributes of some of the more advanced Continental states: there was no standing army for much of the period of the witch-hunts, taxation was low and the taxation machine underdeveloped, bureaucrats and office-holders were rare, and much of the work of local administration and law enforcement depended on local gentlemen serving as justices of the peace. Yet in other ways the English state looked very strong. Obviously, although the old 'Tudor Revolution in Government' debate has long since passed, there were important changes over the middle of the sixteenth century.[44] Yet these changes built on the solid foundations of the English medieval governmental system, which is widely recognised to have been one of the most effective in Europe. Crucially for our present discussion, those parts of the English law enforcement machine which were involved in witchcraft trials were under central control. English witches could be tried before a variety of tribunals: but the overwhelming majority of accusations of malefic witchcraft, a capital felony under the English statutes of 1563 and 1604, were tried at the assizes. And assize judges were centrally appointed, and were usually senior members of the legal profession. The contrast with Scotland was demonstrated in 1582, when the Essex justice of the peace Brian Darcy orchestrated a local witch-craze in which about a dozen women were tried at the assizes. Of these, only one was hanged. As far as its criminal justice system was concerned, the English state was fairly formed by the time that witchcraft was criminalised by statute.[45]

[42] B. P. Levack, 'State-building and witch hunting in early modern Europe', in Barry *et al.* (eds), *Witchcraft in Early Modern Europe*, pp. 103–4.

[43] Cf. J. Goodare, 'Witch-hunting and the Scottish state', Chapter 8 above.

[44] The classic statement in this debate was G. R. Elton, *The Tudor Revolution in Government: Administrative Changes in the Reign of Henry VIII* (Cambridge, 1953). For some suggestive changes in the working of law and order over the mid Tudor period, see J. H. Langbein, *Prosecuting Crime in the Renaissance: England, Germany, France* (Cambridge, Mass., 1974).

[45] The 1582 Essex case deserves further research: the key text is the relatively lengthy trial pamphlet, *A true and just Recorde, of the Information, Examination and Confession of all the Witches taken at S. Oses in the Countie of Essex, whereof some were executed, and some entreated according to the Determination of the Law* (London, 1582); abstracts of the relevant indictments are given in Ewen, *Witch Hunting and Witch Trials*, pp. 143–6. The standard introduction to the workings of the assizes in this period is J. S. Cockburn, *A History of English Assizes, 1558–1714* (Cambridge, 1972). For an overview of developments in the law and state formation, see J. A. Sharpe, 'The law, law enforcement, state formation and national

Such considerations make it clear that historians of English witchcraft must adjust their conceptual framework to take on the role of elite attitudes. Larner put the point well:

> There is a question left open. Given that English society at this time had more than one cultural level, it resembled that of Scotland more closely than any primitive monocultural society. What part, therefore, in the English persecution can be ascribed to clergy, magistrates and gentry? Despite the great differences in intensity and quality, it would seem that the English villager with an accusation to make was as dependent for getting his case heard on the attitude of his local authorities as his Scottish counterpart.[46]

The point maintains its validity even given the knowledge that these local authorities in England were more likely to defuse a witchcraft accusation as to encourage it.

Perhaps the crucial difference was that, possibly because of the existing strength and maturity of the English state, the notion of the godly commonwealth never really took off in the way that Larner perceived it doing in Scotland. Obviously, there were some Englishmen who desired the erection of a more godly state in England, and some at least of them had strong ideas on witchcraft. Consider, for example, the opinions of the most celebrated English theologian of the Elizabethan period, William Perkins:

> It is a principle of the law of nature, holden for a grounded truth in all countries & kingdoms, among all people of every age; that the traytor, who is an enemie to the state, and rebelleth against his lawfull prince, should be put to death; now the most notorious traytor and rebell that can be, is the witch. For shee renounceth God himselfe, the king of kings, shee leaves the societie of the church and people, shee bindeth herself in league with the devill.[47]

Yet Perkins and people like him, even in the what is normally thought of as the period of Puritan ascendancy after 1649, never gained complete control. Godly ideas penetrated English society. At least some of the more active justices of the peace in Elizabethan and early Stuart England conceived of themselves as godly magistrates, in some parishes the members of the local elites from whom constables and other local office holders were drawn adopted godly attitudes, while the charges of that notable justice of the peace and legal writer William Lambarde are full of godly rhetoric.[48] Yet the full-scale programme of moral reform based on a revised legal code which at least some godly Englishmen envisaged remained imperfectly established.[49]

---

integration in late medieval and early modern England', in X. Rousseaux and R. Levy (eds), *Le Pénal dans tous ses États: Justice, États et Sociétés en Europe, XIIe–XXe Siècles* (Brussels, 1997).

[46] Larner, *Witchcraft*, p. 21.

[47] William Perkins, *A Discourse of the Damned Art of Witchcraft: So farre forth as it is revealed in the Scripture, and manifest by true Experience* (Cambridge, 1608), pp. 248–9.

[48] *William Lambarde and Local Government: his Ephemeris and twenty-nine Charges to Juries and Commissions*, ed. C. Read (Ithaca, NY, 1962).

[49] For a useful discussion of the relevant issues see J. R. Kent, 'Attitudes of members of the House of Commons to the regulation of "personal conduct" in late Elizabethan and early Stuart England', *Bulletin of the Institute of Historical Research*, 44 (1973), 41–71.

In Scotland, with James VI, the push from the godly state came very much from the top. James showed little of his witch-hunting propensities after he came to England, while his predecessor had shown little interest in witchcraft. But there are clues that concern over witchcraft as a threat to the monarchy did affect the Elizabethan regime. A recent essay has sought to demonstrate that the English statute of 1563 was a response to a perceived threat created by a coming together of fears of papists and of treason cum sorcery.[50] The execution of a number of witches in Berkshire in 1579, who had, *inter alia*, allegedly dabbled in image magic, was made more certain by privy council interest in the case resulting from an incident in the previous year when puppets representing Elizabeth and two of her councillors had been found stuck with pins on a London dunghill.[51] And in 1581 there came an act 'against seditious words and rumours uttered against the queen's most excellent majesty' which included provisions aimed at ensuring that the life and security of the monarch, along with the security of the realm, should not be endangered by occult practices.[52] Concern over witchcraft in Elizabethan England was evidently not restricted to Essex villagers.

Larner saw the emergence of the godly state in Scotland as being of central importance to the rise of witch-hunting. In this, she was in many ways making a more sophisticated and elegant restatement of earlier writers' insistence that the blame lay squarely on the kirk.[53] Larner was attracted by the work of Jean Delumeau, and argued that the Scottish experience fitted his model of Christianisation, claiming that for many Scottish peasants 'the preaching of the reformed clergy was their first contact with Christianity'.[54] It is now widely accepted that the burgeoning interest in witchcraft from the mid sixteenth century onwards was connected with the new notions of Christian belief being spread in both reformed and counter reformed territories. Certainly in England many clergymen felt that they were bringing the Christian word to the populace for the first time, and that the resultant struggle was very much an uphill one.[55] Yet the process did not necessarily result in a heightened sense of worry over witchcraft, or to an increased propensity to hunt witches. Many advanced English Protestants felt that the popular belief in witchcraft was a delusion, the result of a tendency to attribute to witchcraft misfortunes which were in fact the result of divine providence, a tendency which would be eradicated once a correct understanding of right religion eradicated ignorance and superstition.[56] Thus English clergymen, among them the impeccably godly Ralph Josselin, were as

---

[50] N. Jones, 'Defining superstitions: treasonous Catholics and the Act against witchcraft of 1563', in C. Carlton *et al.* (eds), *State, Sovereigns and Society: Essays in Honour of A. J. Slavin* (Stroud, 1998).

[51] Sharpe, *Instruments of Darkness*, p. 46.

[52] Statute 23 Eliz. I, cap. 2.

[53] E.g. Scott, *Letters*, pp. 245–9.

[54] Larner, *Enemies of God*, p. 57; J. Delumeau, *Le Catholicisme entre Luther et Voltaire* (Paris, 1971).

[55] These and related issues are delineated in P. Collinson, *The Religion of Protestants: the Church in English Society, 1559–1625* (Oxford, 1982).

[56] J. Teall, 'Witchcraft and Calvinism in Elizabethan England: divine power and human agency', *Journal of the History of Ideas*, 23 (1962), 21–36.

likely to try to defuse witchcraft accusations as encourage witch-hunting.[57] The English evidence suggests that a reappraisal of the role of the kirk in Scottish witch-hunting is essential. One would like to know more about the recruitment, social background and education of the Scottish clergy, and how far individuals among them felt able to resist local witch-hunts. And, given the current interpretation of the English Reformation as a gradual and piecemeal process, there is perhaps a need to question the impression of rapid and complete religious indoctrination which seems to have accompanied the Reformation in Scotland. By 1597 according to Larner 'the witch doctrine had … taken an almost complete hold of the clergy, gentry and legal profession of Scotland'.[58] Given the resources for ideological control at the disposal of the kirk, this does seem rather sudden and rather total.

But perhaps this problem of the impact of the state, of godliness, and (to run these two together) of the godly state can best be illustrated by the one big witch-hunt which England experienced, that associated with Matthew Hopkins which afflicted the eastern counties from March 1645 onwards. The Hopkins episode has never formed the subject of a full scale scholarly study, but even on our current level of knowledge it constitutes a powerful corrective to any 'tame' image of English witchcraft.[59] In the course of this particular witch-hunt, some 250 witches were tried or at least subjected to initial investigation, and, on a conservative estimate, upwards of a hundred were executed. The presence of Hopkins as a witch-hunter was obviously a powerful catalyst. But the elements upon which this catalyst acted were of vital importance. The context was provided by the strains imposed on local society by a war effort, the war in question being increasingly conceived of in ideological terms. But there were two more definite factors. One was a temporary dilution of control through the assize courts, so that local officials operated without the normal checks, and somebody with no official status, Hopkins, was allowed to play a leading part in witch-finding. And the second was the eruption of a powerful popular puritanism, which had already been unleashed in the form of a campaign of ideological cleansing against unreliable clergymen in the eastern counties, and in a remarkable and semi-official outbreak of iconoclasm in Suffolk, the county most affected by this bout of witch-hunting. A region of England had experienced those elements of decentralised justice and intense godliness which were a recurrent theme in witch-hunts in the Scottish Lowlands: the resultant witch-craze was on a par with anything Scotland produced.

V

Studying English and Scottish witch persecution on a comparative basis thus demonstrates that, while undoubtedly there were differences between the two

---

[57] *The Diary of Ralph Josselin, 1616–1683*, ed. A. Macfarlane (British Academy Records of Social and Economic History, new ser., 3, 1976), pp. 379, 404.

[58] Larner, *Witchcraft*, p. 17.

[59] For a recent reappraisal of the Hopkins episode, see Sharpe, *Instruments of Darkness*, ch. 5.

national experiences, there was perhaps more by way of common themes than what might be described as the standard interpretations indicate. Similarly, if we allow ourselves the luxury of speculating on where research might go in the future, it is possible to discern clear areas of overlap in the most likely agendas.

Perhaps the key issue is that, surprisingly, there is still much which we do not know about witchcraft. There is a need for detailed studies of individual or regional witch-hunts. In England, a monograph has been published on a well documented case involving a young woman named Anne Gunter,[60] research is currently in progress on the Warboys case,[61] and a volume of collected essays on the celebrated Lancashire trials is projected.[62] Little work of this nature exists for Scotland, although Isabel Adam's 1978 study of the 1697 Paisley witch-hunt, while not a full scale scholarly monograph, does reveal the potential for detailed local studies in deepening our understanding of Scottish witchcraft.[63] The mass trials of 1661–2 have been subjected to an incisive yet short analysis by Brian Levack,[64] but the hunts of 1628–30, noted as being especially problematic by Larner in 1984,[65] still await detailed research.

We must also deepen our understanding of witchcraft as a cultural entity, as part of the popular belief system of the period. In January 1591 Agnes Sampson, one of the alleged witches at the centre of the North Berwick trials, confessed about her pact with the Devil. She told how he came to her late one night shortly after her husband had died, and she was worried for 'the sustenation of her and her bairns'. The Devil told her not to worry, for if she would serve him, 'she nor they sould lack nothing. And being movit with her povertie and his fair promisis of riches and revenge of her ennemies, tuik him for her maister and renunceit Christ'.[66] Twenty-five years earlier, in the earliest surviving English witch-trial pamphlet, we find Elizabeth Francis making her confession at the Essex assizes. She learned her witchcraft at the age of twelve from mother Eve, who 'counselled her to renounce God and his word, and to give her blood to Satan', 'Satan' in this case being the name given to a familiar spirit in the shape of a white spotted cat. The familiar, like the Devil as described by Agnes Sampson, helped the witch achieve modest wealth in the form of sheep, and helped her revenge herself on her

---

[60] J. Sharpe, *The Bewitching of Anne Gunter: a Horrible and True Story of Football, Witchcraft, Murder, and the King of England* (London, 1999).

[61] A. R. de Windt, 'Witchcraft and conflicting visions of the ideal village community', *Journal of British Studies*, 31 (1995), 427–63.

[62] In the form of the proceedings of a conference held in April 1999, under the editorship of Robert Poole.

[63] I. Adam, *Witch Hunt: the Great Scottish Witchcraft Trials of 1697* (London, 1978). These trials were the subject of an earlier work, J. Millar, *A History of the Witches of Renfrewshire* (Paisley, 1809). See now M. Wasser, 'The western witch-hunt of 1697–1700: the last major witch-hunt in Scotland', Chapter 9 above.

[64] Levack, 'Great Scottish witch-hunt'.

[65] Larner, *Witchcraft*, p. 25.

[66] *CSP Scot.*, x, p. 464.

enemies.[67] These statements obviously owe much to the input of the witches' respective interrogators: but clearly they also refer to a rich folklore about witchcraft, the Devil, and the occult. Unpicking this folklore, and establishing how popular beliefs on witchcraft interacted with those of their educated betters, is still an unfinished process.[68]

It is also worth noting that one of the more marked, and perhaps most unexpected, developments in English witchcraft studies over the last few years has been the re-opening of witchcraft as a political issue. This has involved not just a consideration of witch-hunting as a by-product of the formation of the godly state, but also the way in which witchcraft was used as a political metaphor, or entered political rhetoric, or was regarded as a component in a cosmic world-view, in which what modern terminology would describe as the political, the religious and the scientific ran together.[69] The types of printed works on which such studies are founded are comparatively scarce for Scotland,[70] but this would nevertheless be a potentially fruitful area for future research and speculation among Scottish witchcraft scholars. Let us take two examples to illustrate the point.

As we have noted, it is now a commonplace to interpret the interest of James VI in witchcraft in terms of his interest in divine right monarchy. Somebody else with an interest in divine right monarch, who was also a figure of some importance in Scottish witchcraft, was Sir George Mackenzie, from 1668 King's Advocate and hence a key figure in the Scottish legal administration. Mackenzie was a keen supporter of monarchy, his theoretical statements to this effect[71] being matched by his harsh treatment of traitors and covenanters. But for Mackenzie, belief in divine right monarchy did not equal belief in witchcraft, a point which is demonstrated in the extended discussion he gave to the crime of witchcraft in his *Laws and Customes of Scotland in Matters Criminal* of 1678. Mackenzie did not deny the reality of witchcraft; he attacked the views of Weyer, 'that great patron of witchcraft', and he cited biblical references, among them Exodus 22:18 and the story of the Witch of Endor to buttress his case. But he also urged caution in the trial of witches:

> Yet from the horridness of this crime, I do conclude, that of all crimes it requires the clearest relevancy, and most convincing probation. And I condemn next to the witches themselves, those cruel and too forward judges, who burn persons by thousands as guilty of this crime, to whom I shall recommend these considerations.[72]

---

[67] *The Examination and Confession of certaine Wytches at Chensforde in the Countie of Essex, before the Quenes Maiesties Judges, the xxvi Day of July Anno 1566* (London, 1566), Sig. A6.

[68] For an important initial discussion of such issues see C. Holmes, 'Popular culture? Witches, magistrates and divines in early modern England', in S. L. Kaplan (ed.), *Understanding Popular Culture: Europe from the Middle Ages to the Nineteenth Century* (Berlin, 1984).

[69] I. Bostridge, *Witchcraft and its Transformations, c.1650–c.1750* (Oxford, 1997).

[70] A point made by C. Larner, 'Two late Scottish witchcraft tracts: *Witch-Craft Proven* and *The Tryal of Witchcraft*', in Anglo (ed.), *The Damned Art*, p. 227.

[71] E.g. Sir George Mackenzie, *The Institutions of the Law of Scotland* (Edinburgh, 1684), p. 17.

[72] Mackenzie, *Laws Criminal*, p. 85.

Mackenzie was clearly one of that growing body of educated people, among them many judges, who, although unable to deny the existence of witchcraft in the abstract, were fully aware of the probable unreality of specific accusations.

Mention of this supporter of divine right monarchy who advocated moderation in the trial of witches suggests an obvious parallel to the historian of witchcraft in early modern England in the shape of Sir Robert Filmer.[73] Although obviously not a legal figure of Mackenzie's standing, Filmer was legally trained, and was a justice of the peace of considerable experience and standing in his native Kent. He is best known for his *Patriarcha*, a justification of absolutism which achieved fame through attracting the odium of John Locke, but he also, shortly before his death in 1653, published his *Advertisement to the Jurymen of England, touching Witches*. This unrelentingly sceptical work has recently been re-evaluated by Ian Bostridge. On Bostridge's analysis, Filmer's tract, which contains a lengthy critique of William Perkins' *Discourse of the damned Art of Witchcraft*, 'formed part of a general attack on Calvinism as he conceived it, both in its covenantal and original forms … in his central task of destroying Perkins' covenantal theory of witchcraft, Filmer also undermines the fundamentals of covenantal theology itself'.[74] Had Filmer and Mackenzie ever had the chance to meet, one suspects that they would have found a lot to talk about.

Interest in pursuing Anglo-Scottish comparisons of witchcraft on an intellectual and political level is further encouraged by another work published in late seventeenth-century Scotland, George Sinclair's *Satan's Invisible World Discovered*. This was continually reprinted into the nineteenth century, becoming 'long a favourite with the labouring classes', and 'for a long time a constituent part of every cottage library in Scotland'.[75] It was, as its subtitle put it, 'a choice collection of modern relations, proving … that there are devils, spirits, witches and apparitions', a claim which obviously invites comparison with Joseph Glanvill's *Saducismus Triumphatus*,[76] a work, indeed, from which Sinclair cheerfully admitted having borrowed. Yet Sinclair, like Glanvill, was no obscurantist theologian. He was probably the first person to study physics in its modern sense in Scotland, was the author of *Hydrostaticks*, and in turn professor of philosophy and mathematics at Glasgow university, as well as being a man who was to demonstrate the practical aspects of

---

[73] For brief discussions of Filmer, see Sharpe, *Instruments of Darkness*, pp. 220–2, and Bostridge, *Witchcraft and its Transformations*, pp. 13–21.

[74] Bostridge, *Witchcraft and its Transformations*, pp. 13, 15. The full title of Filmer's tract was *An Advertisement to the Jury-Men of England, touching Witches. Together with a Difference between an English and an Hebrew Witch* (London, 1653).

[75] George Sinclair, *Satan's Invisible World Discovered; or, a choice Collection of modern Relations, proving evidently against the Saducees and Atheists of this present Age, that there are Devils, Spirits, Witches and Apparitions, from authentick Records, Attestations of famous Witnesses, and undoubted Verity* (Edinburgh, 1685). The quotations on the book's popularity are taken from T. G. Stevenson's edition of 1871: this also provides biographical details on Sinclair, which I have augmented from *DNB*.

[76] Joseph Glanvill, *Saducismus Triumphatus: or full and plaine Evidence concerning Witches and Apparitions* (London, 1681).

his knowledge by participating in attempts to use a primitive diving bell to raise treasure from an Armada wreck, by carrying out schemes to drain Scotland's coal mines, and, at the invitation of the city fathers in the mid 1670s, by helping improve Edinburgh's water supply.

It is now generally accepted that Glanvill's thoughts on apparitions and witches were lodged firmly in the context of the ideological and intellectual conflicts of post-Restoration England, and were aimed at providing an Anglican defence of the reality of the spirit world as a bulwark against atheism.[77] Sinclair's work, although located in the rather different context of Scottish ecclesiastical politics, was clearly hoping to achieve the same objective. Sinclair lambasted the spirit of drollery which he thought to be rampant in his age, attacked atheism, excoriated the English sceptics Scot, Webster and Wagstaffe, reserved a special odium for Thomas Hobbes, and refuted fifty-six 'absurd and dangerous' principles advanced by Cartesian philosophy. But Sinclair's mental world, like that of Mackenzie, Filmer, and perhaps most relevantly Glanvill, was imbricated with the political issues of his day. His brother John, a minister in East Lothian, had left Scotland for Holland in 1682, and before his death at Delft in 1689 was regarded as a dissident by James VII and II's regime. Sinclair himself had resigned his professorship in 1666 because he refused to comply with episcopacy, and resumed in 1688 or early 1689 when happier times returned. In both England and Scotland elite witchcraft beliefs were firmly embedded in contemporary politics, demonstrating in Scotland that there was more to such beliefs than a propensity for rabid witch-hunting, and in England, once again, that there was more to witchcraft than village disputes. Ian Bostridge, indeed, has commented of post-Restoration Scotland that 'as so often, witchcraft theory indicates a trauma about the relationship between the secular and the divine order, and the religious constitution of the state'.[78]

So our comparison, which began with a restatement of two historiographical traditions which suggested differences between the English and Scottish witch-hunts, has ended with a brief discussion of a set of issues in which the experiences of the two nations seem to converge. This exercise in comparative history has, above all, demonstrated that witchcraft was a phenomenon with multiple meanings: we have the politics, with James VI and I interpreting witchcraft as an attack on the godly commonwealth, and Sir Robert Filmer regarding belief in it as a distasteful side effect of Calvinist theology; we have the religious aspects, with William Perkins attacking witchcraft, Ralph Josselin defending alleged witches, and George Sinclair and Joseph Glanvill trying to maintain belief in witchcraft and the spirit world as a bulwark against what they perceived as a rising tide of unbelief; we have the legal aspects, with Sir George Mackenzie worrying about the conduct of Scottish witch trials, and English assize judges bringing in one of the highest acquittal rates of accused witches found anywhere in Europe; and, perhaps most importantly and

---

[77] Sharpe. *Instruments of Darkness*, pp. 244–7.
[78] Bostridge, *Witchcraft and its Transformations*, p. 23.

certainly most elusively, we have the problem of reconstructing the mental maps of the common people, of what witchcraft and the occult meant to them.

So many questions. If nothing else, the agenda for future research for historians of both Scottish and English witchcraft is an exciting, if dauntingly broad, one. This research will best be carried out on a comparative basis, or, at the very least, with historians of witchcraft on either side of the Anglo-Scottish border maintaining a dialogue with each other. Historians of what once was usually called the English Civil War are now beginning to interpret the political problems of the seventeenth century in terms of the shared and interacting experiences of the component parts of the British Isles, and it seems that other historical topics, among them witchcraft, would also benefit from such a perspective. It is hoped that this chapter, however imperfectly, has made some contribution to this process.

The last of the witches?
The survival of Scottish witch belief

Edward J. Cowan and Lizanne Henderson

– CROSBIE: An act of parliament put an end to witchcraft. – JOHNSON: No, sir! witchcraft had ceased; and therefore an act of parliament was passed to prevent persecution for what was not witchcraft. Why it ceased, we cannot tell, as we cannot tell the reason of many other things.

James Boswell

> Haply 'tis weened that Scotland now is free
> Of witchcraft, and of spell o'er human life;
> Ah me! – ne'er since she rose out of the sea,
> Were they so deep, so dangerous, and so rife.
>
> *James Hogg*[1]

Both Samuel Johnson and James Hogg lived in an age which had something of an obsession about the last of things – whether lamenting 'the last of the race of Fingal', dazzled by 'the last of all the bards', bemused by *The Last of the Lairds*, or sentimentalising the last of the Mohicans as ambiguously as they threnodised the demise of the Jacobite cause at Culloden and the apparent passing of the Gaelic way of life.[2] There were numerous accounts of the departure of the last Scottish fairies.[3] Clearly many commentators would have liked to detect a similar type of closure for witches, but, although the attempt was made and 'The Last of the Witches' became a familiar theme, finality proved elusive. There is, of course, a problem about knowing precisely at which point the last of anything actually occurs. How do we know for certain that the last is not actually the antepenultimate?

A suggestive parallel is offered by the case of the 'last' wolf in Scotland. Wolves, like witches, represented wild, primitive barbarity. The central concern was not with

---

[1] *Johnson's Journey to the Western Islands of Scotland and Boswell's Journal of a Tour to the Hebrides with Samuel Johnson, LL.D.*, ed. R. W. Chapman (Oxford, 1924), p. 188; James Hogg, 'Superstition', *The Works of the Ettrick Shepherd: Centenary Edition*, 2 vols (London, n.d.), ii, p. 394.

[2] James Macpherson, *The Poems of Ossian and related works*, ed. H. Gaskill (Edinburgh, 1996), p. 18; Walter Scott, *The Lay of the Last Minstrel* (various editions); John Galt, *The Last of the Lairds* (1826; Edinburgh, 1936); J. Fenimore Cooper, *The Last of the Mohicans* (1826; various editions).

[3] L. Henderson and E. J. Cowan, *Scottish Fairy Belief: a History* (East Linton, 2001), chs. 1 and 7.

Canis lupus itself but with the notion that the extinction of wild animals indicated a country's 'advance in civilisation, and of the appropriation of its soil for economic purposes'. Wolves are said to have been gone from the Southern Uplands by the sixteenth century. The last wolf in the north east was supposedly killed in Kirkmichael, Banffshire in 1644 but a specimen shot by Cameron of Lochiel in 1680, either at Killiecrankie or in Lochaber, and put on sale by the London museum in 1818, was claimed as the last in Great Britain. The last known in Sutherland were exterminated between 1690 and 1700 but at three different locations. There are competing claims from Lochaber as well as cairns commemorating the ultimate wolf from Galloway to Sutherland. One, Macqueen, is credited with slaying the last wolf of all, which had allegedly killed two children, in Moray, in 1743, while Lord Morton, president of the Royal Society, asserted in 1756 that wolves still existed.[4] But while hunters celebrated the slaughter of the last wolf they could not be certain whether another still roamed free in the mountains. It was a similar story with witches; the execution of the putative last of their kind by no means destroyed the last believer or the final practitioner.

I

During their three month tour of Scotland in 1773 the conversation of Samuel Johnson and James Boswell frequently turned towards the supernatural. A discussion over supper between the advocate Andrew Crosbie and the learned doctor was one such occasion. Crosbie's explanation for the demise of witch beliefs, that an act of parliament was responsible for effecting a sudden change of attitude, was swiftly countered, in typical Johnsonian fashion, as inadequate, if not naive; centuries of witch beliefs could not be dismissed as untenable on the grounds that they were no longer held to be credible, nor could a belief be eradicated by an act of law. Throughout his tour, Johnson was to show, like many visitors who descended on Scotland in his wake, a keen interest in the supernatural, particularly second sight. The Scottish expedition was partly inspired by Martin Martin's *A Description of the Western Islands of Scotland* which contained a great deal of information on Gaelic folk beliefs and many examples of the paranormal. Johnson's interest in such phenomena was certainly greater than at least one of his biographers has allowed.[5] Indeed many travellers expected supernatural encounters, or accounts thereof, during their visits, since Scotland was regarded as a backward country which preserved primitive

    [4] R. Chambers, *Domestic Annals of Scotland from the Revolution to the Rebellion of 1745*, 3 vols (Edinburgh, 1874), iii, pp. 608–9. See also F. H. Groome, *Ordnance Gazetteer of Scotland: a Survey of Scottish Topography, Statistical, Biographical, and Historical*, 3 vols (Edinburgh and London, 1886); I. Pennie, 'Other wild life' in D. Omand (ed.), *The Sutherland Book* (Golspie, 1982), p. 119; J. Ritchie, *The Influence of Man on Animal Life in Scotland: a Study in Faunal Evolution* (Cambridge, 1920), pp. 120–1; D. Stephen, *Alba, the Last Wolf* (London, 1986), prologue, in which novel the subject is a metaphor for the last Jacobite rising.
    [5] W. J. Bate, *Samuel Johnson* (New York, 1977), pp. 352–3, who in our view greatly underestimates the extent of Johnson's interest in the supernatural.

cultures and superstitions in all their supposedly pristine purity. Robert Burns would later satirise such expectations (which amounted to confirmations) of barbarism by contributing his masterly 'Tam o' Shanter' to Francis Grose's *Antiquities of Scotland*.[6] The poet, like many other people, was convinced that superstition was in recession. The Revd Donald M'Queen in Skye told Johnson that when he first took over his charge women were frequently accused of stealing milk from cows by means of witchcraft. By 1773 he had personally eradicated such superstition through a combination of preaching and guile.[7]

Interestingly, most later commentators on the witch-hunts concurred with Johnson, that the repeal of the Witchcraft Act in 1736 was something of an afterthought, as if government had decided to tidy up a messy desk by removing any archaic and unused legal clutter. This assumption seems to be based on the notion that some time around 1700 the belief in witchcraft disappeared almost overnight, at least in the minds of the elite, surviving only in the thoughts of a few fringe eccentrics or as the folkloric curiosity of a bygone age. Scott, for one, believed that learning and knowledge taught the Scottish establishment, in the shape of lawyers and ministers, to reject the credulity of their ancestors, though he had to admit that 'these dawnings of sense and humanity were obscured by the clouds of the ancient superstition on more than one occasion'.[8]

Davenport Adams, however, thought that popular witchcraft beliefs had more or less died out before the repeal of the witchcraft act, and he was perplexed by those who still harboured such beliefs well into the eighteenth century. His puzzled and erroneous comment, 'it is a curious fact that educated Scotchmen ... retained their superstition long after the common people had abandoned it'[9] was, in particular, aimed at men such as Professor William Forbes, of Glasgow, who published his *Institutes of the Law of Scotland* in 1730. Forbes spoke of witchcraft as 'that black art whereby strange and wonderful things are wrought by power derived from the devil', adding, 'nothing seems plainer to me than that there may be and have been witches, and that perhaps such are now actually existing'.[10] Adams was also bemused by the Seceders who condemned the repeal of the laws against witchcraft, as 'contrary', they said, 'to the express letter of the law of God.' Such men were hopelessly behind the times for 'public opinion, as the result of increased intelligence, had numbered witchcraft among the superstitions of the past, and we may confidently predict that its revival is impossible'.[11]

---

[6] E. J. Cowan, 'Burns and superstition', in K. Simpson (ed.), *Love and Liberty: Robert Burns: a Bicentenary Celebration* (East Linton, 1997), p. 235.

[7] *Boswell's Journal*, p. 266.

[8] Sir Walter Scott, *Letters on Demonology and Witchcraft* (London, 1884 [first pub. 1830]), pp. 267–8.

[9] W. H. D. Adams, *Witch, Warlock and Magician: Historical Sketches of Magic and Witchcraft in England and Scotland* (London, 1889), p. 376.

[10] William Forbes, *The Institutes of the Law of Scotland*, 2 vols (Edinburgh, 1730), ii, pp. 28–41, 371–3.

[11] Adams, *Witch, Warlock and Magician*, p. 377. The Seceders published an act in 1743 complaining against the repeal of the witchcraft act. It was reprinted at Glasgow in 1766.

The prosecution of, and the laws against, witchcraft, since the passing of the 1563 witchcraft act, were never wholly synchronous with the witch beliefs of the peasantry, so it should not be assumed that the repeal of the act in 1736 was any more in tune with popular opinion than the initial legislation had been. Neither does it necessarily follow that either learned discourse or popular attitudes towards witchcraft rose and fell with prosecution rates. Witch belief, or unbelief, was emphatically not dependent upon the intensity of witch-hunting, particularly when viewed from a folkloric perspective. For someone living in the eighteenth century the possibility that a witch panic might erupt was not all that far-fetched; to dismantle the mechanisms of witch persecution was not to outlaw belief. The challenge is, irrespective of the correspondence between legislation and folk sentiment, to 'excavate the mental structures that underlie the fragmentary manifestations of popular culture and to analyse the interaction between popular and elite belief'.[12]

II

The problem has been that studies of witch hunting in Scotland, as elsewhere, have concentrated on the ideas and opinions of the persecutors rather than the persecuted. Scottish historiography has, so far, made little attempt to assess the actual beliefs of the accused witches themselves or, indeed, the attitudes of their neighbours towards them.[13] The people (usually women) accused of witchcraft have generally been dismissed as ignorant, senile, and no real threat to anybody. Such interpretations, while no doubt well-intentioned, are also condescending, treating the witch as a passive figure, stripped of all societal and cultural significance. If there has been a near absence of scholarly interest in folk beliefs about witches at the height of the witch-hunt, it is not altogether surprising that there should have been so little curiosity about the survival of witch beliefs after the hunt had ceased.

It is ironic that learned discourse on the reality of witchcraft and the supernatural was not only far from moribund in the late seventeenth century, but was actually on the increase. Indeed there was very little Scottish commentary on these phenomena until this period. George Sinclair's *Satan's Invisible World Discovered* (1685) was a compendium of supernatural accounts, the subtitle of which clearly articulated the author's intention:

> A Choice Collection of Modern Relations, proving evidently against the Saducees and Atheists of this present Age, that there are Devils, Spirits, Witches, and Apparitions, from Authentick Records, Attestations of Famous Witnesses, and undoubted Verity.

---

[12] C. Holmes, 'Popular culture? Witches, magistrates and divines in early modern England', in S. L. Kaplan (ed.), *Understanding Popular Culture* (Berlin, 1984), p. 86.

[13] There is so far no Scottish study to remotely match O. Davies, *Witchcraft, Magic and Culture, 1736–1951* (Manchester, 1999) or M. Gijswijt-Hofstra, B. P. Levack and R. Porter, *Witchcraft and Magic in Europe: the Eighteenth and Nineteenth Centuries* (London, 1999). The omission is surprising given that there is good evidence for a remarkable number of late Scottish cases, only a few of which can be discussed here. For some indication see Larner *et al.*, *Source-Book*, which lists a total of some 434 cases after 1662.

Sinclair was professor of Natural Philosophy at Glasgow, specialising in hydrostat-
ics with reference to the mining industry, for which reason he dedicated his book
to his patron the earl of Winton whose own hitherto invisible and 'subterraneous
world' of coal workings at Newhaven was one of the wonders of the age. He was
concerned to account for the declining belief in witches and was intent upon
attacking those modern Sadducees who totally denied the existence of spirits and
apparitions; people scoffed at witch narratives, being more disposed to believe in a
'World in a Moon'. Testimonials to witchcraft were humorously dismissed as old
wives' tales, the 'melancholious fits of distempered persons', or the utterings of
cheats, tricksters and impostors. While some argued that innocent victims had suffered during witch panics such assertions did not, in his view, invalidate prosecution, for the guilty had perished as well. At root the problem was atheism, informed
by the materialistic unbelief of Cartesian philosophy which questioned the very
existence of God, hence 'No God, no Devil, no Spirit, no Witch'. Sinclair's intention was to turn Descartes inside out; quite simply, he would, in proving the existence of witches, demonstrate the existence of God.[14]

Robert Kirk's manuscript *The Secret Common-Wealth* (1691) which argued for
the reality of fairies and of second sight was motivated by identical sentiments,[15] as
were the anonymous *Witchcraft Proven* (1697) and John Bell of Gladsmuir's *Tryal
of Witchcraft* (1705), both of which dealt with witchcraft generally rather than
dwelling on particular cases.[16] *A True and Full Relation of the Witches at Pittenweem*
followed exactly the same principles in attacking the new sort of Sadducees who 'as
they deny the existence of good spirits, deny evil spirits also, and the possessing of,
and covenanting with witches'. The evidence for witches, overwhelming as it was,
could not be ignored. The anonymous author touched on the classics and the Bible
while alluding to contemporary Lapland and America (he must have had Salem in
mind), the British experience, and the recent cases at Renfrew by way of introduc-
ing the current developments at Pittenweem.[17]

Cotton Mather of Salem notoriety corresponded with the Revd Robert Wodrow
who was minister of Eastwood from 1703 till his death in 1734.[18] Wodrow is now
best known as the author of a four volume *History* of the Scottish Church from
Restoration to Revolution but throughout his life he collected, almost like a folklorist, what he termed 'providences', mainly concerning second sight, ghosts,
charms, and occasionally, demonic possession and witchcraft.

The case of Christian Shaw who figured centrally in the episode known variously
as the witches of Renfrew, Bargarran or Paisley in 1697, was truly sensational and

[14] George Sinclair, *Satans Invisible World Discovered* (Edinburgh, 1685; repr. Edinburgh, 1871), preface.
[15] Robert Kirk, *The Secret Common-Wealth (1691)*, ed. S. Sanderson (Cambridge, 1976). See also
Henderson and Cowan, *Scottish Fairy Belief.*
[16] C. Larner, 'Two late Scottish witchcraft tracts: *Witch-Craft Proven* and *The Tryal of Witchcraft*', in
S. Anglo (ed.), *The Damned Art: Essays in the Literature of Witchcraft* (London, 1977), pp. 227–45.
[17] *A True and Full Relation of the Witches at Pittenweem* (Edinburgh, 1704), pp. 3–7.
[18] The two began a correspondence in 1713 which lasted for twenty years: T. McCrie (ed.), *The
Correspondence of the Rev. Robert Wodrow*, 3 vols (Wodrow Society, 1842–3), i, p. 386.

since it was of the greatest interest to those seeking evidence for their particular viewpoint on both sides of the great debate on Sadducism and witchcraft, it is also the best documented of all Scottish cases. On the evidence of the 11-year-old Christian, daughter of John Shaw laird of Bargarran, seven people were convicted of witchcraft, one of them (John Reid) committed suicide in prison and the other six were strangled and burnt in Paisley. There are several notable features about this case. Its relatively late date is the most obvious, as are the youth of the accuser and the powerful impact of her accusations, all of which echo Salem. It was also centrally concerned with possession, which had been less conspicuous during the earlier phase of the witch-hunts.[19]

The anonymous pamphleteer cited above was delighted to find apparent confirmation of his views in the Pittenweem case of 1704–5. This particularly gruesome and repugnant example involved Janet Cornfoot, one of the witches accused of assisting in the bewitchment of a blacksmith named Peter Morton. The presence of the latter is of interest because blacksmiths were thought to possess magical powers. In 1691, for example, a man in Irongray was rebuked by the session 'for bringing his child to a smith to be charmed with ane forge hammer'.[20] Janet was tortured by the minister and his associates while in prison. She managed to escape but was caught and brought back. A number of her fellow villagers then set upon her, dragged her down to the beach and swung her from a rope between a ship and the shore while pelting her with stones and sticks. In this rare documented example of a lynching they finally covered her body with a heavy door which they heaped with stones and pressed her to death.[21]

The sad yet intriguing case of Elspeth McEwen (variously M'Queen, M'Cowen and M'Koun), an old woman in the parish of Balmaclellan in Galloway, was played out between 1696 and 1698. Her witching included the use of a wooden pin to draw the milk off neighbours' cows. She could also cause hens either to cease laying, or else to produce prodigious numbers of eggs. Upon examination by the local minister she was sent to Kirkcudbright Tolbooth where she languished in such pain and discomfort that she demanded death as a release. She duly confessed, was tried with another woman, Mary Millar, and was executed on 24 August 1698. The bald accounts for maintaining the executioner, William Kirk, before and during the burning, preserve the stark cruelty of the whole affair. He received money, food,

---

[19] See *A Relation of the Diabolical Practices of the Witches of the Sheriffdom of Renfrew* (London, 1697), *A History of the Witches of Renfrewshire* (Paisley, 1877), I. Adam, *Witch Hunt: the Great Scottish Witchcraft Trials of 1697* (London, 1978), and M. Wasser, 'The western witch-hunt of 1697–1700: the last major witch-hunt in Scotland', Chapter 9 above.

[20] J. Maxwell Wood, *Witchcraft and Superstitious Record in the South-Western District of Scotland* (Dumfries, 1911; repr. Wakefield, 1975), p. 121. The smith's hammer was believed to be efficacious in the curing of changelings: G. Sutherland, *Folk-Lore Gleanings and Character Sketches From the Far North* (Wick, 1937), p. 26.

[21] See *A True and Full Relation of the Witches at Pittenweem*, and *An Answer of a Letter from a Gentleman in Fife to a Nobleman* (1705), and S. Macdonald, 'In search of the Devil in Fife witchcraft cases, 1560–1705', Chapter 3 above.

drink and a complete new outfit for the great occasion. The provost of the burgh and his cronies were reimbursed for drink money. The sums were carefully entered for 'peits to burn Elspeth with … twa pecks of coals … towes [i.e. ropes] small and great … for ane tar barle … to William Kirk when she was burning, ane pint of aill'. Poor Elspeth had at least one ally. Janet Corbie was accused of 'endeavouring to dissuade her to confess', stating that 'people sinned ther sowl wha said she was a wich', and she was banished the burgh for her pains.

Kirkcudbright, which was still in the grip of covenanting fervour at the turn of the century, was a dangerous place for women, as was Kirkmaiden where a witchfinder was allegedly at work as late as 1697, but attitudes were gradually changing. In 1701 Elizabeth Lauchlon observed Janet M'Robert's spinning-wheel moving of its own accord. When she tried to still it she was thrown back against the wall, injuring her head. Subsequently in Janet's house 'the Devil appeared to her in the likeness of a man, and did bid her deliver herself over to him, from the crown of her head to the sole of her foot, which she refused to do, saying she would rather give herself to God Almighty'; the Devil had, by this time, been replicating precisely these demands, in exactly the same language, and eliciting identical responses from his intended victims, for over a century. After the Evil One disappeared Janet swore her to secrecy. He appeared again in the likeness of a gentleman and disappeared through a wall when she refused to go with him. It is noteworthy, in many cases, that despite all his supposed powers, many women found the Devil eminently resistible.

Someone else reported that Janet, dissatisfied with the amount of chaff she received to feed her cow, caused a woman's breast to swell alarmingly so endangering her suckling child. She also contaminated a cow's milk, drove one dog mad and crippled another, and swindled a girl out of her money. Eldritch screechings were heard around her house through which ghostly candles drifted. Remarkably however, a commission to try her was denied because the privy council 'judged the delations not to be sufficient presumptions of guilt, so as to found a process of that nature' and Janet consented to being banished to Ireland instead. A request for banishment ended the decade-long witch spells of Jean M'Murray of Twynholm in 1703, a woman who survived multiple accusations, any one of which would have earned her the fire only a few years earlier. She mostly took revenge on people who were less than generous towards her, inflicting a woman with a stitch-like pain which lasted until death, rendering milk useless, and causing the deaths of at least three horses.[22] While the Galloway examples were perfectly compatible with earlier cases, what was novel was the authorities' willingness to spare the accused, Elspeth McEwen excepted.

There is some merit in the suggestion that Scottish resistance to the cessation of witch-hunting and the abolition of the witchcraft acts was in part conditioned by concerns about religion and identity arising from the Union of 1707.[23] It was

[22] Wood, *Witchcraft and Superstitious Record*, pp. 72–91.
[23] I. Bostridge, *Witchcraft and its Transformations, c.1650– c.1750* (Oxford, 1997), pp. 21–37.

undoubtedly felt in some quarters that union threatened the very existence of the presbyterian establishment recently won from William of Orange and, as the union debate intensified, the covenants were more frequently invoked and the pamphleteering literature of earlier decades reprinted. Unhappily, there were those who regarded witch-persecution as both a religious and a patriotic duty. It is probably no coincidence that there was a fairly serious outbreak of witch cases in the south west at this period.[24] Though the incident is poorly documented what is claimed to be 'the last trial for witchcraft by the Court of Justiciary in Scotland' occurred at Dumfries in 1709 when Elizabeth Rule was condemned to be branded on the cheek with a red-hot iron. 'People living in 1790 have been told by their parents, that the smoke caused by the torturing process was seen issuing out of the mouth of the unhappy woman.'[25]

III

Traditionally the incident which has been regarded as providing closure on the whole business of witch persecution in Scotland is the famous 'last execution' which apparently took place in Dornoch, Sutherland, though the whole episode is very poorly documented and even the date is in dispute. It was first reported by Captain Edmund Burt who worked on the construction of roads and bridges in the Highlands between the late 1720s and 1737. He observed that while English people of sense and education no longer had any belief in witches, belief persisted in the Highlands, 'even among some that sit judicially', and he correctly noted the general assembly's interest in charming. According to Burt, in 1727, two poor women, mother and daughter, from Loth in the county of Sutherland, were tried for witchcraft and condemned to be burned; the younger escaped but the old woman 'suffered that cruel death in a pitch barrel, at Dornoch'.

In the matter of witchcraft Burt was inclined to appeal to reason and experience, questioning why it was hardly ever detected in cities while it was often discovered in so many little villages and remote places. He favoured the annulment of the witchcraft acts. Nobody, he thought, could ever prove witchcraft because no honest person would testify to flying broomsticks, bodies disappearing through keyholes or old women appearing in the guise of cats. He suggested that accusations were a way of disposing of unwanted people. But such was the tenacity of belief in such matters that recently two Gaels had threatened the life of an Englishman who questioned the existence of witches.[26]

In the 1790s it was stated that some time between 1717 and 1730 'the last unhappy woman that suffered for witchcraft in Scotland was executed', at

---

[24] Elsewhere, two men in Inverness were sentenced to death for witchcraft in 1706: Larner *et al.*, *Source-Book*, p. 150.

[25] W. McDowall, *History of the Burgh of Dumfries with notices of Nithsdale, Annandale, and the Western Border* (Edinburgh, 1867), pp. 434–5.

[26] Edmund Burt, *Letters from a Gentleman in the North of Scotland to His Friend in London*, ed. A. Simmons (Edinburgh, 1998 [first pub. 1754]), pp. 124–7.

Dornoch; 'the common people entertain strong prejudices against her relations to this day'.[27] In 1819 Charles Kirkpatrick Sharpe dated the execution to 1722, adding the further embellishments that the unnamed victim

> was accused of having ridden upon her own daughter, transformed into a poney, and shod by the devil, which made the girl ever after lame, both in hands and feet, a misfortune entailed upon her son, who was alive of late years. The grandmother was executed at Dornoch: and it is said, that after being brought out to execution, the weather proving very severe, she sat composedly warming herself by the fire prepared to consume her, while the other instruments of death were making ready.[28]

The problem with the much-repeated story about the fire is that it would not have been lit until after the victim was strangled. Sharpe's date was accepted by Scott who added the circumstance that the daughter's son, also lame, 'was living so lately as to receive the charity of the Countess of Sutherland, to whom the poor of her extensive country are as well known as those of the higher order'.[29] Sir Walter, convinced that the countess was the subject of a witch-hunt herself over the Sutherland Clearances, emphasised her good works. His information and the 1722 date derived from the countess who told Sharpe that a porter had recently not dared reject a couple of old women at Dunrobin Castle, 'believing them to be witches'. She mentioned the execution, 'to our everlasting shame', relating that the daughter, a fishwife, 'happened to have burnt her hands when a child, which contracted her fingers, and the common people ascribed that misfortune to her mother's witchcraft'. The very day on which the countess wrote to Sharpe her husband had met the witch's grandson, a beggar 'with his hands in that form ... and the descendants of that family are still feared in the neighbourhood from that old liaison'. However the countess's son, later, could find little information about the Dornoch witch though he knew the story of her seeking warmth at the fire and he claimed to 'have seen people who knew some that were assistants and spectators'.[30] The witch's stone in Littletown, Dornoch supposedly marks the spot where the execution took place. The screams of the dying victim still resounded in Dornoch's oral tradition in 1920.[31]

The presbytery of Dornoch minutes, which unfortunately do not survive for the period covering the execution, indicate that it had been exercised by certain relevant matters since at least 1709 when presbytery outlawed the practice of taking oaths from

[27] Sir John Sinclair (ed.), *The Statistical Account of Scotland*, 21 vols (Edinburgh, 1792–9), xviii, p. 467 (parish of Loth).

[28] C. K. Sharpe, *A Historical Account of the Belief in Witchcraft in Scotland* (London, 1884), pp. 199–200. The material was originally published as the introduction to Robert Law, *Memorialls: or, The Memorable Things that fell out within this Island of Britain from 1638 to 1684*, ed. C. K. Sharpe (Edinburgh, 1819).

[29] Scott, *Letters on Demonology*, p. 272.

[30] *Letters From and To Charles Kirkpatrick Sharpe, Esq.*, 2 vols, ed. A. Allardyce (Edinburgh, 1888), i, p. 344 (15 Sept. 1808); ii, p. 6 (2 Aug. 1812).

[31] H. M. Mackay, *Old Dornoch: its Traditions and Legends* (Dingwall, 1920), p. 110. W. N. Neill, 'The last execution for witchcraft in Scotland, 1722', *SHR*, 20 (1923), 218–21, is useful only for its discussion of human transformation into animals.

persons who were suspected of 'witchcraft, charming and the like'. In 1713 Robert Kirk, son of the author of *The Secret Commonwealth*, became minister at Dornoch. That same year John Baxter in Inchnadamph told a man that the 'Devil would stop his mouth as he hade stoped his fathers'. The matter of oaths was raised again. People who were sick or had lost cattle would insist that those suspected of malice, ill will or evil must swear on the Bible or 'on iron' that they were not responsible for their sufferings, 'a horrid prophanation of the Lord's most holy name, acknowledging the Devil in affiliations which should be taken from the Lord's hand and further a cherishing of a most abominable heathenish superstition'.[32] The presbytery, however, was concerned overwhelmingly with more mundane matters such as schools and the repair of churches. Disciplinary cases mainly involved fornication and adultery; one man was accused of driving his cattle on a Sunday. Music and 'promiscuous dancing' at wakes were condemned. Discussion of the Devil or occult practices was by no means even an annual occurrence. In 1718 several individuals were excommunicated for divination but their sentences were relaxed within a few months.[33]

There were more serious problems in neighbouring Caithness. Robert Dundas, lord advocate, wrote to the sheriff-depute of the county, concerning 'very extraordinary, if not fabulous, discoveries of witchcrafts and using of poisons' as a consequence of which several persons were in custody. Dundas was concerned because, although, by law, all precognitions had to be sent to Edinburgh, there was a rumour that the sheriff intended to go ahead and try the case, an allegation subsequently denied. William Montgomerie, a stonemason in Scrabster, claimed that his house was infested with cats. Their fearful noise terrified his wife who threatened to move out while their servant 'heard the cats speaking amongst themselves'. He killed two of them with his sword and injured others, but there was no sign of blood. When a local woman, Margaret Nin-Gilbert, or Gilbertson, fell ill Montgomerie's petition to the sheriff for an investigation into suspected witchcraft was refused because the allegations seemed 'very incredulous and fabulous'. However when, a couple of months later, Gilbertson's leg dropped off, she was arrested, subsequently confessing to a pact with the Devil, whom she had met in the likeness of a man some time before. Thereafter he appeared to her as a great black horse, or riding on the horse, as a black cloud or as a black hen. She had indeed been in Montgomerie's house in the form of a 'feltered', a shaggy or unkempt, cat; his sword had sliced her leg.[34]

She incriminated other women, such as Margaret Olson. When she claimed that she and her associates meant no harm, the minister of Thurso, Mr Innes solemnly countered that 'the disturbing and infesting a man's house with hideous noises, and cryes of catts, was a great wrong done to him, having a natural tendency to fright the

[32] NAS, presbytery of Dornoch minutes, CH2/1290/1, 72, 123, 125, 127, 130–2, 139.

[33] NAS, CH2/1290/1, 173, 175, 218, 227, 229, 231, 232, 235, 236, 242, 245, 249, 250, 255.

[34] 'In what part would the old woman have suffered, had the man cut off the cat's tail?' Thomas Pennant, *A Tour in Scotland, 1769*, ed. B. D. Osborne (Edinburgh, 2000), p. 110. Pennant attempted to place some perspective on such accounts by citing the case in Tring, Hertfordshire in 1751, and the 'ridiculous imposture' of the Cock Lane Ghost in 1762.

family and children'! After two weeks of interrogation Gilbertson died. Olson was searched for the Devil's mark, the minister and others testifying that when the needle was deeply buried in her shoulder she asked, 'Am I not ane honest woman now?'[35]

An explanation, of a kind, for those bizarre occurrences was offered by James Fraser of Alness to Robert Wodrow, writing in April 1727. First he reported a case from Kilernan, Caithness, where the parish minister allegedly lost his life due to witchcraft during the reign of William II. Fraser was unable to consult any papers on the matter since they had been sent to the lord advocate but he anticipated that Wodrow might have access to them. On the Montgomerie affair he had information from his uncle, factor for the bishopric of Caithness, and Margaret Olson's sometime landlord, until he ejected her 'for the wickedness of her behaviour', installing William Montgomerie in her place. Olson then prevailed upon Gilbertson to do mischief to the factor, but she had neither the power nor the inclination. He did recall that he had much trouble with his horse one night when crossing a bridge and thereafter he was sick for some six weeks but he was not minded to attribute such problems to the accused. He did suggest, however, that Gilbertson was murdered by the other witches in prison. Fraser also noted that there had recently been 'great noise of witchcraft in the parish of Loth, in Sutherland, by which the minister is said to have suffered'; the women involved were before the presbytery. In closing he reported rumours of similar developments at Tarbat in Easter Ross, telling Wodrow that 'if there is any thing in these stories, and you desire to know more about them, I shall endeavour to procure the best information'.[36] Would that he had done so. However, one of the two recent cases he mentioned, those of Loth and Tarbat, may well represent the early stages of the case that ended in an execution in Dornoch. Sharpe's date of 1722 seems unlikely, since Fraser's letter detailed local witchcraft cases back to the 1690s and he would hardly have omitted a 1722 case. Thomas Pennant on his 1769 tour briefly mentioned 'the last instance of these frantic executions in the north of Scotland', dating it, 'if I mistake not', to June 1727, a date which agrees with Burt.[37]

---

[35] Sharpe, _Witchcraft in Scotland_, pp. 184–94. There may be some echo of this case in Burt's account of a Highland laird laying about a collection of feline witches with a sword. One of his victims in human form was found next day bleeding profusely while under her bed 'there lay her leg in its natural form'. Burt, _Letters_, pp. 249–51. On the folklore of cats see R. Darnton, 'Workers revolt: the great cat massacre of the Rue Saint-Séverin', in his _The Great Cat Massacre and Other Episodes in French Cultural History_ (New York, 1984), 75–101.

[36] Sharpe, _Witchcraft in Scotland_, pp. 181–3. Burt noted that 'in this county of Sutherland, as I have been assured, several others have undergone the same fate within the compass of no great number of years': _Letters_, p. 126. For Fraser's letter see Robert Wodrow, _Analecta: or Materials for a History of Remarkable Providences_, 4 vols (Maitland Club, 1842–4), iii, p. 302; cf. NLS, Wodrow MSS, Folio 51, fos. 269r.–270v. He briefly noted the Ross-shire minister who lost his sight but made no mention of the Dornoch case which he obviously knew about and which may be noticed elsewhere in the extensive Wodrow archive.

[37] Pennant, _Tour_, p. 110.

A local historian preserved unverifiable traditions that the victim had in her youth spent time as a lady's maid in Italy, a country long associated with the diabolical.[38] Sensational though the case has subsequently become there are some peculiar features surrounding it. No-one up to and including Scott bothered to record the name of the victim, Janet Horne. Indeed, it is not absolutely certain when this attribution was first made though it is widely cited, albeit erroneously referenced, by virtually all twentieth-century commentators. To complicate matters further, Jenny Horne seems to have been the generic name for a witch in the far north.[39] It is also a strange coincidence that earlier expositors falsely etymologised the placename Dornoch as *dorn-eich*, 'horse's hoof'.[40] It seems likely that the case went ahead in opposition to the wishes of the lord advocate but we cannot be sure because the entire incident is so poorly documented. One thing is certain: the last witch executed in Scotland was not the same phenomenon as the last Scottish witch. Not even in Sutherland apparently for the last murderer executed at Dornoch, on 26 May 1738, was credited in popular tradition with having pole-axed a hare which turned out to be an old woman.[41]

IV

The kirk session records of Kenmore reveal that traditional witch belief, rooted as it was in gossip and rumour, was far from dead. In 1730 one woman was accused of witchcraft, while another denied she slandered John Lumsden as guilty of the death of her children by witchcraft. In 1747 Margaret Robertson complained that she was unjustly charged with such diabolical arts as witchcraft and enchantments, as well as with raining curses and imprecations upon her accusers; she therefore craved that the session should enquire into this scandal by which her character suffered so much in the eyes of her neighbours. Furthermore, she was seen going to the loch with her rock and spindle, intent upon 'some bad designs'. The session unanimously found her not guilty of witchcraft but sentenced her to stand three Lord's Days before the congregation to be rebuked for her sin and scandal. Her complainants were also rebuked for their calumnies. Witchcraft was not specifically mentioned, though perhaps implied, when the two M'Intaggart sisters used charms and enchantments to restore their cows' milk. One of them had 'ane egg shell with a little milk in it, concealed in her breast … an effectual charm to recover

---

[38] Mackay, *Old Dornoch*, p. 93.

[39] Sutherland, *Folk-Lore Gleanings*, p. 50. Janet is not named in C. D. Bentinck, *Dornoch Cathedral and Parish* (Inverness, 1926). Black, *Calendar*, names Janet Horne but gives no reference. Larner, *Enemies of God*, p. 78 and *Source-Book*, p. 229, cites Burt and Sharpe respectively but neither names Janet Horne. Virtually everyone who has written since has erroneously followed Larner. Janet Horn is identified in Mackay, *Old Dornoch*, p. 93.

[40] *New Statistical Account of Scotland*, xv, p. 1 (Dornoch), repeated from Sinclair (ed.), *Statistical Account*.

[41] Mackay, *Old Dornoch*, pp. 100–2. A version of this story is preserved in Sutherland, *Folk-Lore Gleanings*, pp. 75–80.

the substance of their milk which was taken away'. Both women were rebuked for their base practices.

Early in the morning of Beltane 1753, Janet M'Nicol was said to have been acting suspiciously, crossing back and forth over a burn, bending over as if she was extracting something from the ground, or putting something into it. At the same time Donald Thomson complained his wife Margaret was scandalised, when some neighbours alleged that his cows gave too much milk, insinuating she used hairs from her cow's tail to fashion a charm, in order to increase the yield. The kirk session dismissed Margaret with a warning about charms but Janet was 'publickly rebuked for the indecent practices proven against her'.[42]

These cases are not significantly different from a series in Dumfriesshire in the early 1690s which amounted to little more than bitter exchanges between neighbours during which words like murder and witchcraft were carelessly traded. John Charters, named as a witness to the witchcraft of Janet Kirk, denied that he knew of any such thing. Another poor woman was uncertain whether to blame God or the Devil for her bad health. In 1706 the Revd Peter Rae of Kirkbride was accused by a woman of having called her a witch, of having demanded that she return his health to him and of having attempted to break her spell by bleeding her on the forehead, the practice known as scoring or striking above the breath, or the brow. In 1694 there was a similar case in Glencairn where ten years later Janet Harestanes was said to be 'under the *mala-fama* of witchcraft'.[43] That same year John Gray in Pencaitland, East Lothian objected that a mother and daughter had called him 'witches gett', wishing that his soul was soaking in Hell's cauldron.[44] A pair of women were rebuked in 1712 for slandering one another as witches and 'resetters of witches'.[45] A woman in Perthshire (1716) was said to be very ill-disposed to flitting or moving house and many feared her because her mother was 'under the name of a witch'.[46] That a reputation for witchcraft provided some sort of security of tenure is further suggested by a much later reference from Inverness-shire to the goodwife of Barntown in 1794 who was considered 'a formidable personage of supernatural powers in this place of ignorant belief', so much so that the individual charged with evicting her felt himself to be under the influence of her spells.[47]

Witch beliefs emigrated with the Scottish colonists who settled in the Cape Fear area of North Carolina where, in 1794, Duncan MacFarland brought an action in the Fayetteville Court of Equity against the MacDaniel family. The major interest in this case lies in the information it preserves about MacFarland's 'furious zeal' to destroy the witchcraft residing in the persons of Sible and her mother Nancy. He

---

[42] *Witchcraft in Kenmore, 1730–57: Extracts from the Kirk Session Records of the Parish*, ed. J. Christie (Aberfeldy, 1893), pp. 3–19. For more on such practices see J. Miller, 'Devices and directions: folk healing aspects of witchcraft practice in seventeenth-century Scotland', Chapter 6 above.

[43] Wood, *Witchcraft and Superstitious Record*, pp. 120–2, 131–3.

[44] NAS, Pencaitland kirk session records, CH2/296/1.

[45] Wood, *Witchcraft and Superstitious Record*, p. 138.

[46] NAS, GD190/3/279.

[47] NAS, GD23/6/300.

envied, and thus suspected, the rich butter yields of their cattle. To ascertain their guilt he resorted to a form of 'turning the riddle'. This involved balancing a sieve or scissors on the sharp point of a gimlet and uttering the names of the accused in the name of Father, Son and Holy Ghost. When these objects turned he declared both women 'Witches of the Devil, who with another in the shape of cats had attacked him the previous night to take his life'. He attempted to prevent further injury by seizing the MacDaniels and scratching each three times above the eyebrow, causing blood to flow. The women later successfully sued MacFarland for this wounding but what is of interest in this case is that all of the aspects featured were perfectly familiar in Scotland.[48]

If the ministers who compiled their reports for the *Statistical Account of Scotland* in the 1790s are to be believed, 'the credulity of former times with respect to witches is almost extinguished', in the words of the Revd Andrew Bell of Crail, 'and the little superstitious fancies, which so frequently prevail among the commonalty, are gradually losing ground'.[49] His observation can stand for many of similar sentiment. In the course of the eighteenth century popular superstition was under assault as never before. Virtually every major Enlightenment figure celebrated the passing of the old beliefs. David Hume believed that he had discovered an 'everlasting check' upon all types of 'superstitious delusion' which would prove useful, he modestly thought, 'as long as the world endures'.[50] Adam Ferguson, William Robertson, Adam Smith and Lord Hailes were among the many who spearheaded attacks upon the beliefs of the subordinate classes so hopelessly widening the chasm between 'elite' and 'popular'. Robert Burns straddled that gulf, realising with Voltaire that philosophy was the means of quenching the flames of superstition, but admitting that in certain situations philosophy could all too easily elude the terror-stricken or the deluded.[51] In the bard's lifetime a Galloway minister could report that witch belief was not entirely laid aside but that 'the kirk session no longer indulges a spirit of inquisitorial investigation on a train of idle and vexatious processes'.[52]

It is quite likely that the literary interest in witches, as in all aspects of the supernatural, which developed during the post-Ossianic craze, positively reinforced witch belief in certain sectors of society. James Hogg was under the impression that while, in his own lifetime, belief in fairies was declining the number of witches was growing.[53] The antiquarian fascination with folklore almost certainly fostered similar convictions. Supposedly learned books on witchcraft such as those by Sharpe and

---

[48] North Carolina State Archives, Fayetteville District In the Court of Equity: Duncan MacFarland against Mary MacDaniel *et al.*, 188–90. We are grateful to Alex Murdoch for generously supplying us with copies of the records of this case.

[49] Sinclair (ed.), *Statistical Account*, Crail, p. 173.

[50] David Hume, *The Philosophical Works*, 4 vols, eds T. H. Green and T. H. Grose (London, 1874–5), iv, p. 93.

[51] Cowan, 'Burns and superstition', pp. 229–38.

[52] Sinclair (ed.), *Statistical Account*, Kirkpatrick-Durham, p. 249.

[53] Henderson and Cowan, *Scottish Fairy Belief*, ch. 7.

Scott, while adopting a sceptical stance, served to confirm the once, and possibly future, reality of witches. The elite, secure in their reason, cheerfully manufactured tales which, often by manipulating the vernacular, comfortingly conveyed the impression that witch belief was something which afflicted only the lowly, faintly but eerily echoing the deluded statements of the *Malleus Maleficarum* – 'certain abominations are committed by the lowest orders, from which the higher orders are precluded on account of the nobility of their natures'.[54] One example dating from the 1830s is entitled 'The Last of the Witches', a story which opens with young Mary Wilson receiving instructions from the witch. She 'maun trot' to St Martin's Kirk, Haddington and

> pu me the tapmost sprig frae the bonny bush o ragweed whilk grows in the nor-east corner, mang the grass covering the corpse o the man wha last Halloe'en nicht cut his father's thrapple, and then slit his ain craigie by way o reckoning. But beware that ye dinna hash the roots etc etc…[55]

A society in which perhaps at least half the population still believed in witches, to a greater or lesser extent, was not quite yet in a position to distance itself sufficiently to regard such tales as pure entertainment.

V

Jean Maxwell, the Galloway sorceress, was tried in Kirkcudbright in 1805 for 'pretending to excercise witchcraft, sorcery, inchantment, conjuration, &c.' Her crimes were committed at the farm of Little Cocklick in the parish of Urr. They included pretending 'to tell fortunes by tea cups and the grounds of tea'. She also predicted that 25-year-old Jean Davidson, servant to Francis Scott, farmer in Little Cocklick, would bear a bastard to Hugh Rafferton, an eventuality which Maxwell darkly hinted she could prevent 'by certain means'. When she anointed Jean's head with liquid out of a bottle the recipient became so intoxicated that she would have done anything Maxwell commanded, a situation the latter compounded by swearing Jean to secrecy and threatening that if she refused to obey her 'the Devil would speedily appear and tear her in pieces'. Maxwell exploited her position by extorting money from Jean for onward transmission to the Devil. She also terrorised her into making gifts of meat wrapped up in clothing. The money was to be returned to Jean after she had been visited by Hugh Rafferton with a proposal of marriage which, if refused, would drive him insane. Maxwell later claimed that the Devil had reneged and had proved too strong for her as evidenced by the marks of Satan's claws on her arm. The sorceress made increasingly excessive demands but Jean recovered her wits sufficiently to seek help and Maxwell was taken before the local minister and justice of the peace, Dr James Muirhead.

---

[54] Heinrich Kramer and James Sprenger, *The Malleus Maleficarum*, ed. M. Summers (New York, 1971), p. 29.

[55] 'The Last of the Witches', *The East Lothian Literary and Statistical Journal*, 9 (March 1831).

Jean's testimony revealed that Maxwell claimed to be an 'Oxford Scholar' (for which dubious honour an inability to write was clearly no disqualification); she had inherited a book worth £9 'from which she learned her skill'. She conjured several spells involving money, pins, pieces of clothing and rags. Jean was ordered to make a straw doll which was to be given as a burnt offering to the Devil who would appear in the shape of either a swine or a bull, and who would, if she stumbled or fainted, tear her in pieces; she was warned that another young woman had lost her wits through disobeying Maxwell. The latter's stories would have tested anyone's reason. She related how she prevented the Devil from dismembering Jean, sometimes the target of peats which he threw at her. Jean eventually had to borrow money from a neighbour to meet the escalating demands which included pay-offs for one John M'George, another Oxford scholar known as 'The Devil-Raiser of Urr'. It transpired that Hugh Rafferton had also been a servant at Little Cocklick and that although he and Jean had been courting there was no way she could be pregnant by him. When the farmer, Scott, learned of what had been going on he had Maxwell arrested. She was found guilty and sentenced to one year's imprisonment in Kirkcudbright Tolbooth. On market days, once in every quarter, she was to stand in the jugs or pillory for the space of one hour.[56] The case has much interest, not only for illustrating how a simple-minded young woman could be taken in by a bullying harridan, but also for the uneasy suspicion of the scholarly world which is revealed. Maxwell was able to manipulate lore and spells, hundreds of years old, in the interests of her own self-aggrandisement at the expense of a gullible servant. She was perhaps fortunate to receive a sentence of only one year's duration, the maximum allowed by the Witchcraft Act of 1735 which acknowledged only 'pretended witchcraft' and which was very seldom applied.[57]

The Argyll commissary court records reveal that old assumptions were highly tenacious. In 1810 Margaret Mitchell claimed that John McMillan in Glenkerdoch had scandalously declared in front of a number of people that she was a murderer, witch and whore. The problem was the word 'witch' though the outcome is not recorded. When, four years later, Sarah Cameron was libelled as a witch she claimed a recantation, damages and a fine. In the past, such trivial occurrences might have led directly to the stake.[58]

---

[56] *Remarkable Trial of Jean Maxwell, the Galloway Sorceress; which took place at Kirkcudbright on the Twenty-eighth day of June last, 1805; For Pretending to Exercise Witchcraft, Sorcery, Inchantment, Conjuration, &c.* (Kirkcudbright, 1805), pp. 1–24. Remarkably the incident is not mentioned in D. Frew, *The Parish of Urr, Civil and Ecclesiastical: a History* (Dalbeattie, 1909), which has a fairly full discussion of Muirhead, pp. 248–54, and a chapter on 'Old Customs and Manners' from a distinctly Christian and sanitised point of view, pp. 187–99.

[57] It was the passing of the 1735 act which made possible the repeal of pre-existing acts in 1736. Larner, *Enemies of God*, p. 78, states that no-one was ever prosecuted under this act, an understandable oversight. The Scottish medium Helen Duncan was tried under the 1735 act in 1944. M. Gaskill, *Hellish Nell: Last of Britain's Witches* (London, 2001).

[58] NAS, Argyll Commissary Court, 1700–1825, CC2/2/109 (1810), CC2/2/113/6 (1814).

Traditional witch practices figure conspicuously in the Ross-shire case of 1822 when Isabella Hay in Invergordon was imprisoned for witchcraft. She advertised herself as a 'cow and horse doctress', but she also had a reputation for fortune-telling and the recovery of stolen goods. Reasonably enough she charged for her services and it was the failure of one client, John Wallace, to pay her which led directly to her predicament which was almost certainly exacerbated by her reputation for causing quarrels in the community. When Wallace's horses began to die, one by one, it transpired that Isabella had threatened that non-payment would result in the death of one horse for every shilling in the pound he owed her. When the two consulted, the alleged witch claimed that she could cure the horse disease with a black hen but John spurned her offer. As a result of his petition she was placed in the tolbooth at Tain, accused of witchcraft, but was released when she agreed to banishment. When she changed her mind and delayed in the district seeking other monies owed she was reconfined for a period of some two months. The lord advocate, Robert Dundas of Arniston, would have none of it. On his pronouncement that 'the charge of witchcraft is really too ridiculous', Isabella was freed.[59]

Sometimes, however, the outcome could be quite serious. The *Dumfries Weekly Journal* (7 November 1826) carried an article giving details of a woman in the neighbourhood of Annan, who was suffering a nervous reaction as a result of witchcraft. 'We did not believe that people within sixteen miles of Dumfries laboured under a state of such superstitious ignorance in the nineteenth century as we are about to mention.' The sister of the bewitched woman attacked an old woman believing her to be responsible. Armed with a knife, she tossed her victim to the ground, and 'cut her across the brow!!! – a mode of dissolving the spell considered by the witch-believers of former ages, and, it now appears, even at the present day, to be altogether infallible'.

Isabel or Bell M'Ghie, described as 'the last of the Ayrshire witches', was born at Kelton, Kirkcudbrightshire in 1760. She later resided at Beith in Ayrshire where she was believed by many to have supernatural powers. She was interviewed by a local archaeologist, Mr James Dobie, in 1835, the year before she died. Bell herself claimed that 'I don't pretend to skill. All I do is in the fear of the God, and if He blesses the means the praise is His'. At the age of six or seven, according to her own account, she was a victim of the evil eye, for which her mother secured a counter-charm. This involved removing the child's shift, outside-in, over her head, and turning it three times 'widdershins' or against the direction of the sun. A piece of burning coal was then dropped through the shift three times after which it was put back on the child and she was cured.

Bell's reputation mainly derived from healing both humans and animals, or from counter-magic such as an elaborate ritual involving stalks of yarrow, as well as spoken and written versions of the Lord's Prayer, in order to restore the curdle in milk for cheese-making. Dairy problems seem to have been her speciality. Like

---

[59] J. Brims, 'The Ross-shire witchcraft case of 1822', *Review of Scottish Culture*, 5 (1989), 87–91.

Bessie Dunlop of Lyne over two hundred years earlier she was consulted by the well-to-do as well as the lowly. That she was rather more than a healer is suggested by her own testimony that she had known many a witch and warlock in her younger days, notably a warlock named Douglas whom she feared. He brought a dead horse back to life and achieved the equally remarkable feat of casting a spell upon a minister with whom he had quarrelled, rendering him unable to preach in his own pulpit for a year, though he could do so in others. Bell's reporter, however, may be deemed as credulous as herself for repeating the hoary tale of a man who shot a hare which turned out to be an old woman known for witchcraft.

Bell did not quite qualify as the last witch in the south west for Joseph Train, excise-man and antiquary, who lived at Castle Douglas in the Stewartry of Kirkcudbright, recorded a gruesome account of witchery in 1848, 'of a darker shade of benighted credulity than has perhaps taken place elsewhere in this country so near the middle of the nineteenth century'. It concerned a farmer in Buittle who, having had an arm surgically amputated, was in poor health. A few weeks after the limb had been buried a 'cannie wife' advised that it should be dug up and boiled until the flesh was separated from the bones, whereupon 'the middle joint of a certain finger should be taken' and used as a talisman to dispel pain and restore health. The instructions were followed to the letter using an open fire in the old parish churchyard. The story acquires credibility from its anti-climactic, but all too believable conclusion:

> The unfortunate yeoman informed me afterwards, that though he had kept the bone in his pocket for a considerable time, he was not sensible that it had done him any good. In the eastern portion of the ivy-covered walls of the old church the curious visitor may see a spot darkened by the smoke raised by this unhallowed incantation.[60]

In the cases discussed above most of the essentials of witch belief were present as they had always been. The possession case involving Christian Shaw, with its echoes of Salem, demonstrated that child testimony could condemn suspects to the fire. Pittenweem seemed to indicate that there was still symbiosis, at least in Fife, between elite fanatics and the folk. The Galloway cases show a return to concerns about parochial economics in minimal diabolical dress which did not convince the rele-vant authorities. Good old-fashioned fears about serious diablerie surfaced in the Caithness and Sutherland cases, counties which thereby confirmed the reputations they had long enjoyed for the tenacity of superstition. In Caithness the scare was rooted in community disputes, ecclesiastical prejudice and, possibly, legal rivalries; Sutherland appears to exemplify similar conditions, as well as a local conspiracy, possibly elite-inspired, to destroy a 'deluded' old woman. Many cases, as at Ken-more, seem to have involved defamation, careless speech, rumour and scandal about which the ecclesiastical authorities were clearly more concerned than they were about accusations of witchcraft, or for that matter, the lesser charge of charming.

[60] A. MacGeorge, *An Ayrshire Witch* (reprinted from *Good Words* for private circulation, London, 1886), pp. 1–12. On Joseph Train (1779–1852) see J. M. Watt, *Dumfries and Galloway: a Literary Guide* (Dumfries, 2000), pp. 286–91.

The case of Isabella Hay represents the commercialisation of witch practice and the response of a client who refused to pay for shoddy service. There had doubtless always been opportunities for persons suffering from some sort of personality disorder to exploit witch belief for their own material or psychological advantage, as in the case of Jean Maxwell who behaved like a school bully. Bell M'Ghie perhaps yearned for the supposedly more powerful practitioners of the past while still occupying a recognisable and, so far as the community was concerned, a useful niche, in rural society wherein failure of the dairy herd might mean financial ruin.

It is clear from several sources that popular or community witches survived in many parts of Scotland until well into the nineteenth century and probably beyond. People growing up in Caithness and Sutherland in the 1870s 'all believed in the reality of witchcraft' because they all personally knew witches. Bell Royal used her evil reputation to extort fish from the fisher folk. She was often consulted by lovesick girls and was welcomed into farm houses in the district. Fortune John was a tramp who teased a bare existence out of the threat of invoking his occult powers. Spells and anxieties involving milk, butter and cheese remained common. Witchcraft it seems was overwhelmingly concerned with the individual, the local and the mundane. One boy acquired a copy of Sinclair's *Satan's Invisible World* but to his chagrin his father 'did with the book what the authorities used to do with the witches themselves – he burnt it'.[61] In 1878 the folklorist James Napier personally knew of a woman who was bewitched.[62] Practitioners of witchcraft undoubtedly continued to function in many parts of Scotland, particularly in the Gàidhealtachd. In 1886 it was reported:

> The belief in witchcraft is by no means dead in Gairloch, and to the stranger the very appearance of some withered old women almost proves them to be witches. Cases actually occurred in 1885 where persons were charged with the practice of these arts in connection with poultry. It seems better not to give details of them here, especially as it is said the poor folk are yet under suspicion.

Most accusations concerned dairy products, farm animals or sea-fishing while some accounts recall shamanistic practices[63] as Dr John MacInnes has pointed out. Folk belief about such matters, left to itself, might have returned to where it was before the witch-hunts, but too much cultural baggage from learning and literature had intervened. So far as a majority of the population was concerned people who lived in fairy tales did not belong in the real world.

VI

While Dr Johnson believed in a kind of perpetual recession of superstition, James Hogg considered that witches were actually on the increase. Throughout the

---

[61] Sutherland, *Folk-Lore Gleanings*, pp. 49–86.

[62] J. Napier, *Folk Lore in the West of Scotland* (Paisley, 1879), pp. 77–8.

[63] J. H. Dixon, *Gairloch in North-West Ross-shire: its Records, Traditions, Inhabitants, and Natural History, with a Guide to Gairloch and Loch Maree* (Edinburgh, 1886), pp. 163–73.

eighteenth and nineteenth centuries witches were fictionalised, factionalised and fantasised by hordes of writers, in Scotland as elsewhere worldwide. At the latter century's end Sir James Frazer warned that people were deluded if they thought that witchcraft was dead. There was ample evidence to suggest that 'it only hibernates under the chilling influence of rationalism', ready to start into life if that influence was removed.[64] The mistake he made was to assume that his observation applied only to the peasantry and not to the educated but the unprecedented evils of the twentieth century would prove him wrong.

Just as today many secular-minded and otherwise cynical people cannot quite bring themselves to totally abandon a belief in God, so many folk in the past, particularly perhaps, devout Christians, were reluctant to completely give up the old beliefs, even if their adherence to such was highly selective, or spasmodic. The case of the Buittle amputee was diagnostic. The spell was powerless but the shadow of belief was reflected on the smoke-blackened wall of the kirk. We can never conclusively demonstrate for the witches, as we can for the wolves, that the last of their kind has gone. It is, as it has always been, belief which confers reality upon witches, beyond proof, beyond reason and beyond history.

[64] Quoted in Black, *Calendar*, p. 20.

Further reading

The standard work on the subject is Christina Larner, *Enemies of God: the Witch-Hunt in Scotland* (London, 1981), supplemented by a collection of essays, Christina Larner, *Witchcraft and Religion: the Politics of Popular Belief* (Oxford, 1984), and by a listing of witchcraft cases, Christina Larner *et al.*, *A Source-Book of Scottish Witchcraft* (Glasgow, 1977). A more general collection of reprinted essays was later made by Brian P. Levack (ed.), *Witchcraft in Scotland* (New York, 1992); this contained a high proportion of older material, much of it still valuable (notably its reprint of Black's *Calendar*), but indicating that few recent scholars had tackled the subject by that date. However, since then the subject has undergone a remarkable revival of interest, and a number of scholarly works have appeared. The most important of these are discussed in what follows.

Perhaps the broadest recent work is Stuart Macdonald, *The Witches of Fife: Witch-Hunting in a Scottish Shire, 1560–1710* (East Linton, 2002), looking at all aspects of witch-hunting throughout the period by means of a regional study. In addition, Macdonald's *Scottish Witch-Hunt Data Base*, a revised version of Larner *et al.*, *Source-Book*, will shortly appear on CD-Rom.

The general issue of why women were prosecuted, and the relationship between witch-hunting and wider issues of social control affecting women, are discussed by Julian Goodare, 'Women and the witch-hunt in Scotland', *Social History*, 23 (1998), 288–308. One aspect of women's experience is investigated using techniques of literary scholarship by Diane Purkiss, 'Sounds of silence: fairies and incest in Scottish witchcraft stories', in S. Clark (ed.), *Languages of Witchcraft: Narrative, Ideology and Meaning in Early Modern Culture* (London, 2001). Another study combining literary and folkloric elements focuses on the elaborate witches' sabbath conjured up by Alexander Montgomerie, a leading member of James VI's 'Castalian Band' of poets: Jacqueline Simpson, '"The weird sisters wandering": burlesque witchery in Montgomerie's *Flyting*', *Folklore*, 106 (1995), 9–20. Lizanne Henderson and Edward J. Cowan, *Scottish Fairy Belief: a History* (East Linton, 2001) deconstructs a number of the witch confessions for the first time. One of the most original recent studies has argued for a relationship between the Calvinist conversion experience and demonic possession: Louise A. Yeoman, 'The Devil as doctor: witchcraft, Wodrow, and the wider world', *Scottish Archives*, 1 (1995), 93–105.

A number of the most significant sixteenth-century witchcraft cases are drawn together, with discussion of their cultural and political background, by Peter G. Maxwell-Stuart, *Satan's Conspiracy: Magic and Witchcraft in Sixteenth-Century Scotland* (East Linton, 2001), which unfortunately appeared too late to be used by the contributors to the present volume. It is complemented on the North Berwick witchcraft panic of 1590–1 by Peter G. Maxwell-Stuart, 'The fear of the king is death: James VI and the witches of East Lothian', in W. G. Naphy and P. Roberts (eds), *Fear in Early Modern Society* (Manchester, 1997). The North Berwick panic has been studied in more detail by Lawrence Normand and Gareth Roberts (eds), *Witchcraft in Early Modern Scotland: James VI's* Demonology *and the North Berwick Witches* (Exeter, 2000), which reproduces much valuable source-material. The role of James VI during the 1590s is the subject of Jenny Wormald, 'The witches, the Devil and the king', in T. Brotherstone and D. Ditchburn (eds), *Freedom and Authority: Scotland, c.1050–c.1650* (East Linton, 2000). A detailed study of a related but later local panic is offered by Julian Goodare, 'The Aberdeenshire witchcraft panic of 1597', *Northern Scotland*, 21 (2001), 17–37.

The idea that special procedures were used for witch-hunting in the 1590s is criticised by Julian Goodare, 'The framework for Scottish witch-hunting in the 1590s', *Scottish Historical Review*, 81 (2002, forthcoming). Procedural issues are also addressed by 'The trial of Geillis Johnstone for witchcraft, 1614', eds Michael Wasser and Louise A. Yeoman, and 'Witchcraft commissions from the register of commissions of the privy council of Scotland, 1630–1642', ed. Louise A. Yeoman, both in *Scottish History Society Miscellany*, xiii (forthcoming). The process of witch-pricking has been discussed from its physiological aspect by Stuart W. MacDonald, 'The Devil's mark and the witch-prickers of Scotland', *Journal of the Royal Society of Medicine*, 90 (1997), 507–11.

For the later stages of the witch-hunt there is R. L. Harris, 'Janet Douglas and the witches of Pollock: the background of scepticism in Scotland in the 1670s', in S. R. McKenna (ed.), *Selected Essays on Scottish Language and Literature: a Festschrift in Honor of Allan H. MacLaine* (Lewiston, NY, 1992). The 1697 case of Christian Shaw is discussed by Stuart W. McDonald, A. Thom and A. Thom, 'The Bargarran witch trial: a psychiatric reassessment', *Scottish Medical Journal*, 41 (1996), 152–8, and by Hugh V. McLachlan and J. Kim Swales, 'The bewitchment of Christian Shaw: a re-assessment of the famous Paisley witchcraft case of 1697', posted in 2000 on the website of the Scottish Women's History Network at http://swhn.gcal.ac.uk/shaw.html. Witchcraft features in the mental world of Robert Kirk, a minister who wrote a scientific treatise drawing on fairy lore in 1691. This has recently been the subject of Michael Hunter, 'The discovery of second sight in late 17th-century Scotland', *History Today*, 51:6 (June 2001), 48–53, and Michael Hunter (ed.), *The Occult Laboratory: Magic, Science and Second Sight in Late Seventeenth-Century Scotland: The Secret Commonwealth and Other Texts* (Woodbridge, 2001). A remarkably late attempt to prosecute a witch has been discussed by John Brims, 'The Ross-shire witchcraft case of 1822', *Review of Scottish Culture*, 5 (1989), 87–91.

The Survey of Scottish Witchcraft, a project based in the University of Edinburgh, is expected to produce additional information on the subject. The project's website is at www.arts.ed.ac.uk/witches.

Index

Asterisks* denote persons accused of being witches.